MUSICAL CHAIRS

A LIFE IN THE ARTS

MUSICAL CHAIRS

A LIFE IN THE ARTS

Schuyler Chapin

G.P. PUTNAM'S SONS

NEW YORK

Library of Congress Cataloging in Publication Data

Chapin, Schuyler.
  Musical chairs.

  Includes index.
  1. Chapin, Schuyler. 2. Impresarios—United States—Biography. I. Title.
ML429.C497A3   780'.92'4 [B]   77–5814

SBN: 399–11970–1

PRINTED IN THE UNITED STATES OF AMERICA

*For Betty
who knows all the reasons why*

CONTENTS

Foreword

As a start I should say that I was born with neither a gold nor a silver spoon in my mouth; if anything I was born with one made of very heavy silver plate, the kind made in England before the first World War and sold, at great expense, by Tiffany. The plate lasted until I was fifteen, when with my father's death the weathering and acids of life wore through and we were down to the greened copper underneath. This was not bad for me; it wreaked havoc on my two brothers but I escaped. The reason I escaped was that I had something to hold onto, something, however ill-formed at fifteen, that lodged within me. I knew, instinctively perhaps, that at some point it would emerge. I loved music; I loved the theater; I loved books and pictures and movies and sculpture and tapestries. I loved the arts. And I knew that somehow or other I was going to spend my life with them.

As I write this I am in the midafternoon of my life. I look back with the bittersweet mixture of regret that I did not know my parents better; wishes that I'd not been so prissy as a child because I wanted to avoid anything that smacked of trouble, and gratitude that at least my parents did not stand in my way, even though their idea of what my way might be was as vague to them as it was to me. I look back on thirty years of a happy marriage, four interesting sons and a promising grandchild, and a professional life that I adore. I look forward to more of the same, in whatever adventures or avenues the new experiences may come. I've survived the silver-plated spoon; I've survived a war, ulcers, malaria, abrupt changes in my professional career, and various other banana peels of life. Best of all, perhaps, I've had a wonderful time making my avocation my vocation, despite occasional pitfalls, brickbats, boomerangs, and disappointments. It has been joyful and I hope that I've been able to bring some of that joy to others. This is what the book is all about really. Read it and share my adventures with the arts and some of the great artists of our time. And remember, as Katherine Anne Porter so eloquently put it, "The arts are what we leave behind when all the cities fall."

I

Crescendo and Denouement

July 1, 1975, was the kind of day in New York City that the Better Business Bureau, the Convention and Visitors Bureau, the Chamber of Commerce, and God create to display the magic of the Big Apple. The sky was cloudless; it was cool, a gentle northeast breeze kept the air sparkling, and the forecasts for the evening were for more of the same. I hoped this was to be the case because, as my last official duty as General Manager of the Metropolitan Opera, I was to open our 1975 season of free performances in Central Park. For eight years the Metropolitan had finished its performing seasons with these al fresco events, paid for, in large part, by the city to bring the glory of the operatic literature to as many people as possible. That year the season almost had to be abandoned because of the city's growing fiscal crisis but in large measure this had been prevented by the intervention of City Council President Paul O'Dwyer and the stumping of the five boroughs that he and I did together in order to keep our program in the city budget. Not that the city paid all the costs: it did not, but it did pay for a part of our expenses and made the job of finding additional funds that much easier. To balance the budget I had to find some $200,000 more than the city allotted and in large measure, thanks to a transplanted New Yorker named Ralph Corbett, I was able to do so. Ralph Corbett and his wife live in Cincinnati, Ohio, and have been generous and supportive of ar-

11

tistic activities in that area. But the Corbetts lived in New York shortly
after their marriage and had attended free concerts of one kind or
another in the parks and remembered their pleasures. They had given
me money for the new production of *Gianni Schicchi* the year before
and we had become friends. They knew I was in trouble with the Met
Board and wanted to help. We were opening our park season with *Madama Butterfly*. Renata Scotto was to sing the leading role and we expected a big crowd.

We were not disappointed. At about 8:00 PM, with the performance
due to start at 8:30, the police estimated about 100,000 people were
stretched out across the Sheep Meadow, sitting on blankets or portable
chairs or just on the ground. As my wife Betty and I approached the
park it looked for all the world to be an unending sea of people. We
held each other by the hand as we made our way along the edge toward
the portable stage at the east end. We were both silent, locked in
thought. This was to be my farewell from the Met and I wanted it to be
a good one. In a far more real sense it was to be "our" farewell after
almost four years of working together as a team for the Metropolitan.
We had all just returned from a fabulous tour of Japan, where the company had scored an unprecedented international triumph, and a week
at Wolf Trap Farm, outside Washington, D.C., where the news of my
impending departure had become public. I had not been with the company since our Wolf Trap opening the previous Monday and by this
time each member had received a letter from me sent out after the
board of directors meeting that had sealed my fate. In it I thanked them
for their support during my stewardship and urged them to continue
the spirit and achievement that they had brought about starting with
the tragic death of Goeran Gentele in 1972, when, under those horrible,
melodramatic circumstances, I suddenly found myself their leader.

Betty and I were wholly unprepared for the reception we got backstage. In groups of two and three and five, sometimes more, the chorus, orchestra, comprimarios, stagehands, security people, and house
staff came up to greet us. Many were close to tears; some crying outright. Two of our children, Ted and Miles, were also there and many
spoke to them. As the groups grew so did the passion and after a few
minutes things were starting to get a little out of hand. To the best of
my ability I tried to tell all of them the same thing, that the board had
decided to take professional control of the company themselves on the
theory that the financial crisis could be stemmed by their collective expertise as lawyers and bankers and in one case a professional accountant and management consultant, and that having installed one of their

own as executive director and eliminating the post of general manager, the management structure would be reorganized along the lines of a modern international conglomerate. The artistic affairs of the company were to be divided between two of my appointees, James Levine as music director and John Dexter as director of production, and they, in turn, would be responsible to the executive director solely on matters of money. Their work was to be overseen by the production committee of the board. No one person was to be the impresario. In the board's mind those days were finished and done for. That was a lot to explain in a few moments and I obviously didn't get it all out as carefully as I would have liked. Perhaps this wasn't the moment for it anyway. Many of them wanted a special word with Betty. Her fiftieth birthday had been celebrated on the plane returning from Japan; in fact she had had two birthdays as we crossed the international date line and a large cake had been produced that was consumed by the company in no time flat.

At about 8:25 PM, Osie Hawkins, the veteran Metropolitan Opera executive stage manager, walked out on the stage and made a few preliminary announcements about our park season—Tuesday night the Bronx, please put your papers in the litter baskets, etc.—and then, as was traditional, introduced the general manager. I walked out rapidly, since the distance from the entrance to center-stage is considerable and I did not wish either to dally or, delay the start of the performance. I was overwhelmed by what happened. As I started across, the audience rose to its feet, applauding and cheering and shouting bravos. By the time I'd reached center-stage, people were standing and the shouting and clapping grew. Suddenly I was aware of a terrific racket behind me and I turned to see the entire company on its feet applauding and bravoing as well. I was literally stunned. I stood there not knowing what to do. I went to the microphone and tried to speak but the crowd wouldn't let me. I started to cry. I couldn't help it. After what seemed like hours, but was, of course, only a minute or so, I heard voices begin to chant rhythmically "Don't go . . . don't go . . ." And then, thank God, I was snapped back to reality. One voice, quite near the stage began shouting "Bring back Tebaldi!" Now I was home free. Here was an opera nut, without whom none of us could exist, making his presence known. In that split second I thought of the times that we had talked about that great lady and whether or not she could be persuaded to look at a different repertoire, at roles she could sing so well these days. You can't explain all this in a few seconds.

Still, it brought me back to reality and I stammered out a few words of thanks. I could hear my voice moving across the loudspeakers and it had a curious, detached quality, almost ghostlike, and I had a quick thought about how the performance would sound if the loudspeaker system wasn't better than this. I have no idea what I said, but I finished, turned to the company, shook the concertmaster by the hand, bowed and waved at them all and fled the stage. The applause was again deafening and as I reached the wings the artists, ready to go on, were also in tears. Then they made their entrances and the cheering began all over again, this time for Scotto and William Lewis and the other artists who were, after all, the reason they'd come to the park. The Chapins paused a moment to listen and then, all four of us on the breaking point, headed for the nearest bar.

II

The Beginnings

The name Schuyler Garrison Chapin really tells a lot. Deacon Samuel Chapin arrived in Boston in 1632, felt it too crowded, and pushed west to found Springfield, Massachusetts. He was the inspiration for the Saint-Gaudens statue of "The Puritan" that stands now in Springfield and, my wife assures me, points to the street that gets you out of Springfield. For generations Chapins lived up and down the Connecticut River valley until, with the stirrings of the mid-nineteenth century, they began to move farther south to Long Island Sound and eventually to New York City. My grandfather married the granddaughter of Commodore Cornelius Kingsland Garrison, a moderately full-blown robber baron who unfortunately squabbled with his partner Commodore Cornelius K. Vanderbilt's cross-country railroad plans and got off the train, so to speak, at Garrison, New York. There went the family fortune.

Schuyler, of course, comes from an old Dutch New York family whose most prominent member was General Philip Schuyler, on Washington's staff during the American Revolution and father-in-law of Alexander Hamilton. People who had the old Schuyler telephone exchange in New York are notable to me as they are among the few who can spell and pronounce the name correctly.

My mother's family, the Burdens, came from Scotland to Troy, New

15

York, and started a large ironworks, prospering on a new kind of horseshoe. Her family also included Griswolds: John Wool Griswold, another Washington general, and John Augustus Griswold, the financier and builder of the *Monitor*, the little iron ship that in 1862 changed the history of naval warfare and the Civil War. They, too, eventually came to New York City and I am therefore somewhat of a rarity: the child of parents, grandparents, antecedents, and others who were born and/or lived in New York.

My parents had a lovely, comfortable life in their home on East Seventy-second Street in New York, and in Mt. Kisco, with summer sojourns to Fishers Island. We children never saw much of them, but had a series of stiff, starched governesses and nurses. We ate at a side table in the dining room with these ladies. The table had a small drawer that was directly in front of my place and I used to fill it with all the food I didn't want to eat. The waitress was a friend and never to my knowledge said anything about this to anyone. The drawer would be empty by the next meal. Frequently it was quite full at the end.

At night when we were having our supper, the servants would often be setting the big table for a dinner party. I'd watch fascinated as the lace doilies were put down, the glasses brought out, fresh and gleaming, the silverware polished within an inch of its life and laid on either side of each doily, the linen napkins carefully folded and put down at the center of each place. The huge candelabra, each with three candles, would be put at the head and foot of the table, the candy compotes placed in the same area and filled with peppermints and chocolates. Every once in a while the cook would serve us some of the same things she was preparing for the dinner party and that is how I became a life-long fan of lobster newburg. When it was first given us, it looked like so much pink spaghetti and was absolutely delicious. Mother found about this, though, and said we shouldn't have it as we were too young for lobster and it was too rich for our digestions.

After meals we always retired to our rooms for homework or hours spent staring out the window. I liked to read and imagine all kinds of adventures. Roscoe Turner was my hero in 1930. I longed to be an aviator (prophetic, perhaps) with a cloth helmet and beautiful goggles and a plane whose engine spit fire and smoke as it streaked across the country. I would fit out my bed as a plane, a broom handle as the stick, a bedpost as the throttle. I would crash in desolate mountain country by rolling off the bed and landing with a bang on the sparsely carpeted floor. Often this brought the governess running with the threat "I'll tell your father!" and every once in a while she would do so. That meant I had to face him in his dressing room or in the library and these were rarely pleasant confrontations. I always had the feeling that whatever I did was simply inadequate and I was not measuring up to some largely unspecified standards. I wanted to be perfect and never displease my parents.

In Mt. Kisco we had a large, sprawling house on McClain Street surrounded by thirteen acres of woodland. It was here I first learned about music on an old crank-up Victrola in the corner of the sewing room. It was a standing model with room at the bottom for record albums. The pickup used steel needles and the records themselves were thick and heavy. Among them was an all-blue Columbia album of Schubert's Unfinished Symphony performed by Sir Henry Wood and the London Promenade Orchestra. Perhaps it was because the color was so vivid, perhaps the almost sensual feel of the record itself; whatever the reason I asked my nurse to put it on the machine. Once the music started I listened, transported to another world. I heard that record over and over again, probably driving the nurse mad, but she was one of the better ones and never seemed to complain. Only Father complained, particularly when he was next door in the children's bathroom concocting bathtub gin. For some reason he had little trouble obtaining pure grain alcohol and this, when blended with Halloway's Gin Essence, produced a more than passable drink. I know because only a few years ago we used up the last of the brew and it was still good. Somehow Schubert and gin did not mix for him, and as a result I got to know Caruso and opera at a tender age. He would come out of the bathroom, remove the Schubert, and put on "Over There" sung by Caruso. Caruso never spoke English and had learned the song for a World War I war bond rally. "Johnee git yourrr gonn . . ." I can hear it to this day. And of course the arias. *Pagliacci, Rigoletto, Martha, Bohème*—I met them all in the Mt. Kisco sewing room, between bouts of Schubert and bathtub gin. This nurse, Nanny Pendle, was the exception to the general rule of dried-up virgins in dark dresses. She truly loved music. Alas, our relationship came to an end when I was ten. She left us to go off to California and later worked for a rising Hollywood couple whom she once described to me as not being "quite the right sort." The couple eventually divorced, the husband remarrying and leaving the screen to devote himself to other activities. His name was Ronald Reagan. I kept in touch with Nanny Pendle over the years and when I first began my concert managing career I would always call her whenever I was on the West Coast and we would pick up where we left off. I've always been grateful for her interest and ability to share enthusiasm, and for being the first person who gave me friendship.

The Mt. Kisco property also included the caretaker's cottage and a large white barn with an old hayloft from which we children tried to jump, using umbrellas as parachutes. Why we were not killed doing this I do not know; but we weren't, and we kept on jumping time after time to see if we could conquer the problem of the collapsing umbrellas. We also had a grass tennis court that had been abandoned for tennis but made a good playing field. On every July 4 Father would come down the hill from the big house throwing torpedos to his right and left scaring my brothers but delighting me. It was the one time of year when he really abandoned himself to playing with the kids and we looked forward to it year after year. Shortly after the 4th I was usually shipped off for a month or six weeks to a boys' camp run by some of the masters of the Allen-Stevenson School up at Queechy Lake, New York. It was called Boyville and I hated every blade of grass in the place. Father and Mother would visit once a summer and I particularly remember the summer of 1931, when Franklin D. Roosevelt was governor of New York and they went to visit him in Albany before coming to see me. Father and FDR had been friends at Harvard, and had various business connections. When they arrived, they were full of stories about the Executive Mansion, particularly about the purple toilet seats that were supposed to have been put there by Al Smith. The purple toilet seats seemed a lot more romantic than the weeds and mud of Queechy Lake, and I spent a lot of time after they left trying to imagine what the seats looked like and what it would be like to live in such a place. My romantic, dramatic streak took over and sustained me for the rest of that summer.

Fishers Island, on the other hand, was a wonderful place and I always eagerly awaited our visit. The Mansion House was an old summer hotel built along the lines of the great United States Hotel in Saratoga Springs. The island was idyllic: green and lush with Long Island Sound on one side and the Atlantic on the other. Father and Mother were inveterate golfers and would spend most of their days at the Fishers Island Club in intense tournaments. We were taken by the governess and nurse to swim, sometimes at the Hay Harbor Club, where we were thrown with lots of other little boys and girls and made to play tennis together and enter swimming races, or to the wilder and more desolate Chocamount Beach, where the breakers were high and rough and the beach stretched endlessly. I loved Chocamount: I was free to roam by myself and over each sand dune there might be a pirate or a ship or some magic moment that would guarantee unlimited happiness.

It was on Fishers Island one summer that I first found my interest in music brought into fierce focus. One of the other families staying at the

Mansion House was named Coleman. They had a son a little older than I who played the piano beautifully. He would practice in the mornings in the Mansion House ballroom and I would sneak in to listen. I didn't know what he was playing but all of it seemed exciting. One day he caught me sitting there and seemed visibly embarrassed. I asked him to continue, and this was very difficult for me to do because I was extremely shy. Nonetheless I did, and he played a Chopin waltz. I know this because I asked him what it was. After that meeting I would come in every day to listen, and after a week or so he saw me coming in one morning and stopped playing. He said he was doing me a favor every day and now it was my turn to do something for him. He asked me to carry his golf bag as a caddy that afternoon. I demurred; it was to be an afternoon at Chocamount, but so much did I want to hear him play that I agreed.

At around two we went out on the little Hay Harbor course and when we came to the third hole, I stepped in the way of his driver and the club hit me hard on the left temple. Blood gushed out all over the place and I dimly remember lying on the ground with people hovering above me. I was taken to the only hospital on the island, at Fort H.G. Wright, where an army surgeon cleaned the wound and stitched it up. I was lucky. The blow had come at the only point on the temple where I neither lost the sight of my left eye nor had a main blood vessel cut. Bud Coleman was beside himself with apologies; so was his family. It was my own fault and I knew it, and so, thank God, did my father. He blamed the governess for letting me go at all but this was foolish. I'd just stepped in the way and to this day I have what many people think of as a Heidelberg dueling scar. I heard a lot of piano the rest of that summer. Bud played for me any time I asked!

Fishers Island was also the setting for another musical experience in my early life. In 1938 John Nicholas Brown built a modern beach house with a raised platform in the living room in order that chamber groups might play there comfortably. The room looked out on Long Island Sound and there was nothing more delightful than the Brown's recitals, with the music in your ears and the water in your vision. As I recall, he inaugurated the house by inviting the Budapest Quartet, and I had my first introduction to Beethoven in this ideal setting. The house didn't last very long, however. In September of the same year New England was battered by the worst hurricane on record and the house, even though "hurricane-proof," was one of the first to blow down. I understand it was rebuilt the following year or two but I was never invited again. No matter—the house had done its work for me.

My early schooling was in New York and that meant the Allen-Stevenson, where I was far from a spectacular student. I hated math, loathed French, was incompetent in Latin, and didn't see the point of all that running around the gym.

However, we did have a school "orchestra." It consisted of ten banjo-uke players, drums, and a frizzle-haired lady who played the piano and nodded her head to keep tempo. We had a music coach who rehearsed us and also taught tap dancing. Some days the "orchestra" would be split up and half would play while the other half tap-danced. I learned the time step and approximately the first eight bars of "East Side, West Side" in a proper Palace Theater routine while plucking away at the banjo-uke. Visions of a vaudeville career would run riot across my imagination and I was happiest of all on the once-a-month days of performances.

The rest of school was nonsense for me and so was home. I was not allowed to travel the Lexington Avenue trolleys alone. They were considered too dangerous for a little boy and I was hideously embarrassed when my governess picked me up at school and escorted me home.

Allen-Stevenson lasted until I was eleven, when following an old family tradition, I was shipped off to boarding school. This meant being pushed out of the house at the earliest possible moment and this, in turn, meant my arrival, on a warm September afternoon in 1934, at the Millbrook School in Millbrook, New York, in the company of my parents. Except for two brief periods at a summer camp I had never been away from home before. I was shy, awkward, scared, unsure, and desperately anxious. I wanted to make friends, something that I had seemed unable to do, unless I counted my immediately younger brother, who was forced to play with me and always looked at life as if he had just been hit in the eye by a squirt of lemon juice. I wanted to succeed at something, even if I had no idea of what that something was.

Earlier that summer, in preparation for boarding school life, my father had taken me for a ride in our blue Chevrolet two-door and told me about the "facts of life." After the ride he'd given me a book to read that had numerous pictures of female insides, some with babies and some without. The pictures were accompanied by a highly technical text and left me confused and embarrassed, as had my father's talk. To me women were terrifying. They were either like my mother, wispy, vaguely beautiful, and remote, or like our nurses and governesses. I hadn't the vaguest idea what life was all about.

While Father was dealing with sex Mother was coping with my wardrobe. On a hot August afternoon she took me on a clothes-buying trip to DePinna and Best & Co. A blue suit was required, as were so many white shirts, so many ties, a raincoat, rubbers, thick socks, underwear, handkerchiefs, gray flannels, a blazer, two sweaters, and a windbreaker. At one point my eye fell on a thick tweed suit. I'd never owned anything as grand and I wanted it. Mother was hesitant, wondering quite rightly what use I would have for it. But I was adamant: I wanted it. We had a contest of wills and I won. Not a usual thing in our house. When it came down from the hanger and I tried it on, the suit was even thicker than it looked. It enveloped me and prickled and was horribly uncomfortable but it was all mine and I would wear it in a blast furnace if necessary.

The thought of that suit sustained me as we drove to Millbrook. I could wear it wherever and whenever I wanted. I could wear it that very night if I wished even though it was hot and sticky and the hills of Dutchess County showed no sign of cooling breezes.

Our arrival at the school was unnoticed. We drove up to what turned out to be the South Dorm, an attractive imitation Georgian building, and pushed our way upstairs to the next-to-top floor that contained cubicles, on one side blue and gray and on the other green and yellow.

The blue and gray section was for the smallest boys and I was one of them. Each cubicle contained a bed and a built-in chest of drawers over the top of which was a closet. Near the bed was a small shelf for books and pictures and a small writing table and chair. The window was good-sized and sunlight flooded in. This gave the place an air of cheerfulness that helped get one started. My parents deposited my bags on the mattress and we walked downstairs and out to their car.

On the way we met some of the masters and I shook hands with all of them in what I hoped was a forthright and manly manner. I was beginning to be overcome by the terrifying feeling that I was actually going to be left there all on my own with a bunch of people I'd never laid eyes on before in an atmosphere that, however cheerful, was increasingly terrifying. My mouth became dry, and at an unfortunate moment, because a large, imposing figure of fierce handsomeness and deliberate stance was rapidly approaching us with his hand outstretched in what I took to be a welcoming gesture. It was, of course, the headmaster, Edward Pulling, whom I had met the previous spring when we drove up to look at the school. I remembered him then as tall and intense and now he seemed more so, not only because of the way he was walking to us but by the way he was simultaneously greeting other new boys with the same reined-in heartiness. When he reached us my courage had all but left me and I took his hand weakly. He fixed me with a good stare that seemed to say we would be friends but only on his terms. My mouth got drier. He murmured something about tea at his house and we walked over the campus toward it.

On reaching his house we were greeted by Mrs. Pulling and given tepid tea in a beautiful cup and a piece of cake. It all tasted cardboard to me but my parents seemed to be making conversation and that left me alone with my increasing misery. Presently tea was over and we all moved out of the house to the campus and the various parents began to move to their cars. My fears welled up again but I kissed my parents goodbye and watched them climb into the car and start off down the driveway. I watched until the car was out of sight and then the realization of my aloneness hit me full blast.

I ran up the dormitory steps and into my cubicle. I began to unpack and the first thing that came out of the suitcases was my tweed suit. I hung it up in the closet, put my socks and shirts and underwear and handkerchiefs and ties into the drawers. For a moment the loneliness left me as I realized that from this time on my clothing, at least, was to be my own destiny. In minutes I was dressed in *the* suit, vest and all, and I started out into the hall.

A friendly voice—and one that was destined to become more and more friendly over the years—called out to me. I stopped and saw approaching the master in charge of the floor. He was of medium height, wore glasses, and had a warm if perplexed look on his face. "Aren't you going to be a little warm in that?" he asked. I felt myself blushing furiously. "I don't know," I replied. "Well, I think you will," he said. "Why don't you save that for the winter? It can get mighty cold here." His whole attitude was friendly but his message was unmistakable. I stood looking at him for a moment, embarrassed and unsure. "My name is Mr. Abbott," he said, and put out his hand. "I'm Schuyler Chapin," I said, almost in a whisper. I turned and went back into my cubicle, drew the curtain closed, and took the suit off. I thought to myself it's too hot anyway and I proceeded to put on a pair of gray trousers and blue blazer. I returned to the hall and went down the front steps and outside. Some of my classmates were throwing baseballs, some wrestling, some sitting around talking. I stood watching for a moment not knowing what to do next and scared out of my wits. Mr. Abbott appeared and tried to ease everyone into conversation. Looking back I realize that everyone in his own way was scared and fearful that day, but at the moment all I could think was that I was absolutely alone in these feelings. The dinner bell sounded and we wandered over to the dining room. The food was served by maids in black uniforms with white aprons. It was plain, overcooked, and not very good. I didn't care, though. All I wanted at that moment was to go home. I began to think about running away and the more I thought about it the easier it seemed. But what was I running away to? I really didn't know. I suppose I thought to go home because I had always lived there and it was an automatic focal point. Besides, I knew instinctively that the governess would take care of me but I was not so certain about my father. My father was a terrifying figure to me. He seemed so perfect, so well turned out, so in command of everything he did. I felt the last thing in the world I wanted to do was to was get him upset. Too many outside things did this already. I knew this by virtue of his state of health, which was not good. He had days of terrible pains, stomach mostly, and would come home from his office gray and drawn. I never wanted to do anything to upset him. I didn't want such a sin on my conscience. And if I were to run away from Millbrook, I felt certain he would view this as a personal insult and one more angry blow from an already tottering world.

My mother would do exactly what my father wanted. She might be a momentary comfort, but basically he ran the show and if he didn't like something or someone, that was that. If I were to return home unannounced, the household would be upset and Father would be hurt and that was out of the question. No, I had to stay. I knew this somewhere in my heart of hearts, but the plotting was in its own way a pain-killer.

After dinner we gathered to find out about classes and assignments. I was in the first form, the very bottom, comparable in junior high school to the seventh grade. Within a week of my shaky arrival, Mr. Abbott began a music appreciation class. Nowadays the phrase "music appreciation" is considered inaccurate, old-fashioned, nondescriptive, and passé.

I still think it says what it means: an opportunity to hear music and learn something about it from the standpoint of being a member of the audience. Many musicans seem to forget that there is an audience to play to and that they have responsibilities to that audience, if they have the nerve to climb onto the stage in the first place. After all, music is the only art that requires a middle man. One can look at a painting without being told what it's all about. One can read a play and react to it in the mind, but unless you know what those dots and tails mean on a piece of music paper, you're lost. I'm all for reinstating "music appreciation." I could be run out town for this but that's the way I feel.

At any rate, Mr. Abbott assembled the class and we sat while he began a gentle lecture on the joys of the art. The first piece I remember was the Haydn "Clock" Symphony and his marvelous description of Haydn and his music. From the "Clock" we moved to the "Surprise" and I remember vividly the shock and pleasure of that loud chord in the second movement. We all really were surprised. I loved this forty-five-minute period twice a week and I was the brightest boy in the class. As we moved along during the year, Mr. Abbott had to keep my enthusiasm in check by letting the others answer some of the questions. I was happy, joyful, moved, complete, when involved in music. Complete, however, only while listening. At the same time as the appreciation classes, it was decided that I should have piano lessons and these started under the guidance of a rather bored young man named Gerald Tracy. Tracy seemed to deal with me as a nuisance, and I was at war with him over the exercises and little pieces he demanded I play. The only thing I wanted was to hear him play instead of pounding out my lessons. I think he, too, was put off by me and responded eagerly when I asked to hear him. Tracy and I were together in our love-hate relationship for six years, during which I did learn some of the easier Beethoven sonatas and a smattering of Mozart, Ravel, Debussy, and Chopin as well.

After the first two years at Millbrook, I began to get encouragement from my teachers, especially from the headmaster, who had to worry about me anyway as part of his responsibilities. Mr. Abbott not only taught music appreciation but was a hopeless music buff and played the piano for chapel services. He also taught music history in a course designed to accompany the Carnegie Foundation Music Library. That library was awarded to a number of schools during the 1930s and consisted of a history of music on records and a beautiful two-piece console phonograph. The phonograph was of advanced design and the sound that came forth from the speakers was truly remarkable. The records themselves were carefully selected from every company in the world and cross-indexed by composer, performer, type, and form. It was then, and still is, one of the best packages of musical research that has been devised for anyone interested in the art. Mr. Abbott used it masterfully, and before long, he had created a special class for one other boy and myself, a class of music analysis that was fully up to college standards.

There was one other teacher at Millbrook who turned on lights for me, and that was Cornwall B. Rogers, a history professor at Columbia University who taught two days a week at Millbrook. Rogers had a quiet approach to his subject, although he was seething with passion underneath his gentle exterior. He was a stickler for good work but nothing was too much trouble for the student who was really interested. His American history class really awakened me to the extraordinary saga of this country, and it was he who pointed out that history can be the logic that keeps us all from going crazy with modern problems. Human beings change so little, he implied, and history makes it easier to see ourselves in perspective.

In September, 1938, two days before I was due back at Millbrook to start my fifth form year, my father died, very suddenly. At his death he had no debts but he had no money either and our lives underwent an immediate change. He had spent most of his inherited capital in the investment counseling business. His firm was to continue into the forties and fifties, merge with another, and become one of the biggest in the country. His investment would have paid off well but he never lived to see it and my mother was forced to sell his interests at a fraction of their value. She was left with a life insurance policy and very little else. Through some family properties owned abroad he stood to inherit two small trust funds and these were deemed to be part of his estate at his death. As a result the little he had, with the exception of his insurance, was taxed away by both the State of New York and the federal government.

When the estate was settled my mother set out to rebuild her fortunes. She took a job to support her three young sons, moved out of our large apartment on 72nd Street to a much smaller one, with one old family retainer instead of the four or five she had been used to. I cannot say we ever really suffered in the physical sense, despite scenes and recriminations about money that were right out of Victorian novels, but with attention focused on economics there was a continuing lack of stimulation in any other area of our lives. I sought it out for myself.

Mother rose to the challenge of the situation beautifully. She had always been fascinated by the world of finance and the stock market, in fact the whole machinery of money. She was constantly bent over the stock pages, making long columns of figures on yellow pads, rattling on at a great rate about debentures, options, stock splits, dividends, interest rates, and the like. With the help of a former partner of my father's, Douglas Newbold, she gradually began to rebuild a small estate, and even weathered a financial disaster two years later when one of her brothers, caught in the same net as Richard Whitney, paid his dues at the Harvard Club of Sing Sing and all his relatives made good his bad debts.

She never remarried, although she was only thirty-nine when father

died. I asked her about this once and she said she just couldn't; she had
had her life and that was that. She was lonely and grew old ahead of
her time. I never knew her really. We had almost no interests in common, although she liked to go to a concert from time to time, and was
enormously proud of anything I did, albeit sometimes with little knowledge or judgment of what that was.

So I was left on my own. When I say "on my own," that is really not
quite right. There were two sets of relatives who had an enormous
influence on my life and from a very early age encouraged me to move
ahead in the worlds in which I felt most comfortable. My father's sister, Katherine, and her husband, Francis Biddle, was one; my mother's brother, Chester Burden, and his wife, Eleanor, was the other.

Chester and Eleanor Burden were childless and traveled a great deal,
mostly to Europe and the major music centers. Music was their great
passion. Eleanor as a young girl had studied the violin with Georges
Enesco in Paris, and Chester snared Eleanor in Paris during World War
I. When Chester was mustered out of the service (he'd been in the Signal Corps) he took a job with Postal Telegraph, where he remained all
his working life. This left him plenty of time for music. Eleanor teamed
up with Anita Damrosch Littell, daughter of Walter Damrosch, to form
the Burden-Littell Bureau, which rapidly became the leading New
York organization dealing with society weddings, debutante parties,
receptions, and all the tribal rites of the rich.

Every summer the Burdens sailed off to European festivals; every
winter they haunted Carnegie Hall and Town Hall and the Metropolitan Opera. Chester served on the board of the New York Philharmonic
for many years as assistant treasurer. Their charming and beautifully
furnished apartment was a civilized haven for musicians, writers, critics, and friends who were equally passionate about the arts. Eleanor is
to this day a woman who knows her own mind. The whole vogue of
women's lib must give her wry amusement; all her life she did what she
wanted to do with utmost confidence and determination and let absolutely nothing stand in her way. Chester was milder but devoted to her
and she to him. They were a splendid couple, and brooked no nonsense
when it came to the things they both cared about. Nephews and nieces
were all very well but housebroken, please, and no fidgeting.

Early on they discovered I was interested in music. It must have
been around 1936 because from that time on whenever I was home on
vacation, they would aks me to concerts and the opera and I accepted
as many invitations as I could. Eleanor would always weep at Richard
Strauss and knows more about his works than almost anyone I know. I

once heard Olin Downes, the great critic for the New York *Times*, talking to Eleanor about Strauss. "Whenever I want to know anything
about him, you're the one with the information," he said. I thought he
was being polite and asked him. He looked at me and shook his head.
"She is more knowledgeable on Strauss than anyone I know," he replied. And he meant it. They would ask me to dinner, too, when they
were having people like Downes or Artur Rodzinski or Marc Connelly
or Jarmila Novotna. It was always black tie and almost always the
same menu of clear soup, veal, beautifully cut long string beans, sweet
potatoes, a creamy dessert accompanied by a decent claret and champagne. The dining room table and chairs were Duncan Phyfe and
glowed softly in the candlelight. The conversation was measured but to
my young ears sounded desperately important, even world-shattering.
This was the world of music and the arts; this was what I wanted. This
I was determined to have.

Katherine and Francis Biddle were different. She, a poet whose
books, particularly *Outside the World* and *Time Has No Shadow*, made
a deep impression on me, was Father's younger sister. There were
three sisters, all of whom were artists in their own ways—Katherine
the poet, Cornelia the sculptress, and the oldest, Marguerite, who was
the family impresario. Marguerite married an Italian, Prince Roffredo
Caetani, himself a pianist and composer. She made her mark as the
Serge Diaghilev of literature, first in the 1920s in Paris with the literary
revue *Commerce* and later in Italy after World II with *Botteghe Oscure.*
In both periodicals she published short stories, poems, essays, cri-
tiques, and plays by new and, in most instances, unknown authors. She
discovered the talents of T. S. Eliot, Rainer Maria Rilke, Dylan Thomas, and Truman Capote, among others. The three sisters looked to Father as their guide in the practical world of affairs and treated him with
something approaching reverence. Cornelia, the sculptress, never married and turned out a body of work usually carved from raw materials.
She concentrated on animals, often huge beasts. Her largest was a
baby elephant carved in ebony which won a grand prix in Paris in 1936
and later floated out to sea in a Florida hurricane. Her frog sits in Rit-
tenhouse Square in Philadelphia. Her crucifix for the main altar of the
Cathedral of St. John the Divine always annoyed her because it was
made for a Byzantine chapel and transferred after the late Bishop Man-
ning took a look at it and ordered all the detail work to be filled with
putty. He got an imposing altar piece but a ruined artistic creation, and
Cornelia never forgave him or the cathedral.

Francis Biddle, Katherine's husband, had a brilliant career as a law-

yer and public servant. He was the first chairman of the National Labor Relations Board in 1933, general counsel for the TVA in the later
thirties, Solicitor General in 1940, Attorney General from 1941 to 1945.
After Roosevelt's death, Truman appointed him the American judge at
the first Nuremberg trials and in his later years he wrote what many
consider the definitive book about the Roosevelt years. He was almost
the last of that rare American breed, a patrician to his heart's core with
a deep love of country and sense of public service. He was brilliant,
amusing, perceptive, passionate, colorful, and impatient with people
and ideas that did not measure up to his high standards. No man to
have as an enemy, he was the ideal friend, and from a very early age he
was one to me. Francis encouraged my interest in the arts, introduced
me to the world of letters, and always had time for my young problems. The Biddles' Washington house was a salon that took in some of
the best minds and talents of the day. I met St. John Perse there, as
well as Edmund Wilson and Conrad Aiken, Harlan Stone and Felix
Frankfurter, T.S. Eliot and Archibald MacLeish, Aaron Copland, Walter Lippmann, and many others; painters, statesmen, and women;
dancers, actresses—a cross-section of the world I loved and wanted to
be a part of. Katherine and Francis moved among their guests with
grace and wit and even in the most difficult days they never showed
anything except interest in the subject or person at hand.

Years later, when I wanted to make the plunge into the music world,
I lacked the funds to do so. I had been reasonably successful right after
World War II and had gotten trapped in the broadcasting business and
was making a very decent salary. To make the change would require a
financial sacrifice and by that time I was married and had three children
under the age of two. I went to Washington to ask for help and for two
days was put through a cross-examination by Francis that could have
stood the test of the Supreme Court. He really wanted to know whether I had thought the matter out carefully and realized the risks I might
be taking. I had to justify and answer every question put to me and
when the interrogation was finished, I knew beyond any measure of
doubt that I wanted music, opera, and the performing arts as my life's
work. "You'll be all right," he said. "Your head seems to be in the box
office and your feet in the clouds. It's better that way!" I agreed.

Between the Chester Burdens and the Francis Biddles I began to
think that my feelings about music and art were worth strengthening.
Both couples took pleasure in watching my career develop almost as
much as I took pleasure in sharing it with them.

I graduated from the Millbrook School in 1940 but "graduate" is perhaps too grand a word for the actual facts. I finished six years of Mill-brook but I did not receive a diploma. Instead I was given a certificate stating that I had completed six years of a "special course of studies." This euphemism was employed because I had not completed in a satis-factory manner the high school requirements for entrance to college. College was out of the question anyway. I wanted to get on with my life in music and already had visions of a big career. Exactly how and what this big career was to be was quite cloudy, but I knew there would be the moment when I stepped on the stage of Carnegie Hall to tumul-tuous applause and, standing there, bowing modestly, I would embrace the public. It was all very vague yet all very definite. The only problem was how. Mr. Pulling and the others felt that music school was the an-swer.

He pondered the problem and came up one day with the idea of the Longy School in Cambridge, Massachusetts. We made a trip there together and much to my pleasure I was admitted as a general student. I think this was in large measure because of Miss Elsie Buckingham, the school secretary, who was a determined-looking lady with firm iron hair and horn-rimmed glasses but eyes that twinkled and encouraged. She was my first example of that unique specimen, the Cambridge, Massachusetts, maiden lady-with-heart. Miss Buckingham and I decid-ed to wait until the fall to determine what my studies should actually be and Mr. Pulling and I returned to Millbrook, both relieved to have something about my future assured. His educational duties were now done. Even without a diploma, I felt good, too. I was going to be in the music field and whatever else happened, this at least was a certainty.

III

School, NBC, the War

Follen Street, Cambridge, Massachusetts, is tree-lined, quiet, and clean. The houses are all set back from the road, the tree branches in summer and fall make an archway filtering the sun, and little disturbs the look of tranquillity. Number One, the home of the Longy School of Music is a nineteenth-century stone mansion with a gabled roof, bay windows, a wide lawn, and imposing steps. At this building I arrived in early September, 1940, as an enrolled student. The Longy School had been founded by the great French oboist of the Boston Symphony, René Longy, and from the outset had set very high standards. In 1940, it was destined to take a big leap into musical history as the wartime home of the great French teacher of composition, Nadia Boulanger, who had been forced to flee her county after the surrender to Hitler and had been given a home in the United States by Winifred Hope Johnstone and her sister, both firm Boulanger admirers, in the Back Bay section of Boston. Mlle. Boulanger was generally recognized as one of the leading teachers in the world and her American pupils, such as Roy Harris, Aaron Copland, and Samuel Barber, attested to her skills, wisdom, and excitement. While here she was joined by another refugee, Igor Stravinsky, who was subsequently to make his home in California and become an American citizen. Stravinsky had been asked by Harvard University to give a course on the poetics of music in 1939 and remained in the Boston area until moving to California in

the late forties. Both Mlle. Boulanger and Stravinsky were often enter-
tained at the Forbes home in Cambridge, where there were great musical parties with reasonable food, excellent wines and music-making until dawn.

Boulanger made her professional headquarters at the Longy. I would
see her coming and going, her pepper-and-salt hair pulled back, her
black blouse, black skirt, and black hat making her look at a distance as
if she were a nun lost outside a convent. I stationed myself inside the
building occasionally to watch her arrival, trailed as she was by admirers and always in deep conversation with whoever her companion happened to be. I noticed she had an incredible smile that lit up her face
and that she talked with great passion, causing her eyeglasses, which
were attached to her dress by a thin chain fastened to a pin, to wiggle
back and forth at an alarming rate. I was puzzled by her all black costumes until my friend Miss Buckingham told me that she was in per-
petual mourning for her sister Lili, who had died many years before. I
thought this odd but said nothing.

In the normal course of events Mlle. Boulanger's and my paths
would not have been destined to cross. I was a beginning student of
solfège, taught by a spicy French lady named Colette, then the wife of
E. Power Biggs. Mme. Colette was very much of the French school, no
nonsense, and if she had the chance I think she would have used the
rod. My classmates were mainly girls, most of whom aspired to singing
careers. There was one other fellow, with whom I became friendly.
His voice was worse than mine but his ear was unerring and he could
conquer all those harmonic gymnastics with astounding ease. I was always confused and if it hadn't been for a dark-haired contralto sitting
next to me who took pity and would hum the tone in my ear just before
I had to perform I would have been kicked out of the class. I've never
forgotten Eunice Alberts for that kindness and rejoice that she has had
such a distinguished career in this country. We met again many years
later, my first season as acting general manager of the Metropolitan
Opera in 1972, and I shall always regret that I had nothing proper to
offer her. Mme. Colette was also my piano teacher and we had many a
scene about my inadequate practicing and bad preparation.

I felt my Longy days might be numbered and went for consolation to
Miss Buckingham. She told me not to worry, that things were going to
be just fine and that she would take care of everything. I had no idea
what she meant by this until I arrived at school one morning to find my
name posted for a class with Boulanger. I knew there must be some
mistake but Miss Buckingham was adamant. "She will like you," she
said. "But I haven't the right credentials," I cried. "Yes you do," she

said. "I've not put you with the composers. You're to take her course on Beethoven quartets." "But I don't know anything about the Beethoven quartets," I pleaded, "You will," she replied and that was the end of that.

A few days later I found myself seated in a small class of obviously senior students both in age and training and at the piano was Mlle. Boulanger. "We are going to explore the quartets," she began. And before I knew it I was mesmerized. She talked about Beethoven, about the quartets and their place in history, she pounded out examples on the piano, she exhorted the heavens, she pleaded for our understanding, she transmitted the energy, force, and beauty of what she believed in. She became Beethoven. We saw the creative process through her eyes and voice. Some days a string quartet played, some days she just used the piano, but on all days she sent us out of that classroom with new thoughts and new inspirations and new curiosities. My imagination was fired, I couldn't get enough. I asked Miss Buckingham if there were any other Boulanger seminars I might attend and soon found myself in a course on contemporary style and compositional texture. I went to the first meeting of this group and realized in a minute that I was way over my head. But again I was transfixed by her techniques. Here, of course, she would illustrate style points by reading off a full orchestral score at the piano as if it was Book One of beginning piano lessons by Diller and Quaile. Her piano technique and ability to play the notes was faultless, but her touch was something else again. She pounded hard and the sounds weren't pretty but they were effective and got across her points.

I thought the best thing for me in a course that was obviously over my head was to stay in hiding in some dark corner of the room and pray that I never was called on. I did this quite successfully for two weeks until one day she turned and pointed her finger. "You, please, here," she commanded, pointing to a chair beside her at the piano. I quaked. "Quickly, quickly," she added with impatience. I got up and came forward wishing that the floor would open before me or that the whole experience was nothing more than a dream. "Sit here," she said, "and turn pages." There was a huge conductor's score of Beethoven's Seventh Symphony. I've forgotten exactly what she was illustrating but I remember keeping my eyes glued to the pages and running them up and down vertically as I tried to find where the melody was. Sweat rolled off my face but I kept up with her. After about fifteen minutes of this she turned to me and nodded what I took to be a "thank you," and I scuttled back to my seat.

After the class was over I waited until everyone had left and stepped forward to speak to her. "Mademoiselle," I said timorously, "I think there's been a mistake. I don't think I belong in this class." She looked at me straight on. "Why do you say that?" she asked. "Because I don't think I'm skilled enough to be one of your pupils." She smiled. "What is your name, please," she asked. I told her. She took my music book of class exercises from me and before I could say anything she placed it on the piano music rack and opened it up. I was dying of embarrassment but there was nothing I could do. She looked over the pages and then, closing the book, she handed it to me saying: "You're right. You haven't any talent." She saw the look on my face, a combination, I suppose, of hurt and relief. "But you obviously love music. I noticed you in the Beethoven classes. We will get along, you and I." And she handed me back my books.

Then began a wonderful time for me in Cambridge. I became her sort of unofficial aide-de-camp at school, carrying her briefcases, making notes, organizing lunches, and most important of all, turning pages for her at concerts throughout the Cambridge-Boston area. She played a great deal of chamber music and I attended most of the rehearsals. Watching and listening to her work was a whole school experience in itself. She drove at music with an intensity and devotion and single-mindedness that overcame any obstacle that might be in the way. The room might be frigid, it might be a Turkish bath; the fellow artists might be flourishing with health or at death's door with pneumonia; the audiences might be sparse or overflowing. It made no difference whatsoever. Music was what counted and music was all that was important. Her composition students were in awe and, I think, fear of her. She certainly dominated any discussion she was in and, I suppose, was also definite and direct on composition forms and shapes. I don't know for certain because I was not one of them but I do remember talking to one man who seemed to turn a pale green before his sessions with her and always emerged from the room after his time was up looking like a ship that has made it around Cape Horn. Her concerts were always events. She took her place onstage at the piano and whether or not that instrument was the featured one in the program she made it so. The other musicians took their cues from her and so did the audience. I sat to the left and slightly behind her and would spend as much time studying the scores before a concert as the musicians. Tough she was, and unrelenting, but all in the cause of music. Not until Leonard Bernstein did I meet anyone else who had so total a commitment.

During the course of these weeks Mademoiselle and I had various talks on the run and I learned to prepare my questions and opinions quickly in order not to waste her time. We spoke of my enthusiasm for music and frankly about my lack of real talent for either performing or creating it. One afternoon over a rare cup of tea in her classroom between appointments she said, "I've been thinking about you. You should think about another part of music." I nodded, as if understanding what she was talking about. "There is a whole other world in this art," she went on, "and it is the world for you. It is very bad now. Everyone cheats, steals, takes the money away from the artists who do the work. But there is no way of organizing a career or running a concert or planning a tour without the managers and agents and entrepreneurs, and the field needs good people." She paused to take a sip and I sat there staring at her. I'd never thought of that. Even in my highest romantic moments of fantasy I'd always thought of myself somehow as being on the stage, of being a star, loved by the people, rich, successful, sought after, although I'd never come to grips with precisely how this was going to be done. I thought of Carnegie Hall, of the Metropolitan Opera, the Philharmonic-Symphony Society of New York (now mercifully shortened to the New York Philharmonic), of the Boston Symphony, for which I had a Saturday night student subscription in one of the best seats in Symphony Hall, of Town Hall, the Academy of Music, Albert Hall, the Paris Opera. I could manage them all! I could be P. T. Barnum and David Belasco, Sam H. Harris and Edward Johnson. My mental wheels whirled. The possibilities were limitless. "What an idea!" I said. "Of course," she replied. "The sooner the better."

And that was, literally, that. I carried her briefcase a few more times, turned pages at one or two more concerts, but as far as she was concerned she had rendered unto Caesar and now Caesar better get about his business. I had no idea how to go about becoming a manager but I thought that Chester and Eleanor Burden ought to know something about this field so I arranged a meeting with them over the Thanksgiving recess and told them the whole story. They had young friends named Richard and Kay Leach, whom I had met a few months before. The Leaches were New York's golden couple of music. He was a representative with the NBC Artists Bureau, then one of the two largest agencies in the concert field, and she, a tall and strikingly beautiful blonde with a wide smile and picture-book looks, stood by his side ready to kill if anyone got in the way.

At that time the NBC Artists Bureau was a wholly owned subsidiary of the National Broadcasting Company. The Columbia Broadcasting System, too, had its concert bureau, Columbia Concerts, Inc., and between the two of them they controlled virtually all the artists and therefore most of the musical life of the country. They also had created, during the depths of the depression, an organized-audience system for concerts that guaranteed fees in advance. The brainchild of onetime Chautauqua circuit bookers named Ward French and Dema Harschberger, a tough lady who took little nonsense and loathed failure, the system was baby simple. A representative of the organization came into a small town or city and sought out the local civic leaders. He or she persuaded the leaders that music was needed in the town to increase the cultural life and could be done on the basis of no profit but no loss. Leading citizens were asked to a meeting to form either a Community Concert Association (if organized by Columbia) or a Civic Concert Association (if organized by NBC). A dinner meeting was usually held at which both the local leaders and the concert representative would extol the virtues of music for the community and the representative would show how a subscription campaign could be organized by the people sitting in the room and money raised before a single artist was engaged. The representative usually had a good talk about the Horowitzes and Heifetzes and Elmans who would come flocking provided the community raised enough subscriptions to pay their fees. The series was entirely by subscription: there were no single admissions. The subscriber could lend his card to a friend if he was not planning to attend a concert, but no one could be admitted on a one-time-only basis; it was a subscription or nothing. After the campaign was held and the money in the bank the representatives then whipped out lists of artists managed by their respective companies and worked out a series with the new Community or Civic association. The town benefitted by having real music performed by first-rate artists, and the artists benefitted because they knew that on Civic or Community dates there was no chance of a vanishing local manager. Their fees were safe and guaranteed.

The organized-audience movement was what really saved the concert business during the 1930s depression when all kinds of traveling theater and vaudeville were dead or dying rapidly and the family moved into the movie palaces. Community and Civic concerts saved the musician, preserved the coast-to-coast tour, and perhaps most important of all gave a platform for both the stars and the newcomers to practice their arts. Most of the Community and Civic cities did not scrape together large budgets and that meant that their series had to be fleshed out with inexpensive talent. This gave the newcomers their chance. And what a chance! Harsh as it may sound, if someone strives for a career as a soloist, either instrumentalist or singer, there is hardly anything better than having to perform for audiences who know nothing about you and care less. The only way to succeed is to move them with your talent. If you can do that you might survive in the solo field, and the more chances you have to perform in public, the stronger your stage presence will be and the more professional your approach. A lot of young artists complain about the restrictive programming of the or-ganized-audience cities, feeling put upon when they are not en-couraged to play Beethoven Opus 111 or to sing a song cycle of Alban Berg. I suppose one can make an argument that repetitious playing of the Moonlight Sonata dulls one's artistic perceptions; nevertheless, I think one better bloody well know how to sell the Moonlight to strang-ers before trying to move them along with a more demanding reper-toire. The organized-audience cities, as imperfect as they are, still pro-vide a priceless opportunity for exposure and development.

In any event I had my meeting with the Burdens and the Leaches. At that time Dick Leach was just finishing an assignment as script writer for the Toscanini NBC Symphony broadcasts and invited me to visit him at his office to discuss my future. I went to 30 Rockefeller Plaza and up to the second floor of the NBC Studios to his office and my romantic streak came out again. Here were the halls of radio, of Jack Benny, Graham McNamee, Jessica Dragonette, the "Voice of Firestone," the "Telephone Hour," and all the great soap operas that spilled out of the speakers every day of the year. And here, too, was the radio home of the Metropolitan Opera. I got off the elevator that morning behind a tall, somewhat heavy-set man with curly brown-black hair and glasses. I heard him clear his throat and my heart leapt. He spoke to someone at the elevator landing and I stared after him as he went down a corridor and turned a corner. Milton Cross! I was in the home of the stars.

Dick Leach received me graciously and explained that NBC had a policy about youngsters. Everyone was supposed to take a turn at be-ing a pageboy. He explained that the pageboys were chosen for their potential as future managers and officers of the company. I explained that I could not quite see what a pageboy had to do with entering the music world but he was clear and definite that one could not have the NBC Artists Bureau without the Page Squad. He took me to meet someone in the personnel department and I began filling out forms and smiling a lot while being questioned about my background. I began to get very excited.

The interview that morning led to another and another and finally the moment came when I was telephoned and told that I had a job and should report at four the next afternoon. I thanked the caller and re-minded him that my basic interest in NBC was in the Artists Bureau and I hoped someone would watch out for my interests in that area.

This all took place in October, 1941, and by the end of that month I was in my well-fitting blue and gold pageboy uniform ready to meet the world.

And it was quite a world, my first real taste of show business, and I loved every minute of it. My post was either the sixth-floor page desk, where studio 6A and 6B housed such greats as Fred Allen and the "Telephone Hour," or the eighth-floor desk, where Lowell Thomas passed by every night to his studio and where, special of specials, studio 8H housed the NBC Symphony. There were smaller studios, too, on that floor and I got friendly with the cast of "Henry Aldrich," the company of "Manhattan Merry-go-round," and Phil Spitalny and his All-Girl Orchestra, featuring Evelyn and Her Magic Violin. It was the first and I hope the last time I ever saw a white violin. Evelyn played it passably but while under her chin it looked as if a giant false tooth had fallen askew.

The high point of the week for me was Saturday night when the NBC Symphony played. I ushered on the main floor, helping people to their seats, and handed out the programs, which were printed on cork so they would not rattle and be picked up the microphones. Toscanini's entrance made my knees buckle every time. He walked onto the stage with his hands clutching his coat lapels, the baton firmly held in the right hand. There seemed to be an almost saintlike look on his face which may have had something to do with his nearsightedness, for he cocked his head at an odd angle and seemed to have great spiritual messages in his eyes. He may have just been looking for the podium. Once he took his place, though, and the green light on his music stand flashed on, he plunged into the music and one forgot about everything and everybody else. The studio itself was an odd place to hear him. It was acoustically dry and every note in every section of the orchestra stood out without much blending. One heard all the parts almost antiseptically, and I believe the theory was that this produced a melded sound when transmitted over the airwaves. I believe the studio was wrong, a disaster for sound, but no one ever said a word about it. You have only to listen to some of the recordings Toscanini made in that room to realize that something was not quite right about it. In any event, imperfect as the room was, he was there, and he more than made up for the acoustical shortcomings with the depth and passion of his music making.

On nights when the symphony wasn't playing, my attention was on less weighty matters and I soon realized that I had an instinctive love for performers. I'd never been around professionals before and they were, as a rule, generous in asking me to share in the off moments of rehearsals. This way I came to have a pleasant relationship with people like Garry Moore, Hugh James, and even Walter Winchell, and more important, began to see how emotionally insecure most of them were. In a sense they all put their lives on the line each time they got up before a microphone. They were only as good as their last broadcast and this included not only the announcers and actors but the musicians as well. I found I shared their fears and anxieties and sometimes their successes. My empathy for them increased and also the feeling that I was a part of their world.

I particularly empathized with the newcomers, and there was quite a large number of these who were introduced to the music public through either the "Voice of Firestone" or the "Telephone Hour." Both programs featured the biggest stars as a regular part of their presentations yet from time to time slipped in a newcomer. One was a young baritone who made his "Telephone Hour" debut with the help of several cups of coffee fetched by the page. I lingered on for a few minutes as the program was getting ready for its dress rehearsal and was knocked out by the sound of his voice. Years later I reminded Robert Merrill of that night and while he had forgotten the coffee, I think he still remembered his nerves. He sent me a bottle of champagne on my first opening night as acting general manager of the Metropolitan Opera with a note apologizing that it wasn't coffee. I liked him then and I like him now.

About a month after my pageboy career was under way I came in one day to face the worst possible news. The government had ordered both NBC and CBS to divest themselves of their concert bureaus under the Sherman Anti-trust laws. They could not continue to be both a buyer and a seller of talent. In addition, NBC was ordered to divest itself of its second radio network, the "Blue," on the grounds that two networks were one too many for any one company. Never mind about the "Red," as the first one was called, and the "Blue." The concert bureau action stabbed right at the gut of my reasons for coming to NBC in the first place and I had no idea how this was going to affect my future. I tried to see Marks Levine, who was the director of the bureau, but he was too busy, and the personnel department of NBC suddenly became very cold on advice. For better or worse it looked as if I was stuck at NBC as the artist bureau floated out of my grasp.

The radio newscasters and commentators as well as the newspapers seemed to be warming up to the possibility that the United States might go to war with Japan. I was paying very little attention to that. I came in every day and went about my pageboy duties though my heart was not in it to the extent that it had been in the beginning. On a Saturday night, shortly after the breakup, I was stationed in the lobby of the NBC quarters to help handle people who were coming to a very special Toscanini concert, marking the signing of a new contract for the maestro's services by RCA President David Sarnoff. The ladies and gentlemen were arriving in evening clothes. My friends (and future in-laws) the Theodore Steinways swept by looking cheerful and elegant and shortly thereafter the familiar figure of Mlle. Boulanger appeared clutching her invitation and looking straight ahead. "Good evening, Mademoiselle," I said, bowing low from the waist. She looked up. "Ah, Chapin! What are you doing here?" "Helping you to the Toscanini party," I replied. "Ah yes, the other side of music. The other side. Well, well . . . good luck." And she waved to me as the elevator doors closed.

On December 7, 1941, I went to the Trans-Lux newsreel theater on Madison Avenue in the afternoon and returned home to find my mother in a state of collapse. I promised I wouldn't do anything rash and tried to assure her that the Japanese were not outside on 79th Street and that I intended to pursue the long process of becoming an aviation cadet. I felt that this was the perfect moment to indulge my boyhood dream of becoming a second Colonel Roscoe B. Turner. I told her I would continue at NBC until at least the time when I had followed through on the cadet program.

With the NBC Artists Bureau now moved to 711 Fifth Avenue and having acquired a new name—National Concert Artists Corporation—I was stuck at the old parent company. Before I had a chance to look into moving myself I was offered a new job with the International Department as what was called a night news editor. It sounded frightfully grand and the talk I had with Fred Bate, the NBC London correspondent who had returned home to take over this department, made me feel that perhaps, until called up to the Air Corps, my destiny lay in playing a home-grown Richard Harding Davis. I accepted, swollen with pride, and went out immediately to buy a crushed fedora in order to look like Ray Milland or Jimmy Stewart playing a newspaper type. What Bate did not tell me was that my duties called for me to man the teletype machines from midnight to eight AM six days a week, tear off the several copies from AP, UP, INS, and Reuters, and distribute those to the various language desks. The international department of NBC ran its own short-wave network broadcasting overseas in English, French, German, Italian, Portuguese, Spanish, and Turkish, and my job was to provide the copy fresh off the machines in order that the reporters could write their own stories. I was a glorified copy boy whose hands were constantly black from carbon paper and whose ears were dimmed by the close clatter of all the machinery. Gradually I became accustomed to the din and the dirt but I never could get used to the hours. I would finish work at eight and stagger my way home as the mobs began arriving for the day. I would sleep from about 10:00 AM until 4:30 PM or 5:00 and get up, bleary-eyed, for breakfast. I would sit around listlessly until 6:00 or 7:00 and then have dinner, followed perhaps by a movie, where I would fall sound asleep, and then into the studios half dead by midnight.

I did see another side of New York life, however, when I "lunched" at 4:00 AM with the whores, pimps, and gamblers. I grew very fond of the "night people." They had a world and a society of their own and I loved observing it. My favorite viewing spot was a Hayes-Bickford cafe across the street from the Sixth Avenue entrance of the RCA Building. Over endless cups of coffee the tight-waisted girls and the wide-brim-hatted men would move from table to table talking, laughing, and occasionally crying. It was the era of the zoot suit with its baggy pants and exaggerated lapels, watch chains looped from the waist to the knees, shoes of various hues wildly shaped. It was the era of Damon Runyon, of Minsky's and Lindy's, the *Daily Mirror* and the *Journal-American*, 5-cent coffee and subways. I saw New York in a new light and despite my continuing exhaustion I felt exhilarated. I was also deep in the midst of preparations for the air cadet exams and I wanted nothing standing in the way here. That meant daytime study, particularly in math and physics, both of which I hated but both necessary for flight training.

But despite the upside down hours, the job was not without its adventures. On the morning of August 20, 1942, at about 3:00 AM the bells rang on the teletype machines as they had done so often before. I got up and went over to look at the AP machine and a bulletin came through about an Allied raid on the French coastal village of Dieppe. The story was not "flashed," as the really big ones were, that is, a series of bells and a one-line "Flash—"but something about it made me go to the map and pick out Dieppe. I looked at the distance between Britain and this small seacoast town and realized that the raid must have had some special significance. I telephoned Fred Bate, got him out of bed, and read him the bulletin. At once he was wide awake and told me to summon all the language desks and get them in as soon as possible. I did the necessary calling and at about 4:00 AM the key staff was assembled. All regular programs were cancelled and special material on the Dieppe situation began pouring out. Only at that moment did I realize that my gut instinct must have been correct. A few days later

Bate called me to his office for special congratulations and I began to feel a touch of the Richard Harding Davis glow.

Eventually I was promoted from the copy desk to the English-language section, given an audition, and put to work as an announcer-writer. I had done a little radio work while I was a page on the so-called radical station WEVD, but this was the first full-time mike job I ever had. My duties included three fifteen-minute newscasts in the morning interspersed with talking and playing records. I joined two colleagues, Lee Emmerick and Bill Lewis, on a show called "Service Serenade," aimed at overseas soldiers and sailors. I became the butt of the program, the fellow who couldn't pronounce baseball players' names unless they were of one syllable. No one heard us at home but we were very big with the Arabs.

I had a moment of great pride in October, 1942, when Francis Biddle, then U.S. Attorney General, picked Columbus Day to announce from the stage of Carnegie Hall that the Italians were no longer enemy aliens. Bate had made a great civil rights issue out of the citizenship question as indeed he should have, and Francis became the hero of the day in our offices. Not only in our offices but in just about every Italian business in New York. The city, then as now, was filled with Italians, many of whom had neglected to take out citizenship papers. Francis and I went to lunch at a favorite restaurant of mine, Giovanni's on East 55th Street, and as we entered, the place erupted with cheers and applause. Busboys dropped their trays, waiters left their customers, the bartender whipped around his bar, and everyone, it seemed, was crying. The proprietor clasped our hands and kissed them. Francis was touched by all this and began speaking to them all in Italian mixed with French. We were ushered to a table and that was the last we had to do with the meal. The corks were pulled endlessly, the pasta and piccata of veal, salads, fruits, and desserts appeared one after the other, and we both gave in to the situation. At about 4:00 PM we left, stuffed and bagged and useless for the rest of the day. The Italians had a new hero; I had a new hangover.

The next day Francis and Katherine, together with my Aunt Cornelia, paid a state visit to NBC. They came to my studio and listened to me broadcast and then were taken on a tour of the place. I joined them in studio 8-H, which was empty at the time, and as we were standing there an aide to Toscanini spotted us and went running back to the Maestro, who was evidently in his dressing room. Minutes later the aide returned and asked Francis if he would please come with him. Francis did and later told us that Toscanini leapt up when he entered and threw

his arms around him. He also had apparently thrown his arms around
the radio while listening to the Columbus Day speech at his home in
Riverdale. There were tears in his eyes and exclamations of gratitude
on behalf of his country and his countrymen. It was an altogether moving occasion.

Shortly thereafter I went to Governor's Island for my Air Corps
physical and passed. I then took the academic exams, trembling all
over, and after what seemed like an eternity passed those, too. Some
days later I raised my right hand and became a full-fledged aviation cadet. Notified that I would be called up in December or at the latest January 1, 1943, I proceeded to wind up my job. Right on schedule the call
came and on the morning of December 31, 1942, I took a ferry from
New York to Jersey City and boarded a Central Railroad of New Jersey commuter car for a four-night three-day trip to Miami Beach, my
first but by no means only experience of spending a lot of time without
changing my clothes or sleeping in a bed. Thus began what was to be
many months of flight training at various places around the country.

My career in the Air Corps really got under way on April 15, 1944,
when I finally, after months of harrowing training, received my wings
as a pilot and my commission as a second lieutenant. We trooped into
the post theater at Altus, Oklahoma, for the ceremonies and this
marked a major turning point for me: at long last I had started out to do
a project and seen it through to completion. And I had done it on my
own.

We were given graduation leave and I headed for Washington to visit
the Biddles. On my first day Francis took me to the Senate for lunch, to
the office of the senior Senator from Florida, Claude Pepper. Senator
Pepper had assembled a group including Lister Hill of Alabama to discuss a constitutional amendment to lower the voting age. Also seated
in the room was a portly figure with the darkest eyes I'd ever seen on
anyone. Whenever the Senators and Francis agreed on a point they
would look over to the figure who would nod either yes or no. They
seemed to be guided by his reaction and I had the sudden feeling I was
in one of those smoke-filled rooms where decisions of power and might
were always supposed to be made. After lunch Francis gave the portly
gentleman a ride and I met Ernest Cuneo for the first time. Cuneo was
a lawyer of Italian background, an intellectual who, like Francis Biddle, moved in and out of realpolitik with grace and favor, carrying
tough tools and fearless about using them. He had been general counsel to the Democratic National Committee, a law assistant to Fiorello
La Guardia, and at this time was an officer with the OSS and chief liaison between British intelligence and the FBI and the OSS chief, Gener-

al "Wild Bill" Donovan. When he smiled his face looked like a faintly naughty saint caught in the act; when he scowled all of Italy was in a black fury. In addition to his credentials he also carried one other job. He was lawyer for Walter Winchell, who at that time was at the peak of his powers as a columnist and whose energies had been engaged by Roosevelt to help the war effort. He had been made a lieutenant commander in the Naval Reserve and given a direct line to the Attorney General. Cuneo was part of the liaison and in the process he and Francis had become friends. So powerful was Winchell's position that the Senators at lunch were trying to make certain that whatever plan they developed would have Winchell's approval, hence Cuneo's presence.

That night I went to Constitution Hall to hear the National Symphony, not a first-rank group but that night the greatest orchestra in the world as far as I was concerned. The sound washed over my ears and latched firmly to my heart. Oh yes, I knew what I wanted to do, after the war was over. I was going into the music business, to make all this beauty possible. I was young, romantic, and prepared to believe the best of everyone.

In New York my mother was proud of my uniform and wings but a little vague about what I actually did. I had written regularly explaining the training process step by step but these things were somehow not immediately translatable to her. I think she had me flying B-17s on unending Walter Mitty-like missions over Germany and there was not very much I could do to persuade her otherwise. While home I went to the opera as often as I could, to the Philharmonic, and to the Toscanini broadcasts. It was thrilling to be back home, even if for a brief period.

When the leave was over I reported to Randolph Field in Texas for training as a twin-engine flight instructor and this led, with immense army logic, to training as a pilot in the Troop Carrier Command. I was shipped off to interior Missouri to learn to fly C-47s and master the CG-4A gliders. I stayed at this for three months at which point we were shipped to a marshaling field to prepare for transfer overseas.

At this base I fell passionately in love for the one and only time in my army career. She was a clerk at the post bank, a girl poured into her clothing, with breasts of Rubens-esque size and lips that pouted sex. Everyone around was after her and I didn't think I stood a chance. Nevertheless I waited patiently at the back door of the post bank, hoping that someday she would notice me. She noticed me all right, the one time I was there with a friend, whose tall body and green eyes caught her fancy immediately. I was left out in the cold, as she proceeded to have a hot affair with him. But I was no fool. I knew he was going to be moved out before I was and I didn't mind waiting. He did go, about a month after we arrived, and I lost no time in commiserating with her about her loss. She asked me to her house for a drink, and sometime along in the commiserating process I leaned over and kissed her with what I thought was properly sympathetic pressure. When our mouths met sympathy went out the window and plain raw sex came in. At one point she pulled back and asked whether I thought she was being too forward since my friend had only just left her bed. I said that I didn't think so at all, and drew her closer. I was at this time a virgin and I found the whole seduction process absolutely lovely in every respect. We saw each other from time to time after that momentous evening. I know she saw others as well and it didn't bother me one bit. She had a big heart and a gorgeous body and if she wanted to spread a little of it around, why not indeed do so. It wasn't until many years later when the film *Never on Sunday* hit the silver screen that I realized Melina Mercouri was playing my Missouri girl and I had warm pangs of memory.

Aside from my lovely wench, Missouri was a complete washout and nothing seemed to happen about moving into action. I finally decided to take matters into my own hands and wrote to the Undersecretary of War, Robert P. Patterson, whom I had known slightly. Judge Patterson, as he was known because of his place on the Circuit Court of Appeals before his appointment to the War Department, was a man of high morals, famous for being incorruptible and the scourge of war profiteers and grafters. But I figured that a request to be sent overseas rather than into some other kind of job might not sit too badly with him and I pointed out in my letter that the taxpayers had a considerable investment in me and it might as well begin to pay off. Within ten days of mailing I was called to the post administrative headquarters, rushed through a processing, and on my way to the China-Burma-India theater. Two weeks later, when I was sitting in a tent at the edge of the Ledo Road with the monsoon rains pouring down, I wrote him a letter of thanks. Some months later, the China-Burma-India mails being what they were, I received a one-sentence reply: "You're welcome."

China, Burma, and India were fascinating. I arrived in time for the last of the British 14th Army push down the Irrawaddy River to recapture Burma. We flew into narrow, newly cut fields with mail, food, and ammunition. We also flew the Hump, from Ledo, India, to Kunming, China, over the Himalayas. On these flights we rarely saw the ground. Everything was on instruments from the moment we took off until we came over the ridges toward the plains before Kunming.

China itself moved me deeply. The colors of the countryside, the sights of thousands of people doing the work of machines, their humor, all contrived to grip my mind. The Chinese knew how to laugh at themselves and everyone else. They might laugh at and with you while stealing you blind but one never really minded. Part of lend-lease here was that Chiang's government was to supply food and housing to the Americans. The food rarely appeared and the housing was the crudest sort, but American ingenuity quickly took over and we all got accustomed to powdered food. One table article of food, however, never seemed to be in short supply and that was eggs. At one point for a two-month period we had eggs every day, morning, noon, and night. I love eggs, fortunately, but even I began to pale at the thought of this diet going on indefinitely. One day a Chinese merchant came to our camp and after considerable talk and a lot of bowing and smiling we sensed a major bargain had been struck. In exchange for, I believe, some gasoline, fresh vegetables, meat, and chicken began to appear at our mess. A perfect example of Chinese-American practicality solving problems in the most direct way.

While flying on one of the few clear days across the Hump in August, 1945, my radio operator called over the headset to report something about a new bomb that had just been dropped on Japan. We tuned in our sets and heard the first news of the atom bomb. The whole tale sounded like bad science fiction, but on our return to Ledo that night, our squadron intelligence officer opened sealed envelopes and took out information about the weapon to brief us all. The shock that man could have devised such a sure way to end his own existence was counterbalanced by the very real possibility that the war might be over sooner than anyone thought. And indeed it was, and the news was gratefully received by everyone in the world, including members of the 317th Troop Carrier Squadron Commando, who assumed that their duties were over and that everyone would be on his way home. That was not to be for a while. We were transferred to China, there to fly back and forth across the country carrying men, materials, VIPs, and, later on, Chiang's soldiers in the abortive attempt to station Nationalist troops throughout the country.

My real China experiences began with a midnight flight from Chunking to Shanghai, two days after the official end of the hostilities and before any clear communications had been reestablished between the east coast and the western sectors of the country. We were loaded with gasoline and destined for the airport north of the city. The only maps available were 1936 U.S. Coast and Geodetic Survey antiques and the best these could do was give us a general idea of what direction to go. We took off in threes, on the theory that we'd keep each other in sight. There were absolutely no navigation aids and no lights on the ground, and as we became airborne I suddenly realized that we had to cross a whole country with nothing to go on except a vague direction and the seat of one's pants. Once up at our cruising altitude my two buddies on either wing decided that we'd all do better on our own and we agreed to shut down our radio for fear of any lurking and suicidal Japanese. We then flew on toward the coast, hoping for the best. About 7:00 AM we reached the sea. I knew it had to be the sea because there was no more land ahead and this brilliant deduction was quickly agreed to by the rest of my crew. There was only one problem, however, and that had to do with the fact that there was no Shanghai under us. In fact there was no city or town or hamlet or anything. Just coastline. I looked at our fuel gauges and realized that we'd better find Shanghai soon or we would be forced down. I ordered the radios reactivated and we could hear very faintly some crackling at a great distance away. We tried homing in on the talk but the needles didn't thrill us with steadiness. I had to make a decision: turn right or turn left. Whichever way I'd better be right and we'd better pray that Shanghai was not too far off. The directional needle seemed to indicate right and with the grudging agreement of my co-pilot I turned right and flew down the coast. We spent five very tense minutes until it became evident that we were approaching the city and indeed we did so, only thirty minutes off our estimate. After we landed I tried to reconstruct how we'd gotten so miserably off our already vague headings and soon realized that the winds aloft, which we had no way of computing, had driven us due north.

At Shanghai all was confusion. Planes were arriving from other parts of China and big C-54s in from Okinawa. The MPs and the Air Transport Command were in charge of the field and we were forbidden to leave the base. I had been wearing a Chinese army officer's hat for many weeks as a good-luck charm and I was promptly hauled before a pale-faced MP major and asked what army I was in. We had a bit of an argument and at the end I thought the only sensible thing to do was to get the hell out of there and back to the other side of the country. There was only one problem: the authorities would not let us have any fuel. I remonstrated with the captain in charge of the fuel dump but it did no good. I then protested to my major friend and asked him how he expected us to leave his field. He was excessively uncommunicative. We were denied a visit to Shanghai, we were denied fuel to leave. We were trapped, as it were, by post-surrender confusion. Resourcefulness, I thought, resourcefulness. We decided that the only thing to do was to get enough fuel to fly to Nanking, where we knew the Japanese air force remnants in China were all based and presumably there would be some gasoline along with the planes. At night, the co-pilot, who was one of the smoothest con men in the CBI theater, and the crew chief commandeered two drums of gas and somehow brought them into a position where we could siphon out enough to partially fill our tanks. This gave us about one-third of a fuel load and it meant that if we were planning to fly to Nanking we would have to do so as low to the ground as possible. For this we needed daylight. We holed up in the plane after getting the fuel drums put away and waited.

With the first crack of sunlight I went to the dispatcher's room and announced that I was leaving for Nanking and had figured out that by flying at ground level I had just enough fuel to make it. He looked at me long and hard and said, "Get the hell out of here, lieutenant, before I do something rash." I took the hint and within minutes we were roaring down the runway and airborne. We set up our course for Nanking and our altitude at about fifty feet. Then came a problem. The C–47 was not designed for hedgehopping. You couldn't see where you were going and fly the plane at the same time. The co-pilot became my eyes and I kept my head in the cockpit trying to keep us at a steady height. Every once in a while the co-pilot would say "Pull it up" and I'd do so, glancing out the windows as a picturesque Chinese garden bridge flew by at eye level. Outside Nanking there is a mountain, not a very high one, but it has to be crossed if you hope to land in the city. I knew we were going to use fuel climbing up to get over it but there wasn't any other way. As we approached we decided the best way to make the climb and expend minimum fuel was to gain as much speed as possible and pull up at a sharp angle that would be helped by our forward momentum. Accordingly we pushed the throttles to the fire wall and built up a maximum ground speed. At the right moment I pulled back on the wheel and we did indeed shoot upward at a fast enough rate to plug up my ears completely. We seemed to hop over the mountain and bear in on the Nanking airport even as our fuel gauges were registering zero. Once on the ground in the three-point position of the C–47, the gauges registered absolute zero and in fact the engines stopped within yards of our touchdown point.

Presently we saw lights heading for us and in minutes we opened our door to be received by two Japanese soldiers in uniform, carrying rifles. For a wild moment I thought they had not heard about the end of the war but that turned out not to be the case. They bowed politely and turned their rifle muzzles to the ground. I thought this a touch odd but bowed back and made gestures about our empty tanks. They understood and raced off to bring help. Presently we were hitched up to a tow truck and gently hauled along toward the center of the airport. There we found many more Japanese, all in uniform but functioning as

air crews. I went inside the airport office to be greeted by two young
American navy officers who had, that very day, flown into Nanking to
participate in the surrender of the city. We decided to stay the night
and together with various naval personnel were driven into Nanking
itself.

I expected to see the place in ruins, remembering the newsreel pictures of the thirties, but it was not. We were taken to the Wagons-Lit
Hotel, which was swarming with navy people and looked for all the
world as if it had stepped straight out of a Somerset Maugham novel.
We were assigned rooms of comfortable size and furnishings and the
first thing I did was head for the bath. I turned on faucets but no water
came out. I rang for a bellboy and one appeared in an instant. I showed
by gesture what my problem was and he smiled, indicated that I should
take off my clothes and get into the tub. I did this and seconds later he
was back with a bucket brigade that proceeded to fill the tub with a nice
balance of hot and cold water while I scrubbed my back with the lon-
gest back brush I'd ever seen. After the bath a drink. The boy brought
a bottle of Johnny Walker Black Label and I couldn't believe my eyes.
But it was not Black Label, it was totally concocted out of something
unmentionable by the Japanese as a gesture of defiance. We settled for
some whiskey that one of the crew had carried all the time. We dined in
the hotel dining room on delicious Chinese cooking and I fell asleep the
minute my head touched the bed.

I made many such visits to Nanking over the next few months. We
were based in Sian, in Shensi province, famous as the city where
Chiang was kidnapped. We were fifteen air minutes in a C–47 from the
Communist headquarters at Yenan. Sian during the pre-Boxer and prewar days had been administered by the Germans, who were responsible for building its effective aerodrome. Concrete hangars, some several feet thick, dotted the field, and the runway was hard and packed and
capable of handling the heaviest traffic. The Communists knew this and
were anxious to have it. During that fall we flew almost regular runs
from Sian to Peking to Shanghai to Hankow to Canton to Nanking to
Chungking and back to Sian. Sometimes the route varied and other cities such as Kwelin and Kunming were added and even once in a while
Mukden. The Sian field meanwhile began to be crowded with surplus
American fighters and light bombers. P–38s, P–40s, B–25s, and even
few B–26s piled up row upon row, adding to the Communists' interest.
One day we awoke to the fact that the city had been taken over during
the night. There were Communist soldiers everywhere and a few frag-
ile-looking jeeps made over as weapon carriers. Our commander, a major from West Point who was newly arrived in China, dealt with the

Communist officer in charge and worked out an understanding that the city was theirs but that we would not accept them on the airfield or a specified area around it. We immediately set up guard posts along the perimeters and this was not easy when you consider that we had a total of 200 officers and men and the airfield stretched at least two miles. We set up two light machine guns at the entrance and the Communists moved right up to within a few feet of them and set up a camp. The two sides stared at each other across a visible white line but nothing untoward happened. Our major was in radio touch with higher headquarters and the word came back for us to pack up and move out. Relays of Chinese Nationalist pilots were sent to fly out the planes but most of them were undertrained and incapable of handling sophisticated machinery. One by one they would take off and as often as not plow straight ahead into the ground. We got everything ready for our departure and the day we left we withdrew our guards and guns, loading them into the last of the squadron planes, and took off for Kunming. My last sight of Sian was watching groups of blue-clad men swarming over the planes that were left behind. I have a feeling that some of those machines are probably still flying.

We headed for Kunming, where we, in turn, parked our planes on a wide field alongside the Kunming runways. Row upon row of transports were already there lined up, wing tips almost touching. I'd never seen as many planes in one place and I soon realized that this was where they were going to stay. I took the identification plate from my cockpit to keep as a souvenir and as I looked around I thought that Chiang couldn't lose if he made use of all the equipment we were leaving behind. I was too young to realize that it takes much more than material goods to fire up an army and a people.

We were flown by the Air Transport Command back to India to await transportation home and sent to Kanchapara, a vile replacement depot outside Calcutta. We were told it would be some weeks before we had transportation home and I settled in for what was bound to be a gloomy, dull period of mind-boggling boredom. I did not reckon on either my brother Griswold or the U.S. Navy.

In mid-November I received a letter from Mother saying that my brother Gris's ship was due in Calcutta sometime in December. This prompted me to visit the tiny naval office at the Calcutta waterfront and make inquiry. The office I talked to did indeed have news of the ship and was very friendly about keeping me informed. One day the ship did arrive and Gris and I had a nice if somewhat quiet reunion. After the ship sailed the naval officer who had befriended me invited me to dinner with his two apartment mates, both of whom were vice-con-

suls at the U.S. Consulate in Calcutta. I told them my story of replacement depot blues and nothing would do except that I move immediately into the spare room in their flat. Dallas Coors and Robert Towers arranged everything with the Air Corps, including the availability of an
airplane in order that I might fly the required four hours a month to be
entitled to extra pay. Coors and Towers were the souls of kindness and
gradually I learned what it was like to have a cocktail again and take a
bath in a bathtub while being watched over by attentive servants.

My visit coincided with the Christmas uprising in the city and we
were virtually barricaded in our rooms for three days of savage rioting.
When calm returned we toured the Calcutta streets and alleyways and
saw death and destruction far worse than anything I'd experienced in
the war itself. Mahatma Gandhi came to the city to see for himself and
hold prayer and meditation meetings in Barrackpore. For one of the
meetings, Dal Coors, as the political observer among the vice-consuls,
was asked to talk with Gandhi and invited me to go along. I changed
out of uniform, borrowing a mixture of clothes from both Coors and
Towers. We drove to Barrackpore in time for the meeting that was held
in a great open field jammed with the faithful as far as the eye could
see. We stayed on the edge of the crowd and were instantly aware that
we were being looked at with scorn and contempt, perhaps even loath-
ing. We were foreigners, impure and contaminating. We made it our
business to stay as far out of the way as possible. The Mahatma looked
for all the world as if he were sitting suspended in mid-air. He sat on a
square, plain wooden platform with only a microphone in front of him
and a lighting effect behind that gave the impression of a halo. When he
spoke every eye was on him, giving Coors and me a chance to look
around at the crowd. There was no question that he had them firmly
under control. Coors knew enough Hindi to follow the general drift of
what he was saying and he was speaking of the deplorable riots in Calcutta and the need for peace and nonviolence. There was nothing new
in his message but it was an unreal feeling being there while he was delivering it. After a while there were some responsive questions from
the platform and shouted answers from the crowd and eventually the
rally was over and the crowd dispersed quickly.

We made our way up to the platform and I noticed immediately that
it was a masterpeice of theatricality. Four thin wires held the platform
in place and at a close look they seemed to be piano strings. Two lights
on the rear were angled up to create the halo, helped in this case by the
setting sun. There were quite a few people waiting to greet the old man
and we waited our turn toward the rear. After a few moments he
emerged from a tall bush and began greeting people. I stared fascinat-

ed. Here in front of me was one of the seven wonders of the world and at close inspection he looked as if a small breeze would blow him away. He was small but I had not expected his spindliness. His white hair, what there was of it, framed the round face and set off the wire-rimmed glasses at a slight angle. The most arresting feature was the big Ingersoll watch pinned to his dhoti. He had his hands on the heads of two small boys and began a walk around the garden with everyone following. We'd been at this for perhaps three minutes when there was a rustle of branches and a young woman emerged, flinging herself on the ground in front of him and wrapping her arms around his legs. He immediately leaned down and helped her up, muttering something that I could not hear, and she smiled into his face as if she'd seen God. Maybe for her she had.

The walk resumed and no one seemed to make any comment about the incident. One by one the visitors came up to the great man, had their turn with him, and left. Dal Coors finally arrived in position and the two walked on slightly faster than the rest for what was obviously a serious conversation. I watched from behind and could see much animation flowing from both. Presently Dal motioned for me and introduced me as a young member of the American Air Corps. Gandhi shook hands and in English with an Oxford accent spoke about the Americans in India as being men with good consciences. "You are too loud, you laugh too much, and you make too free with women," he said. "But you have good hearts." I was stunned not by what he said, which sounded like a pat statement meant for media consumption, but by both the timbre of his voice and his accent. He sounded like an English university professor about to give a mighty lecture in front of a learned society. And his voice was low, with wonderful theatrical overtones. I had an instant picture of him on a stage. He went on about America and India and free peoples and worked himself up to quite a pitch while doing it. I was mesmerized. It was only on the way back to the city that on trying to recapture the moment I could not remember one significant thing he had said. Everything was as safe as a church and almost a string of clichés . But, oh, how he put it across. And the obvious love, devotion, even worship for him that the crowd had had! A powerful, engrossing, clever, practical, shrewd, cunning, and, I suspect, devious man. And a God to India.

Some years after this meeting, my wife Betty and I were lunching with the last full-time viceroy, Lord Linlithgow, the father of one of our closest friends. Lord Linlithgow was sitting at a luncheon table in the River Club in New York, overlooking the East River. With bursts of sunlight filtering through the windows, the light hit him in profile, outlining his craggy face, which became deeply animated when I asked him about Gandhi and the war. In 1942, when Britain was at her most desperate in Europe, Gandhi visited Lord Linlithgow, who was facing critical problems in India. On the entire subcontinent there were only four antiaircrafts guns and a scattering of the British Army. The rest of the troops were Indian of one sort or another. On the eastern border a rebellious general named Subat Chandra Bose was poised with the Japanese, ready to invade the country. Gandhi suggested to Linlithgow that now was the moment for Indian independence, that it made little difference to him whether his country was occupied by the British or the Japanese, but it might make a difference to Britain. "This is blackmail," Linlithgow recalled saying. He paused after telling this, his face flushed with remembered anger and his jowls moving slowly from side to side. "What did you do?" I asked timorously. "Do? Do?" he said, growing louder. "Do? I clapped the bugger in jail, that's what I did!" he said, looking over at me and fixing his eyes into mine. And indeed he had done just that, and later on encouraged a Muslim fanatic named Mohammed Ali Jinnah to espouse the cause of a separate Muslim state on the theory, I suppose, that Jinnah and Gandhi would fight among themselves while the British got on with the war. He was right. They did and so did their successors. Pakistan and India were the result. Gandhi was a real seventh wonder.

My Indian and Chinese adventures came to an end in January of 1946 when I boarded the troopship *General William S. Hase* and set sail for home. Our route took us to Sumatra and Java, the Philippines and into San Francisco. We were thirty-two days at sea, hit a typhoon in the South China Seas that almost upended us, and arrived in Manila as thousands of Japanese sailed passed us on overcrowded ships that looked as if they were going to sink and smelled of filth. As we entered San Francisco harbor on a cloudless and fogless February morning, listening to a rebroadcast of Churchill's recent speech at Fulton, Missouri, where he created the phrase "iron curtain," I was convinced we'd be at war with the Russians the next week and I was not looking forward to being kept in the service. The trip had been useful in one respect: I had read, among other books, Emil Ludwig's biography of Bismarck and Foster R. Dulles's treatise on Russian-American relations from 1776 to 1945. *Bismarck* fed my romantic sense of middle nineteenth-century European history. Dulles's book made me feel an expert on a highly difficult and subtle part of our history. Mr. Churchill's speech disturbed my newly formed ideas that America and Russia were natural partners because of size and common interests and, even if different politically, had no real cause to fight each other. I was confused by being back, and when I stepped off the ship I half expected to see guns and tanks and jeeps full of soldiers hurrying along the streets. Instead I saw traffic and civilians and banners and headlines that talked about baseball and the clothing shortage for men. The horns honked, the bells clanged, the air smelled of the sea and city, and I was touched, perhaps, in a way that I never imagined. Back in 1854 my great-great-grandfather. Commodore C. K. Garrison, had been a reform mayor of San Francisco and I felt a kinship to the city. Oscar Wilde said in *Dorian Gray* that sooner or later everyone ends up in San Francisco and perhaps these thoughts added to my general feeling of euphoria.

I took a taxi to the Mark Hopkins Hotel, that unique tall building on top of Nob Hill with a bar that commands a total view of the San Francisco bay and countryside. I went to that bar and ordered a drink and when it came I quietly lifted my glass in a toast to what I saw. I was profoundly glad to be alive, to be back in the United States, to be unharmed either physically or mentally, and to be ready to take up my life again. And that night I was overwhelmed with a redetermination to get back to music as quickly as I could. I was lucky—and grateful.

IV

Early Management,

New York Pops, Heifetz

I was released from the service in late February, 1946, and arrived home a livid yellow color thanks to the Atabrine I'd taken overseas as a suppressant against malaria. I weighed something like 130 pounds, had a crew cut, and couldn't wait to begin civilian life, even though it became a problem to find clothes in the first postwar days.

My second problem developed about six weeks after I returned home. I awoke one morning with a raging fever and a slicing headache. A thermometer in my mouth ran up to 103.5 in no time at all. I felt weak and dazed. A call to the family doctor and a description of my symptoms brought an invitation to come immediately to his office. By clutching at the walls and moving slowly alongside the buildings I managed to make the seven blocks between our apartment and his office. Once there I collapsed and a series of tests was begun immediately.

I was poked and prodded and drained and punctured by two doctors and after an hour or so they said they wanted me to go to the hospital for further tests. They suggested Mt. Sinai. I said no. I said that I would rather die than be sent to a hospital where everyone would have at my racking body attempting to probe the answer. I said I thought I had malaria. They said they thought I had spinal meningitis. I said I'd gone through too much to have everything end now. I said I was going home to bed. A nurse took me back to the apartment. That day and that night I got steadily worse. My temperature stayed up around

103.5–104, the headache wouldn't go away, I couldn't eat, and I couldn't focus my eyes. I called the doctor and he must have heard something in my voice because this time he said he would be right over. He arrived with a great satchel filled with equipment and standing at the foot of my bed he turned to our terrified maid and said, "Boil these." Shades of Paul Muni as Louis Pasteur! When the equipment was boiled and rigged up over my bed, a needle was inserted in a vein and liquid quinine was dripped into my bloodstream. "You may be right," he said. "If it's malaria this ought to give us a good indication." And to my surprise he settled down to wait.

I fell into a restless sleep filled with snatches of dreams and nightmares and suddenly I felt calm and rested. I woke up and he was still there. My ears were ringing slightly, a sure sign that the quinine was doing its work. I felt cooler and when he saw that I was awake he stuck a thermometer in my mouth and smiled as he took it out. "You sleep now. I'll be back tomorrow. I think we're over the hump." And with that he picked up his coat and bag and left. I had no idea how long he had been there, but the maid told me later that he'd not moved out of the room for close to three hours.

In his office a few days later he resumed testing, including a spinal tap, and was becoming more and more convinced that it was malaria but could find no proof. "If it is, it will return," he said, "and as soon as you feel an attack coming I want you to get into this office wherever you are as quick as you can. I think we'll find the proof only during an actual seizure."

I made careful note of everything he said and set about returning to work. Under the wartime law NBC had to give me my job back and they proceeded to do so. Since I'd left, the International Department had grown dramatically and had taken over most of the work of the New York office of the Voice of America. I returned to my desk in the English-language section and once again became a newswriter, broadcaster, and correspondent.

The United Nations was in its first home at Hunter College in the Bronx and within weeks I found myself assigned there as a reporter. Once every hour or so I would broadcast a live report on what was happening and most of what was happening was, I'm afraid to say, boring beyond imagination. The plenary sessions of the Security Council were showcases for propaganda. Each member insisted on speaking in his own language, which then had to be translated into French before any reply or comment could be made.

One day a delegate was talking on and on about the value of some fishing books. He was droning and the Council was drowning. At one point Andrei Gromyko, tireless then as he is now, blurted out in English: "What iss all dese talk? Fish are fish and belong in the ocean." I thought that remark had deep significance but my boss didn't and after I'd reported it on the air the phone rang and I was given a dressing down. And not just a light one either. When the action got hot, as it did when the Russians walked out of the Council briefly, NBC sent more experienced reporters, much to my relief and agitation.

I was better off with a musical program I was allowed total freedom to devise and present. It was a weekly program of classical music. The music librarian of NBC was very helpful and between us we worked out programs that covered a wide range of tastes. This was before the LP record, of course, so everything was on 78 rpm shellacs. I also supervised the rebroadcasting of the NBC Symphony, which was recorded on big glass discs coated with acetate. I did the announcing and made up vivid descriptions of Toscanini's entrances and exits. I kept the talk to a minimum, particularly because there was really very little opportunity for it, but what I did was fanciful, and I'm afraid, unabashedly worshipful. I kept thinking that it was time I took up my commitment to music in a more practical way.

In the middle of a music broadcast one afternoon I felt a sudden backache coming on and within minutes I was sweating like a shower and my temperature rose. I was coming down with another malarial attack and this time while on the air. I called a colleague to take over for me. I had not said very much about this problem to anyone at NBC and he was surprised to see me looking so odd. Still, he didn't ask any questions and as soon as the next record began playing he took over and I took off for the doctor's office. There was only one problem: when I reached the street there wasn't an empty taxicab in sight. My fever was mounting steadily as my legs became disjointed and more and more I resembled a drunk. I went up to a cop on Fifth Avenue, and weaving to and fro, asked him to find me transportation. He tried to turn me away but I wouldn't let him and I made him feel my forehead. "I've got malaria," I said, "and I must get to the doctor." One touch and he put his whistle in his mouth and stopped traffic. He went to the first cab and asked the passenger to give it up. He put me inside and told the driver to take me to 73rd and Park and stick around to see if I was all right. Who says New York cops don't care!

I arrived at the doctor's office shaking with fever and barely able to move. My teeth were chattering so much that they were afraid I might damage my tongue so I was made to clamp on a rubber mouthpiece like a prizefighter. Blood was taken from my arm and in seconds I heard a "whoop" from the laboratory. Both doctors converged around the microscope and one came to me, his voice bubbling with excitement, to explain that they'd found it! He helped me up and insisted that I look for myself. I lurched into the lab and lowered my eye onto the scope and did indeed see a swarming brown object swimming in the blood. "A female!" said the excited doctor, "and very hard to find." I think I smiled wanly. In any event I was taken back to the examining room, given a massive dose of quinine and Nicomen, and sent home to bed.

Some days later I asked the doctor how long these attacks were supposed to go on. "Oh, indefinitely," he said with something approaching smugness. "There is no cure at the moment. We can only hope to keep things under control with the quinine." I had visions of Kipling and India and the Khyber Pass, to say nothing of Ledo and Calcutta and my own recent past. I went back to work and it turned out that I would have the attacks about every five weeks. I made notes on all my calendars and tried to be reasonably near bed when the dark week approached.

During this time I was very busy doing something else of lifelong importance. While at Millbrook one of my best friends had been Fritz Steinway of the piano family, a gregarious, eager fellow who loved many of the things I did and who befriended me at a time when shyness and insecurity threatened to be my way of life. In the summer of 1938 he had invited me to visit Long Pond, the Steinway summer home near Cape Cod. There I met his warm and welcoming family, including his sister Betty. Betty and I did not hit it off, in fact it would be fair to say that we cordially disliked one another on sight. We did, however, keep up a slight spitting acquaintance until after the war, when, right after my return to New York, I called on the Steinways and found a grown-up, intelligent, and provocative woman instead of the brat I remembered.

During the war I had inherited $5,000 and I decided to put this money to good use. I began an intense courtship, with flowers and dinners and theaters and concerts, in a well-planned attack to persuade Betty to marry me. She said that she'd rather go around the world on a tramp steamer. There were several other suitors hanging around and I never did find out what she told them. Eventually I wore her down and at a little bar one night she said that if she were to marry at all she might consider the possibility of marrying me. I showed her the lovely diamond solitaire that my grandmother had left me for my intended and asked if I could tell my mother. She sighed and realized she was beaten. Our engagement was announced later that month and on March 15, 1947, we were married in the first postwar marriage in both our families. We had a wonderful time at our wedding. Francis Biddle was my

best man, Betty's sister Lydia her maid of honor. We were married in
the Church of the Epiphany, with her brother, Theodore D. Steinway,
arriving in an open victoria, lots of marvelous music, and a reception at
Steinway Hall. "Elsie Sloane wouldn't have her daughter's reception
in the front window of W. & J. Sloane," sniffed my aunt Eleanor Burden before the event. Afterwards she asked my father-in-law whether
the place might be available for other receptions.

We went to Florida for our honeymoon and both promptly got sick.
Betty had a heavy cold and I developed impacted wisdom teeth. We
stayed in what is now Cape Kennedy and spent our days in the sun and
our nights in the little bar at our inn. We returned to New York, brown
and blond, and settled into our one-room $65.00-a-month apartment on
the corner of Park Avenue and 64th Street.

My malaria hit on schedule and our new life together began with Betty watching me shiver and shake on my bed while trying to keep her
good New England spirits up. The malaria began to take its toll and I
lost weight steadily no matter what I ate. One day the doctor called
with the news that the government had just released a still not perfect-
ed cure for the disease and he had a supply if I wanted to be a guinea
pig. I leapt at the chance and began to take chloroquine. It did cure the
malaria after a while but it damn near did me in. That meant lots of other tests and doctors and I was beginning to get mighty discouraged
about the whole thing until one day my mother-in-law suggested that I
visit an osteopath. I did, and after a careful examination, he put forth
the theory that I had been so filled with medicine that most of my normal physical processes had gotten jammed up. This sounded quackish
to me but I agreed to come twice a week for treatments that consisted
of massage and osteopathic exercise. Within a matter of weeks I began to feel human, gain weight, and brighten up for the first time since
coming down with the disease, and I could face the attacks with much
more stamina. The chloroquine finally worked and I was pronounced
cured about a year after treatments began.

In the meantime I continued to work at NBC, as the music business
faded more and more into the background and the corporate machinery
began its work. Our son Henry arrived in November, 1948, and I had to
be certain that I had a job that could pay for his upbringing. I moved
from the International Department to the local station as director of
field exploitation. Once a month the station saluted a city in its listening
area and I had to pick out the city and arrange with the powers that be
for lots of publicity in return for doing a day extolling the virtues of
Elizabeth, New Jersey, or Bridgeport, Connecticut, or whatever place
it was. This led to appointment as station publicity director just as the

infant television industry was bursting forth and the birth of WNBT as an independent programmer.

My only brush with music in those years was a special program arranged with Leopold Stokowski to mark the two hundredth anniversary of the birth of J. S. Bach. Stokowski would come to a little studio, deliver some fascinating words about Bach, and play some of his own recordings. *Time* did a big article on him and we became pleasant aquaintances. When his then wife, Gloria Vanderbilt, was about to deliver their first child, Betty was once again pregnant and it was a neck-and-neck race to see who would deliver first. Mrs. Stokowski won and furthermore gave the maestro a son after his three daughters by other wives. Betty followed in a few days and topped her: she had unexpected boy twins.

The twins saved me from a return to the service for Korea. I had stayed in the reserve because I loved to fly and this way was able to do so with Uncle Sam footing the bill. Of course, I was called up. However, the twins arrived, as did the realization that I had four dependents. I knew that no one could be involuntarily recalled to the service with four or more dependents, so I called the adjutant of my squadron and explained the change in my status. He didn't believe me but when he got the birth certificate he sent me my discharge papers. I was out of the military woods, hopefully forever.

That same year (1950) I left NBC to work for the husband-and-wife team of Tex McCrary and Jinx Falkenburg. They were nice people, Tex and Jinx, but their basic interests were not mine and I began to look around for another job.

Through my parents-in-law I secured an introduction to Arthur Judson, then manager of the New York Philharmonic-Symphony and head of his own concert division within Columbia Artists Management. Judson received me affably but pointed out that I had no experience whatsoever in the music world. He suggested that I get some before talking with him again. I left his office accepting the wisdom of his words but wondering how exactly to get what he required.

I talked it over with my friend Skitch Henderson one night and he told me that he had been approached by one of the members of the New York Philharmonic to start a series of spring concerts with the orchestra to be modeled after the highly successful Boston Pops. "Have you ever done anything like that?" I asked. "No," he replied. "Good," I said, "let's do it together."

We met with Daniel Rybb of the orchestra, whose interest was largely in seeing the musicians employed for additional services. I think Rybb recognized two suckers who were ready to take on the project.

My first visit was to the Philharmonic's lawyers to see if we could use the name New York Philharmonic, then to the president of the board. I was looked over very carefully and finally given the green light with the absolute understanding that no money of the Philharmonic's was to be involved in any way. That meant a trip to the boondocks to raise the money for a first season.

We planned an ambitious one-week program. Monday night was to be a performance of Marc Blitzstein's Airborne Symphony, the first in New York since the work was premiered by Leonard Bernstein and the New York City Symphony. We asked Tyrone Power, an ex-Marine pilot, to narrate and we persuaded the Air Force to lend us the Singing Sergeants as the airchoir. Lehigh University provided the considerable chorus. Tuesday was to be a Romberg-Viennese night; Thursday a Gershwin program; Friday a Tchaikovsky night with Eugene List as soloist; Saturday morning a "Lollipops Concert" for children with Faye Emerson as the narrator for "Peter and the Wolf."

It was my first adventure as a manager and Skitch's first with a symphony orchestra. Between us we raised the money and got the venture under way. We made a lot of mistakes but one we did not make was to take the orchestra for granted. On the first day of rehearsal, after an hour had passed, Skitch called for a break and announced that coffee and rolls were being served in the lounge courtesy of the New York Pops management. With one whoop the stage was empty and everything was consumed in seconds. The orchestra was surprised and even, I think, touched and did everything in their power to see that the musical parts of the week were going to be successful. Our ticket sales lagged, partially because I had no idea of how to scale a house and partially because we were trying to appeal to the widest possible public and misfired.

When the week ended we had the satisfaction of reviews that praised our artistic intentions and some of the results The week after we closed I went back to see Judson and asked for a job. "You told me to get some experience," I reminded him, "and I have. Now I want a job." He looked at me quizzically for a moment or two and then smiled. "Fair enough," he said. "I'll talk to my colleagues at Columbia Artists and see what we can do." I left his office feeling better.

Nothing happened for several weeks except that the post of assistant manager of the New York Philharmonic opened up and Judson indicated to me that there was a very good chance of my getting it. I didn't. It went to George E. Judd, Jr., the youngest son of George E. Judd, who was for many, many years the manager of the Boston Symphony.

George, Jr., had been with Columbia Artists and when he moved to the Philharmonic his job at the firm became vacant. Somewhat to salve his conscience Judson offered the post to me. I would be in charge of publicity activities for the artists managed by the Judson, O'Neill & Judd division of Columbia. The Judd was George, Jr.'s, older brother William, who had been a Judson partner for some little time. The O'Neill was Ruth O'Neill, one-time secretary to Leopold Stokowski in his Philadelphia Orchestra days. The salary was $6,500 a year and there was one additional kicker: I had to be willing to travel three months of the year as tour manager for Jascha Heifetz. Such was Heifetz's position that he demanded and got a private tour manager for his domestic engagements. So did Lily Pons, but they were unique at Columbia.

I thought that starting out to work for the greatest violinist of his day was a good omen. The only problem was how to break the news to Betty, who would then be faced with the full responsibility of raising the children in the tough winter season. I also had to tell her that we were going to have to go into debt to satisfy my craving. I had been making over $15,000 a year with the McCrarys and this, in 1953, was still a lot of money. There was no way out, though. This was the break I'd always thought about and I had to do it then and there or I would always shy away from the final commitment. I told Judson I would take it and we shook hands. I went home to break the news.

Betty was stoical. She asked, quite properly, where the money was going to come from to pay for our family. I said, bravely, that I'd find it somewhere but I really pleaded my case about music and asked her to gamble with me for ten years. At the end of that time if I had not been able to make it, I promised that I'd give up and return to broadcasting, something by this time I knew something about. As I spoke I realized that I meant every word. This was to be the opportunity at last and I would push heaven and earth to get it. Betty understood and agreed.

I began with Judson, O'Neill & Judd in November, 1953, and from the moment I walked into their offices in the Steinway Building on 57th Street, I knew I was home. J.O.J., as it was referred to, was part of the Columbia Artists Management organization. Columbia Artists had been created in the thirties by Arthur Judson and William Paley. Judson, who was also manager, together with Bruno Zirato, of the New York Philharmonic (and at one time simultaneously the Philadelphia Orchestra) was, in truth, the most powerful man of music in America. Part of his power lay in the fact that he personally managed the conductors and that meant power with the individual symphony boards on the subject of music directors. He also took his responsibilities seriously and gained the confidence of the various boards by always trying to match the right conductor to the right orchestral situation. He took a lot of abuse for this from frustrated maestros who always felt that when they could not get ahead it was Judson's fault.

Physically Judson was a powerful and commanding man, standing well over six feet. His face could reflect anger, sadness, joy, and compassion in easily readable terms. He was not somebody I ever wanted to cross.

His partners, Bill Judd and Ruth O'Neill, were a curious pair. Ruth O'Neill had the look and color of her Irish ancestors. Bill Judd was all New England on the outside and I suspected very like me on the inside when it came to a belief in music and artists. He was a closed book in many ways and when he was pressed too hard his eyes stopped smiling and his smile became set. Both of them welcomed me and I found myself plunged into work that seemed almost as if I'd been doing it all my life.

I had not been in the office three weeks before Bill Judd came to me one morning and asked if I'd mind very much taking on an assignment that my duties did not call for but one that he thought I might do well. It seemed that soprano Eleanor Steber was scheduled to sing somewhere near Hartford, Connecticut, that evening. As she had only just returned from a heavy concert swing around the country and was tired, Bill felt it would help if a manager was along to look after the details. I was overjoyed. Miss Steber was in those days a prima donna assoluta at the Metropolitan and I had enjoyed many performances of hers both in the opera house and on the radio. I agreed immediately. "Fine," he said. "And you'd better get started." "Now?" I asked, somewhat naively. "Now," he said. "It's a long drive." I just had time to call Betty to say I wouldn't be home until very late that night, and snatch an advance from Ruth O'Neill, who among other things was the treasurer of Columbia Artists, before I set out for the Steber apartment.

There, all was madness. Bags and hatboxes all over the place, fans standing outside to catch a glimpse of the diva, her accompanist looking the worse for wear, her driver running around with vases of flowers, the phones ringing, people all over the living room. Steber herself moved from group to group, laughing and shouting and having a wonderful time. It was hardly the atmosphere I imagined for a diva before a concert. I half expected shades drawn and servants on tiptoes and above all calmness and peace. I lost these misconceptions quickly. At about 2:00 PM the driver, accompanist, and I, together with several suitcases and piles of music, were in the car waiting to go. Steber appeared a few minutes later, climbed into the car while waving to her fans, and we were off in a cloud of laughter and what I believe must have been Chanel #5.

The ride to Connecticut was fast and the talk flowed, mostly about musical matters and gossip. I listened to every word, asking an occasional question. Finally I made some remark that they all thought was very funny and at that point Steber turned around and looked at me, saying, "What did you say your name was?" I told her again. "And where have you been before? Why haven't we met?" I told her that I was three weeks old at the office and that we had met before only she wasn't aware of it. She liked that.

At about 4:30 PM we arrived at a large country house and were warmly greeted by our hostess, who was preparing to feed us at 6:00 before the concert. I thought this strange as I always had believed that singers never ate before performing. I was totally unprepared for the size of the meal Steber consumed. Soup and lots of roast chicken, potatoes, vegetables, several glasses of wine, ice cream, and coffee. I picked away at the repast but she approached everything with gusto. After dinner she retired to rest a few moments, change her clothes, and warm up. I didn't see how she was going to be able to stand up, let alone sing for an audience, but I reckoned without the Steber constitution.

We arrived at the concert hall only a minute or two before the performance was to begin. The manager was not happy with this and made no bones about saying so. I tried to calm him, explaining that the artist had been deep in preparations for the evening and time had somehow been overlooked. "These expensive dames—who do they think they are anyway?" he asked, almost rhetorically. "They fill your house," I replied, thinking him an insensitive boor for asking such a question.

When the program got underway, I was seated in a side seat in the auditorium and thought that Steber got off to a rocky start. It lasted only a minute, perhaps, and then her voice warmed up and she proceeded to deliver what the audience had come to hear. At the end the applause was long and steady. When I went backstage she was bathed in sweat and signing autographs at a rapid rate. "Perhaps I shouldn't have had that last helping of chicken," she said quietly to me. "Was it that or the ice cream?" I asked and then suddenly realized that I'd overstepped my bounds. She turned and looked at me for a moment and then started laughing. "They need more of you around that damn office," she said. I was immensely flattered but puzzled. I hadn't said anything world shattering, just commented in an oblique way that I thought she was right about eating too much. "You're okay," she said, giving me a hug and turning back to her fans. I thought the same thing about her. We drove back to New York that night and on the way stopped for a few drinks. We were all feeling no pain when we arrived. I'd had my first experience as a tour manager and had evidentally passed muster with some degree of success.

Shortly after the Steber trip I was presented with a project that from start to finish was an absolute delight. Burr Tillstrom, the talented and extraordinary creator of Kukla, Fran and Ollie, had been an ongoing delight to millions of television viewers during the early days of the medium. His program had brought pleasure to all ages. Kukla and Ollie and their friend the singer Fran Allison created a whole world of fantasy that seemed a direct counterpoint to the real world and especially to the cut and dried formulas of network programming. Burr and I had met briefly during my NBC days but did not know each other too well until Bill Judd had the idea of presenting Ollie in recital at Town Hall. Ollie was the rambunctious member of the group who aspired to worldly success, particularly as a singer, and Bill thought to capitalize on this character. Burr was delighted with the idea and a date had been booked. The "recital" was to be held on Thanksgiving night, 1953, and a great deal of work had to be done to assure its success. Burr's manager, Beulah Zachary, was also enthusiastic about the project and shortly after I arrived at the firm a large amount of the detail from Columbia's end was put into my hands.

From the beginning the concert experts assured us that we were headed for disaster. No one ever booked a concert on Thanksgiving night; it was considered sure and sudden death. On top of everything else it was all very well to respond to Ollie in front of a television set at home, but the live-audience situation might prove to be inhibiting. Arguments flowed on; after all, Ollie was only a puppet character created out of Burr's imagination, as was everyone else in the company except Fran Allison, and this simply might not stand up to a stage presentation.

Burr, Beulah Zachary, Bill Judd, and I felt differently and proceeded to arrange the concert as if it were, in fact, a real vocal recital. We created flyers with fantasy texts about Ollie's career, took ads in the papers on the music page, and played the whole thing straight. It worked beyond our wildest dreams. The demand at the box office was brisk and the concert was completely sold out. On Thanksgiving night, we closed the curtains on the Town Hall stage as the audience filed in and opened them with lowered lights just as everyone was seated. For a moment or two the stage was empty with only Burr's folding theater on view and at exactly the right moment Ollie appeared, framed in the puppet proscenium and bathed in a white spotlight, dressed in white tie and tails. The audience broke into cheers and the whole evening was an enormous success. The next day the critics, playing it straight as well, gave wonderful reviews and only at the end of their comments did they acknowledge Burr Tillstrom as the creator of the whole company. It was a tribute to his success as an illusionist, but I kept wondering if any of them had any idea of the amount of work that flowed out of one man. Burr and Beulah were happy with the results, as were we, and that, after all, is what really counted.

On December 28, 1953, Betty and the boys came to see me off at Grand Central Station as I embarked on the Twentieth Century Limited, bound for California on the first leg of my journey to Jascha Heifetz. I was sad at leaving home, now that the moment had actually come, and nervous at the prospect of meeting Heifetz. Our farewells were tremulous. Betty was terrific: here I was about to journey out across the country leaving her in New York with three small children and very little money. She put on a brave front and sent me off "as if to war." I was excited and scared: I was to take responsibility for one of the great artists of our day, heading out around the country on one- and two-night stands and, at last, starting out in a business I knew I wanted. In my heart of hearts I was terrified of failing and creating even more problems for my family. Too late for all that now, I thought, we're off on the road and we'll see what happens.

In Chicago I had several hours to kill before boarding the Super-Chief for Los Angeles and I spent most of them at the Chicago Art Institute. I arrived at the Dearborn station in plenty of time, however, as high romanticism had taken hold once again and I wanted to be there in time to see the stars board and the flashbulbs pop. I reckoned without the season of the year and the airplane because as far as I could see there were not going to be more than a slim handful of passengers and most of them were traveling salesmen. I settled into my roomette, however, with the feeling of a great impresario on the way to California for a world-shattering tour.

The train was like a seedy but respectable boarding house. Everything needed dusting; the windows had grime on them that cut down the view, the dining car silver was slightly tarnished, the dishes chipped, the linen looked yellowed, the flowers wilted. The waiters' coats were slightly gray and the smiles on their faces were not up to the standard of, say, *The Harvey Girls*. But the food was wonderful and I ate my way across the country in style. I had my hair cut in the barber shop and spent lots of time looking out the rear observation car dome. I'd never crossed the country by train before and I wanted to make this trip on the theory—correct, as it turned out—that the days of cross-country railroading were numbered. I also wanted to get again the feeling of space and distance that so many of us who live in the East are apt to forget. But the dining car and the bar car, however genteelly shabby, were still expensive and my expense account figures mounted up.

Our arrival in the downtown Los Angeles station was anticlimactic. The station was deserted. Sunlight poured into the main passenger area, piercing the dust and looking like great theater spotlights cutting through years of neglect. There couldn't have been more than a dozen people wandering around and most of them didn't look like long-distance travelers. I couldn't find a porter so I lugged my bag, which was extremely heavy, and my briefcase outside where I had to wait some minutes to find a cab. When I finally caught one we rode on nonexistent shock absorbers to the Beverly Hills Hotel, where I was to stay for two days before the tour got under way.

All my life I'd read about the Beverly Hills Hotel, playground of the stars. The fan magazines always showed pictures of the screen greats moving in and out of the entrance, around the swimming pool, on the tennis courts, or sitting in the cabanas. As we bounced along I had visions of chatting casually with Vivien Leigh or Rita Hayworth or some new nubile starlet or perhaps being asked to fill out a foursome with Cary Grant, David Niven, and Ronald Colman. As the taxi pulled up to the main entrance everything was almost as I had imagined it. The flowers grew all over the place with southern Californian vulgarity, the grass was too green, the palm trees too palmy.

I stepped out, paid an enormous fare, and walked into the hotel. A man was hosing down the main steps and I stepped right into a large puddle. I gave him my widest smile and entered the lobby. Aside from the desk clerk the place was empty. I registered and was handed over to a bellboy who started down a long corridor without saying much. On the top floor we came to a door at the end of the corridor and the bellboy opened it. The curtains were drawn and I couldn't see too well but I did notice that the room was small. My bags were put down and I handed out a tip that I thought was adequate. He looked at it and at me, shrugged his shoulders, and closed the door. I went to the window and drew the curtain. I opened it and found myself coughing in a cloud of steam. The windows looked out over the hotel laundry. I closed it again quickly. I looked at my watch and realized that it was barely 8:00 o'clock in the morning and much too early to call the Heifetzes. I called room service instead and a sleepy voice told me that I couldn't get service until 9:00. I wondered what kind of a place I'd come to and then realized with a start that it was New Year's Day. No wonder the place was empty and the staff haphazard. But the laundry was going and the steam was pouring through my window. At 9:00 I reentered negotiations with room service and presently a bright tray with sparkling silverware and crisp pink napkins was brought to the door. The food was perfect: the scrambled eggs fresh and hot, the bacon crisp, the tea made in a teapot. I couldn't believe my eyes. Suddenly Hollywood began to look better. So did the Beverly Hills Hotel and the world.

I waited until around 10:00 and nervously picked up the phone to call Heifetz. I gave the hotel operator the number and a lilting voice with a Southern accent answered. I gave my name. "Oh, Mr. Chapin!" she said. "Welcome to California. Jascha is so anxious to meet you. When can you come to see us?" I was touched by the warmth.

That was my first contact with Frances Heifetz, the ebullient second wife of the great man, a Southerner with long smooth black hair, a quick smile, and a wonderful ability to bend with whatever wind was blowing at the moment. "Whenever you like," I replied, with what I hoped was the proper amount of individuality and Jeeves-like politeness.

"Why don't you come at noon," she replied. "Jascha usually is ready to leave his study by then." She gave me directions to find their house, which was quite far up in the hills of Beverly, and in my newly rented car I started out. "You'll know you're in the right direction when you hit Schuyler Road," she had said, and I wasn't certain that I'd heard her right. But there was a Schuyler Road and it did lead up a hill toward their house.

Heifetz lived on a bluff high up over the city of Los Angeles, which at that time was just beginning to cope with the smog problem. But there was no smog in their area. The air sparkled, the sun was bright, the colors vivid and varied. The house was a one-story ranch with a good-sized lawn and a separate studio building. I was taken to the patio and asked to wait a few moments. One had a sense of color and comfort and a certain formality. You didn't want to put your feet up on the nearest stool yet you were perfectly comfortable without a necktie. I had brought with me a special letter of introduction from my father-in-law, who was an old friend of Heifetz and, as a first-rank stamp collector, had certain items that Heifetz wanted badly for his own collection.

As Frances and I were chatting a figure came out of the studio door and started slowly on the path toward the house. I recognized him instantly. He walked onto the porch and came toward me. "How do you do." he said, formally, extending his hand. I shook it. "How do you, sir," I replied. A slight smile appeared on his face. "Welcome to California," he said. I thanked him and gave him my father-in-law's letter. He went to a sofa, sat down, and began to read it. His smile broadened for a moment and then disappeared. "I hope he is well," he said. "I look forward to seeing him when we are in New York." "He's fine," I replied. "I want to see some of his newest musical stamps before Grischa does," he said, referring to cellist Gregor Piatigorky. "We are both collectors." We chatted on about this for a while and presently the conversation turned to the upcoming tour. I took a copy of the itinerary from my pocket. We were scheduled to leave the next day by train for Salt Lake City, where he was to play the Beethoven Concerto with the Utah Symphony under the direction of Maurice Abravanel. "I will send a car for you tomorrow at 1:00 PM," he said. "Please do not be late." With that he got up, shook hands again, and disappeared into the house. Frances Heifetz walked me to the door, smiled, and said something about seeing me tomorrow.

I returned to the hotel and wondered what I was going to do until 1:00 PM the following day. The phone rang and it was Frances. "Don't be upset by Jascha's formality," she said. "He's always tense before starting a tour." I thanked her for her thoughtfulness. "And one more thing," she said before hanging up. "Don't be late for the car tomorrow."

I spent a pleasant evening with some friends in Bel Air and the next afternoon at 12:45 PM checked out of the hotel and stood at the entrance, my suitcase and briefcase at my side. Car after car pulled up; I watched Arlene Dahl sweep up the ramp, smiling tensely at her escort. Fred Astaire arrived, so did Ginger Rogers, but no car for me. At 1:00 I began to sweat. By 1:15 I was sweating and beginning to panic. At 1:20 I went to the phone booth. Frances Heifetz answered. "Where are you?" she asked with barely suppressed hysteria. "Standing at the Beverly Hills Hotel entrance waiting for the one o'clock car," I said, "and it looks as if he's forgotten." "Get a taxi right away and tell him to drive fast. Mr. Heifetz will be upset."

Now really sweating I climbed into one of Los Angeles's finest cabs and gave the address. "And as fast as you can," I said, sounding as desperate as I felt. "It won't be all that fast," he replied quickly. "The cops are murder and the hills are mean. But we'll do our best." "This is the address of the great Jascha Heifetz," I said by way of an explanation that I hoped would impress him. "Really," he said, concentrating on his driving. I sat back and tried to relax.

Once we had turned off Sunset Boulevard and started into the hills we really began a horrendous drive. The cab swayed, not only from side to side but from front to back and in between. We rounded corners with tires screeching, roared up hills, churning gravel and dust at a great rate, honked the horn incessantly, and finally pulled up to the house with everyone, car, driver, and passenger, panting. The Heifetz bags were stacked with precision outside and I was dismayed at the number. I leapt out of the cab, paid him off, and turned to go in. "Heifetz, uhmm," he said. "I prefer Milstein myself." He wrenched his car around a tight circle and shot off. So much for one southern California music lover.

The door opened and the Heifetz group came out. "I'm sorry," I said. "I waited for the car but it never showed up." "It had a flat tire and called here," Frances said, "just after you called. Another one is on its way." And she turned to introduce her daughter and Gregory Ratoff, the director and actor, a fellow ex-Russian and devoted friend. The car, a great gray Cadillac with a gray-uniformed chauffeur, appeared. It stopped and we began loading the bags. No easy task. There were seven of them and Frances was not even coming on the first part of the tour. I had two and that made nine, not counting the violins. Somehow we got them all in and when this was done the house door opened and Heifetz himself emerged. He got in the front, his violin case firmly between his legs, and Frances, her daughter, Ratoff, and I piled in the back. "We haven't much time, you know," she said to the driver. And we leapt forward.

We were scheduled out on a Union Pacific special, brown and yellow cars all looking clean and eager, and we boarded quickly, saying goodbye to everyone and waving a great deal. Presently the train started and, with last hand waves and handerkerchiefs, we were off for Salt Lake City. Heifetz turned to me. "Do you drink?" he asked. "Why, yes," I replied. He looked at his watch. "Meet me in the club car at six PM," he said.

I sat down in my roomette and opened my briefcase. There staring at me was my unfinished expense account for the trip across the country. I added the Beverly Hills Hotel bill, the Hertz bills, and miscellaneous cash and totaled everything up. It came to something close to $500. I had visions of Ruth O'Neill's face when she saw it but I signed it and stuffed it into an envelope. I looked out the window and thought that only now, on this train, riding with Heifetz and really beginning the career I'd always wanted, was I truly happy. My only sadness was not being home with Betty and the boys but this was countermeasured by the simple fact that I was now in the music business for real and had at last begun to make my avocation my vocation. I stared at the passing countryside and mused. The whole world was a stage, a concert platform, applauding crowds, masterful artistry, and there, in the background, making it all happen, was Schuyler Chapin, homburg at a slight angle, overcoat thrown casually over the shoulders, cigarette loosely held in the right hand while the left fondled the top of a goldheaded cane. Perhaps I would out-Hurok Hurok or become the general manager of the holy of holies, the Metropolitan Opera. The visions danced, the world whirled, and suddenly I awoke with a start, my head hitting against the window with a smart rap. I looked at my watch. It was 5:55 PM. I quickly splashed water on my face, ran a comb through my hair, smoothed my tie, straightened out my coat, and made my way to the club car. My life with Heifetz was about to begin.

He was already there when I arrived. I saw him glance at his watch. "Sit here," he said, motioning me to a chair beside him. "I will buy your first drink. It is my custom to do this for my tour manager on the first trip. After this you will pay for your own." I ordered a dry martini. His face lit up. "I make a wonderful martini," he said. "I will show you when we get home after the tour is over." "I'll be delighted, sir," I replied. He seemed friendly yet aloof, but I noticed one thing immediately. When he smiled his face took on a wholly different look. His eyes warmed, he seemed to lose the impassivity and aloofness of his looks when not smiling. But the smile didn't come too often.

The drinks arrived and we raised our glasses to each other. "Good luck," he said, and took a good swallow. I did the same. "We must talk of the tour," he said. "There are certain things I want to make clear so that we don't have any problems, or as few as possible." "I'm here to make things as easy for you as I can," I replied. "Bill and George Judd briefed me rather thoroughly before I left New York." Indeed they had, as both of them had previously held this job. They filled me in on many habits and preferences of the great man, including the information that Heifetz liked to play gin rummy. "But he doesn't like to lose," they said, "and if you play be certain to let him keep the upper hand." I had replied by saying that I hardly played the game and did not think this was going to be much of a problem. That at least turned out to be the truth. Heifetz was a good gin rummy player and except for the occasional freak game I never won. We played regularly for three tours but I never really took him. I think he liked that.

We chatted casually but directly as we sipped our drinks and I began to feel some of the tension leaving me. "May I offer you a refill?" I asked at the appropriate time. He looked at me impassively. "I find one martini is like one leg. Rather hard to walk on," I said, with a trace of a smile. He continued to look impassive. "Sir," I said, "I like two martinis before dinner. I'd be happy if you'd join me." A brief flicker of smile appeared on his face. He nodded. The waiter caught my eye and his drink appeared on cue. "Let us take these to the table," he said, rising and walking ahead. I followed.

The club car was one away from the diner and as we walked into the restaurant the headwaiter opened the door for us. "Good evening, Mr. Heifetz," he said. "How nice to see you again. Time for another tour?" He chatted briefly as he showed us to a center table for four that was immediately stripped down for two. "Yes, another tour," he said. "I hope it's a good one," the man replied, handing us the menus. Heifetz nodded. We ordered on separate checks. "From here on you pay for everything except my hotel bills," he said. "You keep a daily account. On Fridays you submit it to me. On Saturdays I will review it and ask questions if I have any. Then I pay you. Be sure to carry lots of singles and I suggest you fold them like this." And he took out a handsome money clip with each bill folded precisely in half and stacked one on top of the other. "This way you know you are giving only one dollar at a time," he said. "And switch ends to separate the various denominations. That way you will not give a five-dollar bill when you only want to give one." He returned the clip to his pocket. "Now I further suggest that you be careful with the press. I do not like to see them except by pre-appointment and I will tell you those I wish to see and those I do not wish to see. Also I like a clean dressing room. Please buy yourself a little canvas bag—we'll call it the concert bag—and keep a fresh towel, a bottle opener, and some paper cups. I find that soda water is best to drink on the road. You never know about local water." And he went on with other details, all quite precise. Finally he paused and glanced out the window. "And one more thing," he said, turning back and fixing his gaze on me. "Don't tell me it was a nice concert. I do not need to hear that." "Very well, sir," I replied. We rose from the table and shook hands. "Good," he said, "I will see you in the morning." And with that he bowed slightly and left the car. I stared after him, thinking what a strange, distant man he was. Everything I'd heard about his reticence with people seemed to be borne out. And yet, I wondered, where did his power to make music come from? It would be a question that was to fascinate me for many months to come. "Don't tell me it was a nice concert." What an odd thing to say to a manager.

When I got back to my roomette I took the itinerary and travel plans out of my briefcase for careful study. Columbia Artists had in those days an almost unflappable Irish travel expert named Mary Crennan, whose job it was to arrange all the artists' hotel, train, and airline reservations. What she was not able to do in fact she made up for in kind; she always had smiles and greetings for everyone and if occasionally an artist found himself stranded in East Overshoe, Nebraska, because the train he was booked to ride had ceased running six months before he usually forgave her, even if before doing so he had hung her in effigy from East Overshoe's only hardware store. For Heifetz she had laid on both train and airplane tickets and these had to be carefully prepared to prevent the East Overshoe Syndrome.

By 1954, of course, American railroads were plunging fast on the downward slope, accelerating rapidly, and it took some expertise to find passenger trains along our entire route. As I unfolded the tickets I saw a lot of blank spaces on them and realized that I was going to be responsible for tracking down the missing trains. I also found holes in the airline schedules and it dawned on me that one of my extra duties was going to be that of travel agent. It had been a long day, the first of many, and I put the travel plans away and turned out the light.

Early the next morning our train slipped into the Salt Lake City station. It was a bright, blue clear day, the sun pouring down, the light intensely bright because of the deep snow. There was a welcoming committee on the platform, all Mormons, as it turned out, dressed soberly and quite formally. All of them were wearing hats. We shook hands, a porter appeared with a large cart, and we bundled all the bags aboard and started for the station interior. A tall, soft-spoken man came up to me and handed me his card. He was a reporter and very politely asked for an interview with Heifetz. I replied that I thought not at the moment, the train ride had been tiring and I knew he wanted to relax before his rehearsal. I would ask later and telephone him at the paper. He had a photographer with him and asked us all to pose. I helped him get the picture arranged but out of the corner of my eye I saw a glare come into Heifetz's eyes. He posed with the rest and then allowed a few to be taken alone, but I could see he was not happy.

We arrived at the Hotel Utah, a wonderful rambling place built at the turn of the century with a wide, high-ceilinged lobby and public rooms and bedrooms of generous proportions. Heifetz was taken upstairs to a suite and there began what became a routine ritual—a thorough examination of each room. With practiced eye he took in the plumbing, the closets, the furniture, the curtains, and the cleanliness. He checked the view, the writing paper, the telephones, the bed, the pillows. He took his time doing it while I made small talk with the Utah Symphony representatives and the conductor Maurice Abravanel. I had never met Abravanel before but I knew and admired his work in the Broadway theater, particularly his association with Kurt Weill. It was Abravanel who created the musical conditions in *Knickerbocker Holiday* for Walter Huston's haunting "September Song," thereby setting a precedent for talk-sing that was used in later years by Rex Harrison in *My Fair Lady.* I knew Abravanel to be a musician of sensibility and told him so. He looked pleased.

In the meantime Heifetz had decided that the suite was all right and the bags had been placed in the appropriate places. The rehearsal was scheduled for later that afternoon and after details were set everyone retired, leaving Heifetz and myself alone. "Do you remember our talk last night about newspaper reporters?" he asked. "Yes, sir," I said, "but the reporter and photographer were there at the station and I couldn't very well refuse any comment." "I will not see him," Heifetz retorted. "You better take care of it." I must have looked crestfallen and upset—I was both—but he came over to me and smiled. "This is your first tour," he said. "I've been making these trips many, many years. I know what's best. You will learn." And he turned away. I started for the door. "We'll have lunch downstairs at one PM," he said. "I will be ready for you here a few minutes before." "Yes, sir." I replied, and went off to my own room.

At 12:55 I appeared back at Heifetz's door and knocked. It was opened promptly and he was ready. I noticed that he was now dressed in a blue suit, with a medium dark blue shirt and tie, the rosette of the Légion d'honneur was in his buttonhole. He looked well turned out, sober yet colorful enough to obviously come from somewhere else. I automatically assumed the military position of walking two paces behind and one to the left and we journeyed thus to the elevator and the dining room. The dining room was like the other public rooms, spacious, with tables set far enough apart for plenty of room and the feeling of privacy. We selected a table a little out of the mainstream and were courteously seated and handed menus. "I must tell you one other thing about touring," he said, while we were studying the cards. "Be very careful of the food. If you ever have doubts order ham and eggs. It is the one thing that is safe almost everywhere." "We don't have to worry here, do we?" I asked. "No," he said, "this dining room is very good. Eat simply, avoid the fancy dishes, which are usually four parts chi-chi and one part flour. And watch the drinking water. It is better to use soda or the bottled spring kind." I felt like a prelunch drink and

asked Heifetz if he would join me. "In Utah?" he said, his eyebrows
rising. "You cannot buy a drink in Utah." I learned later that day that
you could not only not buy a drink but on the grounds of the Temple,
including the Tabernacle, where the concert was to be given, you could
not bring in any stimulant whatsoever, including tea, coffee, Coca-
Cola, or tobacco of any kind. This was to pose some interesting problems.

Our lunch was good. Heifetz talked about previous visits to Salt
Lake City and filled me in on details about the construction of the Tabernacle. "The acoustics are extraordinary, you will hear," he said.
"There is no metal anywhere, no nails. All of the pieces are fitted
together and joined by pegs. The effect is one long bending piece of
wood forming a great shell." He was fascinating on the subject and I
listened carefully. Every once in a while a smile might come to his face
but most of the time he talked on impassively, displaying practically no
emotion. At the end of lunch we rose, I signed the check and escorted
him out of the room. "The rehearsal is at four," he said. "Pick me up
at three-thirty." And he bowed slightly and went off to the elevator. I
went upstairs to get my coat. I wanted to have a look at Salt Lake before the work began.

Salt Lake City is one of the few American cities that laid out its
streets for the convenience of its residents rather than its cattle. Its
main arteries are wide with broad sidewalks. Everything looked clean,
and with the Rockies framed in the background the effect was almost
magical. The people all looked neat and organized and seemed to be
going about their business in a brisk manner. They all looked the same,
though, and I wondered how interesting they might be over the long
pull. I walked to Tabernacle Square and looked carefully at the Temple. Unless you are a Mormon you are not allowed in it. The only major building open to the public was the Tabernacle and this was famous
to me as the home of the Mormon Tabernacle Choir whose Sunday
broadcasts had been part of my regular radio listening pattern. At 3:00,
I returned to the hotel, took a bath, and changed into slacks and a blazer. I felt this was right for rehearsal clothes. I had bought the little
"concert bag" and into it I put a bottle of soda water, some paper
cups, and two hotel towels. I found a bottle opener in a drawer and put
that in as well. I felt prepared for the moment and went down the hall
to tap on Heifetz's door. He was ready, his overcoat and gloves on. I
reached for the violin case. "Oh no," he said. "Thank you very much
but I always carry this."

It was only a block from the hotel to the Tabernacle; nevertheless we took a taxi and drove to the stage door. It took some minutes to do this because of the one-way streets but Heifetz wanted to preserve his energy. We walked into the building and were directed to his dressing room. Inside I took his coat and hat and hung them up in a closet. I opened the concert bag, spread out a towel, and put a bottle of soda water in one corner, together with the paper cups and the bottle opener.

Heifetz found a sturdy table and opened up his violin case. It was the first peek I had into this treasure chamber. There were two violins, one a Stradivarius and the other, the one he preferred playing, the "David" Guarnerius del Gesu. He gently pulled the "David," named after Ferdinand David, one of its earliest owners, out of its silk casing and laid it gently in the open case. He took off his suit coat and handed it to me. Turning to a small additional bag he had brought, he opened it and took out a blue jacket. I held it for him and he put it on. Parts of the sleeves and the body were shiny from use and cleaning. This was his rehearsal coat and as far as I know he never used any other on our tours together. He buttoned the coat and glanced in the mirror. His trousers were perfectly creased, his shoes shined. He was in order. He picked up the violin and began a scale. He was absorbed in what he was doing and I left the room to check the state of the rehearsal and find out exactly when he would be needed.

Abravanel was rehearsing the orchestra and the sound rolled out into the empty auditorium. He caught my eye as I stood in the wings and from the expression of his face I gathered he was asking whether the great man was ready. I nodded. Immediately he stopped the orchestra and declared a break. He came out toward me. "I would like to resume in ten minutes, if that is all right," he said. "I should like to go to Heifetz now." Heifetz was still playing the scale when we arrived in front of the door. I knocked lightly and entered. "Abravanel is outside and would like to see you," I told him. "Have him come in," he replied. I opened the door and bade the maestro enter. "I've been looking forward to this all season," he said. "Thank you," replied Heifetz. They began discussing the score.

When the ten minutes was up I opened the door, and the two of them started out toward the stage. The orchestra had reassembled and at the sight of Abravanel became absolutely still. "Ladies and gentlemen," he began, "Jascha Heifetz." And Heifetz walked out on the stage as the orchestra rose and applauded. He turned, unsmiling, and bowed to them. They sat down and I scurried out into the house itself to listen. A few whispered words between conductor and soloist and Abravanel raised his baton. The four tympani notes of the opening measure of the Beethoven concerto floated out into the hall and the rehearsal was under way.

Heifetz watched Abravanel, turning three-quarters to do so. The orchestra were all sitting straight, on the alert. The music moved and built and the moment approached for the soloist to enter. Heifetz tucked the violin under his chin and at the moment drew his bow across the strings. A sound, unique in the world, came forth. I was stunned. Certainly the Beethoven concerto is one of the most beautiful in the entire violin repertoire and this was not my first hearing of it, but it might just as well have been. The work was excitingly new, electrifying, moving, breathtaking. The sound filled the hall, there was no escaping it. I looked to see if there were others present. There were not. The whole performance was for me and I focused on it.

From time to time in the first movement there were stops for corrections but basically the work progressed without major problems. I got the measure of the sound and its mellowness in the hall and found it seductive, a much richer and enveloping sound than halls I'd been in before. At one point Heifetz looked out at me and cupped his ear, in a gesture that asked about the balance. I circled my thumb and index finger in the okay sign. At the end of the first movement the orchestra applauded. Heifetz bobbed his head in response, touched his strings to tune them briefly, and nodded his head for the second movement. Here there were several stops. The second movement is tricky, very exposed for the soloist and the balance between the forces must be perfect. It was easy to see that everyone wanted the same thing, perfection, and great attention was being paid to achieving this. The second and third movements of the work are interconnected and played without pause. This finale is a rondo written in the style of music of the chase. It's the movement that drew the admiration of Donald Francis Tovey. "To find the right finale," he wrote, "to a scheme so subtle and delicate as that of a classical concerto is of itself a crowning stroke of genius. And there is no finale which more boldly and accurately gives the range, so to speak, of the whole, than this most naïvely humorous of rondos." And the humor and the bounce burst forth, unbounded and joyful. The movement was played without pause and as the closing measures approached I was brought abruptly back to earth by the sudden realization that I had to be backstage after the rehearsal to take care of my artist.

At the last note the orchestra again burst into applause. Heifetz turned to face them and bowed formally. He shook hands with Abravanel, bowed again, and came off the stage. I was about to say something but checked myself, remembering our talk on the train. I handed him his ring and watch. He put his violin down in the case, picked the whole thing up, and we started for his dressing room.

When we arrived he took out his cigarette case, and carefully placing a cigarette in a holder, lit it. I reminded him that smoking was not allowed in the building. "Watch out for me," he said. And I went to the door, locked it securely, and opened the window. The dressing room was on the second floor with windows that opened out onto the Temple grounds, highly exposed to any passer-by. I felt as if I were back in boarding school keeping a sharp lookout for any master while we all shared a cigarette up the chimney of a vacant master's study.

Heifetz busied himself with putting away his rehearsal jacket, putting on his tie, sipping a glass of soda water, and was amused, I think, by my role as tobacco cop. Presently the cigarette was finished and we were ready to go. There was a knock on the door and I went to unlock it. Abravanel entered the room, paused, sniffed the air and hurriedly closed the door behind him. He seemed to pale. "Have you been smoking?" he asked. "No, don't answer that. Open the windows wide. Let out the smell. This is very serious here." And he obviously meant it. "They are so strict," he said. "My worst problem was always Oscar Levant. You know how Levant is about his coffee and cigarettes. He would not rehearse without the coffee and I had nervous young people passing it back and forth in milk containers. The cigarettes were a nightmare. He finally took to a rubber tube which he stuck out the window and blew the smoke through. I was glad when his concert was finished." Heifetz didn't say anything but I assured Abravanel that we would do nothing to cause difficulties.

We all left the auditorium together. Abravanel dropped us off at the hotel. "Won't you both please come to lunch at my house tomorrow? It would be an honor for us." "I'd be delighted," Heifetz replied, looking over at me. "And I would be too," I said. "Thank you for including me."

I discovered another Heifetz that night when we met in his room before dinner. I had foolishly forgotten to pack any liquor and was facing a dry patch with no cocktail. When I arrived at the suite, he had laid out soda, ginger ale, ice, glasses, and scotch. I do not ordinarily drink scotch but with nothing else in sight it looked just fine to me. "Will you join me in a drink?" he asked. "Oh yes, sir," I replied. "I'm very grateful. I forgot to pack any booze." "That is one mistake I'm sure you will learn not to repeat." And we toasted each other.

After lunch the next day Heifetz took a rest and I picked him up in the evening a half hour before the concert was to begin. I had bought an empty medicine bottle into which I poured some scotch. I had also bought a set of paper ashtrays that could be emptied quickly into the toilet and a spray can of air freshener to circumvent the tobacco smells. As we walked into the Tabernacle I began to feel that all eyes were on me. The stage doorman, looking me over carefully, seemed to be nodding his head as if he knew what was going on but was not going to interfere. I set up the dressing room with ashtrays planted and the toilet door ajar so that I could make a quick dash, empty them, push down the handle, close the door, and smile, all, practically, at the same time.

When all was ready I left Heifetz alone and walked to the wings to look out into the auditorium. Every inch was packed with people, including the choir stalls. I asked Abravanel about the choir and he said that taking their normal places was the only way they could hear the concert.

The concert started on time and the audience was responsive but not overwhelming. Heifetz always played last on any program—it was written into his contracts—and when he finally appeared the audience was ready for him. I watched as he bowed; there was not a trace of a smile on his face. He could have been caught up in a high-stakes poker game. He bowed both to the audience and, turning, to the orchestra and the choir. He tuned and looked over the orchestra while he was doing so. I noticed something odd about his tuning. It seemed sharp but before I had a chance to think too much about this the tympani began the four notes and the concerto was under way.

Again I went into the house to listen. To me the opening of the Beethoven concerto is one of the sublime moments in all music and as the sound poured from his instrument and as the concerto moved along I forgot about everything and everybody. My soul was filled with the beauty. Every once in a while I looked out over the audience and they too were caught in the spell. Orchestra and soloist were one.

With the beginning of the coda I went backstage again to be ready for the great man when he came off. As he did he looked unruffled. He shook hands with Abravanel and then walked out to take a solo bow. The ovation mounted. The poker face never changed. Was he indifferent to that burst of affection? I didn't think so. He came back for Abravanel and the two walked out together. Abravanel motioned for the orchestra to stand and the applause increased. Heifetz shook hands with the concertmaster, nodded his head at the other players, and continued bowing to the audience. Never once did his expression change. And curiously never once did the audience really let go. It was almost as if they were waiting for a cue from him to do so and they never got it. I didn't say anything but I was curious and puzzled. From what they heard the applause should have continued. But it stopped after a reasonable length of time and never really reached an impassioned climax.

We returned to his dressing room and I helped him out of his tailcoat and into his overcoat. This was to be an unchanging ritual after every performance. As I took his tailcoat I noticed that it was warm but not wet. He put the violin away after carefully removing all the resin dust and cleaning the strings. I watched him doing this and was caught up by the sheer beauty of the fiddle itself. I asked him for a closer look and he moved it toward me. One marveled at the exquisite carving and the scrollwork. I knew it was one of the most famous instruments in the world and I doubted if it had ever sounded as beautiful even after it was first finished.

I poured him a scotch and lit his cigarette. "Now the manager, please," he said, all business. I'd been briefed that he wished to receive his fee by check from the hands of the local manager right after a performance and I had alerted the manager of the orchestra to this. I brought him in and discreetly left.

"There are many people waiting backstage to see you," I said, when I returned. "How do you want to handle them?" "No more than three at a time. I like that because it does not crowd the room and the public likes it because it gives them a sense of personal contact." I went outside again and gently lined them up. I let in three at a time and he stood talking to each one, signing autographs if asked, shaking hands, and from time to time smiling faintly. If someone seemed to be overstaying their welcome he would look up and I would steer the person away. We never discussed this point; I just sensed it and Heifetz, while maintaining his composure, moved his eye in something that might be taken for a wink.

With the last autograph seeker finished Heifetz changed his clothes and we were ready to leave. The Abravanels were waiting to take us to a post-concert supper. I had told Abravanel to tell our hostess that Heifetz ate very lightly before a performance and liked supper afterward. This was to be my first but by no means last experience about what many hostesses view as a post-performance supper. It was hardly a classic "supper," for there was no real food; just crackers and cheese and nuts and candies. And being a Mormon household, there was no liquor, just a sweet punch, water and milk. The people were nice enough, but to each other, not the guests, and consequently they talked among themselves, leaving us to fend for ourselves.

I still had a little scotch left in my medicine bottle and went off to find the kitchen. I took a paper cup that I found there and filled it partway up with the liquor and carried it back into the living room, exclaiming how delicious I thought the punch was. "Here, sir," I said to Heifetz. "Taste this. I think you'll like it." His face became instantly poker. "Oh, do try it, sir," I said again, staring straight at him. He took the cup and tasted. His expression did not change. "Thank you," he said. And looked straight ahead.

We left just as soon as we could and when we reached the hotel I scrounged around to see if there was any way of getting some food. There wasn't. We then started out to find something. The city looked deserted and abandoned, as if swept clean of people. A taxi driver told us of a diner and we got in and drove for what seemed like ages, finally reaching a tiny wagon where the hamburgers and coffee tasted as if they'd been prepared the day before. Heifetz ate ham and eggs, reminding me that this was the safest dish while on the road. And it turned out that he was absolutely right. My aged hamburger kept me awake most of the night while I gathered the next day that his eggs and ham had put him to sleep like a baby.

V

On the Road

The following day we headed east and south to Texas. I hadn't been to Texas since World War II and had vowed that I would never voluntarily return again. But the first recital of the tour was slated for Beaumont, Texas, where we were joined by Heifetz's then accompanist Emanuel Bay. I had not met Bay yet; he had not been in Los Angeles when I was there at the start of the tour, but I knew him from phonograph records. He had been Heifetz's pianist for a long time. Bay was Russian, a little older than Heifetz, and a little more outgoing. He was a champion bridge player and bristled when Heifetz would talk about the game.

From Salt Lake City we had flown to Dallas for a performance with Walter Hendl and the Dallas Symphony. Later we were to return here for an adventure that made the headlines all over the country. The first Dallas experience was marked by another new discovery: Heifetz was a movie buff. The night before the concert he hinted around about the movies and I looked up everything I could find about Dallas's cinema life in the papers. We finally settled on one of those endless 1950s costume dramas, starring Robert Taylor in beard and baritone as Ivanhoe. We blew ourselves to a good dinner at the Old Warsaw, a kind of Texas version of Chasen's and 21, and came into the theater for the last show. There must have been all of ten people in the place and we took center seats about halfway back. Heifetz was instantly glued to the screen and so was I for a few minutes until I realized what was up there was the drivel of the world, despite Cinemascope, Technicolor, costumes, and blaring trumpets. I looked over at Heifetz looking at the screen and he was absorbed. The picture ended after what seemed like weeks and as the lights came up we were the only two people in the place. We were sitting surrounded by spilled popcorn and damp pools of soda. "That was terrible," he said, looking at me. "Terrible. Terrible." "But you seemed to be enthralled by it," I said. "Terrible," he said and we made our way out of the theater.

On the way back to the hotel he began to talk about Hollywood before the war. "We had wonderful times," he said. "There wasn't any smog. Everyone came there and we all knew each other." He sounded almost wistful. At the hotel we heard sounds of well-played popular music coming out of the bar. "I love good jazz and popular songs," he said. "George Gershwin was a good friend of mine. We often played together. I asked him to write a concerto for the violin but he died before he had a chance to do it. You will hear two of his preludes. I use them as encores at my recitals. Did you know that I once wrote a popular song?" I replied that I did not know that. "Oh yes," he said, "I'm a member of ASCAP, under an assumed name, of course." "What's the name?" I asked. "Jim Hoyl," he replied. I didn't confess that the name was a new one to me. "When we return home after the tour I will give you a copy." I thanked him.

By the time we reached Beaumont I was beginning to feel like a veteran impresario. The dressing room in Dallas had been filthy and I'd cleaned it up before the concert to the spit and polish of my aviation cadet days. Hiefetz was impressed. I'd even bought a set of skeleton keys that promised to be good for all locks.

In Beaumont the theater was an old one and the dressing room was again a pig sty. I went over early on the day of the recital and cleaned everything in sight. To make certain that no one would come along and touch things I locked the door with one of my skeleton keys and went out into the auditorium to hear Bay practice. I felt smug and professional until I reached around for my wallet. I suddenly remembered that I'd left it on the dressing room table. I ran backstage and took out my key. I put it in the lock and nothing happened. The lock would not turn and I couldn't get the key out. When I finally did work it loose the door was still locked and I couldn't see anyone around the theater who might be able to help. I began to get panicky. I tried again but nothing happened. Bay came off the stage and I explained my plight. He shook hands and left. I tried once again. I thought about breaking the door down but abandoned that idea. I saw that the hinges were on the outside and might be removable if I had any tools. I went out looking for some kind of janitor or watchman and finally found an old-timer dozing in a side office off the basement. I asked him for a screwdriver and hammer and he looked at me with grave suspicion. He finally agreed to come upstairs and have a look. Knowing that skeleton keys were illegal and that I had been technically trespassing in the first place I was at some pains not to tell him how the door happened to be locked. "Ain't never seen this door locked before," he said with a Texas drawl that seemed like a caricature. We wrestled with the door, removing the hinges accompanied by loud squeaks and groans and stirring up of long-abandoned dust. It was heavier than we thought and as it came free it crashed to the floor with a resounding roar. Before the confusion righted itself I nipped in and grabbed my wallet. "Need some help gettin' this back," he said, and went off to find someone. I looked at the lock and handle and, taking the hammer, rapped the lock itself back into place. By the time my friend returned with help the door was lying flat and the lock in place. "Can't figure out what happened," I said, "but everything seems to be okay now." The three of us lifted the door and returned it to its hinges. I threw away the skeleton keys. Once was enough.

That night the program included Beethoven's Kreutzer Sonata as the big piece closing the first half. The Kreutzer is one of the world's most played violin sonatas and was never one of my favorites. I changed my mind after hearing Heifetz and Bay.

After the concert and the post-concert backstage ceremonies of fee and public we waited outside the theater to be picked up before going to supper. Heiftez, Bay, and I were standing when Heifetz turned to me. "Don't you like music?" he asked. I stared at him. "Of course I do," I replied. "I love it very much indeed. It is why I'm in this business." "But you never say anything," he went on. "You told me the first day not to tell you it was a nice concert," I said. "Oh well," he said, "everyone wants to know if someone *likes* something." I said I'd tell him if I liked something. "And another thing," he went on. "You never wish me good luck." "Good luck?" I said. "I was brought up to believe that you never say 'good luck' inside a theater." "But I like it," he said. I promised him that I would do so from that moment on.

Next day we left for Chicago via San Antonio. It was a crackling Texas winter day, not a cloud in the sky. We boarded our Trans Texas DC–3 and I was overcome with waves of World War II nostalgia. I sent a note up to the pilot and presently he appeared at my seat and asked me forward to the cockpit. I sat in the co-pilot's chair, which is strictly illegal, and had the time of my life watching familiar countryside slip below the wings. As we approached San Antonio the co-pilot reappeared, standing between the two seats, and I made a motion to get up. "Stay put!" he said. And we started our descent. At the appropriate moment I lowered the landing gear, moved the mixture controls to full rich, and opened the cowl flaps. We touched down perfectly and taxied up to the small Trans Texas terminal. I shook hands with the crew and thanked them and went back to join Heifetz. He looked quite pale. "Did you fly this plane?" he asked. "Well, not really," I said. "I handled the controls while we were in the air but the pilot made the landing. I flew as co-pilot." He looked at me with suspicion. "That's the truth, sir," I said, "and I do have a lot of flying time in the planes. I wish I had a chance to do more." The look he gave me did not quite square with my feelings. I thought we better drop the subject.

At San Antonio the weather was also crisp and clear and I watched our bags being transferred from Trans Texas to American for our connecting flight. We walked into the terminal, had a cup of coffee, and arrived at the American gate in plenty of time. As we boarded I thought what a simple trip this was and how much I was looking forward to Chicago, where Heiftez was scheduled to play the Brahms with Reiner and the Chicago Symphony and to record it. We settled into our seats and played a little gin rummy. I was worse than usual and this put Heifetz into a great humor. As lunchtime approached I realized that we had, for some time, been flying on instruments. The white light look of solid fog was all around. I thought nothing of it. We had a drink and our food and an occasional glance out the window still showed instrument conditions. I'd just settled down for a post-lunch nap when the pilot came on the speakers telling us that there were bad weather conditions all over the midwestern part of the country and he was not at all sure that we would be able to get into Chicago. He said he would keep us advised. I tried to nap again but not for long. The white fog had now been replaced by dark gray to gray-black and the light reflected back in the passenger cabins was anything but pleasant. The pilot's voice came back on the speakers. "I'm sorry, ladies and gentlemen," he began, "but we are not going to make it to Chicago. Chicago is totally closed. We've been ordered to Kansas City and we should be there in about thirty minutes."

I rummaged through my briefcase and took out our itinerary. Mary Crennan had provided me with a basic railroad schedule of the entire country before I left New York and I had tucked it into my case, occasionally cursing at its size and heaviness. Now it was going to prove its usefulness. I looked up trains from Kansas City to Chicago and red-circled those I thought might be useful to us. Presently the seat belt sign went on and we were descending toward the runway. We landed without incident but I noticed that we braked very swiftly and in an extremely short time had come to a dead halt. Then I saw we were turning and I also saw that there were airplanes everywhere one looked, parked at every conceivable angle. We deplaned and were put in cars and trucks and old busses and driven toward the Kansas City air terminal.

In those days Kansas City had a perfectly adequate airport for the 1930s, but not one up to date for the '50s. The terminal building was small, cramped and in the throes of enlargement. When we arrived it looked like Grand Central Station on New Year's Eve. I've never seen so many people before or since jammed into such little space. Luggage was piled up everywhere and clusters of people were sitting on bags or on the floor, taking turns leaning against the walls and looking miserable.

Into this maelstrom we came, bringing in our luggage and carving out some kind of space. I elbowed my way into a corner and piled our suitcases into a pyramid, putting two of them into position to act as a chair. By the time I had everything arranged I was sweaty and dirty. Heifetz sat down on the cases, tucked his violin case between his knees, folded his hands over the top, and looked at me. "Do something!" he said. There was a faint smile on his face but none in his eyes. I looked at him for a long moment. "Yes, sir," I said, and went off pushing my way through the people.

I worked my way down toward the airline ticket windows, which were crowded by people trying to get the attention of the clerks. I saw a hole in the line in front of TWA and blatantly shoved my way past several people who were at that moment reading timetables. I touched the clerk's sleeve and asked, wanly and exhaustedly, if there was any chance of sleeping car space on any train to Chicago. As he stared at me I played out my only trump. "I am Jascha Heitfetz's tour manager and we are due in Chicago tomorrow for a concert with Reiner. Heifetz is sitting over there (I pointed) and this is a matter of professional life and death." I spoke without pause, gambling on the fact that the man might have heard of Heiftez and might be impressed. I was not prepared for his reply. "Heifetz?" he said. "You're kidding!" "No, I'm not," I replied. "He's right over there." And the young man craned his neck to look. "I see him!" he said. "I heard him a few years ago when he gave a recital here. I love music and he's the greatest!" I'd won, far beyond my wildest hopes. "What about the Chicago trains?" I asked. He grabbed a phone and called someone. He turned his back and engaged in what looked to be a conspiratorial conversation. Finally he took pencil and paper and began writing, looking at me and over my shoulder toward Heifetz while doing so. The other passengers on the line began to get impatient, as well they might, since I had slipped in ahead of them. He finally put down the phone and turned the paper he'd been writing on toward me. On it I saw 10:00 PM train to Chicago. Two duplex roomettes, and then a car number. "Take this to the railroad station within the next half-hour and go to the first window on the left as you enter the building. Give them this. The space will be held for only thirty minutes so you better get going." I grabbed the paper and shook hands.

I worked my way back to where Heifetz was still sitting looking unperturbed. "We must go quickly," I said. "Fortunately the TWA clerk is a fan of yours and we've got roomettes on the ten PM to Chicago." "Roomettes?" he queried. "Duplex roomettes," I replied. "I've no idea what they are but they sound luxurious. We've got to get to the terminal building in thirty minutes or they will not hold them for us." And I started to pick up some of the bags. Heifetz walked toward the entrance. I had the feeling that roomettes were not exactly what he had in mind. We pushed on toward the door and the outside ramp. There were no cabs in sight. I knew that the airport was only minutes away from downtown and was prepared to walk to find one when with a screech and lurch one pulled up to discharge passengers. As the passengers got out I held the door and as quickly as possible thrust Heifetz inside. Our bags were draped all over the car and I gave the porter a large tip. He smiled. The taxi started off for the railroad terminal.

"What's going on here?" I asked the driver as we made our way in crawling traffic. "Don't you know?" he asked. "Every plane in the Midwest has been ordered down here. There's a huge storm belt with snow and fog that has closed down most of the airports. Kansas City seems to be the only one still open." "Not for long," I said. "I don't think there is any more space to park even a Piper Cub." "Do you guys have train tickets?" he asked. "If not, forget it. The terminal's almost as crowded." "I have reservations," I said, "but I must pick them up in the next few minutes or I will lose them." "I'll get you there," he said. "Hold on." He took off through side alleys and byways, down small streets, avoiding the main traffic snarls and getting us to the terminal with remarkable skill. When we pulled up I leapt out and unloaded the bags. He helped me. Heifetz stood on the sidewalk watching. "Many thanks for your help," I said. "We would never have made it here without you." "That's okay," he replied, and then, turning toward Heifetz, he said, "And have a good concert, Mr. Heifetz. I enjoy your playing!" My God, I thought, the power of recognition. Heifetz didn't say a word.

We entered the terminal, found the right window, and I laid out the money for the tickets. "What exactly is a duplex roomette?" I asked the clerk. "It's a little smaller than a roomette," he replied, "and they are staggered in the cars so that there are twice as many of them per car as of the ordinary roomette." The ordinary roomette has hardly any headroom, I thought. This duplex business is going to be even tougher. I took the tickets and saw Heifetz standing alongside of me. "What are the duplex roomettes?" he asked. "Well, sir," I replied, "they're kind of smaller versions of regular roomettes." "We are going to be crowded," he said. And there was no further comment.

I glanced up at the station clock. It was just past seven and I was suddenly starved. I also remembered that this was the famous Kansas City station where the Fred Harvey restaurants started. Before I could say anything Heifetz tapped my sleeve. "Let us have an early and good dinner," he said. "It's been quite a day." I gave the porter our roomette numbers and paid him a fat fee. "Don't worry," he said. "I'll take care of everything." And he pushed the luggage off.

We found the restaurant and were seated promptly. The place was empty and this surprised me as the terminal was jammed with people. We ordered cocktails, Kansas City steaks, baked potatoes, and salads. The cocktails were generous, and after two, both of us were feeling a great deal better. The steaks arrived tender and juicy and cooked just right and the salads were crisp and fresh. A Nesselrode pie slice finished off the meal and we washed everything down with strong black coffee.

We both felt better and drifted slowly toward our train. I felt that we were over the worst. No matter how small or uncomfortable the space, we were at least bedded down on the train and would not have to sit up all night. Small was right. It was midget, with absolutely no place that I could see to put the luggage. And where was our luggage anyway? Heifetz sat down on his bed, the fiddle case stuck between his knees as usual, and looked at me. I know, I thought. Do something. "I'll find the porter and see about the bags," I said bravely, and went back onto the platform.

There was no porter in sight. I started back toward the station. He was nowhere to be found. I began to sweat again. I pushed my way through the crowd, looking everywhere. I finally found myself outside the station near the taxi stands and over the heads of lots of people I caught sight of what I believed to be our man. I elbowed my way toward him. "Where are our bags?" I said. "You told me you'd take care of everything." He looked at me with no sign of recognition. "Don't you remember me?" I asked. "I'm the fellow with all those bags who paid you well to take them to the ten o'clock to Chicago." He still stared. "Look," I said in desperation, "the train is leaving in ten minutes and I need to stow away all that stuff." I took out my wallet again. He glanced at it and then at me. I took out five dollars. "Oh yes," he said, pocketing the money. "I remember. I'll be right with you," "And I'm staying right with you," I said, and looked at my watch.

We were now down to seven minutes before the train was due to leave. Slowly the porter moved toward a large room and reappeared with our luggage piled up on his handcart. He moved very slowly but I didn't want to make a fuss. We moved toward the platform and finally to the car entrance. With three minutes to go, we started to put the bags on the train but in no time at all we'd used up all the available space. Throwing everything on board as best we could, we had bravely lifted the last bag when the train whistle hooted and we started off.

I now faced the problem of what to do with all our luggage. The train porter looked disconcerted and angry. "I've a full train tonight," he said, "and what am I going to do with all these?" I reached for the faithful wallet and pulled out ten dollars. Without breaking stride he pocketed the money, took out a key, opened a small closet, and began stuffing it with our suitcases. A vision of the unforgettable ship's cabin scene in the Marx Brothers *A Night at the Opera* filled my mind. The porter pushed and pulled and finally stuffed in everything that would fit and shoved the door shut, locking it firmly. "There," he said. "now the rest will have to go under things." By "things" I knew he had to mean other people's accommodations. I looked the other way.

The duplex roomette was as small as it looked and I spent a restless night. So, I gather, did Heifetz for the next morning he didn't look happy and we had a gloomy breakfast together before moving on to Orchestra Hall, where he was scheduled to begin recording the Brahms Concerto with Reiner and the Chicago Symphony.

I had never been in Orchestra Hall before and was unprepared for its intimacy and beauty. The orchestra was already onstage when we arrived and sitting in the auditorium was Frances, who had flown in from Beverly Hills. She looked cool and radiant and I saw Heifetz's spirits pick up immediately.

Presently we were joined by a tall dark-haired man with a comfortable smile wearing a stopwatch around his neck and carrying a clip board. He was introduced as Jack Pfeiffer, recording producer for RCA Victor. Over the years I was to see a great deal of Jack, between his activities for Heifetz and Horowitz and others of the RCA stable. This day, however, he sensed that Heifetz was not in the best of moods and I noticed he handled him with the greatest skill. I walked back to the dressing room while Heifetz donned his rehearsal jacket and heard how gentle but professional Pfeiffer was being in his approach.

As we reached the back stage area we were joined by Fritz Reiner. Reiner was not only a great conductor but an absolute autocrat in every respect. He tolerated no nonsense from anyone, star or line player alike, and the stories of his temper, cynical humor, and mannerisims were rampant. My favorite was of the double bass player who claimed he could not see the maestro's beat from the back stands and took out a telescope to see. Reiner was aided and abetted by his indestructible wife Carlotta, whose humor and affection Reiner seemed to respect. In later years Reiner asked me to work for him as assistant manager of the orchestra and I was tempted.

Brahms' violin concerto is one of the towering masterpieces of the literature. It is curious that Beethoven, Mendelssohn, Brahms, and Tchaikovsky each wrote only one concerto for the instrument and that all four are cornerstones of the violin repertoire. To them must be added the Mozart concertos as well as high romantic favorites such as the Sibelius, the Weiniawski Concerto Number Two, Saint-Saens Introduction and Rondo Capriccioso, Ravel's Tzigane, Bruch's Scottish Fantasy, Prokofiev's First and Second Concertos, and William Walton's Concerto that was commissioned by Heifetz in the late thirties.

The recording of the Brahms that Heifetz was about to make was his first of that work in the newly developed stereo sound and there was great interest in it from all sides of the musical world. It also was my first recording experience. I sat in the auditorium with Frances as things got under way.

It was a tedious and exhausting process. Soloist and orchestra would play through a large part of a movement, perhaps the whole of it, and then go back to repeat sections or measures that were not perfect. I feared that out of all the work there might emerge the perfect Brahms but one with very little life. At the first take of the second movement,

Ray Still, the oboist, began his long, sweet solo passage, and sounded as if he played the entire section without taking a breath. So haunting and beautiful was he that I saw Heifetz turn to observe him and at the conclusion of the phrases tap his bow on the back of his violin. Even Reiner applauded and orchestra men shuffled their feet in the time-honored method of showing approval to a colleague. This was all lovely but it seemed to me to ruin a take. Not at all. They all knew their man. At a signal from Pfeiffer they began again and Still repeated the passage without a fault and just as beautifully as he had done the first time. With the entrance of the solo violin it was evident that whatever tiredness and ill-humor Heifetz may have had at the beginning of the session he was now in top form and even enjoying himself.

But he is a perfectionist, even more than Reiner, and the session dragged on all morning. Suddenly Reiner looked up and barked for the manager. "There is a matinee today," he said, when the manager appeared. "I'm too tired. Get the associate conductor to conduct." Turning to Heifetz, he said: "This is enough. I am going home." And he left the building. I expected Heifetz to show some annoyance but he shrugged his shoulders. "We'll play the piece in concert tomorrow tonight and record again on Monday." And he packed up his violins.

With Frances's arrival my life became a little bit easier and I decided to take time off to see the Larry Howes and my friend Burr Tillstrom. For the first time since the tour began I left Heifetz on his own. I sat with Burr while he did his nightly show and that night the whole program was devoted to his impresario friend who traveled with a violinist but whose heart really belonged to an aging dancer and singer. It was extremely funny to everyone except, I suspect, Heifetz. But then I don't know to this day if he ever saw it. On one of the free evenings I asked Tina and Larry Howe to have dinner with Heifetz and myself at the Cape Cod Room of the Drake Hotel and we had a hilarious time. Heifetz obviously liked the Howes and it was a relaxing evening for everyone.

The next night Heifetz played the Brahms in concert with the Chicago and I was staggered once again by his performance. The music poured out as if it were being composed on the spot. The fiendishly difficult cadenza, written by Joseph Joachim, the Hungarian violinist for whom Brahms composed the work, sounded totally easy and the expression on Heifetz's face never changed. Toward the end I made my way backstage and he came off looking cool and unruffled. The audience, as in all the other concerts, gave him warm applause and seemed to be waiting for some sign from him, a smile or a gesture, to pour out its collective heart. But this he never gave and as a consequence never received what he so desperately wanted. We spoke of this one day. I asked him why he never smiled on stage. "They come to hear me play not to see me smile," he said. "But you want them to like what they hear and you always seem disappointed in their response. It seems to me that they would respond with love and abandon if you invited them to do so." He looked at me without expression. I thought I'd crossed the line with that remark and indeed I almost had. "I've been playing for a long time," he replied, after a pause. "I must do things my way." And it was obvious that conversation on that subject was closed.

The recording of the Brahms was completed and we moved on to New York, where he was scheduled to play the Mendelssohn with the New York Philharmonic under Guido Cantelli. This gave me some days at home and I welcomed them. It was like returning from the war all over again, and as in wartime, I knew I would have to be off very shortly.

The Mendelssohn was one of the first pieces of music with which I fell in love. It was the recording of Fritz Kreisler that introduced me to the work and it has occupied a special place in my affections ever since. It was to be the first time I would hear Heifetz perform the work and I was looking forward to it. I had no idea it would turn out to be probably the fastest performance since the work was composed and one played as a competition between soloist and conductor.

I should have realized there was an indication of this the morning of the first rehearsal when we arrived at Carnegie Hall and the conductor was nowhere to be found. We went to the soloist's dressing room and as always I helped Heifetz on with his rehearsal coat and stood by ready to walk him down to the stage. Usually at this point the conductor would come to greet the soloist and the two go out together but this morning no conductor appeared at all and at the appropriate moment I escorted Heifetz down the stairs to the stage. We'd just gotten down about halfway when I looked over my shoulder and saw Cantelli a few steps above us. He was wearing a flowing white silk shirt with bubble sleeves and looked like a Spanish dancer ready to spring into action. He was in a hurry and as he approached us from behind reached out his baton and touched Heifetz on the shoulder. "Excuse me, please," he said, and moved the baton in a manner to clear passage. He walked right past Heifetz without a glance or a word and proceeded out onto the stage. Heifetz and I looked at each other. The rudeness was obvious. Heifetz looked through the wings and saw him standing on the podium. He walked out himself and advanced to the soloist's spot on the stage. Cantelli looked around and stepped down to shake hands. The poker face was more poker than ever and the jaw firmly set.

The rehearsal began and right away it was obvious that the conductor and soloist had very different ideas about tempi. Cantelli wanted the concerto slow and Heifetz wanted it at the tempo called for in the score. They played a few measures and stopped. Heiftez advanced to the podium and had a few words in Cantelli's ear. They began again. The same thing. Cantelli too slow, Heifetz at the proper tempo. They stopped a second time. Cantelli came down from the podium to confer. I could see the members of the orchestra whispering to each other. They realized that a real row was in the making and were waiting for it to begin. Cantelli got back on the podium and they tried again. This time Heifetz matched his tempo with the conductor and the rehearsal dragged on in this manner. Every once in a while Cantelli would look down at Heifetz. At the end they shook hands politely, Heifetz bowed to the orchestra and as he came offstage I saw his expression set and grim. I didn't say a word as we went up the stairs to his dressing room. Frances was there as well as his sister Pauline and brother-in-law Samuel Chotzinoff and all except Frances began to talk in Russian .

Pauline, Heifetz's younger sister, married Samuel Chotzinoff, one of his first accompanists and later the critic largely responsible for getting Toscanini to accept David Sarnoff's invitation to form the NBC Symphony and in persuading Sarnoff to begin the NBC Television Opera Company. It was obvious that Pauline, Jascha, and "Chotzie" were in agreement on whatever they were talking about and I suspected it was the concerto.

The first concert was the next evening and I arrived at Heifetz's hotel in plenty of time to take him to Carnegie Hall. On arrival we went to the dressing room and through the usual pre-concert procedures. Since he was playing last, the concert was already well under way and when the intermission arrived Cantelli came up the stairs to his room looking sweaty but pleased. He greeted Heifetz politely and closed his door. Heifetz looked after him with what I thought was a look that lacked love.

The intermission ended and I walked him to the stage. We were joined by Cantelli and the two of them walked out to a very warm greeting from the orchestra and the public.

The concerto began and it was obvious immediately that Heifetz intended to play it his way and that if there was not to be absolute chaos on the stage Cantelli had better keep up with him. As the work unfolded Heifetz got faster and faster, and Cantelli kept looking over his shoulder with increasing horror on his face and whipping the orchestra along. Between movements Heifetz paused only long enough to make certain that his violin was still in tune and off he went with Cantelli a desperate second.

By the time they arrived at the finale it was obvious that something was going on but you could not tell it from the expression on Heifetz's face, which was, as usual, enigmatic. The finale began at breakneck speed and grew faster and faster with each bar. It was like a horserace. Every time they drew neck-and-neck Heifetz would step up the tempo and Cantelli's looks became ever more desperate. Finally with another burst of speed the concerto ended with the soloist and orchestra at least two measures apart.

The audience, whipped to a frenzy by the performance, burst out cheering. Heifetz, keeping his usual demeanor, bowed politely and left the stage. Cantelli followed behind looking like a defeated thoroughbred. Offstage not a word was said. Heifetz returned for his solo bow and then Cantelli reappeared for the routine bow of conductor and soloist. The applause kept up but never crested. It was the same story. If he had smiled they would have been with him.

The concert over, we went back upstairs to the dressing room. There waiting for us was a fierce old man sitting on a straight chair, his black eyes staring hard and angry. A flow of Russian began as soon as we arrived and it was strong and directed at Heifetz. For the first time I saw him look a little pale and he replied firmly but with great control. I wondered who this marvelous old person was. He was certainly someone who had great power over Heifetz and this evening he was using every bit of it. I judged him to be in his late eighties or early nineties and as the conversation went on, I was glad that the man was talking to Heifetz and not to me.

When Pauline and her sister Elsa arrived the girls went up to the old man and kissed him affectionately. "Do you know our father?" Pauline asked me. I replied I did not and was introduced. He put out his hand and as he did so it was obvious that his anger was spent. "How do you do," he said in heavily accented English. And he folded his hands away and looked straight ahead, almost as if I had been the conductor. I backed away without saying anything. Heifetz received his public as usual and our routines proceeded as if nothing had happened. But as the Heifetz family was leaving he turned to me and, gesturing toward the conductor's room, said: "I wonder who knows that concerto better?" And without answering he went down the stairs and out of the hall.

Most of the orchestras with which Heifetz played seemed not to have problems between conductor and soloist. With lesser organizations, such as the Wichita Symphony, Heifetz would go out of his way to help, answering any questions put to him by the members of the ensemble and gently suggesting ideas and solutions to the conductor. Wichita, Kansas, is not, perhaps, a place one envisions a symphony but there is one and it is not bad at all, largely supported in the fifties by an extraordinary ex-German aeronautical engineer named Samuel Bloomfield.

Mr. Bloomfield came to the United States shortly after the First World War fascinated by the relatively new science of aviation. He put his good mind to work on a problem that had been baffling the experts of his day—how to increase the size of airplanes. His part of the problem had to do with landing wheels or, more properly, landing carriages, which were, at the time, rigid, small, and narrow. Their very smallness restricted airplane weight and a way had to be devised to allow for expansion and the building of heavier machines. Bloomfield came up with the design of the cantilever gear and his fortune was made. He settled in Wichita, the home of some of the important aviation factories, and proceeded to bring culture to the city with taste, discretion, and, above all, passion. He played the violin himself and had a rare collection. Every year he brought in special coaches for the various orchestra sections. He also brought in instrument makers and as conductor he engaged James Robertson, a pupil of Pierre Monteux and a careful, precise musician.

Bloomfield did not restrict his cultural pursuits to music alone. He built a museum into which he put most of his first-rate classical painting collection. His home, on the outskirts of the city, contained Titian's Portrait of His Landlord, as well as several beautiful Rembrandts, Rubenses, Gainsboroughs, and a few scattered Van Goghs. Bloomfield was a very shy man and one of his heroes was Heifetz, so we journeyed to Wichita for a pair of concerts with the orchestra.

The scheduled work was the Tchaikovsky concerto in the high school auditorium. The orchestra looked smooth and disciplined sitting on neat blue seats in front of identical music stands. The tuxedos of the men and the gowns of the women looked freshly pressed and neat. I asked the conductor about this and was told that among other Bloomfield gifts were decent chairs and music stands and dry cleaning services so that the orchestra looked neat, precise , and attractive.

During the first part of the concert Heifetz and I stood backstage, and after a few moments I felt a pull at my sleeve. "Look there," he said, pointing out the last stands of both the first and second violin sections. I looked and saw four players slouched back in their seats, hardly playing at all. "It's very hard to cure that," he said, indicating the players. "Those people will always behave that way. They do not belong in music." With that he tucked his violin under his chin and began to play along with the first violins. As I recall, it was a Beethoven symphony and he either had extremely good long-range vision to see onto the stage music stands or knew the work by heart.

When the time came for his performance, however, the slouching disappeared and the orchestra played as if possessed. Heifetz gave them no artistic quarter because they were a young organization. He worked in close rapport with the players and their conductor and created a memorable concert.

A few weeks later that same season, though, he had another almost Cantelli-like clash with another conductor that added up to the public's benefit. We had traveled to Buffalo, New York, through a real midwinter blizzard. Our train moved ahead very slowly with the snow swirling around and the wind leaking through the windows. I thought of all those wonderful Currier and Ives prints of "Winter on the Railroad" and the like, but we made it through the night and arrived in Buffalo with the sun out and the plows cleaning up the mess. When we reached our hotel we saw in the lobby a big sign welcoming Josef Krips to his new home as permanent conductor of the orchestra. Our arrival coincided with his, and the city had declared something like Krips Week.

We settled into our rooms and I'd just started to unpack when the phone rang. "Come at once," said Heifetz and I could tell that something was very wrong. When I arrived he showed me a copy of the program. It announced the beginning of a Beethoven Festival, the first concert of which was to consist of the Coriolanus Overture, the violin concerto, intermission, and the Eroica symphony. "There must be some mistake," I said. "I'm certain that the manager read your contract carefully. I'll go and see him."

I went to the Buffalo Philharmonic office and to its then manager, Ralph Black. Mr. Black was busy when I first arrived and after waiting what I considered to be long enough I told his secretary that unless Mr. Black could spare a few moments I thought he might have to find another soloist for his next scheduled concerts. Mr. Black came out immediately and I pointed out to him the violation of Heifetz's contract. "You know he always plays last," I said. "There's nothing new about that." Black looked annoyed. "Why should he do that?" he asked. "It's always those big stars who make life complicated." And he launched into a lecture about the star system, their fees and peculiarities, whims and illogicality. I waited patiently until he was finished and returned to the point at hand. "Heifetz always plays last," I said again, "and I suggest you rethink the program to take that matter into account." Black's face became darker. "Krips won't like this one bit," he said. "You know that these concerts are his first as our new music director and he set the program up in a very special manner." "I'm aware of his new position," I said. "You could not miss it from what I saw in the hotel lobby and in various store windows and on lampposts. But Heifetz plays last or he doesn't play. Period. That's the way it is going to be. Will you talk it over with the maestro and let me know the results. I will be waiting for your call." We shook hands and I left his office.

About an hour later he called, sounding meek and exhausted, to say that Krips was changing the program and the concerto would be last and that we'd all meet the next day at the first rehearsal. I communicated this to Heifetz. He nodded.

The next morning we went to the auditorium early in order not to be delayed by the still remaining heavy snow. The Buffalo Philharmonic's home is an imposing contemporary auditorium, Kleinhans Hall, that works beautifully in all respects—acoustically, architecturally, and, surprise of surprises, for the public. There is plenty of space to move around and one doesn't feel hemmed in by neighbors. The colors are natural wood, the whole atmosphere conducive to music making and listening. The backstage area is designed for the comfort of the performers.

We were settled into a spacious dressing room when there came some imperious knocking at the door. I opened it and there standing framed in the doorway was Krips himself. He was a big man, almost as wide as he was tall, bald with a fringe of hair around the base of his head and thick glasses out of which he peered like a barn owl. He stared at Heifetz and didn't say a word. I went to him and put out my hand. "Maestro," I began, "I'm Mr. Heifetz's tour manager Schuyler Chapin." He took it and gave one violent jerk. "And this is Jascha Heifetz. Mr. Heifetz, Mr. Krips," I said, gesturing an introduction. Heifetz put out his hand, Krips took it for one moment and dropped it like a hot Japanese stone. "Ach, so, you're Heifetz," he said, with his heavy Austrian accent. "I've never heard you play." And with that he turned on his heels and walked out.

Heifetz looked at me and without saying a word went to his violin case and began putting away his fiddle. "We will leave now," he said after a moment's pause. "We do not need this behavior." His face was expressionless. I waited a minute and then suggested that perhaps Krips was put out about the program change and why not give him a chance to see what Heifetz's music making was like. "Besides," I said, "people are coming from miles around to hear you and it wouldn't be fair to them. And look at all the snow they have to get through to get here." Heifetz looked at me, still expressionless, and finally said, "We'll see. If there is any more trouble we will not stay." He took out his violin again and we proceeded to the stage.

Onstage the orchestra was assembling and presently Krips came on from the other side and the players gave him a warm reception. Ralph Black appeared at my elbow and I introduced him to Heifetz. He escorted Heifetz onto the stage. The orchestra applauded when he was introduced and all was ready for the rehearsal.

I went out with Black to sit in the auditorium just as the first tympani measures signaled the start of the concerto. Krips stopped the proceedings immediately after the tympani and started again. He stopped a second time at the same place and again a third time. Heifetz's face began to show his annoyance. He had found a cardboard match on the stage and was moving it to the right and left with the tip of his bow. Finally after the fourth pause at the same place he stepped back to speak to Krips and while I couldn't hear what was being said I knew it must be strong because I could see the color rising in his face. They stared at each other for a moment and Krips motioned to go on.

The concerto proceeded smoothly after that, with only little pauses for minor corrections, and when it was finished the orchestra gave Heifetz a tremendous ovation. He left the stage, bowing to them as he did so. We went to the dressing room; he put the violin away, changed into his street clothes and overcoat without saying a word. In short order we were in a cab going back to our hotel. We lunched together and talked about stamps but not a word was said about the rehearsal.

The next evening was the first concert and as usual I picked him up a half-hour before we were due at the hall. We taxied in silence and arrived just as Krips was walking out to begin the program with the Choral Fantasy. He had found a chorus and pianist and had switched to this work to be followed by the Seventh Symphony and then the violin concerto. Krips saw us come in and inclined his head briefly in a formal bow. Heifetz acknowledged his greeting with the same gesture.

At the end of the intermission Krips came to the dressing room and together they walked toward the stage. I walked along behind. I wished Heifetz good luck and he turned to me. "Thank you," he said, and walked out onto the stage. I ducked into the auditorium to hear the performance.

If I thought that I had heard great performances of the Beethoven before they all paled alongside what was happening on that stage. The sound poured out in flowing lines, measured to the ear as if the piece were being played for the first time. Like the rest of the audience I sat transfixed. With the approach of the coda I got up and went backstage. As the last notes died away the house exploded in an uproar. Heifetz stood there taking his time, as usual, and acknowledging the reception in his usual impassive way. Krips looked as if someone had hit him; he stared, shaking his head from side to side. The two joined hands, bowed, and walked off. Heifetz put his violin down and walked back out for a solo bow. The audience rose to a man and woman and the ovation increased. Krips, meantime, with sweat pouring out of him and looking as if he'd just run a record mile after too many beers, grabbed my arm in a viselike grip. "Do you know what happened out there?" he almost shouted at me. "Do you know?" I said that I had never heard a more moving performance. "No, no. That's not what I mean," he went on. "Do you really know what happened? He played all the notes! All the notes! Every one! Impossible, impossible!" By this time Heifetz was back and took him by the hand and they returned together to acknowledge the applause. As they came off Krips looked at me again, accusingly. "All the notes! All the notes!" he repeated.

When the applause finally died down we went to the dressing room and through the by now familiar routine: into the overcoat, receive the manager for his fee, greet the public three at a time. Not a word was said about the performance until all this was finished and finally, when I closed the door on the last visitor, I turned to him and held out my hand. "May I thank you for an unforgettable performance," I said. "I am too moved to say more." Heifetz smiled. "It went well," he replied. "Krips had never heard me play. I thought he should." "You did," I said. "You did." And he finished dressing. We packed up the concert gear, got into a cab, and went off for some supper. That performance was never mentioned again.

Heifetz the infallible; Heifetz the unperturbable; Heifetz the perfectionist; Heifetz the cold one. How many times have I heard these or similar phrases as we criss-crossed the country over three seasons. And in a sense all the comments were right. Heifetz is essentially a very lonely and unhappy man.

Once, in Pittsburgh, an old friend of his, Dr. Isidore Lattman came to a concert. Heifetz told me that Lattman knew more about chamber music than he'd ever know. On the way to the rehearsal Lattman happened to be waiting to cross the street within view of our car. "You see Lattie?" Heifetz asked. "See him there?" I said I did. "He trusts people. I don't." And he turned to look the other way.

At that same Pittsburgh concert there occurred one of these incidents that illustrate Heifetz the implacable. Early on in our tours together Heifetz explained that he did not ever want a spotlight on him while performing. "It gets in my eyes and gives too much attention," he said, in describing his feelings, and I always made certain that no spotlights were around at his performances. However, at this particular concert with William Steinberg and the Pittsburgh Symphony I forgot to say anything to the house manager and just as he walked out to begin the Tchaikovsky concerto a bright pink light flooded down from the balcony onto the stage and caught him dead center. He took his violin away from his chin and turned to say something to Steinberg. Steinberg looked over his shoulder and made motions offstage to kill the light. It happened I was the only one standing in the wings at that moment and I turned around trying to find someone from the house who would know how to control the offending light. I could find no one at all and shrugged my shoulders toward Steinberg, who, in turn, relayed the information to Heifetz. Heifetz shook his head and turned, glaring, toward me. By this time I was beginning to realize that he would stand there all night until the light was put out. I rushed to the stage doorman and asked him where the light booth was. He told me, pointing to the opposite side of the house, and I took off at a dead run. I raced around corridors, up stairs, across lobbies, in my desperate search for the source and in the meantime everything on stage had stopped, waiting for my success. I finally located a door marked "Booth" and opened it. Inside were two men training the spot onto the stage. "For God sakes kill that light," I said. "Heifetz never plays with a light." The technicians looked down and saw that everything was at a standstill. One of them reached for the switch and the light went off. Applause broke out immediately. Heifetz turned to Steinberg, nodded, and the concerto began.

I retraced my steps backstage and listened. When the work was over a grim Heifetz came off the stage. "What in the world happened?" he asked," not too pleasantly. "I'm sorry, sir," I replied. "I forgot to say anything to anyone here about a light. Frankly it never occurred to me that in Pittsburgh they would resort to such a theatrical trick." He went back onstage, acknowledging the applause, but standing in a spot where he was able to continue half a conversation with me. He was clearly angry.

When we returned to the dressing room I apologized once again but he was still fuming at what he rightfully thought was an oversight of mine. I figured that the less said the better. I'd confessed my failings and I hoped that with a little time all might be forgiven. We had to go on to a fancy supper party after the concert and at this party were Skitch Henderson and our old friend Capitol records executive Richard Jones. Of course they pounced on me, full of glee and it wasn't too long before one of them came out with the Lady Macbeth line about spots. Heifetz heard this and came up to me. "Out, out, damn spot," he said. "And it better stay out!" I nodded agreement.

Heifetz the infallible. That myth was broken in Dallas not so long after the spotlight incident in Pittsburgh when in the middle of a performance of the Sibelius concerto with Walter Hendl and the Dallas Symphony Heifetz forgot.

The concert had begun with great style . Heifetz liked Hendl and enjoyed working with him. The vast university auditorium was sold out for the concert and this was unusual in Dallas, where the orchestra was not strongly supported. I walked Heifetz to the stage, as usual, and wished him good luck. I then returned to the dressing room, where with the door left open I could hear the concerto. The first movement proceeded smoothly enough. The Sibelius concerto is technically one of the most difficult in the entire violin repertoire and I always marvelled how Heifetz made it sound so flowing and easy. The second movement began and had not proceeded for more than three or four measures when everything stopped. The hush was deafening. I rushed to the stage and peeked out through a flap in the stage entrance door. I expected to see a collapsed soloist or conductor but instead the two were talking together as if nothing had happened. Presently Hendl motioned for the beginning of the movement again. The work went on and at the conclusion of the finale the audience gave its wholehearted approval. Both men came offstage at the same time and were smiling at each other.

At the appropriate moment I asked Heifetz what had happened. "Nothing," he said. "I just forgot my place." There were a number of reporters present that afternoon and they lost no time crowding backstage. I held them off as best I could and asked Heifetz what he wanted to do about them. "If I might say, so, sir," I said, "I think you ought to tell them the truth." "That's what I intend to do," he said. "Ask them in." And in they came and he told them the truth.

The next day it was front-page news on half the newspapers of America. "Heifetz Forgets" was the headline in the New York *Herald-Tribune*. Other papers had similar banners. The radio stations carried the story; for two or three days it was a great novelty. But Heifetz could not understand what all the fuss was about. "I just forgot," he said. "Others do." "Yes," I replied at one point. "But others are not Heifetz."

Our association together included some delightful times. There was a dinner in Los Angeles, hosted by two brothers who shared interconnected houses. These two men worshipped Heifetz and would do anything in the world for him. On one occasion, at the end of a tour, they gave a large dinner party for the musical elite of the area and I was invited.

I arrived on time to be greeted by the brothers' wives standing each in her own house. The doubled-up rooms were spacious and high ceilings gave the place an atmosphere of a small mountain castle. The guests poured in and poured down the vodka and champagne, ravaged the caviar and the smoked salmon, and talked in every recognizable language except English.

Clutching my vodka firmly, I went over to talk with the Piatigorskys. He was a huge man, well over six-foot-two, and generally recognized as one of the world's great cellists. He and Heifetz often played chamber music together at their respective houses and later, joined by other artists, created a chamber music ensemble and recorded as well as played a few public concerts. Piatigorsky's English was larded with a Russian accent of such thickness that I've often suspected him of trying to imitate Mischa Auer. His wife, a member of the French Rothschild family, was as gentle and retiring as he was flamboyant and dazzling. "How is Theodore Steinway?" he asked the moment I came into sight that night. "Fine," I said. "He's looking forward to showing you some of his latest stamp acquisitions." "Shhh, shhh," he said, looking around wildly. "Don't let Jascha hear. He will be very jealous." At that moment a lady dressed in what looked like high fashion of the nineteen twenties in a beaded dress with a headband across her forehead, a long cigarette holder balanced in her right hand and a drink in her left, came toward us. "Grischa my dahlink," she purred at him, "you are vunderful as alvays." She slinked past much to the annoyance of Mme. Piatigorsky, who asked, "Who is *that* ?" "A friend, my dear, a friend," he murmured. I sensed a little tension between them and slipped off to find the woman, as my curiosity was thoroughly aroused. Just then dinner was announced and we trooped into the dining room.

The table was sumptuously set with at least four glasses at each place. The tablecloth was of rare Russian lace, the china of exquisite workmanship, and the effect was dining at the table of the Tsar. And that, indeed, is practically what it was, for most of the appointments came, in one way or another, from imperial houses. Heifetz looked over at me, as if to say that this whole evening was styled to my romantic nature. The strange beaded and banded lady was on my right, her bracelets dangling and clanking against everything in sight. It was obviously to be a pre-1917 Russian evening and I settled back to enjoy it.

At first more caviar was served and glasses filled with chilled vodka. Toasts were proposed and the vodka kept flowing. Plates were changed, courses came and went, wines were poured into the various glasses, and the conversation became louder and freer. Finally it was obviously my turn to toast. Before doing so I turned to the lady on my right, who by this time was feeling no pain at all. "Would you like some more vodka?" I asked, holding the decanter in my hand. She looked at me for a long moment. "No, my dear," she finally got out. "If I have vun more wodka I vill slide under de tabel." I turned to the lady on my left and asked the same question. She took some and with my table companions' glasses charged I rose to speak. Just as I did so I felt a little rustle at my right elbow. I looked around and the lady of the beads and the bangs was slipping slowly, like a ship launching, under the table. Her face was smiling but it was all over for her that night. I reached to pull her back but it was too late. She was on the floor. I looked around. None of the guests seemed to be in the least perturbed. I looked at my hostesses and they were talking away without taking any notice. So were my hosts. I shrugged. If this is the way the Russians play, I thought, who am I to say anything. I toasted one and all and sat down. The lady stirred a little and I felt hands around my ankles. Soon one was climbing up my leg. I kept as straight a face as I could but began to wonder where she'd stop. Finally I felt a weight on my lap and I glanced down to see her head there, about to go to sleep. "Dahrling," she said, "no more wodka." And she fell fast alseep.

She stayed there during the rest of the dinner. At the appropriate moment we all rose to toast the chef, who appeared with his assistants to take well-deserved bows. The lady slept on. When the meal was over everyone started out to the library and living rooms for cognac and coffee and dancing. My two hosts appeared at my side and without saying a word picked up the lady and carried her off to another room. I moved toward the library, thinking surely that someone would say something. Not a word. I went over to Heifetz. He didn't say a word either. We toasted each other in cognac this time and I suddenly realized that I too had consumed quite a measure of potent spirits during the course of the evening and that it might be a good idea for me to make my exit before too long. I bade my hostesses good night and went to get my overcoat. Everyone was having such a loud and sociable time that I did not want to disturb my hosts and therefore sought out the coat by poking my head into all the doorways I could find. At last I opened a door to find myself in a bedroom with a sleeping figure on the bed. I recognized the dress at once and tiptoed in to retrieve my coat, which was thrown over the back of a chair. "Dahlink," she murmured, "dahlink." I beat a hasty retreat.

Heifetz was always very careful to see that his tour manager was included in all post-concert parties and sometimes these were the most difficult part of the day. Hostesses were for the most part alike in securing the lion of the moment and then after introducing him to her friends leaving him to fend pretty much for himself. We devised a system that made certain that Heifetz was not trapped with the party bores and we got pretty good at carrying it out. The parties were, for the most part, a tremendous effort but they were also the only guarantee of getting supper after a performance and for this alone they were worth it. Every once in a while we would be in for pleasant surprises.

In Winnipeg, on a fierce, cold night, with the snow six feet deep, we left the auditorium after a performance to drive into the country. I had no idea at all where we were going except that Heifetz had told me earlier in the day that we were going to the home of a friend of his who was the wheat baron of the city and who was a champion shot. We drove for what seemed like endless miles and eventually arrived at a lovely house, set back from the road. Every light was twinkling and the reflections on the snow gave the place an unreal look. We went inside and there were six people plus the host and hostess. "You asked for a small party, Jascha," his friend said as we were helped out of our coats, "and this what you're going to get!" Fires burned warmly and invitingly in the living room and the library, and as we were handed our drinks I found myself in conversation with a very pretty girl. We walked slowly into the library, chatting pleasantly, and took seats in front of the fire. I was just settling in when I detected a presence standing alongside of me. I looked up and it was Heifetz, drink in hand, smiling down at the girl and giving me a look that I understood immediately. "I don't think you've met Mr. Heifetz," I said, with a smile on my lips but hate in my heart. She rose, they shook hands, and he put his arm out to take hers. They walked toward the dining room, leaving me in front of the fireplace. A moment later our hostess appeared. "Shall we have supper?" she said charmingly, and we walked to the dining room. RHIP, I thought to myself. Rank Has Its Privileges.

The dining room was a thing of beauty. Spread out before us were pheasants, grouse, duck, wild rice, steaming gravies, fresh jellies, and opened bottles of Château Lafite. We helped ourselves and walked back to the fires to chat. I'd found another attractive woman by this time and we settled down to the incredible supper while she asked me about myself.

After about an hour we rose to take our leave. Our host produced a limousine with driver and fur lap robes. We got in, wrapped ourselves in the robes, and were whisked away back to the city. The moon was out, casting our shadow on the snow, and for all the world we might have been on the steppes of Asia. Heifetz was in a good mood and I brought up the matter of the girl at supper. He smiled at me. I looked at him. "That was a dirty trick, you know," I said. "I know," he replied. And looked out the window.

Canada was the scene of part of our last tour together, a tour that indicated the many sides of Heifetz and the complexities of working with him. In Toronto that year he played a Sibelius concerto with Sir Ernest MacMillan and the Toronto Orchestra that still haunts my ears. It was the night before his birthday, always an important event for him, and he was feeling happy. Usually birthdays made him gloomy but for some reason this one did not. The performance was hair-raising. Frances and I sat together and could not believe our ears. Neither could the audience because when it was finished there was at least thirty seconds of dead silence before the audience and the orchestra rose, to a man and woman, and cheered their lungs out. Frances and I were both in tears and tried to pull ourselves together before showing up backstage. This was not an easy thing to do, but somehow we controlled ourselves sufficiently well to greet him and help with the crowds. After everyone had left we closed the door of his dressing room and I started to stammer out something. The tears were very close to the surface. He looked at me and said something about it being a "not bad" performance. He then picked up his violin and kissed it. Frances and I looked at each other.

The other side of the man came to the fore a week or two later again in Winnipeg. His friend the wheat baron was abroad and this time he was giving a recital, the first of several to be presented by Canadian impresarios in the northwest part of the country. Our itinerary included Moose Jaw, Saskatoon, Medicine Hat, and Calgary, as well as Winnepeg, and it was a trip that included trains and planes with performances to be given, for the most part, in ice hockey arenas. I met with the impresarios at some length just after we arrived in Winnepeg and soon discovered that tickets were not selling too well upcountry, largely because there had been very little promotion. I also detected the fact that the impresarios were having some financial problems and I thought it best to get all the fees in advance by certified check. They were not anxious to do this but were finally persuaded. I told them that I would give each check to the local arena manager for presentation after the concert in the usual Heifetz tradition but that I wanted to know the money was in place. In return for this they asked for some extra promotion help, especially on radio, which was still very potent in Canada. I told them that Heifetz never spoke on the air as a matter of principle but that if it would be of any help I would be delighted to go on and talk about being tour manager for the great man and perhaps whet some appetites to hear him. They liked this idea and we made a date to tape a program for later that same afternoon.

I returned to the hotel for lunch and a review of upcoming details. During lunch I mentioned casually that radio was still very big in Canada and that the impresarios needed a little help in northern promotion. I said that they had accepted the idea of having me do a program as tour manager and about the excitement we all felt concerning the upcoming northern swing. Heifetz looked at me and said, "No." "No?" I queried. "No about what?" "No broadcasting. I forbid you to do it." I looked at him to see if he was kidding but he obviously was not. "No broadcasting. No radio. I do not like it." "But the impresarios need help," I said, "and I think we should do all we can." "No," he said. "We will not discuss it further."

We finished lunch and I went to my room. In a few minutes there was a knock at the door and I opened it to find Heifetz standing outside. "May I come in?" he asked. "Of course," I replied, opening the door as widely as possible. He came in, shut the door, and looked around. "Won't you sit down?" I said, gesturing to a chair. "No thank you," he said. "I won't be a minute. I want you to call the office and have them send out someone else to finish this tour. I think you feel yourself too big for the job!" I was stunned. "This is my tour and I wish to do it my way and if you do not like it you may go home and someone can replace you." I saw that he was pale and a little nervous. I did some quick thinking. I felt he was being stubborn and harsh in a professional matter that needed attention but I also realized that he'd been touring for many more years than I and if he wanted to behave this way he was entitled to do so. "That won't be necessary," I said. "Of course it's your tour and we'll do it your way." He seemed to accept this and left the room.

For the rest of that season our relations were polite, proper but cool. I felt he was wrong and he felt I had overstepped my position. At the end of the tour, in Los Angeles, Frances came to me to try smoothing things over. "You don't understand Jascha," she said. "He is shy and deep." I said that I thought I understood him very well and that I was not going to say anything but I thought he had been wrong and I wasn't going to change my mind about that. "But he likes you very much, you know," she said. I said I felt the same but that had nothing to do with the issue at hand.

Shortly after this exchange the tour was over and we all had a grand dinner at Chasens the night before I flew back home. When I arrived back I immediately plunged into other professional matters and began to forget about the incident. Some three months later the Heifetzes came through New York on their way to Europe and we lunched together at the Sherry-Netherland Hotel. After lunch Betty and the children showed up to say goodbye and we all helped pile luggage into the car taking them to the airport. As the car was about to pull away from the curb Heifetz called out to me. I went to the car window and he handed me a package. "Open it when you get home," he said, and the car pulled out into the traffic.

On reaching home I opened it. Out fell a letter addressed to me and in the package itself was a beautiful new briefcase. I opened the letter. It said: "Dear Schuyler, let us forgive and forget and take this present as a sign of my affection and friendship. Yours, J. Heifetz."

The affection and friendship are reciprocated.

VI

Columbia Artists Presents

During the years that I was Heifetz's tour manager I also had other managerial responsibilies: I was the Midwestern booking representative for Columbia Artists, which meant that I was responsible for all Columbia activities in such states as Oklahoma, Kansas, Nebraska, Iowa, Missouri, Arkansas, Indiana, and Michigan that were not part of the Community Concerts circuit. Community had its own sales force; I was responsible for the symphony orchestras, the impresario series in various cities, and the schools and colleges.

The concert business was changing in the fifties; the colleges were becoming important buyers of talent. Student funds often paid for these concerts, held in new theaters and all-purpose auditoriums that were springing up on campuses after the war. The symphony orchestras were then, as they are now, a dominant part of our musical life, and by the end of the fifties there were over a thousand of them. Statisticians were fond of the fact that more people attended orchestral concerts than organized baseball games. It was a time when the country was awakening to its cultural life and this made for a vigorous concert business. Columbia's "list" contained some of the most distinguished names in the profession, ranging from Jascha Heifetz, Rudolf Serkin, Claudio Arrau, Zino Francescatti, Lily Pons, Richard Tucker, and the

like to newer talents, including a tall, lanky, frizzy-haired unknown, a
student at the Juilliard School named Van Cliburn.

I first heard Cliburn in the living room of my mother-in-law, Ruth
Steinway. From time to time she gave small musicales, usually con-
nected with the Olga Samaroff Fund, of which she was a trustee. Olga
Samaroff had been an extraordinary woman. Born Hickenlooper in the
Midwest, she became a concert pianist but gave up her active career
when she became Leopold Stokowski's first wife. After her divorce
she turned to teaching and writing. Her books included the *Laymen's
Music Course*, still one of the best books of its kind, and her pupils included some of the brightest new talents, including William Kapell and
Eugene List. The Samaroff Fund helped young talent and one of its
grantees was Cliburn.

I was jolted by what I heard. Cliburn seemed to embrace the piano,
to subdue it to his will. His ability to communicate musically was overwhelming. His hands on the keys gave the visual impression of someone about to scoop them all up and give them back one by one. There
was no question in my mind that here was a man of gigantic qualifications. What he was going to do with them remained to be seen.

After the recital I introduced myself. He shook my hand warmly and
fixed me with his Texas grin and stare. "I sure am pleased to meet
you," he said, making me feel as if nothing else mattered. "I think
we'll be working together. I think I'm going to sign a contract with Bill
Judd to manage me." "I'm delighted," I replied "I work for him." "I
know," he said, "and that means you will be working with me." And
he turned to greet other guests.

During the next months he finished up at the Juilliard. Word of
mouth began to drift out about him, just as it always seems to do when
major talent is discovered. By the time he'd signed his Columbia contract there were already inquiries for his services.

In consultation with Judd he decided to enter the prestigious Edgar
M. Leventritt Competition. The Leventritt is considered the most difficult competition in the country and next to the Queen Elizabeth of Bel-
gium prize the most distinguished. The judges are always first-rate musicians drawn from various areas of the profession. For many years the
panel was chaired by George Szell, music director of the Cleveland Orchestra and one of the most respected figures in American music. The
Leventritt committee was also snobbish and very inclined to treat casually anyone they did not consider in the proper artistic mold. There
was never any precise definition of what that mold was, outside of artistic excellence, but it was there and many, including Cliburn, felt it.

Nonetheless he entered in 1954 and won. The competition, in addition to prize money, provided its winner with all-important orchestral engagements.

The following fall Cliburn started out on his Leventritt winnings and enjoyed a brisk season. But then, as happens to many artists, he hit a slump. People were interested in hearing him once or perhaps twice but after that they were curious about other new talents. Usually these slumps are overcome after a year or two and the artists goes on to a respectable career, but Cliburn was intensely discouraged by this and convinced that his career was all over even before it had really begun.

Betty and I had become very fond of him and invited him to visit us in the country that summer. Our children adored him. He went swimming with us one morning and dove off the end of our dock. He didn't surface and Betty and I peered into the water looking for him. Fortunately the water that surrounds us is almost crystal clear and we could see him thrashing near the diving board but not coming to the surface. "My God, he's drowning!" I yelled, and dove in after him. I pushed down to where he was and grabbed his shoulders. We rose to the surface and the minute we did so he began flaying about in wild confusion. I managed by a combination of pushing and shoving to move him toward the dock and into shallow water. He partially collapsed when he gained his footing and spread himself out on the dock coughing and spluttering. The children, who could swim well even at their tender ages, gathered around while Betty and I applied what little first aid we knew. Presently he stopped choking and began shaking his head. His complexion was stark white and his eyes were wide and staring. "I can't swim," he said. "I don't know how to swim." "Well, why didn't you say something?" I asked. "There was no need for you to risk your life and scare the hell out of all of us. Lots of people can't swim." He made no reply and the incident was forgotten during the remaining days of his visit. When the time came for him to leave, the children lined up for hugs and embraces and Cliburn was quite emotional about leaving. However he wrote in our guest book: "I feel sure you only wish that you had let me go down the third time." And I had a strong feeling that at the time he meant it.

During the 1955–56 season he played few concerts and continued in a slough of discouragement. I was able to get him some engagements around the country, particularly in South Bend, Indiana, where the affairs of the orchestra were presided over by the extraordinary Mrs. Ernest Morris. I told her about Cliburn and she decided to take a chance. I knew this was one of the few engagements he had for that season and I wanted to make sure he would be invited back the next year as well. I talked to Mrs. Morris and found myself down on my knees pleading his cause. She listened again and agreed on the double engagement, not for the immediately following season but the one after.

The other important appearances he had this season were on television. My friend Skitch Henderson was then music director of the *Tonight* show. The *Tonight* show was in its infancy, hosted by Steve Allen and already commanding a large share of the late-night audience. I thought an appearance by Cliburn, with a few potential clients alerted to listen, could be of enormous help. The *Tonight* show did not normally use classical artists but Henderson had been so impressed when he heard Cliburn that he persuaded Steve Allen to take a chance. The results were all one could have hoped for. Inquiries for his services came from many different parts of the country and he was invited back to the *Tonight* show for a second appearance.

About the middle of 1956 Cliburn received a letter from the concert manager of Steinway & Sons, a refugee from Russia named Alexander Greiner, who alerted Cliburn to an upcoming competition in Moscow. The Soviets were inviting performers from all over the world to compete for prizes in the name of Peter Ilyich Tchaikovksy. The material Greiner sent was in Russian with a translation attached and he urged Van to consider this event as a strong hypodermic to his career. The competition had specific rules and repertoire requirements that meant a lot of study and preparation. Cliburn made the decision to enter and settled down to prepare for it.

The competition took place in Moscow during the late winter and early spring of 1958 and we saw Cliburn off on a gloomy, gray afternoon. He looked lonely and tired as he left. Greiner embraced him and wished him Godspeed in Russian. We didn't think there was much hope, not because of his ability, but because it seemed improbable that anyone but a Russian could win. Nonetheless we all put up a good front and sped him on his way. The worst that could happen would at least add a shadow of exoticness to his experiences.

On April 13, 1958, newsbells rang all over the world. Cliburn had won the Tchaikovsky Competition. An American from Texas had gone to Moscow and pulled the honors away. The press, in America particularly, went wild. Not only was this a good human interest story but at that time we were seeing Russian spies under every bed and this seemed to indicate that just maybe they were human and not committed to unconditional elimination of the United States.

Judd arranged a ticker-tape parade up Broadway for Van Cliburn's triumphant return to New York. The young pianist rode on the back of a city limousine, waving to the crowds on the street and to the many people cheering from the windows of the buildings along the way. Old-timers along the route swore he had more ticker-tape than Lindbergh in 1927. At City Hall he made a gracious speech and was then rushed uptown for an official lunch at the Waldorf, where he was greeted by a standing ovation from officials of the city, the state, the federal government, businesses, the church, and the arts. Every orchestra and concert association in the country fell all over themselves trying to engage him. Record companies lined up at the door, Hollywood besieged the office, the television networks never got off the phone. Everyone, it seemed, needed Cliburn that minute. It was extremely heady wine.

But he kept his head. "I would like to appear on the *Tonight* show, if they'll have me," he said. "And I will play the date in South Bend. Both groups had faith in me before Moscow and I would like to show my gratitude. Would you arrange it?" I went off at a fast clip.

The *Tonight* show appearance was set for a Sunday. It was decided he would play the last movement of the Tchaikovsky B-Flat Minor Concerto and the necessary extra musicians were engaged. The performance was a huge success. Louis Armstrong, a fellow guest-performer that night, stood in the wings shaking his head and saying over and over: "Man, can that Cat play!"

Skitch and Ruth Henderson gave a small party afterwards and here we had our first chance to see Cliburn quietly since his return. We told him of our ten-year-old son Hank's first reaction to seeing his picture on the front page. Hank came running to our bedroom clutching the paper and yelling: "Mummy, Mummy, Mummy, look—my accompanist is on the front page!" Cliburn had encouraged him when Hank began cello lessons, and had several times played with him. Van seemed pleased by the story but looked tired and discouraged. He got into deep conversation with Betty and the next thing I knew the two of them had disappeared. Some time later I went looking but they were nowhere to be found. I went outside the apartment and began walking up Third Avenue. A few blocks away I spotted them in a late-night hamburger shop. I went in slowly sensing that whatever they were talking about was deeply important. Betty saw me enter but with her eyes motioned me away. I returned to the party.

After about an hour they returned. Cliburn looked drained and we urged him to come home with us to spend the night away from the three-ring circus at his hotel. He agreed and we left very late and found a cab going uptown.

At our apartment he flung himself onto the living room sofa and was asleep in an instant. We took off his necktie and shoes, covered him with a blanket, put a pillow under his head, and went off to our bedroom. "What on earth were you two talking about all that time?" I asked, as we undressed. "I'm not sure," said Betty. "He's a very confused young man and I don't know what we can do to help."

The next day we were up early seeing the children off to school. They crept out of the house, not wanting to disturb the sleeping Cliburn, and we went to the kitchen for breakfast. The phone rang almost immediately. "Cliburn's disappeared," said Bill Judd. "We can't find him anywhere." "I wouldn't worry," I replied, "he's sound asleep at this moment on our living room couch. I'll see he gets back to the hotel when he wakes up."

An hour or so later he awoke, no doubt with a stiff neck, although he said nothing about it. We gave him breakfast and then he and I left for the outside world. We had not gone three feet from our apartment house door before he was set upon for autographs and a small crowd gathered to applaud him. We got into a cab and rode to his hotel. He seemed even more exhausted than the day before.

Arrangements were soon made for a special Carnegie Hall concert where he would play both the Tchaikovsky and the Rachmaninoff Third Concerto, the two major pieces of the Moscow competition. The concert would be recorded by RCA Victor and Cliburn very much wanted his Russian conductor, Kiril Kondrashin, brought to this country to conduct for him. Such was the magic of the Cliburn position that within a few days arrangements were completed for Kondrashin to fly to New York.

Kondrashin, an immensely attractive and vigorous man, had a distinguished career in his home country and was married to a beautiful actress-dancer. He had been music director of the Bolshoi Opera and once had his own orchestra in Moscow. During the war he had conducted orchestras at the front lines. Upon arrival in New York he began immediate rehearsals with the Symphony of the Air, which was not in good musical shape. Kondrashin had a lot of work to do to bring it up to what he considered adequate form. He knew the concert was important not only for Cliburn but for himself as well, and he was determined to overcome all problems. The program finally chosen consisted of Prokofiev's Classical Symphony, the Tchaikovsky concerto, intermission, and then the Rachmaninoff Third.

On the night of May 19 a packed Carnegie Hall heard the concert and responded with overwhelming enthusiasm. I was standing in the wings listening and I felt the energy and passion that went into the performances. Just after the Rachmaninoff, when Cliburn and Kondrashin were walking offstage, I heard the latter turn and in his almost nonexistent English say, "Dot vass better dan Moscow!" Cliburn looked pleased.

Cliburn's career, of course, now burst into full flower and hasn't slowed down since. We see him from time to time and always greet each other with genuine bursts of affection. One of the last times we met he took me aside to tell me something of great importance. "I've learned to swim," he said. "Invite me to Long Pond again. I know what to do." He is welcome anytime.

One person during those years whose life seemed to be moving along preordained paths to the top of his profession came to American through Columbia Artists almost by accident—Herbert von Karajan. The late André Mertens, a Columbia manager, had been working ever since the end of World War II to have the Berlin Philharmonic make a tour of the United States, not only because it is one of the world's greatest musical ensembles but also as a gesture of friendship between West Germany and America. Finally, in the late fall of 1954, the tour was set. Wilhelm Furtwängler, the orchestra's musical director, was to conduct but two weeks before the tour was to open Furtwängler died.

The music world was stunned, the management was wringing its hands. The tour had to be saved but who could be found at the last moment to conduct? Meetings and telephone calls continued almost around the clock and at the eleventh hour a proposal was put forth: the orchestra would come with Herbert von Karajan provided Columbia agreed to bring Karajan's Philharmonia Orchestra of London the next season. Both Karajan and the Philharmonia were known in this country only by phonograph records. The commercial risk was enormous; while the records were beautiful they were released by Angel Records, a then new subsidiary company of England's giant EMI, and their distribution pattern was just being established. Nonetheless, the Berlin Philharmonic tour had to be saved and this seemed the best way to do it. Columbia agreed and Karajan was signed.

Immediately after the news of his signing became public a hue and cry went up from certain parts of the press. Karajan had allegedly been an active Nazi, they said, and had no business being invited to this country. There were rumors everywhere of his active support of Hitler and photographs supposedly showing him in Nazi uniforms. Various columnists began steady campaigns and it soon became obvious that we had a very tough problem on our hands. Inquiries to the State Department and other agencies seemed to indicate that as far as the

American government was concerned Karajan was in the clear and we proceeded with the arrangements.

Not much was known about him except his growing artistic reputation, which began to be internationally recognized just as the war broke out. Born in Austria in 1908, he had started his career in Ulm and moved on to become opera director and general music director in Aachen, kapellmeister of the Berlin State Opera, conductor of the Berlin Philharmonic, and director of the Berlin Staatskapell. Following the U.S. tour he was named artistic director of the Berlin Philharmonic. Eventually he became intendant of the Vienna State Opera and at the same time director of the Salzburg Festival. At one point he was referred to as the generalmusikdirector of Europe.

The Philharmonia Orchestra of London was put together after World War II especially for recording by the brilliant English innovator-impresario Walter Legge. Legge's idea was a recording orchestra of the best players available in London. He was shrewd: what better way of assuring sales than to tour the United States with his master conductor at the helm. If Karajan could be introduced to the public one year ahead of time so much the better. Legge pushed hard for the Berlin Philharmonic-Philharmonia scheme and helped to pull it off.

During the negotiations we learned of Karajan's passionate interest in aviation. He was just learning to fly and insisted that an airplane and pilot be chartered for him. This was to be at his own expense but it was a must in his arrangements, and in this area André Mertens had no knowledge whatsoever. He discovered that I had been a transport pilot during the war and asked me if I still flew. When I told him that I kept a valid commercial twin-engine license his relief was visible. "May I ask you to handle the Karajan aviation matters?" he asked. "Certainly," I replied. "You just square it away with Bill Judd and Ruth O'Neill. It will require time and I don't want them miffed." He said he would take care of any problems. He did, because soon after that I was made a one-man aviation bureau to set up all the necessary arrangements.

The Berlin tour began in Washington and I went down to be on hand when the orchestra arrived. It was my first meeting with Karajan and I had no idea at all what he would be like. He was one of the first off the plane and our meeting was brief but polite. At the appropriate moment I told him that I was an ex-pilot and was making the arrangements for him to fly from city to city. His entire attitude changed. From being stiffly polite he turned on the charm and we launched into an intense discussion about planes. The questions he asked, some of which I could not answer, were direct and knowledgeable, and I could plainly see that flying was indeed an obsession with him. All matters pertaining to the tour were brushed aside or turned over to his loyal and patient secretary-manager André von Mattoni. Mattoni hated flying, was scared to death of small planes, but resigned to his boss's enthusiasm. He joined my colleagues in a sense of relief that one problem seemed obviously under control.

The press had continued its anti-Karajan campaign and we were all anxious that he not know too much about it. We spirited him away to a special hiding place until just before his first rehearsal. He fretted at this but was persuaded that it was for his own good. He came in and out of hiding only for rehearsals and performances in Washington and nothing untoward happened. When we moved to New York the campaign reached a new pitch. Walter Winchell screamed that Karajan was practically a combination of Hitler and Goering and various organizations were prepared to boycott. At the first concert a flight of doves were let loose in the hall but they were quickly rounded up. Karajan didn't say a word through all this but when he mounted the podium and gave his downbeat it was obvious that a great new talent had come to America.

After a few concerts in New York the tour proper got under way. I had arranged with a flying company in New Jersey to charter a Piper Apache. The Apache is a twin-engined airplane with a cabin for three plus pilot and co-pilot. After careful search I engaged a professional pilot named Jack Chapman, who I felt would meld with the Karajan character, but for the first leg of the trip, from New York to Baltimore, I wanted to fly with him myself and Jack Chapman was banished to the rear compartment. We boarded the plane early in the afternoon and both Chapman and I explained the complexities of the eastern seaboard flying rules. Fortunately it was a brilliant, clear day and we were able to proceed visually. Karajan listened to everything intently and taxied us out onto the runway. He made a smooth takeoff, climbed to our assigned altitude, and set off on course. He had his head locked in the cockpit, a common action of inexperienced pilots, and I warned him to look around at where we were going. I reminded him that traffic was heavy and we had to be constantly on the alert. He would nod, as if understanding, but kept his head glued to the instruments. I repeated my warning, even making him look up at a plane passing us closely but at a safe distance. "Keep looking around," I said. "This is one of the heaviest traveled air routes in the world and you must watch where you're going." He nodded again, looked around a bit, and once more buried his head in the cockpit. He seemed not to get the message and I was getting hot under the collar and beginning to forget that he was the great Karajan and was reverting to my brief wartime assignment as an instructor. "Look around, damn it," I said, after a few more minutes of head in cockpit. "It's dangerous around here." And my voice had new authority. He jerked his head around a few times, smiled at me, and within a predictable few minutes he was once again immersed with the gauges. I looked out my window and saw a plane approaching us at what looked like a very chancy distance. I looked back at Chapman for his reaction. He, after all, spent his professional life flying and I wanted his judgment about the danger ahead. He leaned over to me and said he thought we'd be all right and then I knew right away what I was going to do to get Karajan to pay attention. I waited until the plane was close, then tapped Karajan on the shoulder at the same time jamming the wheel forward and putting us into a steep dive. "God damn it," I said. "I don't care about you but I went through the war flying all kinds of machines in all kinds of places and I'm damned if I'm going to be killed by you today. Will you stop fooling around and get your head out of the cockpit and into the sky." He was startled. The dive had pushed him hard against his safety belt and for a moment he seemed to panic. But he recovered quickly and for the rest of the trip kept his eyes on the route.

As we approached Baltimore I began to feel a little chagrined at my behavior. He made a beautiful landing. After parking the plane at the visiting aircraft ramp we climbed out and drove into the city. All was quiet on the trip until we reached the hotel. Karajan got out quickly and entered the lobby. As soon as he had his room key he turned to me and said: "I am going upstairs right now to write down one hundred times 'You must look around while flying in America.' I'll give it to you at the concert tonight."

At the concert, just before his entrance, he handed me a folded sheet of paper. The words were on it. "That way I'll never forget," he said.

In later years I've seen Karajan from time to time and always enjoyed his company. He is now part-owner of a Lear Jet, flies everywhere in the most sophisticated equipment, and has often asked me to join him. The merger of Karajan's interests, at once musical, scientific, and artistic, makes for a complex but curious man. Shortly after the death of Toscanini we were riding together in a train, the weather having prevented flying. We were talking about the Maestro and suddenly Karajan said that when the time came for him to retire he would not die because of lack of other interests. "The problem with so many colleagues is that they have nothing else but music. I have the world."

And in the sense he said it he was right. For Karajan there is always another hill to climb, another mountain to explore.

The Berlin Philharmonic tour was an enormous success and the following season Karajan was back with the Philharmonia of London. This time the public was not quite so responsive to an unknown orchestra. The company scheduled four concerts in New York and we were all expected to see that the houses were full. In casting around for some likely candidates I happened to remember that Eleanor Roosevelt was a music lover. Having the briefest of acquaintanceships with her because of Katherine and Francis Biddle and my father, I nonetheless wrote and asked if she would like to go to the first concert and as an afterthought scribbled on the bottom of the note an invitation for dinner if she happened to be free. Not two days later I received a reply saying she would love to come and love to have dinner and could I call her secretary with the details. We took her to the Coffee House Club, and also invited Bill Judd and our dear friend Liza Glendevon and the five of us arranged to meet at 6:30.

I was at the club a few minutes early and at 6:30 on the nose Mrs. Roosevelt's footsteps could be heard on the stairs and she entered the room right on schedule. She settled down with a sherry and I with my vodka martini and we chatted away at a great rate. Betty, Liza, and Bill Judd all arrived a few minutes later and we went to the dinner table. I had ordered the meal ahead of time, and having heard from many people that Mrs. Roosevelt paid little or no attention to food, ordered a good one so that the rest of us would be properly fortified for the evening ahead. Mrs. Roosevelt attacked her meal with gusto, eating everything in sight and exclaiming how good it was.

The conversation ranged over politics, world affairs, art, New York, and music as well as a good deal of talk about families. The Roosevelts, the Chapins, the Biddles and my wife's family, the Steinways and the Davises, were, in one way or another, loosely interconnected, and Mrs. Roosevelt was fascinated by genealogy. The time passed quickly and when I glanced at my watch as the ice cream was being served I realized we had fifteen minutes to get to Carnegie Hall if we wanted to be there on time. Everyone got up to get coats except Mrs. Roosevelt, who was not finished with her dessert and was not going to let it go to waste. I paid the bill and presently we were all ready to leave.

We walked out to the street and, of course, there was not a taxicab in sight. By this time I was getting quite nervous and was about to suggest that we walk the ten blocks when Mrs. Roosevelt stepped out into the street, one arm raised. With a screech of brakes and a scream of tires, a taxi pulled over to her. "Ain't you Mrs. Roosevelt?" the driver asked in awe. "Yes, I am," she replied calmly, "and these friends of mine and I are late for a concert at Carnegie Hall. Do you think you could get us there quickly?" "You just get in," he said, "and we'll make it." We all piled in and the driver moved out into the traffic. "You better hold tight back there," he said, and we started off. The driver weaved in and out between cars, buses, and even trucks and turned into 57th Street just two minutes before the concert was scheduled to begin. When we pulled opposite the hall she said, "Don't turn around. We'll all get out here." Which we did, and ran, dodging cars, across the street to the entrance of the hall. I paid the driver and he looked out at Mrs. Roosevelt's disappearing figure with love and admiration. "She's some dame," he said. "The best. And I hope she enjoys herself tonight." I think she did.

In 1955 Columbia embarked on a project that excited me very much indeed. For some time Bill Judd had been in contact with Samuel Chotzinoff about touring the NBC Television Opera. Judd felt that because of television exposure there would be an audience across the country ready to respond to live opera and I agreed with him completely. The two of us worked together with Chotzinoff and later with Alfred Stern and Robert Sarnoff to put a touring company together. Peter Herman Adler was to be artistic director.

We planned a first season around two works, Puccini's *Madama Butterfly* and Mozart's *The Marriage of Figaro*. The operas were to be sung in English with casts who were appropriate to their roles musically and dramatically. Adler felt that many people would be seeing opera for the first time and he wanted to give them the perfect theatrical balance that opera is supposed to represent but seldom does.

Judd and I booked a route around the country and I persuaded Sister Mary Madeleva, president of St. Mary's College, South Bend, Indiana, to let us have her new theater to prepare the company and open the tour. Sister Madeleva was an acute, alert, and artistically curious woman who was a fine poet in her own right and one of my favorite clients on booking trips. I had told her two years previously that we were working on an NBC Opera tour and she was encouraging and supportive. She was in the process of building a new fine arts center on her campus and it was her pride and joy. I walked over it many times during the construction, accompanying her inspections, which she took regularly and thoroughly, her habit flying behind her. I asked her how she was going to pay for it and she would roll her eyes to heaven, wink, and change the subject.

St. Mary's agreed to have the NBC Opera open the auditorium and to putting up the company during the rehearsal and preparation period. Bill Judd engaged Chandler Cowles, the actor and producer, to become general manager of the company. Cowles's productions of the Menotti operas on Broadway and elsewhere had earned him a rightful reputation as a skilled man in the arts. Chandler and I were the two who bore the brunt of the responsibilities after the contracts were signed, starting out with a pre-tour promotion trip to all of our scheduled cities. We were accompanied by Alfred Stern, who had been delegated by RCA and NBC to watch over the operations. The three of us were joined occasionally by local RCA and NBC types who would shepherd us through the press conferences, TV appearances, local lunches, dinners, meetings with the Chambers of Commerce, and anything else that seemed appropriate to get our message across. We were gone for a month in the summer just prior to the fall tour and it was an object lesson for anyone wishing to enter, among other things, politics. We were almost always tired. Ceremonies might start at 8:00 AM and finish up past midnight. We always had to be on our best behavior and look as if we'd just stepped out of the shower. It was a good training course for my years at the Metropolitan.

We opened at St. Mary's with great ceremony. The days before had been filled with the usual theatrical crises, including the fact that William and Jean Eckart had designed too much scenery for both productions and there was no way we could use it all without bringing the curtain down sometime after 1:00 AM. Their work was beautiful but had to be cut. In addition, we had allowed for one ten-ton trailer to carry the productions and this was obviously not going to be enough. Trucks cost a lot of money and an additional one was not in our approved budget. Stern had to be persuaded of the validity of our problem. He was charming but a fierce keeper of RCA's keys. One day he decided to tell Peter Herman Adler that an added truck was out of the question and he came into the theater, sat by me, and waited for the moment to speak. Adler was concentrating on the stage. At a pause in the proceedings Stern leaned down and told Adler that the extra truck was out of the question, just too expensive, and that he would have to make do with one. Adler stared straight ahead and Stern, thinking he'd not heard, repeated his remarks. Adler still stared ahead and finally rose, directing his attention to the stage. "The words, the words!" he shouted. "I can't hear the words!" And he stomped down the aisle. Stern looked at me and shrugged. "I surrender," he said. "You can have the two trucks."

The opening brought out many RCA and NBC officials who had obviously never been in Middle America before. One of these was Emanuel Sachs, talent coordinator for both organizations and at home in 21 or Romanoff's, but certainly not St. Mary's. Sister Madeleva took him and some others on a tour of the college, including the chapel. With a twinkle in her eye, she said, "We like to keep the girls on their knees from time to time. It keeps them out of trouble." Manny Sachs looked at her and then at the floor. He shook his head. It was too much for a good Jewish boy from Philadelphia.

The opening was widely attended by the press and things got off to a good start. The press was enthusiastic about the venture and we saw to it that our tour towns were properly alerted to our initial success. We were received well almost everywhere, with packed and appreciative houses, but I noticed that the audiences were much more responsive to the pathos of *Butterfly* than to the high comedy of *Figaro*. Both were being done in excellent translations by Ruth and Thomas Martin and both were understandable as Adler insisted on clarity of diction. I puzzled on this for a few stops and when we were scheduled to open our run in St. Louis I went to Adler and asked him if I could try an experiment. I told him that I thought people were not responding to *Figaro* because they did not think it proper to laugh in an opera house and that they were not clued in to the idea that Mozart might be funny. I suggested going before the curtain and explaining that *Figaro* was a comedy of the highest order, that it was a comedy of manners and mores which had been banned at its first performances because it took too many potshots at the establishment. He thought it was worth a try and on our first afternoon I went in front of the curtain. As an afterthought I said that *Figaro* was, in a way, the *My Fair Lady* of its day. The audience applauded warmly and one could sense that they were beginning to relax. Which is exactly what they did. The laughter and audience participation were such that at the great denouement, when Figaro is confronted with his mother and father and sister, Adler had to fold his arms and wait patiently for the laughter and applause to die down. The full measure of the piece was finally reaching the audience.

The tour was a success, although the one-night stands were exhausting to everyone. RCA went ahead with the second season as agreed and a third opera was added, *La Traviata*. However, by the end of the second tour both RCA and NBC lost interest and it wasn't until the ill-starred attempt by the Metropolitan in the late sixties to form a national touring company that another major group went around America with first-class opera. By then opera had begun to take a different pattern: regional companies had sprung up with permanent home bases and support drawn from local sources as well as the big foundations, and perhaps most important of all, from the National Endowment for the Arts.

VII

Intermission

By the summer of 1959 Betty and I were both ready for a new adventure. We had been spending our summers happily at our place outside Plymouth, Massachusetts, at Long Pond, but as the children continued to grow we thought it a shame not to give them and ourselves a chance for new experiences. My cousin Kay Garrison had married a delightful Englishman, Viscount Runciman of Doxford, and the Runciman family, particularly Leslie and his brother Steven, owned an island off the northwest coast of Scotland with the unlikely name of Eigg. In 1953 Betty and I had spent two weeks in Scotland and had fallen in love with it. Leslie was kind enough to suggest that he make an extra house on Eigg available to us for a summer, rent free, if we should ever want it.

We had both remembered the conversation and one cold February evening we spoke with our friends the Gary Graffmans about our idea of a summer in Scotland. The Graffmans were frequent visitors to Long Pond and knew our charming but dilapidated house well. "You go to Scotland and we'll rent your place," they said. I wrote Leslie immediately and received a prompt reply that the house, Glamisdale, was available to us as requested. We figured out what the cost of transportation and living might be and agreed on a fee for renting Long Pond that covered most of our expenses.

On July 1 we boarded an Icelandic Airlines Constellation and set out for our great adventure.

Our adventure began within an hour of taking off when one by one our children became airsick in our nonpressurized cabin. I spent a good deal of the time running up and down the aisles looking for airsick bags. The children grew pale and exhausted and so did we and I began to think that this was a bad omen for the weeks ahead. We landed at Gander, Newfoundland, for refueling and the minute we hit the fresh air the children bounded back with pink cheeks, springy steps, new-found energy sources, and fierce appetites. We filled them with Drama-mine and did the best we could to prevent any eating but they managed to sneak a few cookies and goodies. When we boarded for takeoff to Iceland their health and good spirits impressed and seemed to please our fellow passengers. This lasted for about thirty minutes, when again, one by one, the bags were needed in droves. It made for an ac-tive flight.

On arriving at Reykjavik the next morning we were both starved and rather than fight off the perked-up children's appetites we tucked away a good breakfast. I went around to the airline office and obtained as many airsick bags as I could handle and we boarded the plane again ab-solutely certain we would have another seasick ward. It didn't happen; perhaps the daylight, perhaps the excitement of a strange country, per-haps the Dramamine. Whatever it was, we flew on to Glasgow without further problems and landed in the early afternoon ready for our is-land.

We spent the first night in the Great Northern Railway Hotel at the central station in Glasgow. We had interconnecting bedrooms that had a bed for everyone and little distance between them and us. Betty and I figured that Glasgow would be our last chance for a really good dinner for a while, so we put the children to bed and set our for Ruganos, a restaurant recommended to me by my old friend Dick Leach, who knows all about where to get a good meal in cities that are not world fa-mous for their cuisine. There we had a delicious dinner and toasted each other, the boys, and our upcoming unknown summer with a good bottle of Bernkasteler.

The next morning at 5:00 AM we were on board the train headed north. The steam and soot from the engine poured in any open window and I realized with a shock that it was the first time our children had ever seen a steam engine. Breakfast was announced at 6:00 AM and we fell to in the dining car with orange juice, porridge, fried eggs and ba-con, toast, milk, tea, coffee, jam, and butter in great profusion. The countryside as we moved north was incredibly beautiful and barren, with deep gorges and ravines, moors and distant mountains, and colors at once vivid and varied. We pulled into Arisaig around 4:00 PM. The

weather was foggy and misty. The drizzle was steady and when our
bags had been taken off and we had assembled on the station platform
the train pulled out leaving us standing, the fog and mist swirling
around our ankles, with not another human being in sight. Instinctively
we all gathered closer together and tried to peer through the weather.

Presently, somewhere out in the mist, we heard slow footsteps that
seemed to be coming toward us. Out of the fog came two tall rawboned
men, dressed in coveralls with hats pulled down quite far on their
faces. They approached us and stopped. "Ye be for Eigg?" one of
them asked in a hollow voice. I said we were, and without another
word they leaned down and picked up all our baggage and started walking. We followed them to a tiny Morris Minor to which had been attached a small trailer. Our luggage went into the trailer and we were
beckoned into the car. We piled in and so did our two silent bearers and
with a bounce we started downhill. We rode for five or six minutes and
turned abruptly into a farmyard where we bumped and lurched over
some ruts and rocks and came to a halt alongside a stone chicken coop.

We got out and the two men took our baggage once again and this
time headed off to a rocky beach. We followed, no one saying a word,
and slipped our way across seaweed-covered stones, trying to keep the
two men in sight. After a few minutes of this I began to feel annoyed.
We'd come some four thousand miles, gotten on the train at 5:00 AM
and ridden almost all day, and now we fetched up on slippery rocks in
fog and rain and no one had said a word of where we were going or how
we were going to get there.

Just then the mist lifted for a moment and we saw the *Dido* riding at
anchor some fifty yards offshore. It was an oceangoing fishing boat that
had been modified as an interisland carrier, mostly for sheep and cows.
There were the two men rowing a dinghy toward her carrying our luggage. I had a motion picture camera with me and immediately put it to
my nose and started to shoot film. I didn't know that there was a leak in
the body of the camera and not a single foot of film would come out. It
was just as well that I didn't know because the act of filming at that moment used up my energy that might have gone into a useless explosion
of "what-the-hell-are-we-doing-here-anyway" type of conversation.
The dinghy unloaded its cargo and headed once again for the shore. It
came up to the edge of our beach and, still silent, the men motioned for
us to board. Betty and two of the boys went first and the other two and
I went on a second trip.

On board the *Dido* there was a tiny cabin, with a long bench and an
ominous bucket tucked into one corner. Betty and the boys settled in

and I walked forward to inspect the countryside that was slowly coming into view as some of the fog and mist began to lift. *Dido*'s engines were started while I was doing this and we moved gently out of the little harbor toward the open sea. I was about to return to the cabin when our bow made contact with the open ocean and we began to plunge and buck at such a rate that one misstep and I would have been pitched overboard. I clung to a small mast that was fortunately near the bow and held on for dear life as the waves mounted, the spray flew, and I became totally soaked. Between waves I could make out Betty's face in the cabin window beckoning me to join her. I could even see flashes of anger as she made it very plain that she thought I was welching on my duties. I shook my head, gestured with my free hand that such a move was, to say the least, improvident, and hung on for dear life.

After a time we slowed down for an approach to Eigg and as we entered the little harbor the ocean receded behind us. As we approached the dock I let go of my life-or-death grip of the mast and joined the family in the cabin.

We were greeted by the factor, Mr. Rutherford, a bent-over Scotsman with a warm smile and ruddy face. "Welcome to Eigg," he said. "My wife is at Glamisdale making sure your fires are going and Archie and Hugh (at last the two silent ones had names!) will have your bags off in no time. Why don't you get into the Land Rover and I'll drive you up." We gathered the children, all the fishing rods and hand luggage, and stepped ashore into what turned out to be one of the most beautiful and thoughtful summers we ever were to have while our children were growing up. Mr. Rutherford drove us to the house. His wife had indeed gotten the fires going and the beds made and had laid out a supper so that we didn't have to cope the first minute. After welcoming us warmly and almost affectionately the Rutherfords took their leave and we had the house to ourselves.

Glamisdale was a large stone farmhouse which at one time had been an inn, rebuilt and added to in the 1870s. The plumbing had been installed in 1878. There was no electricity, no icebox, none of the household things that we were all accustomed to. The kitchen had a wood-coke stove through the back of which ran the pipes for hot water. The water was hot only if the stove was. The kitchen contained various Victorian and Edwardian instruments of torture that were designed to curlicue, fancy up, and sculpt food but not to cook it. The sink came to Betty's knees. The cold room held the butter and fresh vegtables. Every other perishable had to go in the meat keeper, a house on stilts with slats for walls facing the prevailing wind. The dining room was large with a worn oriental rug, a large oak table, and a good-sized fireplace. The living room was dominated by the fireplace over which hung a menacing claymore. The furniture was Asbury Park 1928. Upstairs the bedrooms were all good-sized, each with its fireplace and each filled with the sound of roaring wind. The one bathroom had an enormous tub, big enough to fit Edward VII comfortably. Right out our windows to the south we had a small but immaculate lawn. To the north rose the powerful and dominating Sgurr of Eigg, a 1,250-foot mountain of basalt. On either side we were surrounded with burns filled with sparkling cold and fast-moving water. We had a telephone, Eigg 3, available in the daytime when Miss MacDonald was not out feeding her chickens, a laundry room filled with tubs that looked like Dr. Frankenstein's laboratory, and fifteen volumes in Danish about the history of the Vikings. We were all set for a splendid visit.

The next morning Betty determined that we had to organize carefully if we were not going to spend most of the summer housekeeping. She decreed two meals a day, breakfast and dinner, and we decided that everyone had to be assigned specific responsibilities. Hank, age ten, helped me bring in the coal, coke, and wood. Sam and Ted, age eight, made up the fires and filled or emptied the stone hot water bottles, and Miles, age four, brought in the smaller pieces of wood. After breakfast, which usually consisted of porridge, kippers, eggs, tea, and toast, beds were made, the house tidied up, and we'd start out to explore the island.

Eigg is about 5 miles long and 3 miles wide with a summer population that swells to roughly 200. Most of the residents are crofters, the traditional Scottish tenant farmers. who in the last century were badly put upon by the invading English and now, for the past sixty years or more, have been taking their full revenge. Their revenge consists of full application of the Croft Laws where the landlord is responsible for everything and the crofter for practically nothing. On Eigg, for instance, the croft farmer had coal delivered to his door from the mainland at less than mainland prices. His rent was £2 a year, his repairs fully funded, again by the landlord; his produce was his and, in truth, if he wanted to (and most of them did) he could sit back and be cared for without doing anything. Most of the crofters were there when Eigg was bought by Walter Runciman, later Lord Runciman, a Scottish shipping tycoon.

Runciman sprang to international fame when he led the ill-starred Runciman Mission to attempt negotiations with Adolf Hitler, negotiations that led to the Munich Pact. For his troubles he was created Viscount Runciman of Doxford. He had a large family, including two sons, Leslie and Steven. Leslie succeeded to the title on the death of his father and took over the steamship company as well. He had been one of the first chairmen of the British Overseas Airways Corporation and largely responsible for the prewar development of this important company. He first married the British novelist Rosamond Lehmann and later my cousin Katherine Garrison. His brother Steven is recognized as one of Britain's finest scholars, having written the definitive books on the Crusades. This task earned him a knighthood. When Walter Runciman died Eigg was left to Leslie and Steven, who shared the responsibility.

Eigg has certain climate advantages. It lies on the outer rim of the Inner Hebrides and is touched both by the Gulf Stream and the trade winds. The cluster of islands in this group—Rhum, Muck, Canna, and Skye—all share in Scotland's bloody history, particularly that of the clans Macdonald and Campbell that brought so much havoc to the wild and beautiful land. One of the sights on Eigg was Massacre Cave. The Campbells, on a women-stealing raid, could not find a single person when they landed and would have left the island alone save for finding, at the last minute, clear footprints in the new-fallen snow leading on a path to what was obviously the mouth of a cave. They followed the prints and realized that the island population had holed up in the cave. With that knowledge they built a great fire at the entrance, killing everyone inside. Even in 1959 you could find bits of parched and bleached human bone in the mysterious caverns. Eigg was dominated by the Sgurr, the mountain behind our house, and on top of it was a stretch of land that included four lochs, jammed with trout. I learned the first day that the tenant of Glamisdale controlled all the fishing rights to the lochs and that no one could go fishing without my permission. From time to time our gate would be tapped and I would go out to find a well-equipped fisherman asking permission.

The Runcimans lived in The Lodge, a lovely but incongruous flat-roofed house that might have looked more at home in southern Italy. The Lodge boasted a splendid tennis court and flower gardens but far more important to us were the kitchen gardens with their unbelievable vegetables growing from the rich but thin topsoil and the raspberry canes that were plentiful, thick, and over seven feet high. In the early morning Donald Campbell would present himself at Glamisdale with a neatly laid out basket of what he considered ripe from the garden and usually later in the day we would journey down ourselves and pick the raspberries.

For other supplies there was a small Scottish Cooperative shop about 2½ miles walking distance from Glamisdale. Meat, clothing, and liquor were available at various shops in Mallaig. The goods would come across, with our mail, twice a week on the *Loch Mor*, a steam ferry that stopped off at the island, if the seas weren't running too high. We had no radio, certainly no television, and lived essentially without regular access to world events. We had a doctor on the island, a fierce lowland Scot who spent part of his days playing his bagpipes and strutting up and down in a kilt. He had the only radio on the island and we took to stopping at his house every few days on our way back from the store to see what was happening out there.

Our days were spent roaming the land, our nights reading, and even without our knowing it, the effects of the island and our life there were drawing us close together as a family. We needed each other and came to depend on each other. We learned, too, to respect each other's quirks and foibles and to share interests of the mind and spirit. Because of Eigg's high latitude the sun never set. It would disappear around 11:30 PM and a half-hour later the sky would be light again. We would all dine together around 7 or 7:30 and then read out loud until the children's bedtime. I found some old Victorian novels in a closet upstairs and took out H. Rider Haggard's *King Solomon's Mines*, which I remembered so well from my boyhood. I decided to read this aloud to the boys just before they went to bed and it wasn't until many years later that Hank confessed the book gave him steady nightmares. It did the same kind of thing to Sam and Ted but I suspect not to Miles, who was a little too young and usually was asleep the minute his head touched the pillow.

Our summer rustication was interrupted one night by Mr. Rutherford arriving in his Land Rover and coming over to us with a look of surpressed excitement. He said there was a transatlantic telephone call for me and would I come with him to his house. He had the only telephone on the island connected to the mainland at night. I looked at Betty and wondered what might be wrong. She said nothing but we both had a moment of fear. I went with Rutherford and entered his house to find at least six other people dressed in oil slicks and rubber boots sitting around the table having a "wee dram," smoking pipes, and looking at me with great curiosity. I went to the telephone that was on the wall and had an old-fashioned hand receiver and separate talk piece. It also had a hand crank that I rang and waited for a moment before an operator came on the line.

"I'm Mr. Chapin on Eigg," I said. "I believe you have a call for me.'' ''Oh yes, Mr. Chapin,'' replied a smooth, rolling Scots accent, ''you just hold on there and we'll get on to Fort William.'' I could hear clicks and voices from Mallaig to Fort William, Fort William to Edinburgh, Edinburgh to London, London to New York, and New York, it turned out, to the office of Goddard Lieberson, the colorful and highly individualistic head of Columbia Records.

I knew Mr. Lieberson by reputation but had never met him. ''Well,'' he started out, ''I had a terrible time finding you!'' ''I'll bet you did,'' I replied somewhat lamely. He continued that of course I knew the news that David Oppenheim, the head of Columbia Masterworks, was leaving to take a new job in television and that he, Lieberson, had to find a new director and while he was not offering me the job, since he hardly knew me at all, he wanted to know whether I might be interested. This was all said at a free-flowing pace and when I could get a word in I told him that I'd been out of communication with the real world for some weeks and knew nothing of what he was talking about. ''Oh, you just fly here tomorrow and we'll discuss it,'' he replied. ''Mr. Lieberson,'' I said, ''I'm flattered by your call. However, I suggest first that you get an atlas and look off the northwest coast of Scotland. There you will see a group of islands including Eigg and you will realize that to fly home tomorrow from such a place is clearly impossible.'' ''I'll have a look,'' he said, and I could hear him calling out to his secretary. ''In the meantime,'' I said, becoming increasingly excited, ''I will be in London in a week's time for five days. Is there any chance of our meeting there?'' ''No,'' he replied. ''I will be in Switzerland in about two weeks to visit Stravinsky.'' And then he paused. ''I see where you are now,'' he said, ''and I guess it would be difficult to come home. Let's arrange to telephone again while you're in London and in the meantime I really don't know very much about you. Would you write me a few details of your experiences?'' ''Certainly,'' I said. ''Very nice to talk to you.'' ''And to you,'' he answered. ''We'll keep in touch.'' And he rang off.

I replaced the receiver and looked around. The men in the room were staring at me. I thanked Mr. Rutherford, who took me out to the Land Rover to drive me up the hill. He was smiling but I didn't think it a good idea to ask why. Finally, as the car pulled away from his entrance, he said: ''That's the first time any of us have dealt with a transatlantic call. The men were curious to see if it actually worked.'' ''It did,'' I said to him, ''and that call may lead to a whole new life for us.''

He left me at the Glamisdale gate and I went into the house to tell Betty. She seemed pleased by the idea and I got out pen and paper to write. I fetched one of the gas lights that we had in the living room, turned the brightness up as far as the wick would go, and sat down. "Dear Mr. Lieberson," I began and realized that I was writing to the head of one of the major communication companies of the world by the light of a gas lantern. The world seemed to have come full circle.

We went off to London for our few days, the high point of which was a day with Clifford and Lucille Curzon that began by their sending one of their sons to pick up our boys and take them off so that Betty and I could have a free morning together. We all met for lunch at the Curzons, and they gave us a wonderful time. I called Lieberson from London and we made arrangements to meet right after Labor Day to discuss matters further. He had received my letter and was a bit puzzled that it wasn't typed. I explained again about Eigg and told him to think about young Abe Lincoln studying before the fire.

We returned to Eigg the night of the beginning of the Bank Holiday. Our train reservations had gone awry but a sympathetic railway clerk found us one first-class compartment into which we neatly fit. It was a long ride from London to Arisaig. The train left London at 5:00 PM and didn't arrive at our destination until 5:00 PM the next afternoon. We were in good spirits, though, after a weekend at Greys Village with our friends Liza and John Glendevon. They had taken us all in and our children were exposed for the first and only time in their lives to the jurisdiction of an English nanny. John and Liza had two boys about the same age as Hank and the twins, and a Miss Glasspool was in charge of them. Our boys grumbled at the idea but were told to look on it as an adventure. At Greys the boys were spirited away and we went out on the lawn for tea. For two days we were treated as honored guests and the boys played with us only by appointment. We did punt on the Thames together, play a little village cricket, and share Sunday lunch, but other times were strictly adult, an informal English country weekend with delicious food impeccably served, our clothing washed and ironed, our shoes shined, and intelligent conversation. When we left for London to board the train for Arisaig, Liza produced a large picnic hamper stuffed with sandwiches, cake, and Coca-Cola "You'll need this on the journey," she said, and how right she was.

On the train we sought out Steven Runciman, who was coming to Eigg for his holidays. Steven, a bachelor, was understandably not overanxious to meet his young American in-law cousins, but polite man that he is he came down to our compartment for a how-do-you-do. The boys were all sitting up straight and clean. Steven sat stiffly, talking to us and presently Hank turned to him with a pointed question about the countryside passing our windows. Steven answered him and this led to questions from the others. In a few moments he was delivering a very interesting history lessson and we were all enthralled. He asked Betty and me to join him in the restaurant car for dinner and we accepted. She turned to the boys and took down the picnic basket from the overhead rack. "There are sandwiches and pieces of cake for all of you." she said, "and two Cokes each. We'll be back after our dinner." We got up and so did the boys, shaking Steven's hand and saying that they hoped to meet again. We left the compartment and I glanced back to see all faces concentrating on the basket. God bless Liza, I thought. She made it possible for us to get off to a civilized start with Steven.

Back on Eigg our last weeks were ideal. Leslie and Kay arrived and Leslie took us all up the Sgurr, explored the back island with us, and took us to watch the golden eagles. When the time came for our departure there were genuine tears on all sides. We journeyed to Glasgow but there, fearing another seasick air trip, I switched our flight to Scandinavian Airlines and a pressurized cabin. We flew home to New York, a family ready for any kind of new adventure.

Lieberson too returned from his various travels and we did meet right after Labor Day. Flattered as I was by the Columbia Records offer, I really was not that anxious to leave Columbia Artists except that I felt my work there deserved more salary and responsibility. Upon my return from Scotland it was abundantly clear that they did not feel the same way and when Lieberson did make me an offer I accepted with pleasure and anticipation. Columbia Artists professed shock. How could I leave them at the beginning of a new season? It was implied that I had no loyalty. I told them that loyalty seemed to me to be more than a one-way street. After I left, the company required its employees to sign contracts, a compliment, I suppose, to the truth of my position.

VIII

Columbia Records, Stravinsky

I joined Columbia Records on October 1, 1959, as executive coordinator for the Masterworks Department. That somewhat fanciful title was dreamed up in order to split the responsibility of the department between two people, John McClure, the music director, and myself. Lieberson and I had a brief meeting that first morning. I discussed some details and just as I was taking my leave I asked him, "How do you really want me to run the department?" "Use your imagination," he replied. "That's a dangerous thing to tell me," I said, "I have a pretty vivid one." "Don't worry," he replied. "So do I. If I don't like what you're doing I'll tell you so. But it is up to you to run your own show." I knew we were going to get on famously.

My duties at Columbia were to select the recording repertoire for a long list of artists, including violinists Isaac Stern and Zino Francescatti, pianists Glenn Gould, Rudolf Serkin, Eugene Istomin, and Alexander Brailowsky, singers Eileen Farrell and Richard Tucker, Igor Stravinsky, the Mormon Tabernacle Choir, the Philadelphia Orchestra with Eugene Ormandy, the Cleveland Orchestra with George Szell, and the New York Philharmonic. The Philharmonic had just the year before engaged Leonard Bernstein to be its new music director, replacing Dimitri Mitropoulos. Bernstein was also a Columbia Records artist on his own.

One of the milestones in Columbia's history was the basic development of a practical, marketable record that turned at 33 ⅓ revolutions per minute and allowed recording of up to 25 minutes on each side of a two-faced disc. The broadcasting industry had long used 33 ⅓ transcription tables but no way had yet been found to reduce these huge discs to a reasonable size and to come up with a unit for playing the results at home. These problems were solved by a remarkable scientist and engineer with a passion for music who had been turned down by RCA Laboratories on applying for a job and snapped up by CBS. His name was Peter Goldmark. When a realistic product was developed in his laboratories, Columbia lost no time in notifying the industry, inviting all companies to use its patents, and launching a campaign to woo the listener away from 78 rpm shellacs and onto the 33 ⅓ microgroove, as it was called. Shortly after this Goldmark emerged with another invention: the stereo recording that allowed music to be played on two channels and be received in the home over two or more speakers. This meant that for the first time those at home could begin to duplicate the sound of a live performance. By the time I joined the company the first major commitment to this new sound had been generally made by the phonograph record industry and this meant that most, if not all, of the giant classical catalogue had to be re-recorded in the new process. I arrived in the record industry at just the right moment.

Lieberson had very strong ideas about the classical catalogue: he felt that the industry took a great deal from music and owed a return debt. The Masterworks Department was therefore required to contribute only a modest amount to the overall company profits, usually one-fifth of the net, and he wanted the repertoire to reflect modern creative work as well as standard fare. At one time Lieberson himself had headed the department and had begun the very first regular recording program of modern music, called the Modern American Music Series, on the theory that recognition should come first to the American composer. The artistic communities around the country took careful note of this venture and Columbia was recognized as a forward-looking company with the strength to experiment on what might not be the hottest properties in the commercial marketplaces.

Perhaps the most important contribution of all that Lieberson made in this area was to sign Igor Stravinsky to an exclusive recording contract. This meant that for the first time in the history of music one of the world's most important composers could record his complete output either conducted by him or under his direct supervision. Future generations of musicians and music lovers will know precisely how the master wanted his works performed. They may not follow his wishes; perhaps they shouldn't, in some cases, but we know how he intended everything to be. The mind boggles when you think what might have happened if Bach, Beethoven, Mozart, Wagner, or Mahler had had the same opportunities.

It became one of my first responsibilites, therefore, to continue this program and I eagerly awaited the chance to meet the great man.

The opportunity came soon enough. One morning my phone rang and it was Robert Craft, Stravinsky's amanuensis. Could I call upon him that afternoon at the Pierre Hotel and be prepared to discuss next season's plans. I talked with McClure, who produced almost all his recording sessions, and we drafted up a plan to include new stereo versions of *Firebird* and *Le Sacre du Printemps* as well as a number of small pieces and *Movements*, a new work for piano and chamber orchestra.

At 4:00 PM McClure and I presented ourselves at Stravinsky's suite to be greeted by both Craft and Madame Stravinsky. The master was not there as yet and we sat down to make conversation. In minutes I realized that Madame was a women of humor, among other qualities, and that Craft was articulate and probing. Madame—Vera as I was asked to call her almost immediately—was Stravinsky's second wife and an important painter in her own right. She was about to open a one-woman show at a prominent Madison Avenue gallery and had some of her paintings around the room. Craft had come into the Stravinsky household some years before when he had written an extremely perceptive and provocative letter that caused the master to suggest a meeting. That meeting led to the relationship that I now found and that was to continue up to the composer's death. I seriously doubt if Stravinsky's creative juices would have continued to flow and produce right up until the end if it had not been for the stimulations, provocations, and suggestions brought by Bob Craft.

I'd been talking with Craft and Vera for about twenty minutes when a door opened and in came the master. We all rose and Stravinsky came toward me, his hand extended. I took it and bowed, looking into his crinkling and smiling eyes. "How do you do," I said, with appropriate solemnity. "How do you do," he replied, smiling. "You are, I believe, the new director Masterworks. I am a Masterwork!" And he bowed toward me. We both laughed. We all laughed and he patted me on my hands. I had no idea he was a short man. I had visualized him almost as tall and as strong as his scores. I also didn't realize how much he depended on his cane and how physically frail he seemed to be. But whatever his physical problems they in no way interfered with his mind. He was quick and bright and even if one thought his attention was wandering he never lost touch for a moment. He had a disconcerting habit of disagreeing with you and then turning at the absolutely right psychological moment and smiling in such a way as to convince you that of course you were absolutely wrong and he absolutely right. It worked many times over in our years together.

The main discussion this first afternoon was the following season's recording plans and Craft, McClure, Stravinsky, and I went over these. It was obvious that McClure and the Stravinsky family enjoyed a very warm relationship and I wanted to do nothing whatever to interfere with that. On the other hand, I wanted to prepare a balanced schedule, not only for actual recording, but for releasing the material to the public in a manner that would give us the best chance for proper sales.

I had been warned that money was one subject not to bring up with Stravinsky. He had copyrighted his ballets *Firebird*, *Petrouchka*, and *Le Sacre du Printemps* first in Imperial Russia and then in France, before the French recognized international copyrights. Therefore, he had lost out on world royalties and had to sit back all his life and listen to the three masterpieces performed anywhere in the world for free. When he came to America he made new copyright editions but these proved useless. An orchestra had only to obtain the score and parts of the originals and sail merrily along without one thought of payment. Understandably, Stravinsky was very sensitive to his losses and he spent a good part of his life trying to make up for it. Unless one was in the mood for hearing the complete detailed account of how he had been badly used, it was better not to bring the subject up at all and confine discussion of business matters to his very astute and shrewd attorney, L. Arnold Weissberger.

The most important new work scheduled for the next year was *Movements for Piano and Orchestra*, a piece that had been commissioned by a wealthy Swiss merchant of Zurich for his wife Margrit Weber, a concert pianist. Herr Weber had paid Stravinsky a considerable sum for the piece and was looking forward to its world premiere in New York and the subsequent recording. It was decided that *Movements* would have its premiere in December at Town Hall as one of a series of new pieces intermingled with older ones that would form a Stravinsky Festival and allow us to gather a strong ensemble of players and go right from the performances to the recording studios. Miss Weber would, of course, be the pianist and, it was assumed, would also make the recording. The other programs and works were discussed and we came up with an exciting repertoire.

Craft and Stravinsky would share the podium and because a performance of *Les Noces* was to be included they thought it would be a fine idea to invite colleagues of the master to play the four piano parts. Invitations were issued to Samuel Barber, Roger Sessions, Lukas Foss, and Aaron Copland. Stravinsky sent notes to each and these were followed up by telephone calls to explain in detail. Mr. Foss agreed enthusiastically on condition that he could play Piano Number One. Mr. Barber conceded gracefully and said "Of course he'd want that." Mr. Copland merely laughed and accepted, while Mr. Sessions was concerned only that he have the easiest part, and he was absolutely sure he wasn't good enough to play it. A cablegram went off to Stravinsky detailing this news and he returned a message that once and for all reduced protocol to its proper level: "All pianos equally important . . . greetings." In the end, Pianos One and Three were played by Foss and Barber, and Two and Four by Copland and Sessions.

On December 20, 1959, *Movements* and *Les Noces*, as well as Stravinsky's arrangements of three Gesualdo motets, the *Epitaphium* and the *Double Canon* (to the Memory of Raoul Dufy) were performed in Town Hall to a sold-out house and standing room only. Several hundred disappointed devotees were turned away. *Movements* was received politely; *Les Noces*, to use the old cliché, brought down the house. The twenty-minute shouting and stamping was acknowledged by Stravinsky only after he turned to encompass pianists, singers, orchestra, and chorus in one superb sweeping gesture of tribute. Only then did he turn back to the crowd, which he thanked with stunning bows from the waist, looking for all the world, in Lillian Libman's phrase, like a little boy bowing to his partner at the start of a dancing class. He was extremely pleased at how the evening had gone and at the reception afterward he was all smiles and grace. Even under Vera's watchful eye, however, he ate and drank too much, because the next day when I arrived at the Pierre he was in bed, looking quite green. "We must change the pianist for *Movements*," he said, opening up the conversation as soon as I entered. "We must what?" I asked incredulously. "Don't you think this will be a little startling, not to say disappointing, to Mrs. Weber?" He looked at me. "We must have a different pianist for the recording," he said again, not really acknowledging my comment. "Have you any ideas?" I asked him. "What do you think of Sanroma?" he replied. "Sanroma is fine except that he doesn't know the piece and we must record during the next week," I answered. "Shall we call him?" He smiled and patted my hand. I placed the call to Puerto Rico. After the usual waits Sanroma came on the line. "I'm here with Stravinsky," I began. "His *Movements for Piano and Orchestra* had its premiere last night and the master is planning to record it. He wants to know if you would be interested in performing the piano part." I could hardly believe my own voice asking the question. Sanroma had not been in America for several seasons and I thought of the near impossibility of learning this very tricky work in time to come before the studio microphones in ten days or so under Stravinsky's supervision. Sanroma paused before answering my question. I could hear him breathing hard on the end of the line. "Let me speak with him," the master said, taking the instrument from my hand. "Hello, Sanroma! How are you, my dear?" And then they launched into rapid French. They had a lovely conversation but the answer was no.

I suddenly had an idea. "I think I know who might be able to do this piece on such relatively short notice. Charles Rosen!" Rosen, a pianist and intellectual of unusual talents I knew to be a quick study and someone who could grasp the subtleties of the work on extremely short notice. Stravinsky looked hard at me. "We will see," he said. "But we must make a decision right away," I replied. "There is not much time." "We will see, my dear," he said again and for the moment that was that.

Later that evening I reached Bob Craft and told him that I thought the whole idea of changing pianists at this late date was ridiculous. He insisted that Stravinsky meant every word and I again pleaded the cause of Charles Rosen. "I'll see him," Craft suggested, and I immediately reached Charles and asked him to get in touch with Craft, meet Stravinsky, discuss the idea, and get back to me as quickly as possible. He was understandably nervous about the whole project but did agree to look at the score and get in touch with the Stravinsky ménage.

A day later Stravinsky sent a message: he agreed to Charles Rosen. After settling details I then wondered how the matter of Mrs. Weber was going to be handled. I had the haunting feeling that I was expected to break the news to her and this was one chore I had no intention whatsoever of carrying out. Neither did John McClure, so we decided that I would bring the matter up with the master and lay our feelings on the line.

The next afternoon I went to the Pierre for tea. Stravinsky was feeling much better and was sitting reading when I came in, the tea service alongside him on a side table. Vera joined us and the cups were filled. That afternoon the likelihood of his making a trip to Russia was the main topic of conversation and I had a hard time steering things around to the Weber family. Finally I said to him, "Mr. Stravinsky, we must talk about Mrs. Weber." He didn't look pleased. I said, "I'm sorry but you must tell her the news. I would like to spare you this but I don't think I can." There was a pause. Then he replied, "You are right. I will tell them. I will do this very soon." "But, sir," I said, "you must do this immediately. She already knows the recording is planned and we have had preliminary discussions about her fee. It must be done in the next day or two." I didn't press the point for the rest of my visit but it was obvious that both of them got my message.

Two days later Vera Stravinsky called and asked me once again for tea. When I arrived Stravinsky was nowhere in sight. "My husband is having a little rest," she said, by way of explanation. "We had lunch today with the Webers." "Oh, wonderful," I replied. "How did it go?" She seemed to hesitate, just as the door to the room opened and Stravinsky entered. We embraced and he sat down. "We had lunch with the Webers today," he said, smiling. There was a pause. "We went to wonderful restaurant. They invite me. We had beautiful salmon, wonderful wines. We talked about everything. At the end I say to her 'You will not make *Movements* for records.' She is very unhappy." I couldn't resist a comment. "You mean," I said, "that you let them take you to lunch and told them the recording was off?" "That is right," he replied, "and it was a very good lunch. In the end they did not mind!" I found this hard to believe.

The *Movements* recording was made with Charles Rosen and was well received by the critics. As a contemporary piano work it did not receive an overwhelming number of performances but it lives today thanks to George Balanchine's extraordinary creation for the New York City Ballet. I often wonder whether Mrs. Weber has performed it anywhere else in the world.

During my Columbia years my relationship with the Stravinskys grew into friendship. We were never intimate but we always seemed to have a good time together and I looked forward to our meetings.

Once, after a concert at Lewisohn Stadium, I rode downtown with Stravinsky to the Russian Tea Room for supper. He had just conducted *Firebird* and as often as I had heard the piece, that night was truly magical. As he approached the climax the tempi remained steady and rock-hard. At the end the audience rose, shouted bravos, and applauded for at least ten minutes. I was among them. I commented on the performance while we were in the taxicab and he took my wrist, putting his fingers on my pulse. "You feel that?" he asked. "Yes," I said. "Distinctly." "That is the way *Firebird* should go. Like the pulse. Strong and steady. Not fast. Not rushed. Not twisted. Strong and steady." He looked flushed but very tired and I asked him why he agreed to conduct at Lewisohn, which was certainly not a place that was going to give him enormous artistic satisfaction. "For money," he said candidly. "I need money. You know I don't have so much of what I should have." And he was about to expand on this when we arrived at the restaurant. Other friends were waiting for him and the money matter was left behind.

But it never was really forgotten by Stravinsky. One hot August afternoon in 1961 I was getting ready to leave my office, around 4:30 PM, when my secretary buzzed me on the phone. "Mr. Stravinsky's here to see you," she said. "Thanks a lot," I replied, "it must be 101 outside and I'm not in the mood for jokes." And I hung up. In two seconds the phone buzzed again. "Mr. Stravinsky is here and would like to see you," she said again and this time I thought she sounded a little tense. I replied, "Tell Glenn Gould to stop with his imitations [he is a superb mimic and one of his specialties was Stravinsky] it's too damn hot." And I put the phone down with a bang. It buzzed again immediately. "Mr. Chapin," she said, and this time I could hear firmness and pleading in her voice, "Mr. Stravinsky is here to see you and he is very anxious." And she hung up. I thought to myself that she must mean it and I rolled down my sleeves, pulled on my coat, and went to the outer office. There indeed was Stravinsky, sitting on a little sofa, his hat by his side, his hands holding his cane handle. "Mr. Stravinsky," I exclaimed. "What a surprise. Why didn't you let me know you were coming?" I went over to embrace him. "My dear, I need to talk to you," he said, and we went toward my office. I glanced over my shoulder at my secretary and tried to apologize with my eyes.

When we got inside, Stravinsky lowered himself onto a chair and looked up at me. We exchanged pleasantries; he asked about my family, and we chatted. After a few minutes his face grew expressionless and very Russian. He put his hand inside his coat and pulled out what I recognized instantly as a Columbia Records royalty envelope. I quickly thought about all the problems we always had at royalty time. While we were busily engaged in creating a unique catalogue of the great composer's work under his direct supervision, the public was not necessarily buying every record in vast quantities, and as a result, his royalty checks were not the largest. This particular pay period had been pretty good, since the Columbia Record Club had recently offered Stravinsky's own recording of *Firebird* and it had sold very well. Usually after the royalty checks were out I would get a call from him complaining bitterly about the amount and asking "Why I do these things? Why I do not go away from the studios." I would always plead about posterity, about the musicians and audiences of the future. I would say to him, "What about Mozart and Beethoven? Suppose they had modern technology? What would we know then?" Usually this calmed him down and he would go back to work. This time, after I sent off the check, I had not heard a word and I began to think that the amount was sufficient to have overcome his usual problems in this area.

With his face now a mask, and a dark one at that, he proceeded to struggle to his feet and cross to my desk. He laid the envelope down with a crisp snap. "I've come here today to thank you," he said, his temper obviously rising. "Oh, there's no need for that," I said hastily. "I was only glad that the amount was approaching what you deserve." The check was for $20,000. "I have come here today to thank you," he repeated, "for my tip!" And he sat down. "I beg your pardon?" I said, looking at the face of the check. "Your tip?" "Da," he replied, "for my tip. How dare you send this for *Firebird*!" And forthwith he launched once again into the story of how he had been cheated all his life by everyone connected with his three early ballets. He grew angrier while talking and I began to think that he might be heading for a stroke. He once paused and looked over at me. My eyes were on him but my hands were resting on my desk, one of them poised over the envelope. He reached over and snatched it back, replacing it in his inside pocket as he continued his story. Finally, exhausted, he stopped. I could think of nothing to say so I didn't open my mouth. When he resumed he was all calm and smiling, as if nothing had happened. He rose, we embraced, and I walked him out of the office and to the elevator. "May I take you home?" I asked. "No thank you, my dear, I am very well." And we embraced once again as the elevator door began to close.

On January 18, 1962, in honor of his eightieth birthday year, President and Mrs. John F. Kennedy gave a dinner for Stravinsky at the White House. It was the first time in American history that a President honored a great creative artist with such an event and I was disappointed not to be asked. I telephoned them in Washington at their hotel before the dinner to wish them well. The Master came to the phone first and it was obvious that he was quite excited. Then Vera came on and she told me what she was going to wear.

The next day I read glowing accounts in the New York newspapers. The Liebersons were there, as were the Bernsteins, Nicholas Nabokov, Marshall Field, Max Freedman, the Arthur Schlesingers, the Pierre Salingers, Helen Chavchavadze, Lee Radziwill, and Bob Craft. Craft, in his book *Chronicle of a Friendship*, gives a vivid description of the evening in which he quotes Stravinsky's comment about the Kennedys: "Nice kids!" At about noon I called the Stravinskys. Both sounded tired, perhaps disappointed would be a better description. They told me bits and pieces about the evening but the master summed up what I gathered were his impressions: "He did not even know *Firebird*."

Later that year the Stravinskys returned to Russia for the first time since the 1917 revolution. Their trip made headlines all over the world. The master conducted in various cities and was received with warmth and curiosity wherever he went, and of course it was a highly emotional experience for both of them. The newspapers kept us well informed, but when they returned to New York I was very anxious to hear details for myself. I was invited to the Pierre for tea one afternoon and both of them were in a very good mood. The tea things were spread out on the table in front of their sofa. Stravinsky sitting on a chair to the right and Vera, with her ever-present embroidery, sat to the left. They put me between them and regaled me with stories. Sometimes during the talk they would look at each other and switch from English to Russian; they seemed excited to be telling of their adventures. After I'd been there for over an hour I thought the time had come to take my leave but before going I had one more question to ask: had they met Khrushchev? "Tell him," Vera said to her husband. "You must tell him." I was all ears.

It seemed that they were in their last full day in Moscow. The telephone rang late in the afternoon and on it a voice said: "Mr. Stravinsky, Minister Khrushchev wishes to see you tomorrow afternoon." As Stravinsky went on: "I said to the voice, no, no, that is not possible. We leave for New York tomorrow afternoon. Our plane leaves at two PM." "Don't worry about plane," says the voice. "Car will come for you." And the next afternoon at 2:00 PM a car did come and whisked them to the Kremlin. They got out at a main gate and walked through the corridors, past the paintings and icons and tapestries, down long halls and through reception rooms until they arrived at the Minister's office. Khrushchev was sitting at his desk and rose to greet them. They all went to settees and began conversation. After a few moments Khrushchev turned to Stravinsky and apologized for not having had a chance to greet him until now. "I have been in Crimea," he said. Stravinsky nodded politely and waited for further comment. "I have been in Crimea while you were here." Stravinsky thought the moment had come to ask what the Minister had been doing in the Crimea all this time. He asked the question. The Minister's eyes widened. He seemed shocked that Stravinsky did not know. "Grapefruit," came the reply. Then silence. "Grapefruit?" Stravinsky asks with eyebrows raised. "Da, grapefruit," replies the Minister. "Also oranges and lemons and limes." And then he pauses for the effect. "Grapefruit, oranges, lemons, limes," he goes on. "We will take the world's citrus markets from America!" And with this he rose, the interview obviously being terminated. The Stravinskys retrace their long steps through the Kremlin rooms and corridors, out to the entrance where their car and driver waits. They drive back to the hotel, pick up their luggage and continue to the airport. The 2:00 PM plane is waiting with a lot of very nervous passengers. The Stravinsky party boards, the doors are closed, jets started, the plane takes off. It is now somewhere past 6:00 PM. Stravinsky wonders what his fellow passengers would think about the delay if he told them it was all about grapefruit, oranges, and limes.

IX

The Conductors

During the Columbia Record days I was concerned not only with the Stravinsky project, although it was a major responsibility. I came to the company at the time of the stereo revolution and found myself in the enviable position of having to remake almost the entire catalogue in this new process. Columbia's sister label, Epic, had been largely created for the popular field but had a classical division which was also my responsibility. The classical line was headed by the Cleveland Orchestra under its brilliant, tyrannical conductor George Szell. Szell looked like the world's most successful banker or a steel magnate from the Ruhr. He stood six feet, with thin body, gray-trimmed hair, and piercing eyes that stared out from round, thick lenses. His clothes were Savile Row; his shirts and ties always unwrinkled, his shoes never unshined. Underneath this somewhat forbidding exterior there was a musician and artist of great sensitivity. It was almost as if he were afraid that showing warmth and passion would destroy him and he took great pains to hide all feelings except anger and outrage. He was a gourmet and wine lover, read extensively, could be hospitable and warm if he knew the person involved. In his years as conductor of the Cleveland Orchestra he had taken an already first-rate group and made it into one of the two or three greatest orchestras in the world. One advantage the Cleveland had on Epic was that they had absolutely no competition and could record the entire basic repertory without any problems except budgets. Over the years we expanded Epic's roster to include the Juilliard Quartet and pianist Charles Rosen. It was a small but elegant label.

Szell and I would have one formal meeting a year to discuss recording repertoire. I often went to Cleveland for these sessions and was usually treated to a superb dinner at the Szells' house before the discussions began. Helen Szell was a stylish hostess; she kept one eye on guests and the other on her husband, always looking over at him if he started off on a tirade that she thought was being overdone. Our evenings usually began with Dom Pérignon and fresh caviar in the attractive drawing room of their house and after dinner and coffee we would retire to his study. This room was strictly for work, a simple room with a desk, shelves for scores, one or two comfortable chairs with good lights for reading, and an upright piano polished to within an inch of its life and stacked neatly with scores, note pads, and pencils. When we sat down he was fully organized for our discussions and would present his requests in a logical manner. I would counter about budgets and the need to keep each year's commitments within careful boundaries. He would argue effectively for his cause and I would do my best with mine. It was all very civilized but in the end his artistic purposes would begin to hold sway. I usually ended up agreeing to much more than I intended.

George Szell would, from time to time, record on the Columbia label as well as Epic, usually in the concerto repertory with artists like Isaac Stern and Leon Fleisher. With Stern he made some memorable Mozart recordings and with Fleisher the Brahms concerti. In my opinion these discs still stand as some of the greatest of their kind.

There was one artist Szell would not work with, and that was the superlative Canadian pianist Glenn Gould. Gould, a performer known not only for his artistry but for his eccentricities, offended Szell's sense of order. Gould had sprung to international prominence at his New York City Town Hall debut where he played the Bach Goldberg Variations and brought the audience and the critics to their knees. He was signed to Columbia by my predecessor, David Oppenheim, who promptly recorded the Goldberg and the disc went on to become a top best seller. Gould made up his mind that he would concertize until he was thirty and at that time would quit the concert platform forever. He was fascinated by records and recording and intended to keep up his work in this area for an indefinite time. He was also keenly aware that television had great potentials for music and he kept on exploring ways of using the medium.

When we first met in 1959 it was on a hot September day and I was startled to see him in a thick winter coat with a cap and ear flaps and thick woolen gloves. I decided not to make any reference to his clothes; my only remarks were to the effect that I was a great admirer and looked forward to working closely with him.

I was anxious to have Gould continue recording the Bach repertoire for obvious reasons and while he was interested in this he also had some bright ideas of his own. One day he proposed that we dust off the old Richard Strauss setting to Tennyson's murky epic poem *Enoch Arden*. I remembered once hearing the piece done in a recital at Eleanor Burden's and being quite moved by it. It happened that at the time of our talk Ormandy and the Philadelphia Orchestra were doing an orchestral transcription of the work with Claude Raines as the narrator and both had been after me to record it. I could not imagine doing the piece with full orchestra but the idea of doing it as written, with piano and narrator, had an appeal and, besides, it was cheap to do. I agreed, contracted Raines, and the two of them met in the Columbia 30th Street studios.

The studio was arranged with a series of screens around Raines and a series of baffles around Gould. They could look over at one another but pursue their individual parts without distraction. At the outset I think the fastidious Raines was offended by Gould's casualness. Mrs. Raines was quick to imagine slights to her husband and right away she picked up the idea that the atmosphere was not right. They set to work with mutual suspicion. Gould would romp through the florid piano part while Raines rolled out the language with suppressed chokes and sobs that were so much a part of nineteenth-century declamation. Mrs. Raines was constantly furious and the conversations between the two artists was peppered with her comments. The studio temperature rose as the work progressed and I began to think that I had unleashed too many furies for a work that really wasn't worth all the trouble. But they did finish it and at the end stiffly acknowledged that they had both done some service to Tennyson and Strauss.

Gould is, however, best known for performances of Bach. We set out to record the complete Well-Tempered Clavier, the Art of the Fugue, the Two and Three Part Inventions, the Six Partitas, the Italian Concerto, and at least three of the keyboard concerti, Numbers 3, 5, and 7. Most of the solo works were recorded on a special Steinway reserved for him by the piano house because, as he said in his own words, "No one else has ever expressed the slightest interest in it. This has enabled me to carry out some rather radical experiments in regard to the action; in effect, to try to design an instrument for baroque repertoire which can add to the undeniable resource of the modern piano something of the clarity and felicity of the harpsichord." And he did just that, much to the fascination of the public and the critics.

Gould's musical convictions have always been original. As a teenager, doing special studies at Toronto's Royal Conservatory of Music (he had been graduated from there at the age of twelve), he moved from baroque to contemporary composers and the twelve-tone technique, which he calls the "only valid linguistic innovation in the twentieth century." He was not partial to public performances but he had no choice but to follow the pattern. He insisted, however, on out-of-the-ordinary programming, and included many esoteric and intellectual pieces in his recital performances. He has maintained a firm position among the dozen or so top pianists of the world but has typically done so by not performing in public since the 1960s. Convinced that "the habit of concert-going and concert-giving, both as a social institution and as chief symbol of musical mercantilism, will be dormant in the twenty-first century," he decided to confine his work to recordings, film, radio, and television. For him, the media of electronic technology guarantees the sound of "clarity, immediacy, and indeed almost tactile proximity" that he finds necessary to his performances.

Every once in a while his interpretative ideas backfire, however, and one such memorable occasion was a performance of the Brahms D-Minor Concerto with Bernstein and the New York Philharmonic that took place in his last year of public performances and was to have been recorded. Gould's ideas on the piece regarding tempo alone were unorthodox but his rethinking of arch and line drove Bernstein to announce to the public beforehand that he disassociated himself from the interpretation and wouldn't conduct at all were it not for respecting Gould's intellectual and artistic capacities and seriousness of purpose. The performance was heard on a Philharmonic broadcast but I did not think it a good idea to immortalize it on disc.

Gould enjoyed working with Bernstein but his choice of other conductorial colleagues was sharply limited. With Bernstein he felt a kindred spirit in musical adventuring and the only other conductor I remember him seeking out was Herbert von Karajan. They never made records together, at least that I know of, but each admired the other.

With more traditional maestri, however, there was little rapport and

Columbia had quite a number to look after, from a recording stand-point. At one time Bruno Walter, George Szell, Eugene Ormandy, Leonard Bernstein, and André Kostelanetz were all under contract. Bruno Walter was, of course, in his twilight years and for him we had a special symphony orchestra in Hollywood drawn from musicians contracted by the picture studios and from the Los Angeles Philharmonic. This group would be gathered together twice a year for recording purposes. Most of the personnel of what we called the Columbia Symphony remained the same over the seasons. The musicians all wanted the rare experience of working with Walter, particularly when we began recording Mahler. Walter was, in his old age, a beloved spiritual figure and for good reason. He had fought his artistic battles heavily and successfully. He had championed Mahler and Bruckner and lived to see both composers gain a hold on the public.

It was the Mahler saga, however, from early assistant to podium advocate, that particularly caught his fancy and I thought it highly appropriate that in the first blush of the new stereo we should capture as much Mahler as Walter felt like recording. My yearly trip to California to discuss repertoire was always a high light although Walter, not wanting to hurt anyone's feelings, often wouldn't say precisely what was on his mind and I had to listen carefully to every word and inflection to be certain not to misunderstand him. After each visit I would get a "Dear Friend" letter that reiterated what we'd gone over and in its gentle language pinpoint specifics that he wanted done. One of his last projects, about four months before he died, was to record *Das Lied von der Erde* in New York with the Philharmonic. I think everyone sensed that the old man's days were numbered and the orchestra played with special care and affection. Mildred Miller was the mezzo-soprano, a young and beautiful singer whom I'd introduced to him, and as the last take of Ewig, Ewig died away I asked him if he wanted to do anything over again. He looked at me, smiling slightly, and shook his head. "No, no, my dear," he said, "it is beautiful. I have finished." And he embraced me. It was indeed his *ewig*. [Forever and ever].

Some days before the *Das Lied* recording Walter had been in New York to give his final approval on some tapes and was upstairs in the engineering rooms listening when all of a sudden the engineers put down their tape cutters, switched off their consoles, and walked out of their cubicles. It was quite a morning for such a display: not only was Bruno Walter in one booth but others were occupied by George Szell, Leonard Bernstein, and Leopold Stokowski.

Stokowski had recently returned to the label to make one record with the Philadelphia Orchestra, his first time with the group since his departure from it some twenty years earlier. We picked for repertoire the Prelude and Love Death from *Tristan* and *El Amor Brujo* of Falla, with the young and then unknown Shirley Verrett as soloist. In addition I agreed to a small Bach orchestral suite which could be included on a miscellaneous record of shorter pieces.

The biggest difficulty I had with Stokowski was over fee. He had a very grand idea of his worth, but there were other considerations that had to be taken into account, including the fee of the regular conductor, Ormandy, and the amount due to the orchestra itself. Stokowski and I went round and round on this matter and I finally had to tell him that our offer was final and that if he was not prepared to accept it, we would have to cancel the project. He thought about that for an hour or two and called me back to say that he would accept, although I knew from the tone in his voice that he was not the least bit happy. I had a hunch he would get his revenge but I didn't know what form it would take.

The first indication of trouble came at the recording sessions. I got a frantic call from the producer, Howard Scott, saying that Stokowski was insisting on starting the sessions with the Bach, small pieces that did not require the services of the full orchestra. At that time we recorded the orchestras on what was known as the symphonic rate. This meant that we had to pay every member a fee for the first two hours, whether they performed or not, but after that we could cut down to the number of players needed for a specific work. We always started sessions with the largest pieces and Stokowski knew this full well. He knew that by insisting on the Bach he was going to cost us money and since he started receiving royalties from the first record rather than having to wait until the costs of the recording had been recovered, he was in a nice position to push the needle into us. I told Scott to tell him that we would start with the *Tristan*. Scott, with Stokowski evidently standing within earshot, relayed back that unless we started with the Bach, for which he felt in the mood, he would leave the session and not return. I calculated quickly that this would be a real waste since we would have to pay the orchestra for the first two hours whether or not we got one note on tape. I told Scott to go ahead with Stokowski's "mood" and surrendered to obvious pressure. Once he won his point Stokowski moved right ahead and completed his work in professionally good time.

Some weeks later he appeared in my office with the request that he personally supervise the editing and cutting of his tapes and he was prepared to do so that minute if an engineer and booth could be made free. I knew that Walter, Szell, and Bernstein were all upstairs at that very moment and I did not think it a good idea to put Stokowski into the middle of that brew. However, a booth and engineer were free and I took him upstairs, reluctantly but resignedly.

The engineer assigned was Fred Graham, a veteran Columbia expert who had known Stokowski since the days of 78 rpm and the All American Youth Orchestra. When we entered Graham's cubicle he rose to greet the maestro and Stokowski indicated that he would personally like to sit behind the console and maneuver the levels. "I am a member of the union, you see. I have a life membership." And he pulled a faded bit of plastic out of his pocket. Graham, sensing the situation, moved over and let Stokowski sit down. The strains of *Tristan* burst forth from the speakers and Stokowski was caught up in the drama of the music, raising a channel here and lowering one there and putting his inevitable Stokowski touch on Wagner's notes.

The door of the cubicle opened during one of the swelling passages and a colleague of Graham came in to borrow a cutter. He saw Stokowski in Graham's seat and went out the door immediately. In a few seconds the door reopened and in walked the engineering department supervisor. He beckoned me to step outside. When I did so, I noticed every engineer in the place standing in the corridor outside his own cubicle. "Get your conductor friend out of that seat," hissed the supervisor. "Until he's out, the men will not go back to work. His sitting there is a direct violation of our contract." "But he's a member of the union," I responded. "He's an honorary lifetime member. He has the card to prove it." "I don't care if he's honorary president of the United States. Get him the hell out of there or no more work will be done around here and it will be my neck." At that moment the door to Walter's cubicle opened and he stuck out his head. "Where is Jimmy?" he asked plaintively. And he smiled his beautiful smile. "He'll be back in a moment, Dr. Walter," I replied. He nodded his head and closed the door. "All right," I said to the supervisor, "I'll get him out."

I returned to the cubicle and Stokowski was sitting behind the console, his hands folded on his lap. "Is there some kind of problem?" he asked. "Maestro," I said, "you will have to get out of that chair immediately. You are not allowed by union contract to touch those levers and while you are sitting here the whole engineering department is on strike for contract violation." "But I am a member of the union," he repeated, "look at my card again." "I'm sorry," I replied, "but union card or no union card you must leave that chair at once." And I went over to him to help him up. He looked at me for a long moment and then rose. "I will sit alongside Graham and tell him what to do." And he pulled up a seat, placed it alongside the console, and sat down.

I went out into the hall. "Mr. Stokowski did not understand the problem," I said in a voice loud enough to be heard down the corridor. "He is away from the machinery and will sit alongside Mr. Graham to indicate what he wants." The supervisor looked into the room and saw that Stokowski was indeed sitting where I said he was. Several other engineers looked in as well and in a matter of moments everyone had returned to work. I fled back to my office.

One of the Masterworks Department's biggest sellers on a year-in-year-out basis was an organization that cost us absolutely nothing to record. They took care of their own work and their tapes were delivered ready for pressing, jacketing, and sale. This was the Mormon Tabernacle Choir of Salt Lake City. The Choir sometimes came east on tours and on these occasions we would pair them up with the Philadelphia Orchestra to record big choral works. A *Messiah* made this way continues to be one of the best catalogue items to this day. I always felt that while the Mormons did very well they might even be spectacular if they could be persuaded to sing some nonreligious repertoire and at the appropriate moment I was invited out to Salt Lake to meet with Mormon officials and discuss the matter.

Our meetings were extremely formal. I stated that we would like to do a series of historic patriotic songs. I said I felt such an album would reach both the regular market for the choir's records and would introduce their work on a much wider scale. The assembled group looked at me impassively and I took my cue from them. "The albums have been very good for all of us," I said in as unemotional a voice as possible. "I believe the change would be advantageous all around." "When you say 'historic, patriotic songs' what exactly do you mean?" I was asked. "Oh, you know," I said. "Civil War songs particularly." I saw them looking at each other. "Civil War isn't a term we use," they replied. I thought quickly. "How about Songs of the North and South," I replied, "any title that will cover the right repertoire." They thought this might be possible and advised me that they would take the matter under consideration and let me know as soon as possible. "How long will that be?" I asked. They looked sternly at me. "In good time," they replied and the meeting was over.

Some three weeks later I received a letter okaying the project. We selected the songs with the choir's music director, told him the sound we were after, and left the rest in his hands. In about two months tapes were delivered and we did indeed issue the album under the title *Songs of the North and South*. It became an immediate best seller.

What really kept our department afloat, though, was an album, with the Philadelphia Orchestra, of Christmas songs. The genesis of this project was a memo I received from the popular album promotion people the day I arrived at the company. In it the statement was made that if I could ever get the Philadelphia Orchestra to record an album of Christmas music, it would be a big seller, in line with any pop album. I put the memo in the top drawer of my desk and two years later I took it out and thought the moment might be right. There were several problems: first, I had to sell the idea to the orchestra trustees and Ormandy, and second, we had to find an arranger who would set the material in the proper manner. I went to Philadelphia and talked to Ormandy, who was naturally rather skeptical until I stuck my neck out and told him that I thought we could double the orchestra's royalties within a year and this meant, of course, an increase in his share. "I will do it," he said. "And I will take it up with the trustees." I thanked him for his cooperation. "But it will depend on how good and tasteful the arrangements are before I give my final okay," he added. "That's fair enough," I replied, and we shook hands.

Tom Frost, the Columbia producer responsible for recording the orchestra, put his good talents to work on the arranger problem but the longer we looked the more discouraging the results. We could not seem to find anyone who understood the specifics of what we were after and we kept at it for many months. Finally one day Frost came into my office with a slight grin on his usually somber face. "I think we've found our man," he said, putting down on my desk a sketch by Arthur Harris for "O Come All Ye Faithful." "I'm too long away from score reading," I said. "How is it going to sound?" He went to the piano and began an analysis. The gut feeling of its being right crept into my stomach. "Okay," I said, "why not give him a couple of other carols and see what he does?" This was done and after we had four good examples Frost went off to Ormandy for the final word. Ormandy approved and sessions were set for early March.

When the tapes were finished, Frost called me to come and hear them. I was knocked out. We had a winner in anyone's books. The arrangements were tasteful, adding something to the overfamiliar songs, and they were bouncy and catchy enough to appeal to the pop album audience and yet were properly symphonic. They were unique: not like any other Christmas music album on the market.

We marshaled the company behind us and the album was released as the major Christmas offering in the 1952 season. It sprang onto the best-seller charts immediately, can still be heard on radio stations all over the world, and did indeed double the Philadelphia Orchestra's royalties. Some years later a comparable album was made with Bernstein and the New York Philharmonic plus the Mormon Tabernacle Choir but it never caught on. Ormandy and his merry men had the marketplace sewn up tight.

Of all the experiences at Columbia Records, however, one stands out in my mind and always will. Simply stated it was the return to the world of performing of a great musician who had elected to retire from the stage, even from the recording studios, and seemed forever shut away from the public. His name is Vladimir Horowitz.

X

Horowitz

On May 9, 1965, Vladimir Horowitz ended a twelve-year self-imposed exile from the concert stage and returned to Carnegie Hall on an afternoon that will never be forgotten by any of those present. The long, tortuous steps to this return were known to many of his friends and go back to the reasons for his stopping in the first place: physical exhaustion caused by years of concerts and the tensions brought on by constantly trying to live up to his own reputation. There were few, if any, who really thought he would play publicly again.

Three years before, he had begun his re-emergence by signing a new recording contract with Columbia Records, leaving RCA Victor after over twenty years of association. I first found out about the possibility of wooing him over to Columbia late one fall afternoon in 1961 when I received a telephone call from Gary Graffman. Graffman, a close friend of the Horowitzes, said that Horowitz was leaving RCA and that overtures were already being made by other record companies. I'd heard these rumors for years but nothing ever seemed to happen beyond the talk.

Through the Steinways I had known Horowitz for many years, but not intimately and never in a business sense. Nonetheless I telephoned his house that night and when his wife, Wanda, answered I came right to the point. Was it true that Horowitz was leaving RCA and if so could we meet to discuss the possibility of his coming to Columbia? I spoke all this breathlessly and without pause since I didn't trust my crust and nerves to do otherwise. Wanda said the news was true and if Goddard Lieberson and I were interested enough to talk they would be interested enough to listen. Two nights later Lieberson and I found ourselves at the Horowitzes' house on 94th Street around 9:00 PM, seemingly their preferred hour for business conversation.

I'd never been in the Horowitz house before and was therefore unprepared for the sight of their living room with the dazzling collection of French impressionists topped by the famous Picasso portrait of The Harlequin. This was over the extra-long sofa that served as both a sitting and lying couch for Horowitz depending on the mood of the moment. One end of the room was filled by two Steinway concert grands, one of which had been presented to him by the firm on the occasion of the twenty-fifth anniversary of his American debut. The other, I believe, was on loan. The furniture was French but not too forbidding.

Wanda ushered us into the room and presently Horowitz appeared, looking fresh, young, trim, and incredibly energetic. He was impeccably dressed, with a subdued silk shirt and bright bow tie, and his eyes were clear and sparkling, obviously anticipating the conversation ahead. He carried two cigarettes, one of which he placed on the table directly in front of him and other he proceeded to light.

The talk started with Lieberson and Horowitz swapping stories— they were obviously old friends—and every so often matters were brought into focus by Wanda, who had her RCA facts and figures marshaled with the excellence and efficiency of a bank auditor. Nothing seemed to get past those wide, sharp eyes of hers and her Toscanini antecedents (she is the Maestro's daughter) seemed to be very much in command. She recited tales of broken promises and professional carelessness and every once in a while Horowitz would nod agreement or lean over in a conspiratorial manner as if to indicate that his wife was a force to be reckoned with. At appropriate moments I talked about how we worked at Columbia, the spirit of the place, and the whole new youth market that was opening up for classical music.

This seemed to catch his attention and he asked me whether I thought that any young people had ever heard of him. I could sense that this was a very important point and might indeed be a key to a more active professional life. I assured him that there was a market out there made up of people who had heard him and also those who knew him only as a myth: the great Horowitz, flying fingers and flying temperament, nervous, tense, and probably the greatest pianist of his age.

The longer he stayed away the more the myth was fed, and while I did not say so that night I felt that it was possible for too much myth and too long an absence to finally remove him altogether from the public mind. I also sensed that he was a very shy man, someone who needed to know that he was going to be loved, admired, and cared for. I was already beginning to think about who on the production staff could be assigned to him and approach the assignment with the right balance of record professionalism and affection. The evening ended with the assurances that they were not going to make any quick decisions, that they were talking to other companies, and would continue to do so, but would not make any final commitment without seeing us once again. As we left the house I felt guardedly optimistic.

The next days were rather anxious ones. Lieberson had other problems to worry about and I felt it was both my duty and responsibility to keep in touch with the Horowitzes and move things along. I did have one important trip to make, however, to Aspen, Colorado, with Leonard Bernstein. I was anxious for Bernstein to adapt his remarkable television series on Bach for records and had been after him for this project over many months. He finally agreed to talk about the idea while on a five-day skiing holiday and said that the only way this could be done was if I went along. I hadn't been on skis since I was sixteen but after finding out there were beginner slopes and extracting a promise from Bernstein that he do his fancy shussing and jumping with his skiing peers I agreed to go. Betty was disturbed by this and kept warning me that I'd break my leg. She was right. I did, on the last day we were in Colorado. And no one felt guiltier than Bernstein. (I confess I used that guilt to move ahead on Bach.) In any event this put me a little behind in the continuing Horowitz discussions. My right leg was put into a walking cast that thoroughly encased the limb and made it mandatory that I walk with a stout cane. The cast was more than a little clumsy and it did bring out a lot of sympathy and made my visits to the Horowitz house a trifle heart-rending.

Finally there came the night that we'd been waiting for. The Horowitzes agreed to come to Columbia and I was moved when he turned to me and said, very simply: "Will you take care of me?" I said a quiet and heartfelt yes.

Lieberson decided the news of his contract merited a special press conference, and the turnout for it was large. We hadn't completed plans for his first record, although we had already been working on a long-range promotion campaign designed for his worldwide fans of middle age and for the youngsters. I thought that the Horowitz artistry would sell itself but needed to be positioned and exploited. I felt that repertoire should in large measure be up to him. Instinctively I felt that this was a major step he was taking and that he'd be extremely selective in what he put forward on his first disc. I also knew that he was going to listen to his tapes with hypercritical ears and would want to feel totally comfortable in our 30th Street studios. We began a series of tests with Tom Frost, who I felt was the right producer for him. Frost is a serious and experienced record man and musician and would understand the nature of the artist with whom he would now be working. He gave me reports as to how the tests were proceeding and I talked almost daily with either one or the other of the Horowitzes. We were making good progress and slowly but surely, over many evenings at their house, the record began to take shape.

Those nights were fascinating. Betty and I would be asked to arrive around 9:00 PM and we left considerably after midnight. Various ideas were discussed and discarded. As often as possible I would try to stimulate his thoughts sufficiently so that he would go to the piano to illustrate his points. One evening we got on the subject of Liszt and I said that I thought most of Liszt was just bombast and vulgarity. He looked at me curiously as I said this and went to the piano. I followed, looking over his shoulder, and on the music stand were some volumes of Liszt that I had never seen before. Very quietly he asked me if I knew anything about late Liszt music. Then he opened one volume, sat down, and played through an extraordinary piece that sounded more Stravinsky than Liszt. He immediately played another, of a simplicity and gentleness that I found absorbing. He said these works had only recently been edited in Switzerland and were an enormous discovery for him. They were for me, too. I asked if he wanted to include any in his first album and he said he was thinking about it but felt that perhaps they should have an album of their own. Then the discussion moved on to Schumann, a composer he felt had basically been neglected or at least underperformed. He began playing the Fantasy in C Major and became absorbed in the work. I was able to watch him carefully at the keyboard and marvel at his economy of movement. There was not an excess gesture, with hands, body, or head.

Later that night, over coffee and cake, I asked if he was considering a return to the stage. He left the question unanswered. He did steer the talk around to youth, though, and kept asking whether I really thought young people would have an interest in him. I kept answering him in the affirmative. I told him that he'd see for himself when his first album was released. He looked at me skeptically and, I thought, anxiously.

Along with the discussions about repertoire we talked about how the album would be merchandised. Wanda was keen on this subject and I outlined what I thought would be a good campaign. On every point she gently but firmly challenged me and I rapidly learned that if she had chosen to do so she could have outmerchandised R. H. Macy himself. No detail escaped her, from the album cover and jacket notes to the smallest program ad in the remotest concert hall. Horowitz would listen to these discussions, rarely adding anything to his wife's comments, but one knew that he too was taking in every word and relishing the whole process.

Finally the moment came when we had to fix the repertoire and set a schedule for recording and releasing the album. One evening Horowitz presented me with a suggested list and the reasons for each selection. One look and I knew that he had chosen cannily, with an eye on the largest public. There was something for everyone who knew his work—Rachmaninoff, Chopin, Schumann, and Liszt—a perfect recital program for the home and maybe, just perhaps, for the concert hall. But one step at a time. And this first step of a new recording contract was a big one.

The press became excited about the potential upcoming events. Articles and "think" pieces about Horowitz began to appear in the New York *Times* and in the national news magazines. All carried the same general theme: Does this mean Horowitz will return to the stage? Is this the "comeback" that everyone had been talking about for years? Will he actually go into the studio and record? The speculations grew each day, the tensions mounted, and the music world waited.

The day finally came when the 30th Street studio tests were finished, the master merchandising plan completed, the album cover picture chosen, the advertising laid out, and there remained only the job of recording. The first sessions were scheduled for 4:00 PM on an afternoon in May, an odd time by union contracts for studio engineers but the time that Horowitz liked to work. About 1:00 PM on that day my phone rang and a message was delivered to me that he had cancelled his first session. I was jolted, for this was the behavior I had heard about for years. The phone rang a second time; now he wanted to speak directly to me. I picked up the instrument, my heart beating and spirits lowering, to hear a choked and stuffed-up voice apologizing for the cancellation and explaining that he had been fighting a spring cold but that it had gotten the better of him. This, indeed, was obvious. I told him not to worry and asked when he thought he would feel like going to work. He said that above everything else he did not want me to have the impression he was cancelling for temperamental reasons. He was ready and eager to work but could not until he was better. He guessed that in four days' time he would be well enough to start work. I wished him a quick recovery.

Now came other problems. We'd moved studio time hither and yon to accommodate his working hours and this had upset other recording artists, particularly in the Pop Department. When I said that Horowitz had canceled, all my colleagues nodded their heads and winked their eyes. I said Horowitz had a cold. They smiled. I said, "No, this is for real . . . " They smiled. One or two patted me on the back, sighed, and rolled their eyes to heaven—and moved in on the schedule. I was in a tough spot. The Pop Department, under the irascible but galvanizing direction of Mitch Miller, was in the middle of one of its biggest hit periods, with Mitch's Sing-A-Long albums accounting for almost half the company's profits. The other half came from Broadway show albums and such artists as Tony Bennett, Doris Day, and Andy Williams. Who was I, the director of Columbia Masterworks—which, if lucky, might account for 5 percent of company revenues—to spread havoc among the musical gold? I waited for the outbursts to cool down and, God love them, one by one my pop colleagues came to my office asking how they might help. All were musicians of first quality and knew who Horowitz was and what he represented. They shared the feeling with me that if we could finally get him into the studio great things might take place. We reworked studio times and set up another 4:00 PM session five days hence. I smiled a lot and thanked everyone but I had my fingers crossed until they hurt.

The four-day period ended. The morning of the fifth day came and all was silence from the Horowitz house. Noon came and still silence. I asked Tom Frost to call and see if everything was all right. On inspiration I told him to tell the Horowitzes that I was sending a limousine to drive them to the studio. Frost called and came into my office beaming. I told him to order a Carey Cadillac and be at 94th Street at least one hour before studio time.

I was too much of a coward to be in the studio myself. I figured that if there were problems I'd be called and I felt that there was nothing I could do there anyway. The chemistry between Frost and the Horowitzes seemed okay and I knew that Fred Plaut, the senior recording engineer of the company, would get along famously with both of them. The only other person there was Bill Hupfer, the chief tuner for Steinway & Sons, without whom Horowitz would not play a note. For years Hupfer was the only one allowed to tune and regulate Horowitz's piano. A quiet, thoroughly professional man who dealt with many pianists, he had an abiding affection for Horowitz and this was returned in kind. Between Hupfer, Plaut, and Frost I felt matters were under control.

It turned out that the only one who wasn't nervous that day was Horowitz himself. He knew just what he was up to and proceeded to go about his job in a workmanlike manner. The session ended with a great deal of tape in the "can" and a feeling of accomplishment.

Recording sessions continued through May until the album was finished, or rather the first part of the album process was finished, because now came almost the toughest part, the editing. Here Horowitz was an even sterner taskmaster. He wanted to retain the feeling of spontaneity, of a live performance that had accidentally been captured on tape. Above everything else he wanted to avoid the plastic perfection of a studio creation. He wanted the best of both worlds and taxed the production and engineering staffs to the utmost to obtain what was right. I didn't interfere in the procedures. My interest was to get the best and get it with Horowitz happily endorsing the whole process. I looked forward to more recordings and to the public reaction that Horowitz was truly at work again.

The album was released on September 24, 1962, and created a sensation. Within days it had climbed to the top of the record charts and reorders were pouring into the factories. Within three weeks the company had earned back its guarantee payments and both artist and firm were in a profit position. A nice way to start an artistic and business relationship!

Work was now begun on a second album. The sales department was pushing for what it considered a more commercial classical product. I reminded them that at the moment Horowitz could record the C Major scale and it would stir up action at the record counters. What we were all hoping for, of course, was the possibility of a big concerto recording. I wanted the Rachmaninoff Number 3, with either Ormandy and the Philadelphia, or Bernstein and the New York Philharmonic. On this subject Horowitz played with us like a cat with a ball of yarn. He knew how badly we wanted such a record and we knew that our chances of persuading him were almost zero. He spoke of his last concert appearances with the Philadelphia Orchestra and said that he had made an informal pact with Ormandy that if he ever recorded a concerto again he would do it with him. This was fine with me, since the Philadelphia was under contract to Columbia and would be honored by such a project. We even discussed repertoire and I had the feeling that my idea about the Rachmaninoff was not falling on totally deaf ears. He would wax enthusiastic and we'd even begin to talk about halls and schedules and once I almost went to the telephone to call Ormandy to make a tentative date but always, at the last second, Horowitz would pull back, smiling, eyes twinkling, and say that he had to think about it some more.

In the meantime we selected the repertoire for his second Columbia album. The sales department was not going to be happy but this didn't bother me because I felt that the Horowitz public was ready for anything provided it was fresh, exciting, and carried forth Horowitz's artistry. The emphasis of the new album was again to be on a balanced program, a recital at home. Schumann's Kinderszenen was a must. Horowitz felt that this work was so often mutilated that it should be heard under ideal conditions. He also wanted to include pieces by Scriabin, a composer he had long championed in his concert days and whom he felt was wrongly neglected. Scarlatti was to be represented with three sonatas, and Schubert's Impromptu in G-Flat Major rounded out the album. Sessions at the 30th Street studio began in November and December 1962 and the completed album was released to the public on April 15, 1963. Again the critics went all out: here was a new Horowitz, a profound artist and musician with even deeper insights than people had heard before. And the public responded. The album headed up the sales charts immediately.

I was very anxious for the momentum to continue and to judge from many evenings of talk it seemed possible that the idea of a public performance was growing. One night, after some superb cognac, I told Horowitz that I was without a doubt the best concert-valet in the business, that I had started my career doing just that for Jascha Heifetz and though perhaps a little rusty I would be happy to do this for him if he ever should decide to try the concert platform again. He said, "I will remember that."

Meanwhile we began planning his third Columbia recording. I was particularly anxious to have at least one work on this record that would keep the sales department happy. Record company sales departments are strange groups: one would think that having had two Horowitz recordings that sold extremely well they would leave the matter of repertoire up to us. We all knew that we wanted to reach the widest possible public, but before each Horowitz album they went through the same kind of commercial war dance. In any event Horowitz understood the situation and agreed to include the Beethoven Pathétique Sonata in the album as well as the Chopin Revolutionary Etude. Also to be recorded were three Debussy preludes, the Chopin Scherzo Number 1 and Etude in C-Sharp Minor.

Between the start of planning for this recording and the actual execution of it my situation at Columbia Records underwent a change. Lieberson promoted me to vice-president for Creative Services, a catch-all name covering responsibility for the company's advertising, art and design, and sales promotion. This was absolutely splendid except for the fact that it took me away from the whole area of artists and repertory, the guts of the record business, and began to wrap me in corporate clothing. I hated the job and when, a few months after my appointment, William Schuman, the president of Lincoln Center, beckoned me back to the artistic wars I accepted and moved up to his provocative campus. While this changed my professional relationship with the Horowitzes it did not change my personal friendship and the offer I had made if he decided to return to the stage.

My Lincoln Center duties kept me pretty much on the international travel circuit but I was aware that Horowitz's fourth recording was released in December 1964 and it was all Scarlatti. I listened to it at home and enjoyed every note.

Shortly after January 1, 1965, the Horowitzes asked us to dinner. We had a lovely time. Wanda provided an impeccable meal and beautiful wine and, as usual, Horowitz himself ate sparingly. The talk at dinner ranged over many topics—politics, painting, literature, and opera—subjects that fascinates him and about which he has a wide knowledge.

A quiet moment arrived and he asked me whether or not I remembered my promise. I said I did. He then said that he had been visiting his tailor and thinking about having a new morning coat made. I had the feeling that the coat was a lot further along than he was letting on. I told him that I would be out of the country a good deal during the rest of the winter and he said that he thought this would not present any problems. We left the table and went upstairs for coffee and champagne and I kept looking at him throughout the evening wondering if in fact he really was going ahead with recital plans. I knew him well enough not to ask directly, or to ask Wanda,who had been quoted some time back as saying, "An artist must want to play. He must feel he has to play. It is no use to talk." In good time, I knew, he would let us all know.

Soon I began picking up rumors and then facts about practice sessions in Carnegie Hall. One day in March he called Julius Bloom, executive director of Carnegie Hall, and came in to play on the stage. He did this several times, bringing Wanda and a few friends, and in early

April started asking about possible hall dates for later in the spring. Despite moving in and out of the country during those months I was kept up to date on what was happening by David Rubin, the concert and artist manager for Steinway, who had succeeded to the post after Alexander Greiner's death. Rubin knew the facts because he supplied the pianos.

I was in Madrid in March and received word from Betty that Horowitz was going to play in Carnegie Hall in May and was anxious to talk to me about his plans as soon as I returned.

Upon my return I called his house and was asked to come immediately. He told me that the concert would be on a Sunday afternoon at 3:30 PM. The date finally selected was May 9. We talked about price scales and student tickets, although here he still seemed to have the idea that students might not come because they had never heard of him. Julius Bloom and I kept telling him that there would be plenty of young people, if there were tickets for them, and Horowitz insisted that there be tickets and plenty of them.

Horowitz had held a press conference and announced that he would return to the concert stage. It was front-page news in the New York *Times* and widely reported on television and radio. The tickets went on sale Monday April 26. They were sold out in two hours to hundreds of people, many of whom had lined up outside the box office on a rainy and windswept Sunday night.

At about midnight on Sunday, after Horowitz had learned of the lines waiting at Carnegie Hall, he and Wanda took a taxi down to 57th Street, saw the by now sodden army of people with their sleeping bags and blankets and bought them cups of coffee from a corner shop. At 4:00 AM the Horowitzes received the following telegram: "Dear Maestro and Madame: The one hundred of us spending the night in line wish to thank you for the heartwarming coffee and to express the joy and anticipation with which we will wait your return. With love and admiration from all of us. Unsigned."

A few days before the concert he called me. "Just a few things," he said. "What about the air conditioning? Is it onstage? I don't want any onstage but we must be sure the people out front are comfortable. It may be a hot day. And one more thing, please . . . I don't want anyone to talk to me before the concert." I replied, "Of course," and went about other details. "But you must know why I say this." "No, I don't need to know," I replied, "it's your concert and should be run the way you want." "No, but you *must* know, because I have a reason. Years ago when I gave my debut recital in America there was a lot of excitement and I was scared. I told my manager, 'Listen, I don't want to talk with anyone before or after the concert. You take care of this for me.' And he did. Well, the concert seemed to go all right. The audience was very warm and I had many bows and encores and bows and thanks and finally it was over and I went to my dressing room and closed the door. I was so glad it was over and I could hear many people outside. My manager came to me and said so many colleagues were there, Hofmann, Rachmaninoff, Lhevinne and Rosenthal, and they were all excited but, he said, most important was an old man from my district in Russia who was so moved and happy and even if I had said no visitors before or after the concert couldn't he come in just to say a quiet greeting, he wouldn't stay a second. He pleaded and I thought of course, for this old man and my homeland. And he came in with tears in his eyes and took my hands and kissed them and said, 'Horowitz, Horowitz, it was wonderful, it was beautiful, I will never, never, never forget you, never, never, but you must continue to play like today. Never change.' I looked at him and said something and then he went on: 'All the great ones are outside your door, they want to see you, but remember you must never change. Hofmann, why he didn't like the way you played the Chopin, and Rachmaninoff hated the G-Minor Prelude, and Rosenthal was upset with the Brahms, but you must never change. Keep playing just the way you do!' ''

As the date approached I was anxious about many things and in the back of my mind was the thought that at the very last minute he might cancel. But things moved ahead smoothly and on the morning of May 9 it was obvious that nature was going to cooperate. It was a lovely spring day and got lovelier—and hotter—as the hours progressed. I arrived at Carnegie Hall around noon to find that Julius Bloom, newly recovered from a heart attack, was not to be allowed out of his house and had sent a letter with his son. I promised that the son and the letter would see the master *after* the concert. I walked through the hall and looked out at the entrance. There, as far as the eye could see, were thousands of people jamming the sidewalks and spilling onto the avenue. Traffic was choked; nothing was moving. I went around to the 56th Street entrance and saw the same thing. I went back into the hall to do a last-minute check on details. It was now 3:00 PM.

The immediate backstage area was a sharp contrast to the streets. Here all was calm and peaceful and quiet. Two of Carnegie Hall's best ushers were assigned to me and stood patiently waiting for orders. Upstairs, the dressing room was ready, the practice piano in position, the water pitcher filled, the room dusted, cool, and inviting. The stage was unlit. I ordered this to keep the heat down, for now, outside, it was turning into a sweltering spring afternoon and inside the temperature was moving up at a rapid rate. I looked into the auditorium and every seat was filled. So was the standing room. I saw people fanning themselves with their programs and taking off their coats but not a sound came from them. They were obviously waiting in anticipation and waiting patiently. It was now 3:10 PM. My knees buckled with the sudden thought that if Horowitz did not appear I would have to go on that stage and tell them. I turned and walked rapidly back to the 56th Street entrance.

The street was a little more orderly. Hurok arrived: the public applauded and he stood, turning to the right and left for the photographers, smiling and bowing. I joined in the applause. He walked past me and said, "Is he here yet?" I said, "No." He stared at me for a second. "He'll arrive," I said, with a lot more conviction than I felt. He moved into the hall. It was now 3:20, ten minutes before the concert was scheduled to begin. I began to sweat. Sweat is for horses, perspiration is for humans, I thought, anything to keep my mind off the problem at hand. At 3:25, no Horowitz; 3:30, no Horowitz. "What are you going to do?" said a voice, helpfully, at my elbow. It was Lieberson. I asked if he had any suggestions.

At 3:35 his car moved up to the door. "It was the traffic, the traffic," he said. "We couldn't move. It took us almost an hour." He didn't seem perturbed. "How does my suit look?" "Beautiful," I said, "but I think we ought to move into the hall. There are a lot of people waiting." A flashbulb went off in our faces. Horowitz turned and waved. The crowds began to applaud and cheer. I kept him moving toward the entrance. "We're a little late, you know," I said. He took no notice.

Once inside we headed for his dressing room. He removed his beautiful gray gloves and sat at the keyboard playing a few scales. "My hands are cold," he said, taking mine. He promptly dropped them— "You're like ice." I nodded. He turned to one of the ushers. "Here, let me try you," and he took the boy's hands into his. "Ah, that's better. You are warm." The boy looked pleased. I said that I thought the concert ought to begin. "What about latecomers?" he asked. I said that there had not been an empty place in the auditorium since 3:00 PM to my knowledge and probably much earlier. "Really?" he said, sounding pleased.

We went downstairs toward the stage. "Hupfer, is everything all right?" he asked of the Steinway man. Hupfer allowed himself a brief smile. "Everything's okay, Mr. Horowitz," he said. We were now onstage, standing in the wings. I turned to the house electrician and noticed that by the clock over his head it was 3:40 PM. "House lights down, please," I said. The murmurs from the house began. "Stage lights up." Slowly the lights settled; onstage the piano looked bare and forbidding and so alone. I turned to Horowitz and bowed him toward the stage. He did not move, just looked at me with a quiet smile. I took him gently by the shoulders and turned him 180 degrees, put my hand on his back, and gently propelled him out.

He hit the lights, the audience saw him, and to a man and woman and child they were on their feet in one bound, clapping, cheering, crying. The sound waves reached us backstage and for the first time I knew what the scientists were talking about when they spoke of the solidity of sound. The wave literally pushed me back as if someone had hit me. Horowitz stood there and I could see, very plainly, tears streaming from his eyes. The roar continued. Then, suddenly, as if on cue, he straightened his shoulders and moved downstage. He turned and bowed to each section of the house, first stage right, then center, then stage left. He was elegant, measured, dignified, and welcoming. The audience sensed his pleasure at being there and the roar increased. Finally he gestured toward the piano and turned his head as if to ask if they would like to hear him play. He sat at the piano bench and the roar ceased. There was a slight scuffle as people resumed their seats. Perhaps two seconds of this, and then the most deafening silence I've ever heard in my life.

Horowitz raised his hands . . . and brought them down on a cluster of wrong notes. Hupfer, the usher, and I froze: my heart literally pounded so that my shirt vibrated.

He was opening the concert with the Bach-Busoni transcription of the Organ Toccata in C Major, a "good luck" piece for him which he played on his debut program some forty years earlier. The chords crashed; the dissonances, like a fingernail on the blackboard, assaulted the ear. And then, in seconds, it was over. Horowitz was back in control. The music moved in proper order. I stood transfixed. Slowly I became aware of someone else standing alongside of me. It was Wanda, staring out onto the stage, tears streaming down her face, her mascara running, saying over and over in a still-like voice: "I never thought I'd live to see this day . . . I never thought I'd live to see this day." I reached out and put my arms around her. Together we watched the stage as Horowitz brought the opening work to a close. With the last chords another roar broke out and he rose to acknowledge the ovation. He walked off the stage, saw her, and his face relaxed. They looked at one another for a long moment and embraced. Gently I went over to him and pointed to the stage. He looked up, straightened his coat, and walked out once again.

Presently the bows finished and he moved toward his dressing room. I followed up the stairs. He said that he would pause a moment for the latecomers to be seated. I reminded him that there were no latecomers. He looked quizzical. I said again that there had not been an empty seat or corner since much earlier in the afternoon. He stepped to the mirror, ran a brush through his hair, straightened his tie, and started down to the stage. We reached the wings and he told me to be certain to listen to the Schumann Fantasy in C Major, the next piece on the program and the one I remembered so well from one of our earliest meetings. "What a beautiful piece it is!" he said, "so beautiful. You must listen carefully." I agreed. "Now you promise?" he asked. "Yes," I said, "I'll listen with all my heart." While saying this I brushed away some imaginary lint from his jacket and moved him into position to go back again onto the stage. He smiled, paused, winked gently, and stepped out into the light.

The Schumann was indeed a magical and moving experience and Horowitz was in total control. The pattern of the work, its harmonies, melodic line, and stateliness had everyone in its grip. Presently it finished and the ovation began again. Horowitz walked off, a smile on his face. "Not too bad, I think," he said. "It will be better the next time." He returned, bowed, smiled at the audience, trying to share with them the pleasure he had had in the music.

During the intermission, Horowitz lay on the couch in his dressing room, coat off, in quiet good humor. Wanda was there holding his hand. "You think they like it?" he asked. I told him that I did indeed think they did. "But I've been away from concerts for a long time. The next time will be better." We spoke for a minute about the recording that was being made of the performance. "Do you think it will have good sound?" he asked. I said that I thought it would. "But all those wrong notes in the Busoni. I was a little nervous, you know." And he paused a second to reflect. "But if the record is released we must keep those notes. It would not be fair to fix them up."

The intermission drew to a close. He rose from the sofa, changed his shirt and tie, washed his hands and face, put on his cutaway, adjusted his handkerchief in the top pocket, patted his sides, and looked at me. "We should go," he said. I led the way.

The house lights went down, the stage lights up, the same feeling of tense anticipation was felt backstage. "Now the public will hear some familiar things," he said. I touched his shoulder and he bounded out, full of energy and eagerness.

And so it went for the formal part of the program. With the last measures of the Chopin Ballade in G Major the concert drew to a close. The roars were, if anything, louder than they had been at the beginning. "Now the encores," he said. "What do you think I should play?" I loved the question: I knew full well that he knew exactly what he was going to play. "Something dashing," I said. He smiled and went out to play Debussy's Serenade for the Doll, hardly dashing. The audience responded warmly but I sensed they were looking for something else. "What now?" he asked. I smiled. He returned to play Scriabin's Etude in C-Sharp Minor. Again, deafening applause, but still, I felt, something missing. He came back to the wings, and waiting just the right amount of time, he re-entered the stage, bowed, gestured toward the piano as if asking, "Should I?" He sat down, waited until there was not a sound in the hall, and launched into the Moszkowski Etude in A-Flat Major. Up and down the keyboard his fingers raced. They were just a blur. His body didn't move, save for a little smile on his face. The piece sped along and ended with a quick group of chords and a run from one end of the keyboard to the other. As he touched the last note he bounded from his chair, his right hand still moving as if at the instrument. If we thought we'd heard applause before that afternoon everything now paled by the deep-throated roars that reached our ears. It was what they had been waiting for. He came off the stage. "I had to show them some of the old Horowitz!" he said. I laughed. So did Hupfer, Wanda, the usher, the electrician. All of us.

He returned twice to bow, then, holding up his hands, he went to the piano and played Schubert's Träumerei. This baby-simple piece that every student has thumped and banged at in early lessons, this maltreated little horror that symbolizes child recitals, stiff collars, nervous mothers, bored teachers, and bored audiences suddenly was revealed for what it is: a masterpiece of a beauty and simplicity that caught the breath. With this Horowitz left the stage. There was nothing more to say.

The lights went up, the yells and bravos continued. Horowitz went out once again and gave everyone a chance to see him. He pointed to the piano and shook his head. Then clasping his hands as a mock pillow, he indicated that it was time to go home.

The world beat a path to his dressing room. Almost everyone who was anyone in the world of the arts was there to see him. So was the general public. The line was endless. On the street, underneath his dressing room window, a crowd began to form and within seconds had grown to a mob. They started cheering and clapping and shouting "Bravo Horowitz!" I took him to the window to look out. His eyes shone like a child's at Christmas. "There are so many," he said. "Perhaps we will have difficulty leaving the hall." He turned once again to greet his guests. Gracious and charming he was, too, to everyone that came. And there were so many; so many, I thought, who, like Wanda, felt that this day would never come.

And under the window the crowd grew. A distraught Carnegie Hall official came to me full of alarms and excursions. "How are we going to get him out of here? There is no room to move out there." I went with him to the entrance. Near the door was the car. The chauffeur caught my eye, and the crowd, sensing that this was Horowitz's car, drew back to make room. The car was brought to the door. I ran back inside and suggested the moment had come. He was ready, and pulling on his gray gloves and adjusting his topcoat, he descended.

We reached the sidewalk and he was spotted. He stood at the top of the stairs, smiling, bowing, waving, taking his time until as many as possible had had a chance to see him. He entered the car, rolled down the windows. Hands were proffered; he clasped as many as he could. Autographs were sought but not given on the spot. He had devised a system years ago where those wanting signatures left their programs, appropriately marked, with his manager. These were signed at leisure and returned by mail. Slowly the car moved away from the curb and started down the street. It was very regal.

Earlier he had asked Betty and me to come to his house later for a glass of champagne. At this point all I wanted was a hot bath, a stiff drink, and no responsibilities. But we could not refuse and after a brief pause for at least part of the above we appeared at his door.

There, in his house, were collected some of his oldest friends. He was stretched out on the sofa, smoking a cigarette and enjoying post mortems. The champagne was delicious, so were the pastries, and the talk flowed. Presently Horowitz looked at his watch and said he was going upstairs to watch the television news to see if there was anything about his concert on the air. We went up with him to his bedroom and sorted ourselves around the set. When the news came on Channel 2 the first item was about his concert. The reporter was seen outside Carnegie Hall interviewing youngsters as they came out after the concert. One after another were brimming over with enthusiasm, boys and girls both. One girl, with long hair and even features highlighted by tears, said that it was all over between her and the Beatles; her new god was Horowitz.

"See, I told you there was a young audience for your art. Now you can believe it." I felt a touch smug. Horowitz looked at me. "I play because of them," he said. And I realized he meant every word.

A door had been closed that afternoon; another had opened. A whole new generation was there to be conquered, just as he'd conquered their parents and, in some cases, grandparents, a generation before. And he was ready for them. A supreme artist at the peak of his talents, a thoughtful musician who'd decided in mid-career to think things over again. He was ready for them.

And they, obviously, for him.

XI

Lincoln Center Festival

I took up my new position, vice-president for programming at Lincoln Center for the Performing Arts in New York City, on January 2, 1964. I hadn't had any intention of leaving Columbia Records. I was enjoying my life there immensely but when I was made a vice-president I got caught up in the corporate snare. The corporate snare is subtle; before you know it you are committed to stock options, officer positions, competition between you and fellow workers for promotions, and, worst of all, the refocusing of your priorities toward personal advancement rather than achievement. I began to find myself bored and restless.

There was an amusing period when Columbia was being wooed by various Madison Avenue agencies to change its advertising ideas and I was wined and dined in the best restaurants of the city. This was instructive and I made it my business to find out as much as I could about the advertising business and particularly about modern design. I was interested to talk with people who were considered the best in their fields and pick their brains. One never knew where this experience might come in handy in the future.

One night during the year, when I was beginning to admit to myself that the corporate life was not for me, I met Bill Schuman, the president of Lincoln Center, at a meeting of the board of directors of the Walter W. Naumburg Foundation. When the meeting broke up, we walked uptown together and he asked me if I knew of anyone who might be interested in a very good job that was opening up at the center. It was to be director of programming. "What is director of programming?" I asked, "the various constituents take care of their own programming." "Yes," he said, "but there has to be more than that to justify the Center as a Center." He turned to me. "When Lincoln Center was conceived, it was to be the home of the New York Philharmonic and the Metropolitan Opera. Then the New York City Ballet and the New York City opera were added to be housed in a building built especially for them. The theater was originally left out and now it too is included. But what happens to all those companies in the summer, when their normal seasons are over? And what about film? Something must be done about the century's only creative art form." And he went on, talking eloquently about what Lincoln Center might become and in his view must become, must add to the cultural life of the city and the nation. I found myself moved by his ideas and philosophy, and as we reached the canopy of his apartment building I turned to him and said, "Yes, I think I know someone who might be interested. Me." He smiled. "That's what I was hoping you'd say!" With that we shook hands and I went home.

On the walk to my apartment I realized that I'd been seduced as surely and cleverly as ever before in my life. I told Betty about the talk and she quite properly suggested that I think it over very carefully. The Schumans called a few days later and asked us to dinner. We went and spent the evening going over the situation in detail.

I was concerned from the beginning that the artistic role of the Center itself would cause a lot of trouble with the professional staffs and the trustees of the constituent organizations. I had no hesitation about the validity of the concept, only about the ability to carry it out. Schuman explained that he accepted the presidency of the Center with clear trustee agreement on his goals. He had insisted that the Juilliard School be included in the Center's plans so that, when the complex was finished, the highest professional and professional training standards would be side by side in an atmosphere of intercommunication. He was optimistic about his chances for success. When we left the Schumans' apartment that night, Betty turned to me and said, "You must try it. You'd hate yourself if you didn't." I agreed.

I went to see Lieberson and told him that the corporate vice-presidential life was not for me, that I missed my direct work with the artists, and that I was going to Lincoln Center to get back in the swim. He was shocked, I think, and putting pencil to paper, made some rapid calculations. "You'll be losing $75,000 profit from your stock options alone!" he exclaimed. "I don't think you can afford that." "That's unfair," I said. "I know I can't afford it. But I'll go crazy here in corporate heaven and then it will cost a lot more to keep me in a quiet institution!" And we bantered back and forth until finally he saw that I had made up my mind. "All right," he said, "if you must go to that nest of vipers—and take my word, it will be a nest of vipers, Bill Schuman notwithstanding—then you must go with rank. I'll talk to Bill about this."

And indeed he did, for the next thing I knew the title of director of programming had been changed to vice-president for programming, my letter of agreement was signed, and I took up residence at the Center in the beginning of 1964.

At that time only Philharmonic Hall was open for performances. It had opened in September 1962 and Betty and I had been there for the opening night, which was a social success and an acoustical disaster. Various attempts were made to patch up the hall during 1963 and plans were under way for extensive revisions in the years ahead. The New York State Theater was the next building scheduled to open and my first task was planning for this event. I was also plunged immediately into a boiling cauldron of wild and ungovernable temperament.

Morton Baum, the effective and peppery chairman of the board of the City Center of Music and Drama, was determined that the State Theater was going to be exclusively in the hands of the City Center; Schuman was equally determined that the building would remain under the control of Lincoln Center. Baum had Lincoln Kirstein, George Balanchine, and Julius Rudel on his side; Schuman had his executive committee, headed by John D. Rockefeller III.

The Vivian Beaumont Theater was also shaping up to an explosion. The Lincoln Center Repertory Company was already launched and a temporary theater built on property of NYU on West 4th Street housed them for their first season. Elia Kazan and Robert Whitehead were the co-directors: Kazan the brilliant and forward-looking director and writer and Whitehead the experienced producer. They had been warned not to start their company until the building was ready but had ignored the warnings and gotten their board of trustees to agree to launch their group ahead of the completion of the Beaumont Theater.

The Metropolitan Opera was protesting everything. Rudolf Bing did not want the City Opera anywhere near his company, let alone in a building a few feet away. In this he was thoroughly supported by the president of his board, Anthony A. Bliss. Bliss was also a trustee of Lincoln Center but seemed to hold no brief for it as an institution in the arts, only as a real estate project.

I met Bliss shortly before joining the Center. Schuman wanted me to meet most of the key trustees in advance and in the case of Bliss he arranged a luncheon at the Plaza Hotel. Bliss tackled his food with determination, hardly spoke to me at all as he was concentrating on Metropolitan matters with Schuman. As we were finishing our lunch a waiter, pale and shaking, came to our table to ask if we'd heard the news. We said no. He told us that President Kennedy had been shot in Dallas and was on his way to a hospital. He began to cry while pouring coffee. After he'd finished we looked at each other. Bliss said he did not like Kennedy but this was no way to behave. And we all rose to go. I think almost everyone in the country remembers where they were when they heard the news. I'll never forget. I was with Anthony A. Bliss.

Still, Lincoln Center's troubles were not just confined to the performing organizations. Schuman's successor at Juilliard was Peter Mennin, the composer and former head of the Peabody Institute in Baltimore. Mennin had firm ideas on Juilliard's role and fought hard for them. The Library for the Performing Arts was having its problems, too, but these were always brought to the conference table in a firm but gentle manner.

The New York Philharmonic was the only organization already working in its new home and was therefore the only one with a firsthand knowledge of the many problems facing the Center. The Philharmonic's arrangement with the Center and Philharmonic Hall was simple: the Philharmonic was the prime tenant and had first call on the time needed for its activities. Other rentals were sought out for the remaining dates. The total of the hall's income and expenses would be balanced at the end of the year and whatever deficit there was would be shared on a fifty-fifty basis between the two organizations. The Center ran the hall. The only problems here were that the hall was a bomb acoustically and despite being occupied almost every night of the year, the costs of operations were horrendous and the deficit at the end of the year far larger than anyone had anticipated. The Philharmonic was, obviously, unhappy and relations grew tense.

In the meantime plans were moving ahead to complete all the buildings and a vast fund-raising drive was under way with John D. Rockefeller III at the helm. Mr. Rockefeller seemed to rise above all the tensions and moved with a singleness of purpose that thrust everything else aside. He believed in creating a great new area for the performing arts and while he was not much of a fan of them himself, he recognized that others were and he felt obliged to do his part. Schuman had convinced him of the necessity for the Center to have its own artistic and educational activities and a fund was created for these purposes. This in itself caused extra resentment on the part of the constituent organizations which felt that any artistic or educational money should go directly to them. They eyed the Lincoln Center Fund like a flock of vultures.

Undaunted, Schuman moved ahead to create the Lincoln Center Educational Department and persuaded a colleague from Juilliard days, Mark Schubart, to head up these activities. Recognizing that film had been left out of the Center's planning altogether, Schuman forced through creation of the New York Film Festival. His selling point on this was not only about the art of film itself but also the practical point of having the festival occupy time in Philharmonic Hall before the beginning of the music season and thus assure additional income.

The trustees agreed and in 1963 the first New York Film Festival was launched under the joint directorship of Amos Vogel and Richard Roud. Vogel was founder of Cinema 16, an early attempt at showing classical films on a semicommercial basis. He was the administrator. Richard Roud, a Bostonian transplanted to London, was the program director of the British Film Institute and, like Vogel, a film scholar and critic of impeccable credentials. He was the New York Film Festival's program director and this immediately put him in conflict with Vogel, who felt his credentials for program work were just as valid as Roud's and must be taken into account. My predecessor as overall programming chief, Richard Leach, had to contend with this problem the first year. It became my responsibility in 1964.

That first year the festival was held in conjunction with the Museum of Modern Art, whose film department under the direction of Willard Van Dyke had pioneered for the proper recognition of film as an art form. Van Dyke was naturally conscious of his contributions and looked on his new association with Lincoln Center in part with pleasure and in part with suspicion and envy.

Beginning with the art work of Larry Rivers, who designed a brilliant poster announcing and promoting the festival, the whole enterprise was headed for success. The media seized on it as a project worthy of the Center's existence, the constituents were silent because it in no way invaded their territories, and the public seemed ready for it. Philharmonic Hall, with its 2,800 seats, played to 90 percent capacity during the two weeks the festival lasted, and the Museum of Modern Art, where special showings were arranged in the afternoons, also played to capacity. The selection of films came in for a great deal of comment and during the festival time there was little else talked about in the cultural and intellectual circles of the city. Passions flared; people had a sense of involvement. Young people flocked to the films and were not shy about voicing their opinions. Many of the film directors who came were treated to heroes' welcomes or villains' defeats.

At the end of the festivities, the first New York Film Festival was pronounced a success, even though it lost money. Schuman covered this from the growing Lincoln Center Fund and the trustees, although completely baffled by its impact, realized that film at Lincoln Center was here to stay.

By the time the second New York Film Festival rolled around I was in office and Vogel and Roud had to report to me. Together we talked over the possibilities of expanding festival activities to take in forums, discussions, debates, and other appropriate dynamics based around the art of film. All during our talks I could see the growing tensions between the two men. Vogel, square and Germanic, stubborn, academic and single-minded, had gone through experiences of trying to keep a nonprofit film enterprise alive despite industry apathy and a loyal but moneyless public. Roud, dark, suspicious, nimble, with impeccable taste and quicksilver mind, had organized the London Film Festival, the pattern of which was followed in setting up the Center's festival. Both men admired each other's abilities; both men jockeyed for prominence. Schuman and I were in the middle, but most of the judgments fell to me because he had to tend to other business. I sensed that the Film Festival could be the beginning of an important new constituent if it could get through the next years without too great a deficit and could keep its growing and administrative pains in the family and not spread all over the media. Basically we were able to do this and most of the heat between the two men stayed in my office.

Meanwhile I had other responsibilities. One of Schuman's dreams was to create a great international festival of the arts during the summer, when the constituents' programs were finished for the season and the buildings could be used for off-season income. The festival idea was one of the things he sold the trustees when he agreed to come as president. Schuman scheduled the first one for 1967, when all the Center buildings, except the Juilliard, would be finished and the Center could provide an opportunity for New Yorkers and visitors to the city to feast at the arts' tables in full swing. Lincoln Center Festival '67 was the working title; I was the officer in charge.

Schuman and I spent many hours together planning the events we wanted. It seemed to us that we should try introducing foreign and domestic regional theater companies of distinction that would not be presented in New York because of the high factor of commercial risk. We also thought the same about certain musical attractions that could not weather the usual route of management presentation. Chamber music

ensembles fitted into this category, as well as some of the underpre-
sented symphony orchestras. Since 1967 was to be the year of the big
Canadian World's Fair as well, it seemed natural to cooperate with the
Canadians and with various other governments who were already com-
mitting funds for overseas artistic activities.

But by far and away the biggest part of our planning centered around
opera. We felt it was high time that New York have a chance to see
some of the great foreign companies whose reputations were significant and whose style complemented both the City Opera and the Met.
The Metropolitan had, of course, primacy in operatic activity at the
Center. It was written into its lease that nothing of an operatic nature
could be produced by the Center without its agreement. The new opera
house was scheduled to open in September 1966 and we planned to
present the first visiting group in the summer of 1967. Our talks were
taking place in the early winter of 1964 and we realized that if we were
to mount our first festival three years hence, we had a lot of planning
work to do quickly.

The idea of Festival '67 was first presented to the Lincoln Center
Council in March of 1964. The Lincoln Center Council was made up of
the professional heads of each of the constituent organizations plus
Schuman, Schubart, the Center's attorney John Mazzola, and myself.
It was a snappish group; everyone defended his own position, heavily
criticized Lincoln Center for every action it took, and jockeyed for access to what was imagined to be the Center's vast financial resources.
The meetings were miniature Security Council sessions; each person
talked politely from his official position and his colleagues listened
without necessarily absorbing anything being said. Schuman and I
knew we were going to have a tough time ahead of us once the idea was
put on the table, but we hoped to counter expected negative reactions
with the invitation of paying for extra season activities of each of the
groups to fit into the total artistic presentations of our season.

The expected negative reactions came in a flood. Each member stated his opposition to the idea and tempers grew heated. At the right moment Schuman introduced the concept of extra paid work for the
constituents and this gave several moments of pause. Finally Carlos
Moseley, the bright and capable managing director of the New York
Philharmonic, took the plunge, indicating that such an idea would not
be detrimental for any of them. The project would benefit everyone
and, as long as it was at the total financial risk of the Center itself,
should be tried. Bing was adamant: there would be no foreign opera
companies lest the press make invidious comparisons. The City Center
was silent. It did not occupy the State Theater in the summertime; a

new unit had been formed called the Music Theater of Lincoln Center under the artistic direction of Richard Rodgers to present classic musical plays for limited runs and 1967 was to be its first season. *The King and I* had been selected as the opening work, to be followed by *The Merry Widow*, and Rodgers had already voiced his enthusiasm for the festival idea many weeks before. The Lincoln Center Repertory Company also relinquished responsibility for the Vivian Beaumont Theater in the summer and was not in a position to produce a special festival production. That left the Metropolitan and the New York Philharmonic in a position of being helped from festival activities and Moseley was not going to oppose the project. That left only the Metropolitan, which generally opposed any idea anyway, and it became my job to see if we couldn't get it to change its mind, give us a three-week special season that we would pay for, and join with us to welcome the presentation of an appropriate foreign company.

Shortly after the council meeting I went to see Bing in his office. He greeted me politely and made his continued opposition absolutely clear. We were joined in our discussion by one of his assistant managers, Herman Krawitz, in charge of business affairs for the company. Krawitz came to the Metropolitan at the suggestion of Anthony Bliss, who felt that Bing needed help in reorganizing the stage departments of the house and that these areas had to be surveyed and reported upon in a manner that could lead to changes. Krawitz's report evidently made some sense to the board for he was engaged by the company and was, to all intents and purposes, the second in command. The other assistant managers were John Gutman, former music critic for a leading Berlin newspaper and old friend of Bing, now artistic adviser; Robert Herman, artistic administrator; and Francis Robinson, in charge of box office and press. Robinson, a very old friend of Betty's family and of mine, was former press agent for the likes of Alexander Woollcott, Katharine Cornell, and Cornelia Otis Skinner, and had worked for Sol Hurok. He originally came to the Met to handle tours when the tours were being booked by the Hurok organization. He gave the Metropolitan a good public image both in New York and across the country.

Krawitz listened as I talked with Bing and soon was adding his thoughts, which I was surprised to find were very supportive of Lincoln Center's position. He pointed out to Bing that a three-week postseason guaranteed by the Center would put the Met ahead economically; in addition to paying the Met for its performances, the Center would have to pay for rental of the house to present a foreign company. This would include the expense of stagehands, ushers, box office, and other front-of-the-house personnel as well. I sensed that it would be wise of me to leave the meeting and let the two of them talk it out.

A few days later Bing called Schuman and indicated that the Met was willing to mount a special post-season festival but was still not in favor of a visiting company.

We felt that the whole concept of an international festival was being jeopardized by this stubborn resistance and that we had to go directly to the Met board to explain the situation and persuade them to change their minds. This action was started between Bliss and Schuman but got nowhere, since Bliss was clearly supporting Bing. John Rockefeller finally had to be brought into the situation because he had received an enormous gift from the German government for the opera house and in return the Germans had indicated that they hoped the first foreign company to visit the new theater might be a German one. Since Schuman and I had decided long before that we wanted the Hamburg company to be the first to come, this presented no problem to our planning and Rockefeller began talking to members of the Met board. Pretty soon the whole matter became a cause célèbre between the Center and the Met; it was resolved only after acrimonious meetings where the Met board was divided into factions and the majority finally agreed to override Bliss and Bing. We had the go-ahead for a visiting company but had incurred the wrath of the general manager and president of the board in doing so. I was determined that we would mend that rift and went to see Bing to discuss repertoire.

Once the decision went against him, Bing was thoroughly realistic and we began to talk over professional matters in a proper way. He thought the Hamburg company was a good idea, particularly since it specialized in modern and unusual repertoire and did not make a habit of engaging international superstars. He agreed that the Center and the Met would present the company jointly, although he would take absolutely no financial responsibility. I realized that he was getting the best of the bargain without any risks.

With the Met's agreement in hand, I set out for Europe to get things organized. Before going I called the German consulate in New York and talked with the cultural officer, a delightful woman named Haide Russell. The Hamburg company would obviously require considerable government support and I wanted to set the wheels in motion for this. My initial meeting with Miss Russell was the forerunner of many more; before we were through, the entire German consulate, UN office and Washington embassy became involved. The Hamburg visit was going to be turned into a major cultural event all over the country, even if it was scheduled to play only in New York and possibly Montreal.

Miss Russell and the embassy arranged for me to meet the acting minister of culture of the Federal Republic of Germany in Bonn and I set out on my fund-raising mission. Upon arrival in Cologne, the airport serving Bonn, I was paged over the loudspeaker system as I was going through immigration and customs. I went to the desk as bidden and there, waiting for me, was a secretary, an aide-de-camp, and a chauffeur. I barely had time to retrieve my luggage when I was whisked into a large Mercedes-Benz town car and was off at a flying clip for the capital. The secretary explained that the minister had agreed to see me at noon and as the plane was a little late we had to make up the time. And we did. At one point sirens blared and the road cleared of any stray vehicles and people. I felt very important, rushing in a government car to the seat of German power.

We pulled up in front of a large building that housed, among other things, the foreign ministry. The chauffeur leaped out, opening the door for me with heels clicking and a short bow at the waist. The secretary and the aide-de-camp ran around to the front of the car, took my bag, and led me into the building. As we entered the guards pulled up to attention and saluted. I felt like all those figures one used to see in countless newsreels, walking into mysterious buildings for grave conferences among unsmiling people. Albert Basserman, the German actor who played a foreign minister in *Foreign Correspondent*, crept into my thoughts and I was inwardly smiling and bowing around each corner.

We arrived outside the minister's door and I was beckoned into his anteroom. I had barely a moment to splash water on my face and comb my somewhat travel-weary hair when double doors opened and I was ushered into the presence. I don't know what I expected in the way of a human being occupying such an important office but I was totally unprepared for the man I met. He was young, tweedy, looking more like a Princeton professor than a government official. He wore gray flannels and an odd jacket, smoked a pipe, and had a warm smile on his face. In faultless English he bade me sit down and asked me what he could do for me. As he did this two side doors opened, as if on cue, and two other gentlemen joined us for what I suddenly realized was to be my big presentation.

I began by reminding them of the enormous debt Lincoln Center felt it had toward the German government, which had given the millions necessary to build the Metropolitan Opera house backstage area. I traced the history of the Met and how it had stood for the best in operatic culture with particular emphasis on the great days of the German wing. I spun stories of Leopold and Walter Damrosch; I spoke of anything German I could think of, except, of course, World War I and World War II. I then led up to my climax: with the building of the new Met there was the opportunity, for the first time, to present a major foreign company in New York, and the Met and Lincoln Center were hoping this might be a German one. I paused at this point, lit a cigarette, and waited to see their reaction.

The three men conferred among themselves for a moment and asked me what year we were thinking of and what company. I had been warned by Haide Russell before leaving that the minister was very partial to Munich, being a Bavarian himself, and would undoubtedly, if at all interested in the project, push the Bavarian State Opera. I replied that we were interested in a visit in June 1967 as the major event in our contemplated Festival '67, and that we would like to discuss the Hamburg State Opera. "Why Hamburg?" he replied immediately. "Why not Munich? The Bavarian State Opera is the best in Germany and perhaps we should be represented by them!" I paused a moment before replying. "No, Mr. Minister," I said, "we do not think so. Please let me tell you why." I could see his eyebrows rising. "Please do," he replied, looking over at his colleagues. I took a deep breath. "There is no question that the Bavarian State Opera is a magnificent company and one that would bring great credit to Germany, but it is very like our own Metropolitan. Its repertoire is similar, its artists frequently appear at the Met, its productions follow traditional lines and in New York it would not represent something different. We feel that the pioneering work done by Hamburg in the last years, work that has made operatic history and brought new theatrical excitement to the art, should be seen by the public and would represent something new and fresh. It would show the artistic vitality of your country as no other organization could."

I paused for breath. I noticed that all three men were looking at me intently. I went on along similar lines, stressing the vitality that I felt was all important for New York to see. I kept my eyes on them, and when I sensed that I was about to overstate my case, I stopped, saying how grateful I was to them for receiving me and that I knew they had many other pressing matters. "No, no," said the minister. "Please continue." "No sir," I replied, "I think I've said enough. The one favor I would ask is to know from you as soon as possible whether or not the German government would consider our request, and if so, for how much money." "But we will consider that immediately!" he replied, and lapsed into German for conversations with his companions. I rose and walked to the window. The view looked up and down the Rhine

River and I could see barges and tugs and small pleasure craft making their way through the currents.

"Mr. Chapin," he called out after a few minutes, "we have a proposal for you." I returned to my place at the table. "We feel your arguments on behalf of Hamburg make sense. We also feel that we must take advantage of your invitation. Our problem is that whatever we do for you must also extend to the Montreal World's Fair. If the fair people will agree, I am prepared to tell you that we will make one million marks available as subsidy from Bonn." With that he rose and put out his hand. "Thank you for coming to see us." We shook hands, the door behind him opened, and he left, followed closely by the two other men. I sat there a touch dazed, trying to make a quick computation about the marks-dollar value. The door reopened and the secretary and aide-de-camp reappeared. "Now it is time for lunch!" they said, and ushered me out of the room and down the stairs to a small dining room. We took a table near the river and I let them do the ordering. They were polite, solicitous, impersonal. After lunch they escorted me down to the main hall, my bag reappeared at my side, they bowed, wished me well, and departed. I was left there, briefcase in hand, bag at feet and not the slightest idea what to do next. Gone was the chauffeured car, gone the aides and secretaries. After three hours, like Cinderella, my coach and four had dwindled to dust.

I asked the guard about hotels. He spoke practically no English at all but we communicated with my schoolboy German and his Hollywood English. He found me a cab, the hotel he recommended miraculously had a room, and I had a well-earned nap. Some hours later I arose, took a shower, changed my clothes, and went downstairs to find the bar.

It was a lovely May night and the breezes from the river flowed gently over the hotel balcony. I took a seat at a small table and ordered a dry martini. I looked over to my right and there, sitting at an equally small table all by himself, was Willy Brandt. He was sipping a beer and looking straight ahead, lost in thought. I ordered some supper and tried to figure out what to do next. With the government promise of a million marks it seemed to me that we were on our way but I had no way of knowing whether or not that indication was going to be honored. I also felt that it wasn't anywhere near enough to cover expenses but it was a first step and the next had to be to contact Hamburg.

I put a person-to-person call in to the Hamburg Opera for intendant Rolf Liebermann, whom I'd never met. I had heard, however, that he was at the opera house almost every night and I was taking a chance that he could be reached. In a few minutes, the phone rang back and when I picked it up a voice said, "Liebermann!" "Mr. Liebermann," I said cautiously, "I'm Schuyler Chapin, vice-president of Lincoln Center in New York. I've just come from a meeting with the acting cultural minister and asked for subsidy to let a German company come to New York in 1967 and play at the new Metropolitan Opera House as part of Lincoln Center Festival '67." And I went on without pausing, "We want the Hamburg Opera. He says that he will make a million marks available for New York and Montreal. I think we better meet and talk!" There was no hesitation. "A million marks, you say?" "Yes, but I don't know whether or not we can depend on that." "I do," he replied. "We can. You better come to Hamburg and we must talk. Can you come tomorrow?" I said I could. "Good. Call in the morning when you've arranged your plane and I'll give you details. A million marks, eh? Not bad for a start." And he rang off.

The next day I booked a flight for early afternoon, and spent the balance of the morning looking around Bonn. I was particularly anxious to visit the Beethoven House, for Bonn had only one meaning to me and that was the site of Beethoven's birth. I arrived there but the house was closed. I then walked around the city, looked at the new concert hall, and realized that Bonn was, to say the least, not very inspiring.

I flew on to Hamburg and found a message from Liebermann to meet him at 6:00.

After unpacking I went for a stroll around the city, looking for signs of the destruction from the Second World War, and I could find almost nothing. The buildings all seemed trim, neat, and ageless. I looked carefully along the Colonnaden, the area directly behind the hotel that was dominated by the new Steinway Haus, the first new office building in the city after the war. Hamburg was the European headquarters for Steinway & Sons which, oddly enough, had never been a German business. It was always American, never independent of New York, and in Germany this had caused troubles in the Hitler days. It was useful after the war because Hamburg was in the British zone and American companies were given all the help they needed to rebuild. Hamburg also is an extremely independent city with people who are very much like New Englanders. They're hardworking but mind their own business and expect others to do the same. I was told that Hitler never came to Hamburg: he feared for his life. I'm prepared to believe it.

At 6:00 I presented myself at the stage door of the opera house and was taken upstairs to Liebermann's office. "So you have a million marks!" he said smiling. "I'll try to spend it!" And he ushered me into his office. "Scotch?" he said, pouring two glasses. "Yes," I said, feeling the need of a drink. We clicked glasses. "To our project!" he called out and we drank.

"Look," he said, after a few moments. "The performance starts at seven-thirty. We can talk for a while, then I show you the theater, and we sit together in the house. Afterwards we will have supper. Does that sound all right?" I said I thought it sounded wonderful. "You must meet some of my colleagues." And he buzzed his secretary. "Send in Paris," he said, and a moment later the door opened to admit a short, thickly set man with iron-gray hair and an infectious grin. "Paris minds the budgets and tells me what I cannot do. But sometimes I do it anyway!" We shook hands.

I knew quite a little about Liebermann, even though we'd never met before. I greatly admired his compositions, particularly his Jazz Concerto. He was a great friend of Lieberson and of Stravinsky. He had been in charge of music at the Hamburg Radio before being offered the opera house and had made quite a reputation for the city in promoting modern music. Rumor had it that when he was given the opera post he made it clear to the city fathers that he intended to champion contemporary opera and to build a repertory company with singers who could also act. He was given the green light and the money to do it. In less than ten years he had made the Hambug State Opera world famous. The public supported him; the good burghers realized that while what he was doing was not necessarily to their taste, it was good for their city. He gave them their needed doses of Wagner, including a yearly *Ring* cycle, and the other classic operatic repertoire as well. For these performances he brought in the best stars available. He presented a balanced ticket and his public were for him.

After a few minutes with Paris we went downstairs to the stage. The opera house had been almost completely destroyed during the war, but the stage had been saved because during the fire-bombing the iron curtain was lowered and water hosed onto it. It heated and glowed but the water kept the temperature under control. Right after hostilities ended the Opera began again with the audience sitting on the stage and a temporary stage erected over the street. A few years later this had all been replaced with a new house but the original stage was kept and returned to its proper use. The house itself was utilitarian. The boxes all looked like opened bureau drawers; the seats were soft and larger than most theater seats. The hallways, corridors, and promenades spacious but impersonal. All the attention was focused on the stage. It was a theater with a minimum of fuss; I missed only the feeling of intimacy that one often finds in more traditional houses. The sightlines were excellent; the acoustics superb.

At exactly three minutes before 7:30 Leibermann and I entered the auditorium and went to seats in the first row. When the lights went down and the conductor entered the pit he looked over at once to where we were sitting and made a slight bow in Liebermann's direction.

During the intermission we walked out to the front lobby and there we stood while members of the audience came up to him and paid their respects. He talked with each one who addressed him, frequently bowing and clicking his heels and kissing the hands of the women. We had a glass of champagne and every once in a while he would introduce me. When he did so I sensed he was introducing me to important Hamburgers and I did my best to give a good impression. As we returned to our seats he asked me to come with him again for the next interval to meet certain officials of the Hamburg Senate.

After Act II we returned to the lobby and this time sought out various special figures. I did my best to talk about Hamburg and New York and Lincoln Center and how we were all hoping that some exchange between our cities might someday be arranged. I stayed away from any specifics regarding the Opera, taking my cue from Liebermann and sensed that we were laying out the groundwork for what might have to be additional monies to assure the trip.

At the end of the opera we went backstage where Liebermann greeted the artists and the stagehands and had a word to say to every one of them. I could see that this attitude was appreciated.

After we'd finished up backstage we went out the stage door and into a small garage behind the theater where Liebermann opened the door of a snappy Mercedes-Benz roadster and we roared out into the streets. In a few minutes we pulled up in front of a modest building on the other side of the Alster, Restaurant Lembkers. "This is one of the great restaurants of Europe," he told me. "I suggest schnapps and beer and you must try the herring in sour cream. It must be the best in the world." I took his advice and it was spectacular. I followed this with one of the best tartar steaks ever and washed everything down with the smooth but dangerous combination of schnapps and beer.

"We must bring a great repertoire to New York," I began. "We must show New York what you've accomplished here." "What does Bing say to all this?" he asked abruptly. "He must be very unhappy." I told him the whole story. He shook his head. "In Europe we travel everywhere and are welcome as guests. I don't want to make the trip any other way." "Don't worry," I said. "You won't be unhappy."

The next morning we met again in his office and began a tentative list of repertoire. We also looked at calendars and made a preliminary schedule for New York. "We must go to Montreal first," he said, and picking up the phone, he put a call in to the mayor's office. "I want to make certain we get this trip, not some other company," he said, and winked. When the mayor got on the line Liebermann explained the whole project and I could see from the expression on his face that he was making progress. After ending the call he said, "We will have his full support; also that of the Senate. They will see that Bonn doesn't change its mind!" And he sat back laughing. "We're going to make this trip and we'll make history!" I couldn't have agreed more.

I flew on that day to England to meet with Lord Harewood, a cousin of the Queen and director of the Edinburgh Festival. Harewood had pulled off a coup at a recent festival when he'd brought the Prague National Opera from Czechoslovakia in productions of *Rusalka* and *The Bartered Bride*. I wanted his operatic advice on our Hamburg project, particularly because I knew of his expertise in this area of Europe. He was immediate and definite in his opinion: Hamburg was the best in Europe, bring them by all means.

London and Yehudi Menuhin were next on my list. I wanted the first festival to have elegant chamber music and I was anxious to see whether Menuhin would be interested in bringing his new Bath Chamber Orchestra to New York. I had met him once or twice and had nothing more than the slightest nodding acquaintance. I did know his manager, the redoubtable Ian Hunter, managing director of Ibbs and Tillet and earlier an assistant to Rudolf Bing in the days when Bing created the Edinburgh Festival. Hunter has four daughters the same age as our four sons and we would often sit speculating how to marry them off to each other. I took my idea to him and he reacted favorably, feeling that Menuhin would like nothing better. The problem was, of course, scheduling and money, but I felt those items could wait until we had Menuhin's endorsement. Hunter called Menuhin and an appointment was made for me at his home later that day.

The Menuhin house is warm, comfortable, and very English. His wife Diana is strong, wiry, sharp-featured, amusing, and bright, and keeps her eyes on everything her husband does. Menuhin is an American but has lived in England for so long he has picked up an occasional inflection of English speech. I was made most welcome, given a delicious cup of tea, and found myself feeling right at home. I launched into the reason for my visit and was pleased by the Menuhins' reactions. "We simply must find a way. It would be absolutely wonderful to participate in such a project!" His enthusiasm was genuine. "I'll get together with Ian Hunter and see what the venture might cost," I said, "and then perhaps we can put our heads together and find the money somewhere." They both agreed.

During the next days Hunter and I worked out budgets and schedules and when we came to the subsidy needed I thought the figure was less than I had anticipated. Taking into account a reasonable box office return, the whole venture could be pulled off, particularly if other dates could be found to offset the cost of transportation. Hunter agreed to take this up with Menuhin's New York management and keep me advised.

I returned to New York and reported to Schuman just as all hell was breaking loose. Bing had had another change of heart and was now fighting again to prevent any foreign company from coming to "his" house. I went to see him to report on my talks with Liebermann and he repeated his feelings that he didn't want the New York critics making comparisons. I told him that the repertoire we were discussing was nothing like his. We tentatively planned *Mathis der Maler* by Hindemith; *Lulu* by Alban Berg; *Jenufa* by Leos Janacek; *Jacobovsky and the Colonel* by the contemporary German composer Giselher Klebe; as well as Stravinsky's *The Rake's Progress.* and a new work by the American Gunther Schuller to be based on a motive suggested by Franz Kafka called *The Visitation*. There would also be a concert performance of Weber's *Der Freischütz* at Philharmonic Hall.

I reminded him that we were talking in 1964; that the new opera house wouldn't be opened until 1966 and that this festival wasn't scheduled until the summer of 1967. I reminded him that we were also adding three weeks of extra Met performances as part of the festival. I suggested that he might have a difficult time explaining to the public why he wished to prevent such a visit and might also have a disagreeable moment or two dealing with the diplomatic problems as well.

He looked at me while was talking and asked me for a cigarette. "I've given up smoking, you know, but this conversation makes it necessary for me to have a cigarette." "Certainly," I replied, lighting it for him. "With that repertoire what kind of sale are you expecting?" he asked. "We are budgeting for 75 percent capacity," I replied. "That sounds high to me," he commented, "but that is, of course, none of my business. I'm glad Lincoln Center is so rich that it can afford the losses." I reported back to Schuman but felt in my bones that we were going to have difficulties all the way until the curtain rose on our opening night.

Meanwhile trouble was developing from another source. The Lincoln Center Repertory Company was running huge deficits at the

ANTA theater on the campus of NYU and its board of trustees was putting the strongest pressure on Kazan and Whitehead to cut expenses. While Lincoln Center itself was to have nothing to do with the inner workings of its constituent organizations, the board of the theater, aware that the Center had set them up in the first place, was now looking for help. Schuman met with Whitehead and their discussions were less than helpful. There obviously had to be a scapegoat for the economic problems there and in this case Whitehead and Kazan were chosen. Schuman asked all of his staff for recommendations on their successors.

Out of several discussions the idea of Herman Krawitz of the Met began to emerge as a sensible managerial possibility. Krawitz was well known around the Center because he represented the Met in dealings pertaining to the new opera house and was admired for his administrative expertise. He was approached informally about his interest in the post to be vacated by Whitehead and replied that he was interested provided he could name his own artistic director. Bliss and Bing got wind of the discussions and without consulting anyone called in a reporter from the New York *Times* and let fly with a barrage of invective and comments about the whole Center idea. Naturally these thoughts ended up on the front page. Bing threatened to resign from the Lincoln Center Council and accusations of raiding and constituent interference were leveled against Schuman.

All the pent-up emotions about the festival and Hamburg in particular came to the fore and willy-nilly Lincoln Center was right smack in the middle of an angry and emotional turmoil. Bing's phrase that Lincoln Center was "apparently deteriorating to a free-for-all jungle" brought emotional responses from members of the repertory company and passionate defenses of Whitehead and Kazan. Murray Kempton used the fracas to symbolize the decline of Western culture and in one article stated that when our civilization was destroyed it would be because of its own weightlessness and underneath it all would be a broken slab of marble with the name Krawitz on it. The whole piece was a gratuitous insult to all concerned but it made Krawitz's name a temporary household word and this, I suspected, he enjoyed very much indeed. I was put to work chairing a small subcommittee to recommend other possibilities as it became increasingly obvious that the Met would not release Krawitz from his contract. We spent time talking about inviting Herbert Blau, one of the co-founders of the Actor's Workshop of San Francisco and author of *The Impossible Theater*, a highly critical survey of the state of the theater arts in America. Blau represented everything that Kazan and Whitehead did not, at least not in the public's mind, and it was felt he might quiet down the critics who continued to complain about the failures to solve all the problems of the theater as the critics saw them.

Looking back now, it is obvious that those of us responsible for the early life of the Center overreacted to the critics in general. We became defensive and felt that nothing must be done to turn the public away from the concept and close up their pocketbooks. And as the months and weeks passed the press kept shoving away until I believe the moment came when people were tired of reading about our alleged malefactions and were discoving that the Center worked and brought a new dimension of pleasure into the lives of New Yorkers as well as visitors to the city.

Meanwhile the problem of the theater continued and it was decided that I would go out to San Francisco and meet with Blau. I was asked to see his work and to report back my findings and recommendations to the president of the repertory theater board.

I telephoned Blau, identified myself, and told him that I would like to fly out that night. He agreed to meet me at the airport but begged that no one know about my visit. I promised silence and flew out uneventfully. As I stepped off the plane two men closed in quickly and walked me to the baggage depot. One I recognized as Blau; the other was his partner, Jules Irving. We picked up my suitcase and walked quickly out the door of the terminal into a waiting car. "We apologize for all the mystery," Blau said, staring straight ahead, "but we do not want to be seen talking to you. The rumors are already around that New York may be offered to us and some of our company and backers are nervous." I said I understood and we agreed that I would come to the theater in the morning for a rehearsal and to a performance at night and we would confine our talking to my room at the hotel.

The next day I went into the Workshop theater and was impressed at the order and discipline of an organization working out of very skimpy quarters. I met Alan Mandell, a young Canadian who had joined the group early in its existence and kept the machinery moving. Mandell took me to lunch and eyed me with suspicion. "Look," I finally said. "I'm out here to see the Actor's Workshop and talk with Blau. I'm not in a position to make any decisions." His eyes never relaxed.

The performance that night was done well with a highly polished company obviously responding to one another as players who had worked often together. After the performance, each of us arrived separately at my hotel and after ordering supper in my room we settled down for a long discussion. At the end of the evening it became obvious to me that Blau alone would not work in New York, that if he was to be considered seriously it must be with his partner Irving and also Mandell. What I was thinking would, of course, break up the Actor's Workshop as then constituted. I said nothing about these feelings that night but the longer we talked the more convinced I became.

I spent one more day and night with them, meeting both their wives, who were important members of the company. Toward the end of my visit Irving told me that the company had been more than curious to know who the person was who seemed to move in and out of rehearsals and performances over the past days and that finally one of them had come to him with the explanation that I was was the richest man in the world and thinking of buying their entire operation. Irving said he replied to the statement by just smiling. I liked the idea of being a modern Medici.

Upon my return to New York I met with Schuman and separately with Robert Hoguet, president of the theater board, and Mike Burke, a vice-president of the board. I told Hoguet and Burke that I thought the Blau and Irving idea was workable but that they should not take one without the other. The decision was made to invite them both to New York for talks and to do this as discreetly as possible. Above anything else we wanted to keep the matter out of the press. Blau and Irving both came and at that point I bowed out of the picture, since the final decisions had to be made by the Repertory Theater board itself. After a day or so of meetings both men called me and came to our apartment for a drink. I asked them what they thought of the theater itself, now nearing completion. "Almost impossible," they both replied, "it will be a bitch to work in. The whole design is poor and someday will have to be completely rebuilt." "Are you thinking of taking the job if it is offered to you?" I asked. "Yes," they both said.

That was that. They came and their appointment was hailed in the press. They opened the theater with a dreadful performance of *Danton's Death*, where all the building's design mistakes seemed to be emphasized; they struggled with inadequate financing and Blau's intellectual impracticality. Blau left the company after two seasons, and Irving carried on alone without much support from anyone, doing an unsung hero's job of raising the standards of ensemble work and tackling repertoire that could not last under commercial auspices. When he finally stepped down he was succeeded by Joseph Papp and the New York Shakespeare Festival. Papp made major improvements in the theater itself and found his usually supportive press barking at him for his choice of plays, players, and attitudes to the public. *Plus ça change, plus c'est la même chose.*

If the problems of the Repertory Company and the Beaumont Theater were dicey, they were a Sunday school social compared to the blowup about care and responsibility for the New York State Theater. In the early discussions about Lincoln Center a decision was made to create a house for dance and as planning went along it was decided to invite the New York City Ballet to become the dance constituent. Later this was extended to include the New York City Opera, a decision that caused Bing so much indigestion, and these two elements of the City Center of Music and Drama were invited to make their headquarters at Lincoln Center in the building to be designed by Philip Johnson. The financing of that particular building was organized along different lines: it was to be built by the State of New York to house attractions in connection with the 1964 World's Fair. After the fair closed it would revert to Lincoln Center, and the Center would agree to sublease it to the City Center for the opera and ballet seasons. The rest of the year, the booking would be the responsibility of Lincoln Center.

With this as a general agreement Schuman turned to Richard Rodgers to fill an important vacuum in the Center's artistic planning, the presentation under bright circumstances of the classics of the American musical theater. Rodgers organized the Music Theater of Lincoln Center and took responsibility for the summer weeks. Between Rodgers and the City Center most of the available time was taken up. There were only a few scattered weeks here and there for the Center's program department to manage.

While the building was still on the drawing boards these plans began to come apart. Morton Baum, the chairman of the City Center's board of directors, and Newbold Morris, the president of the board, insisted that the City Center had the rights to the entire building and that Lincoln Center had to lease it to them immediately following the close of the fair. Baum acknowledged that the Center had the responsibility of filling the theater during the fair but that its involvement ended after that and everything became the property of the City Center. Nowhere in the enabling legislation of the state that allowed funding of the building was there any such provison, but Baum, being a lawyer, read the bill the way he wanted, and Schuman, surrounded by corporate lawyers, read it his way. No amount of meetings seemed to help: Baum was not interested in a compromise. All or nothing, he implied, and as if to underscore his words the ballet management gave strong indications of dissatisfaction, showing truculence and temper in their planning meetings with us.

The problem had to be pushed into the background in 1964 because attractions had to be found to open the theater and play during the World's Fair. It was decided to lead off with the company for whom the theater was originally conceived, the New York City Ballet, and follow this with a number of outstanding events, including the only New York appearances of the Royal Shakespeare Company, under Peter Brook's direction, for performances of *King Lear* with Paul Scofield and *A Comedy of Errors*. This was to be followed by the first productions of Rodger's Music Theater for July and August and the New York City Ballet would begin its first regular season in the fall to be followed by the New York City Opera. On paper all seemed to be in order.

During the actual construction tempers continued to fray. Since the theater had originally been conceived for dance the sightline emphasis was for this art, the orchestra pit designed to accommodate a ballet-size orchestra, and the theater generally geared to the terpsichoreans. With the introduction of the opera, and later the Music Theater, the need for good acoustics became important. In addition, experimental lights, in the form of giant spots affixed to the upper sides of the stage, were supposed to eliminate hand settings and speed up the production procedure. Johnson designed impressive huge lobbies and he and Lincoln Kirstein had two immense enlargements of Elie Nadelman figures brought into the main promenade as the walls were going up, thus assuring that the pieces would remain regardless of any hue and cry.

All during this time the Baum-Schuman battle continued in the board rooms and the lack of progress at these meetings was reflected in the attitudes of the ballet management. I thought it a good idea to try to get Schuman together with George Balanchine and Betty Cage, the general manager of the company, and see whether a direct talk might accomplish more than was coming out of board meetings. The four of us met one late afternoon in Betty Cage's apartment and when we were all assembled I opened the discussion with the observation that since Balanchine and Schuman were first and foremost artists they spoke a common language and should be able to find a workable solution that would satisfy both their needs. Both men accepted the premise but once talk got under way their artistic poles seemed as far apart as their respective boards. After an hour of no progress drinks were served and both men turned to professional matters in a much more relaxed atmosphere. Betty Cage had a black cat that kept moving restlessly around the room and crossed and recrossed in front of all of us. At one point Balanchine conspiratorially turned to me, and pointing to the cat and Betty whispered that both were witches. I smiled. "No," he hissed, "it's true. You wait. You will see." I looked at him and he was deadly serious. The cat continued marching back and forth.

The only result of my attempted compromise session was to firm up the positions on both sides, resulting in an explosion from Lincoln Kirstein and notice that the ballet was pulling out after its initial season and returning to the City Center. The same action was contemplated by the opera. This meant that all of a sudden, apart from the opening weeks, the theater stood empty and I was instructed by Schuman to see that it was filled with appropriate events. This took me to several long meetings with Sol Hurok, whom I had known for a long time and done business with during my record years. Hurok was delighted. To him it meant the possibility of bringing some of his major ballet attractions in the prime of the New York winter season. Together we arranged a brilliant season, with the Bolshoi Ballet and Opera to be the keystones leading up to the period when Rodgers took over for the summer. Over many weeks we negotiated terms and finally, with great flair and trumpets, we signed contracts.

This, of course, enraged Baum, who, despite his colleagues' actions, was still determined to get control of the theater. He moved into high gear and began direct conversations with Governor Rockefeller to put pressure on his brother John to see the light. Baum had done political service for Rockefeller and now called his marker. Quickly the fight was over. Word came from on high that the theater was to be made over to the City Center, taking into account the committed time for the Music Theater and that if anything should happen to the Music Theater its time would also revert to the City Center. Baum won a great victory, but it did nothing for his health and within a few months he died of a heart attack. A great fighter and a stubborn man, Baum left an indelible mark on New York. But he ran the City Center as a one-man operation and the scramble for control of his organization was on, minutes after his death.

The decision to give everything to the City Center left us with a potentially explosive situation. We had signed binding contracts with Hurok and these now all had to be repudiated. Schuman and I went to call on him to break the news of the decision before it became public and I returned the next day to tell him that none of our deals would hold up. He was in a state of shock, particularly as far as the Russians were concerned, and I told him we would do anything we could to help. I was afraid he might sue and I wanted to head him off on this if I possibly could. After the shock had worn off we got down to practicalities and the only solution seemed to hinge on the agreement of the Metropolitan Opera to delay the destruction of its old house until Hurok could present postseason ballets as he had done for so many years in the past. This was going to be tricky, as the Met was anxious to get the building down, and in addition to everything else, Hurok was heading a committee to save it. We had to work out arrangements with the Met or we would, however reluctantly, find ourselves in court.

Schuman took the problem to John Rockefeller and between them they persuaded the Met board to let Hurok have the house after the farewell Met gala. They were not happy about this but they did agree and we were able to stay out of litigation.

The State Theater opened on April 23, 1964, with fanfares and television and was a success from the start. The stage was designed and framed for dance and in this area the theater was an unqualified success. The first test of its effectiveness for drama was to come in a few weeks when the Royal Shakespeare opened its season.

Just before this event I had to make another quick trip to Europe on further details connected with the Hamburg State Opera visit and to finish up details with the Bath Chamber Orchestra. I also wanted to start negotiations in Italy with an eye to bringing the Rome Opera in the summer of 1968. I sensed our path to subsidy was going to be a great deal trickier in Italy than it had been in Germany. I was absolutely right.

In Hamburg Liebermann and I ran into a difficulty with his production of *The Rake's Progress*. This was scheduled to be done by Ingmar Bergman, based on his highly successful version for the Royal Opera, Stockholm. For some reason Bergman suddenly decided to cancel his Hamburg commitment. Liebermann and I wanted to borrow his production from Stockholm, play it in Hamburg, and bring it to New York. I volunteered to go to Stockholm and see what could be negotiated. I also wanted to meet Goeran Gentele, the dashing leader of the Stockholm Opera, whom I knew a little about through a mutual friend, Isaac Stern. Liebermann agreed and I called Stockholm, made a date to meet Gentele, and flew off the next day.

Stockholm in winter can be a pretty dreary place, particularly if the weather is bad, and I arrived on just such a day. I checked into the Grand Hotel and at the appointed hour crossed the square to the Royal Opera House. Gentele greeted me in his handsome office and we took to each other at once. I explained my mission and he listened carefully. When I was done he looked up at me with a smile and said, "I certainly will not lend my Bergman production. I want to bring this to New York myself!" I must have looked disappointed because he immediately rose and, patting me warmly on the back, suggested that we have dinner together after the evening performance of *Tristan*.

The *Tristan* was an interesting one. Isolde was sung by a new young Swedish soprano named Berit Lindholm, and the conductor was Silvio Varviso. The production had been staged by Gentele and was imaginative and fluid. Varviso surprised me in the Wagnerian repertory; at the Met he had conducted only Italian or French works and was indifferent in these. After the performance the Varvisos, Lindholm, the Genteles, and I retired to the Opernkeller and plowed our way through delicious crayfish in dill, venison, and a great deal of Swedish beer.

I returned to the States the night of the Royal Shakespeare opening. When I arrived home Betty didn't have any reports or rumors about how the rehearsals had gone and being exhausted from the flight I went to bed instead of attending the opening. The next morning I looked at the reviews and the very first comments were to the effect that the acoustics at the New York State Theater were impossible. The company could not be heard and apparently there had been several loud reminders to this effect from members of the audience. My heart sank and I dressed quickly and made my way over to the office.

Peter Brook had called a press conference for noon and I was designated to be there representing Lincoln Center. I'd never met Brook before but knew his work and admired it. I was not prepared, however, for his accusatory finger, which he pointed at me when I walked in, and addressing the press, he said something to the effect that I had told them all that the acoustics were perfect. Never having made such a statement in my life I was in a quandry as to how to answer. Before I had a chance to speak Brook went on about the fellow who was supposed to solve all the sound problems instantly in case any arose. "After the first act when no one could hear I sought out the fellow and told him to turn on his magic machinery to solve the problem. There was no such machine." And he glared across the room.

My reply was that I thought we had to find an immediate solution to the problems and hoped that Mr. Brook would work with us to do this. Having blown off his steam he was now in a much more conciliatory mood and agreed to try. I hoped the press would be careful in their stories. Another acoustical problem blown up in the papers might just give the public the idea that the architects and designers of Lincoln Center did not know what they were up to.

Immediately after the conference Brook and I sought out the house manager and a sound engineer and designed a series of microphones and speakers placed judiciously around the theater which we hoped would help. They did, for a little bit, but there was no question that the State Theater had not been designed for drama and we had to do the best we could for the remainder of the run. I had scheduled the Schiller Theater of Berlin for the following weeks and wondered how we were going to fare with them.

The problem never really did get solved. After the Royal Shakespeare completed its run, and we had refunded quite a lot of money to irate customers, the Schiller group took up residence and we continued using a jerry-rigged microphone system that psychologically, if nothing else, gave the impression that something was being done about the sound. The theater was simply never intended for drama, or for opera either, for that matter. For opera there have been modifications but the sound does little to help the singers and is generally unsatisfactory.

While the State Theater problems continued we began having a major difficulty with the Vivian Beaumont Theater and the Library Museum of the Performing Arts. Apart from the Kazan/Whitehead-Blau/ Irving switch serious problems were developing in the building shared by both the library and the theater, really two buildings blended into one. The ventilation problem was especially difficult. The library, for its rare book collections, needed a constant year-round temperature; the theater needed a flexible system adjustable according to the seasons. One air-conditioning unit was put in for the whole building with the understanding that the costs would be shared equally. Immediately the theater's bills soared out of sight. The library reminded everyone that in agreeing to move the theater and music collection to the Center it was promised that the expenses would be no greater than at its old sites and declined to discuss sharing ventilating expenses.

In addition, the Lincoln Center garage placed under the building was found to be a fume trap and much too small to take care of patrons who arrived for performances. Since the city provided the funds to build the garage, it had the parking concession, which it leased out to the Kinney Company. Kinney couldn't have cared less about Lincoln Center and its problems. It filled up the place with New Jersey commuters in the morning, who would park and lock their cars, take the subway or bus to their place of work, and return leisurely in the early evening to drive home. The rates were reasonable. Many local west side residents moved their cars in on a full-time basis and as evening performance times approached the FILLED signs were usually out by 5:30. People who had driven in from any of the suburbs were forced to scour the area for places and usually found themselves some distance away from their theater and charged enormous prices. More than any single problem the garage gave the Center its worst public relations headaches and, I'm afraid, with very good reasons.

Despite the problems, and the continuous mounting expenses, both the library and the Beaumont Theater opened on time, the former an instant success and the latter with many questionmarks, both architecturally and artistically. Architecturally the exterior of the building is a stunning example of first-class contemporary work. Inside, the theater

itself was less good. Jo Mielziner designed an auditorium for both proscenium and stage thrust presentation, and it really didn't work either
way. The stage playing area and the sightlines were so arranged that
you could not put a play under the proscenium with a set wider than ten
feet. It could not be square; it had to be a squashed triangle if everyone
was to be able to see. As a thrust theater it had fair sightlines but
acoustical problems. The actors had to shout to be heard clearly. The
audience had to be careful going to and from their seats; the aisles were
sharply raked and there were no handrails. Both Blau and Irving, as
professional theater men, spotted the basic problems immediately but
there was nothing they could do about them as the budget was way
overspent and no provisions had been made for corrections. They had
to make do with what they had.

Right after the opening of the Beaumont I had to talk with both men
about their participation in Festival '67 and it was obvious they really
did not have time to deal with this properly. That meant that Schuman
and I were back to work. We thought about asking several of the regional theaters, particularly the Guthrie Theater in Minneapolis and the
Arena Stage in Washington, D.C. I met with officials of both and the
scheduling and expenses seemed to rule them out, at least for the first
festival.

Word was getting around New York that we were looking and one
day I received a phone call from Alexander H. Cohen, the Broadway
producer, with an invitation to lunch. At lunch he handed me a script
of a new play by Peter Ustinov called *The Unknown Soldier and His
Wife, Two Acts of War Separated by a Truce for Refreshment.* I took
the script and read it that night and was fascinated. Ustinov had written, in his typically engaging manner, a very serious statement about
the futility and stupidity of war through the ages and a plea against war
in the future. Not a very original thought, perhaps, but one that needs
stating over and over again and preferably with humor. I thought the
play wonderful; the next morning I brought it to Schuman and without
making any comment gave it to him and asked him to let me know what
he thought as soon as he could. The next morning it was back on my
desk with a note saying he thought it was just right for the festival and
that we should try to do it.

I called Cohen and told him we were interested and what were the
terms. Cohen was familiar with the Lincoln Center setup; at one point
between the Kazan/Whitehead-Blau/Irving administrations it looked
as if we were not going to be able to open the theater with the company
for whom it had been built and Cohen had come forth with some
suggestions. The press had gotten wind of this and for a few days

played out a how-dare-Lincoln-Center-be-so-commercial scenario. It made the Center seem careless in its institutional theatrical responsibilities and gave Cohen some extra publicity and an interest in our general problems. The terms we finally worked out for the Ustinov play were rough but fair; Cohen was to produce it for us at the Beaumont and we were to remain partners throughout the various lives of the play. We were to be consulted on artistic matters but the final authority lay with him. I was not completely happy about this but I figured that Cohen and I could work out details.

The play brought together a distinguished company of players—Brian Bedford, W. B. Brydon, Howard Da Silva, Bob Dishy, M'el Dowd, Alan Mixon, Melissa Murphy, Marco St. John, and Christopher Walken. The director was John Dexter, fresh from triumphs with *The Royal Hunt of the Sun*. It was the beginning of collaborative work with Dexter that was to climax six years later at the Metropolitan Opera.

Ustinov proved to be a delight. I had met him a few years before and I knew he was fond of music and the arts in general. I think he and I became friends one afternoon when, as I was leaving his apartment after tea, he put on a recording and asked me to identify the composer. I listened for a quick moment and shot back "Buxtehude!" I'd guessed right and he was not prepared for that. He broke into a wide grin and said, "Come back next Sunday! We'll try someone else." I agreed and did.

Ustinov, as author of a new play, is, to put it mildly, stubborn. *The Unknown Soldier* needed cutting and no amount of persuasion from Cohen, Dexter, or myself did any good. Dexter staged the piece brilliantly, using the Beaumont's problems as assets, but the play was too long, repeated its points too often, and cutting would have made it, in my opinion, much stronger. Ustinov was charming but adamant. We all had to live with it his way.

The festival was now pretty much in place. The Hamburg company sent scenery, costumes, and props by sea containers and the 325 members of the company arrived in New York on schedule. Their season was an enormous success. *The Unknown Soldier* did well at the Beaumont; Rodgers had a beautiful *King and I* at the State Theater, the Philharmonic and various individual and chamber music organizations were holding forth in Philharmonic Hall, the Center plaza was decorated with colorful bunting, the cafés had tables in the open, and the whole atmosphere was bubbling and inviting. Festival '67 was off and running; the public was responding strongly and the validity of the idea of serious summer programming was proved.

One of the sidelights of the festival was the interflow between the various theaters, best demonstrated by Rolf Liebermann coming to me one day and asking if I could arrange for him to meet both Dexter and Ustinov as he had admired both men's work and had some ideas he wished to discuss with them. I arranged for a late lunch one day and brought them all together. The upshot of that meeting was that Ustinov went to Hamburg two years later to design and direct a production of *The Magic Flute* and Dexter went several times, directing *Boris Godunov*, *The House of the Dead*, and *I Vespri Siciliani*. They all might have met anyway but it happened that Lincoln Center was the artistic catalytic agent.

Festival '67 was followed immediately by the 4th New York Film Festival where, as usual, the films were provocative and Vogel and Roud abrasive. Two major talents were introduced to America that year, both Czechs from the famed Czech School: Jan Kadar and Milos Forman. Kadar's *The Shop on Main Street* brought the audience to its feet cheering, and Kadar, fresh off the plane from Europe and visiting America for the first time, was stunned by the reception. Forman brought *The Loves of a Blond* and also found New York audiences warm and inviting. He elected to stay in this country and in 1976 won an Oscar for his direction of *One Flew Over the Cuckoo's Nest*. The artistic track record of the festival continued to grow.

When the final accounting of Festival '67 was audited we found that we were within one percent of our anticipated income and expenses and the trustees were encouraged enough to vote to stage Festival '68 the next summer. True, not all the trustees were enthusiastic, particularly the key members of constituent boards, but they were outvoted and plans moved ahead.

Two major importations were planned for 1968: the Rome Opera and the Théâtre de la Cité of Roger Planchon, perhaps the most provocative company in France. Planchon was based in Lyon, in a theater over a swimming pool, and had assembled a brilliant company. He was often in trouble with various French governments because he was a communist but he never stayed in trouble too long. He and Jean Louis Barrault were rivals; Barrault ran the Théâtre National and Planchon the Théâtre Populaire and they both competed for subsidy and audiences. We felt Barrault was a familiar figure to New York theatergoers and that everyone should have a chance to see what Planchon was all about.

In addition to Planchon we invited the Atalier Theater 212 from Belgrade, Yugoslavia, to appear in the tiny Forum Theater, the 299-seat experimental thrust-stage house under the Beaumont. The Atalier, brainchild of the extraordinary Mira Trailovitch, came to my attention when the Yugoslav government invited me to make a visit and look for Yugoslav artistic activities that might be possible for a Lincoln Center festival. The Atalier seemed like just the right group and they came with a repertoire drawn from their normal work, including Alexander Popovic's *Boris the Tailor*, Jarry's *Ubu Roi*, and Edward Albee's *Who's Afraid of Virgina Woolf?*, all performed in Serbo-Croatian.

Again the trickiest importation was the opera and Bing was less difficult than he had been the previous year, when he found that the Hamburg company did not destroy the Metropolitan. The Rome Opera is not known for its overall quality but the Italians were anxious for it to come because it was Rome. Bill Weaver, the critic and translator whom I had hired to help with negotiations in Rome, and I worked very carefully with its artistic director, Massimo Bogianckino. I was anxious that they bring the Visconti production of *Marriage of Figaro*. Bogianckino agreed if we could persuade Carlo Maria Guilini to conduct and Visconti to come over to stage it. Bogianckino suggested that he would also like to bring Rossini's *Otello*, rarely heard anywhere. His production was a visual spectacular with sets and costumes by Giorgio de Chirico. Lastly we had to have a Verdi work. The Italian government insisted upon it but I was dead set against bringing standard repertoire. Weaver, Bogianckino, and I talked about this problem but could not agree.

One weekend, while I was staying with Weaver at Monte San Savino, he very cleverly laid out a campaign for one of his favorite early Verdi works, *I Due Foscari*. After dinner, when we adjourned to his music room, he had a score and libretto of the work laid out on a table and an old disc of a performance conducted by Victor de Sabata in the late forties. With espresso in hand we sat down and the turntable started. I picked up both score and libretto and was struck by the beauty of the music but appalled by the stodginess of the stage directions. "This is all very well," I said, "but all we have here is 'enter chorus' and 'exit chorus,' 'enter Foscari' and 'exit Foscari' and a lot of sitting around." "I think we can overcome that problem," he said. "I think Romulo Valli should direct it and Pier Luigi Pizzi should design, and between the two of them it will be theatrically exciting without destroying the story or the music." I knew both Valli's and Pizzi's work from the Teatro Giovani and this seemed like a good idea. "How do we get ahold of them?" I asked. "We go to Paris tomorrow. Their company is playing at the Odéon and we can nail them there." And the next morning we took the train to Rome, boarded a plane for Paris, appeared at the Odéon early in the evening, saw both Valli and Pizzi, who agreed, stayed for their performance, had supper at the Méditerranée, the greatest seafood restaurant in Paris, and flew back to Rome, arriving in the early morning hours.

That was about the only thing in connection with the Rome Opera that did work smoothly. I knew we were going to be in for a lot of trouble after my first meeting with the *sovrintendente*, Signore Enio Palmitessa. Palmitessa had been promised the job as mayor of Rome by his political party but when they succeeded to power they gave the job to someone else and offered him the opera in its place. He was not too pleased by this, although he did have respect for Bogianckino, whom he kept addressing as "maestro." He became intrigued with the possibilities of riding triumphantly to New York with his company. He saw the possibilities but had to play the role of difficult, cantankerous, and temperamental impresario to the fullest.

Our meetings took place in the Rome Opera House, an unattractive building in early Mussolini style. Its conference room was long and narrow and difficult to meet in except in the most formal manner. Our discussions would begin at 10:00 AM, break for lunch, and continue until late afternoon. Seated around the table in close clutches were the various departments of the opera house with signs designating who they were. We had representatives from the house itself, also from the Rome city treasury, from the minister of culture and tourism, and from Lincoln Center. Weaver and I were joined here by Robert Brannigan, the Center's technical expert on its various stages. Brannigan could not speak a word of Italian but managed to get his points across by a deft combination of English and a sharp pointer.

The meetings were plays and ploys and we learned quickly to go along with them. The real work was done outside the room; Brannigan and the chief stage technician found a common language, as did the other department heads. I stayed in the background ready to move in at the correct moment. A great deal of my time was spent negotiating with the ministry of tourism, for the subsidy. The offices for this part of the government were also housed in Mussolini architecture, part of the new city of Rome he envisioned building. The area looked like a set; I do not think I've ever seen so many marble corridors outside of the movies. Our talks moved slowly but there came the day when the word was passed that the government approved the visit and the monies to pay for it would come from the Italian treasury. Bill Weaver and I bowed our heads in proper diplomatic thanks.

After the laborious negotiations and preparations of documents we met at the opera house to sign the contracts. Various ministries were represented, the table had been polished brightly, all were dressed in their best. Weaver and I approached the head of the table and I sat down to sign. Palmitessa signed after me and signatures were added from official ministries. As the seals were being affixed Palmitessa turned and through his interpreter said, "Now we have a problem." "Now?" I responded incredulously. "Si, now," he replied gravely. I looked at Bill Weaver and he was as puzzled as I. With a deep sigh I looked over at him and said, "May I ask what problem?" "Pasta," was his quick reply. "Pasta?" I said, trying to see if he was serious. "Si, pasta," he said, and there was not a trace of a smile on his face. "Suppose you tell me more about the problem," I went on, now getting curious. "Si," he answered. "When we went to France last year, there was nothing for the company to eat." "In France?" I rejoined, finding it a little hard to believe my ears. "Si, France," he said. And he paused. "Do go on," I urged him. He continued, "In France, in the cities we played, there was wine, surely, and vegetables, meat, some chicken, but no food. No pasta. For America we are taking no chances. There must be added another crate for pasta and formaggio, oil, and other necessary ingredients. You must allow this." I thought immediately of the conversations that had been going on at home with a leading pasta manufacturer about helping defray expenses in New York. Our talks were proceeding well but all would be over if word got out that the Rome Opera was bringing its own spaghetti. The deal would be off. "Do you know that New York has more Italian restaurants than Rome?" I asked, remembering a statistic I once saw somewhere. "In fact there are several excellent ones within a block of the theater. There is plenty of pasta." "No, we bring our own. And we must also have a place to cook it." "May I think about this for a moment," I said. "We'll discuss it further after lunch." He agreed but not happily. Afterwards I told him that he could of course bring his own pasta and we would find a place for him to have it cooked but there was one condition that he had to agree to. The fact that they were bringing their own must not get into the newspapers. I explained about our delicate pasta company negotiations. He nodded solemnly and we added an addendum to the contract spelling out the details.

Brannigan and I went on to France to button up details regarding the Planchon company visit. We flew to Lyon, the home of the group, and were met by Planchon and one of his staff people.

We discussed all day in the basement of his theater, and at 8:00 I went upstairs to look at the evening's performance of *Tartuffe* and Brannigan stayed below, wrestling with details. At 10:30 PM, when the performance finished, they were still at it. By this time coats, ties, and shirts were off, charts of the Beaumont stage were spread over several tables, the air was thick with gray-blue smoke, and Planchon himself, a cigarette between his lips with the smoke curling up toward his nose, led the proceedings. When I appeared he came to me and began speaking rapidly. He gesticulated around the room, took me over to the charts and, pointing to the drawings of the Beaumont, made it very plain that the whole visit was impossible. "This stage is out of the question," he said. "There is no way for my company to play. We must cancel the tour." I suggested we break for a little supper, it now being around 11:30 PM. They agreed and we went to a peasant restaurant with long, plain wooden tables, and had onion soup and bread with sweet butter and herbs and tall glasses of red wine. The mood changed immediately and afterwards we all returned to Planchon's office and found ways to overcome the problems. At 4:00 AM Brannigan and I were left off at our hotel and collapsed into bed.

That same year I made my first trip to Spain. I was invited on an official visit by the minister of tourism and information, Manuel Fraga Iribane, who had been to the United States some months before and inspected Lincoln Center thoroughly. He was planning on creating a similar project in Madrid and felt that it might be nice if some Spanish artists and groups participated in Lincoln Center Festival '68. Schuman and I agreed and I went off to have a look at what Spain had to suggest.

Arriving in Madrid, I was whisked to the Palace Hotel, given a wonderfully comfortable suite, and told that I would be called for the next morning. I worked out my schedule with Fraga's office and a slight, sweatered, runny-nosed girl with badly fitting glasses showed up in a small limousine to take me about. I was charmed by Madrid, the Escorial, by everything we looked at, but decided that I wanted to see the Prado by myself. We lunched in the country at a bull-breeding ranch and I told her that I had to call on the United States ambassador that afternoon and would like to have the balance of the day and the next one to myself. Fraga was receiving me in his office two days later and I wanted to be thoroughly prepared on my impressions of Spain before that time. She seemed delighted and drove me to the embassy.

Our ambassador was Angier Biddle Duke, a collateral in-law cousin by the remote connection of his relationship with Francis Biddle. Duke was married to Robin Chandler, whom Betty and I had known slightly for years. Duke received me pleasantly enough but when I told him I was in Spain as Fraga's guest he really grew interested. "I did not know anything about this," he said. "We've been trying to get together with him on various matters for weeks now and he's always avoiding us." "I'm seeing him in two days," I said. "Is there anything I can do?" "Not right now but please keep in touch. You may be able to help us in an important way." I promised I would.

When I did see Fraga in his enormous office, we talked at great length about Spanish art. I had been knocked out by the Prado, having spent my whole free day there. He seemed pleased and each time I spoke of something that had impressed me, he touched a bell by his chair, a door would spring open, he'd say a few words to a uniformed attendant, and I would be laden with books, pamphlets, prints, and other material applicable to what we'd been discussing. After an hour it was obvious that our appointment was up and I rose to go. "I've so enjoyed our talk," he said. "Tomorrow I'm giving a little reception here. I would be pleased if you'd come." "I'd be delighted," I replied. "Please invite two or three friends if you like. It is to be informal." I thanked him and then remembering my conversation with Duke asked whether or not it would be all right to include them. He nodded his agreement. I left and returned to the hotel, where an hour later I was due to be picked up to attend the theater. Before leaving I telephoned the ambassador and told him that he was free to come to Fraga's reception if he wanted to. "We'll be there," he said.

And they were. Both Ambassador and Mrs. Duke entered the room just as I was talking with Fraga. "You know Ambassador and Mrs. Duke," I said. "Oh yes, certainly," replied Fraga and bowed stiffly. "It is so nice to have Mr. Chapin in Spain," said Duke, "thanks to your courtesy." "I hope Spain will soon be represented at Lincoln Center," he replied politely. At this point he bowed and left us. Duke looked at me. "Is there anything more I can do?" I asked. "This doesn't seem like very much." "But, oh, yes it is," replied the ambassador. "He hasn't said that much to me since I arrived." And I looked up to see Fraga returning. "Mr. Ambassador," he said, "I believe we should have a talk one of these days." And they both went off across the room.

A few minutes later the Dukes came by to say goodbye. "Thank you so much," Duke said as we shook hands. "You've been an enormous help." And off he went. I never did find out what I had done but I hoped I had solved the vexing problem. I never saw the ambassador again.

As it turned out, Lincoln Center Festival '68 was the last. The expenses were too great and the constituents were beginning to plan longer seasons themselves, having seen that a summer audience was there and having agreed with the unions to extend the yearly guarantee of employment. The Center was reorganized; Schuman resigned as president and my position was eliminated. I had a contract with one more year to go and agreed to work on setting up an independent organization to assure the continuation of the New York Film Festival. Other than that I was free to do what I wanted.

It was the same year that Bernstein was leaving as music director of the New York Philharmonic. He didn't know what he was going to do but over a dinner one evening we agreed to join forces to create our own projects. We shook hands and Amberson Productions was formed to create musical films for television, plays, operas, and anything else that caught our fancy. Bernstein and I were to work together again and nothing could have pleased me more.

XII

Bernstein—

"Accessible Without Being Ordinary"

The National Airport in Washington, D.C., always makes me nervous. This has nothing to do with flying or the horrible, impersonal impedimenta of modern travel. I'm just convinced the minute I enter the terminal that my visit to our nation's capital will be a disaster. I won't be able to find a cab. The hotel will have botched up the reservations. The person I've come to see will that morning have gotten triple pneumonia and been dispatched to recuperate on the presidential yacht. All the others in the terminal building are hell-bent on business of cosmic importance to the nation's future and my poor problems seem unimportant indeed. I grow sad and a little withdrawn thinking about them. I glance up and see that there is a plane back to New York in forty-five minutes and why not call the whole thing off and go back to my nice wide urban womb.

These feelings were especially pronounced on the morning of October 12, 1959, when I flew down to be on hand to greet the New York Philharmonic on its return from a toweringly successful trip to Europe that included the orchestra's first appearances in the Soviet Union. I had just started at Columbia Records and was more than a little nervous about meeting, for the first time, that package of talent, communication, energy, and personality known as Leonard Bernstein.

Only the year before, Bernstein had been appointed music director of the New York Philharmonic, the first native-born American ever to hold that prestigious post, and he instantly brought new life and fire to the organization. This life and fire had spread itself way beyond the concert hall and was reaching untold millions by extraordinary programs on TV, such as *Omnibus* and Leonard Bernstein and the New York Philharmonic *Young People's Concerts*, and of course, recordings. There was only one catch for me in my new job: somehow or other Columbia Records had neglected to notice that his recording contract had expired in mid-September and that the New York Philharmonic's had wound up around the same time. There were red faces and wan smiles but the facts were the facts and they were told to me almost my first day on the job, only three weeks before. I was thunderstruck. I found that over the years the company had been taking an affectionate but paternal approach to Bernstein and he must have begun to resent this attitude. Overlooked, of course, was the fact that he had now become the number one figure of classical music in America and one of the major stars of the lyric theater and television as well and, wunderkind or not, he was bound to want to burst out of restrictive obligations. It was to be my responsibility to see that he didn't leave the label and my first major assignment in my new job.

Our plane landed and I was swept up with the Philharmonic board and management and whisked off to the Butler Aviation terminal to await the arrival of the Boeing Clipper that was bringing everyone home. The press were there too, in droves, because among other things Bernstein had spoken about artistic freedom upon his arrival in Russia. He had also captured the hearts of Russian music lovers not only by his dynamic abilities to communicate his love of music from the podium but also by breaking tradition and talking to his audience.

Indeed the whole Philharmonic tour had been a triumph, in Greece, Lebanon, Turkey, Austria, Poland, Holland, Germany, Luxembourg, France, Switzerland, Yugoslavia, Italy, Norway, Sweden, Finland, and England as well as Russia. *Time* magazine called the tour "likely to go down as the most successful of all time." It was a diplomatic triumph as well. One Western European newspaper commented that with the "New York Philharmonic's playing of U.S. and Soviet music on the same program the international stage was set for the forthcoming meeting of Eisenhower and Khrushchev." A little too expansive, perhaps, in light of Francis Gary Powers and his U-2 spy plane, but that problem was still in the future.

It was understandable, then, that there was restless anticipation at the tarmac on the part of the many gathered for the welcome and that there were rampant butterflies in my stomach.

We stood around making small talk. George E. Judd, Jr., who had succeeded Arthur Judson and Bruno Zirato as the Philharmonic's manager, was on the plane, and ground arrangements were in the hands of Carlos Moseley, the assistant manager, and Silas Edman, a member of the staff. The orchestra was scheduled to play in Washington at Constitution Hall with a program that included the Shostakovitch Fifth and I wondered how anyone would have the energy after the long flight from England. It was much longer in those days before the jet.

"Here they come!" someone called out as the big Clipper slowly taxied toward the area. One could see people crowding the windows looking out for friends. The plane stopped and the health officials boarded for what seemed like an eternity, but finally they came down the ramp, followed, after a brief pause, by a group led by the unmistakable figure of Bernstein, dressed in gray slacks and blue blazer with a smart ascot around his neck, a broad grin on his face and obvious pleasure at being home. A phalanx ran toward him, arms outstretched, and in seconds he was embracing everyone in sight.

Laughter and joyful shouts increased as the group made its way slowly toward the waiting press and one frightened stranger—me. The cameramen started flashing and calling and reporters moved in swiftly. I inched my way forward and stood just behind a radio man who managed to thrust a microphone under his nose and ask about artistic conditions in Russia. Bernstein paused before answering and looked up. Our eyes met head on and for a second I thought I saw a puzzled kind of "who's this?" look. I moved forward to introduce myself and before I could say a word he said, "Ride with me in the car to Washington! We have to talk right away!" I was startled but nodded yes and drew back to let the press proceed with their work. "He knows who you are," said a voice on my right and I turned to see John McClure heading toward Bernstein with arms outstretched. Any further thoughts were interrupted by the arrival of baggage and more reporters and I stepped out of the way.

Within moments a lot of luggage was dollied out to a limousine with two people following, one of whom was a breathtakingly lovely woman, looking organizedly chaotic. Behind her I spotted George Judd, who beckoned to me to come over. "This is Felicia Bernstein," he said and we shook hands. "A great honor," I said, and she flashed an affectionate if weary smile. "Lenny wants you to ride with us to the hotel," she said, "so why don't you hop in here and wait. It may be a bit but he'll get here eventually!" "Of course," I said. "Can't I help with some of these!" I asked, looking at the mounds of luggage. "Oh, no, thank you," she replied. "But you can take these." She handed me a wrap and a small briefcase and a book. I took them into the car and settled them onto the seat. I glanced at the book. It was Pasternak's *Dr. Zhivago* and I suddenly realized that I had read in the papers that morning that Pasternak had come to the last Moscow concert. They must have met and talked.

Before I could think any more about the implications of this there was another great bustle and mound of luggage over the top of which I saw Bernstein, coming toward the car at a slow but steady rate. My hands began to perspire and my mouth felt full of cotton. The door was opened and in came more briefcases and books and scarfs and magazines. Presently he got in and squeezed over to make room for Felicia, George Judd, John McClure, and Frank Milburn. There was hardly a square inch in which to breathe and I was in a quiet panic.

I must have looked uneasy because all of a sudden he turned to me, stuck out his hand, and said, "It's wonderful to meet you!" "It is for me too," I said, somewhat lamely. I looked into his eyes, which were smiling and warm, and I felt better. "We must talk right away," he said. "Is my contract all settled?" Before I could answer McClure said that talks were still going on with his lawyer. "Then I have no contract?" he asked. I said that was right but I thought it was only a matter of ironing out a few details and that there was no serious problem. He looked dark and unhappy with that reply. "But why isn't it done?" he said. I replied that I really didn't know but that this was my top priority. "Did you know George Marek [head of RCA Victor Records] came to see me and offered me an orchestra of my own and my choice of repertoire if I switched to them?" he asked. I said I'd heard rumors of something like that.

"I want to be free to record whatever I wish. I don't want anyone telling me such-and-such cannot be done. Right now I want to make certain we record the Shostakovitch Fifth before we open our New York season. We have some dates in the South next week and then perform at Symphony Hall in Boston. I want to record the work there." He was polite, communicative, and absolutely definite.

I said I was looking forward to hearing the concert tonight and would get to work right away on the Boston arrangements. McClure turned and looked at me, shaking his head. I glanced over to see if Bernstein had noticed. He was looking out the window away from me; if he noticed anything he didn't say a word. Suddenly he exclaimed, "God, how wonderful to be back! Look at those *colors*!" And he went on a few moments about nature and art and excitement and I was swept along by his sentences. The man truly loves life and has an excitement about living. His spirit is contagious. The compelling power that radiates from the podium and galvanizes one in front of the television set is absolutely real. He can say it is raining outside and make one want to go out and stand in it.

The car drew up to the Mayflower Hotel, the doors were opened, and in seconds both Bernsteins were in the lobby, shaking hands with the manager, and off to their suite. The bags followed, and so did I, more than a little mesmerized and more than a little puzzled as to exactly what to do next. I registered (they did have a room for me) and went upstairs to collect my thoughts.

McClure followed and came to my room to talk. "We'll never get Symphony Hall," he said helpfully. "You know that it is strictly for RCA with the Boston Symphony. It's one of the treasures of the world." He walked to the window and looked out. "Of course we did lend them E. Power Biggs to record the Saint-Saëns symphony but I doubt if that is enough for an exchange." I turned abruptly. "When did you do this?" I asked. "Oh, last year, I think, or possibly the year before. I don't remember exactly." "But they did make the record?" I asked. "Yes indeed," he replied.

I went to the telephone to call Thomas D. Perry, Jr., the manager of the Boston Symphony, whom I had known since my Columbia Artist days. As the company's representative for the Boston Symphony, I used to meet with Tod at least once a year for an all-day session at which we discussed and negotiated for many of the soloists for the following season. When Tod came to the phone at Symphony Hall, I explained our current problem. I reminded him that Columbia Records had let its biggest organ star record the only "commercial" orchestra-organ concerto for RCA, Munch, and the Boston Symphony, and that he now owed us a favor. He agreed but said he would have to discuss the matter with RCA. I asked him to do this as quickly as possible. I then called my counterpart at RCA, my old friend Alan Kayes, to tell him our problem and to alert him to expect a call from Tod Perry. I urged Kayes to please reply in the affirmative. He was very careful but acknowledged that RCA owed Columbia a debt and this might be the easiest way of repaying it. A few minutes later Tod called me back, as promised, and said that he'd gotten RCA's consent and we could go ahead with our plans. I then rang McClure's room and told him everything was cleared for the hall and that he should go ahead and arrange for his equipment.

That night we all went to the concert. The hall was sold out to the rafters and every inch of standing room space was filled as well. It was a very grand and gala crowd—Senators, Congressmen, diplomats, the secretary of state, the vice-president, society, the works, as well as music lovers. The atmosphere was festive and anticipatory. When Bernstein came out the crowd roared. He bowed and smiled and at just the right moment turned and raised his hands to begin. The audience quieted down instantly. At intermission everyone was talking about the crispness and precision with which the orchestra was playing and wondering how this could be after such a long and difficult tour. The second half of the program was to be devoted to the Shostakovitch Fifth Symphony and there was a feeling of great anticipation. The papers had been full of its reception in Russia and the composer's remarks about the sweep and sound given it by the Americans.

When the symphony got under way all expectations were fulfilled. The line and tension and excitement of the piece never flagged for a moment and when Bernstein came to the last movement, with its brass fanfares and musical heroics, he made them sound even grander and more heroic than ever. At the end the audience leapt to its feet and the cheers almost brought down the plastered ceiling. I was on my feet cheering with the rest and relieved to know that we were going to get it on record while fresh in the repertoire.

We gathered backstage after the concert and moved on to a party in a lovely house in Georgetown. Once again I rode in the car with Bernstein and as we were walking up the steps of the house, he turned to me and said, "Is everything arranged for Boston?" I looked at him and replied, "Yes." He stopped on the top step and looked at me incredulously. "You mean it's all set?" he asked. "Yes," I replied. "It sometimes helps to have a friend at court." "Wonderful," he said, "and we'll make a beautiful recording." And he swept on into the house to be gathered in our hostess's arms.

That night was my first experience with Bernstein at a party and I watched with wonder the attention he was getting. All the guests flocked around him and he seemed to have the right thing to say to everyone. Felicia, too, was surrounded, mostly by men, and her smiles and sparkle set a charm hard to resist. What is it that these Bernsteins have? I wondered to myself as I moved about from room to room. It's not just success, there's something else, some other qualities that defy definition. I couldn't make up my mind, but whatever it was they had it and all kinds of people responded.

At about 2:00 AM I took my leave and as I was at the steps I heard Bernstein call out, "Wait!" and they both joined me. Their car pulled up and we got in. "Now where?" he said. "To bed," replied Felicia, with some firmness, "at least for me." And she put her head back on the seat. "Aren't you exhausted too?" I asked Bernstein. "You've put in quite a day, quite a few days, for that matter." "I can't sleep," he replied. "I never can sleep. Oh, God! How I wish I could sleep!" He looked driven and pale. I was alarmed by the sudden change in looks and mood. But it didn't last. He soon turned, smiled broadly, and suggested a nightcap. I was delighted and when we reached the hotel and Felicia had gone to bed we poured drinks and settled in to talk.

And talk he did: fascinating talk on all kinds of subjects—politics, literature, theater, movies, and music, mostly music—and out of him poured his love of the art and his passion for it, without bombast or pretension. I grew more and more excited at his unbelievable ability to communicate his feelings, and it was with a start that I saw the sun begin to peak around the window curtains. I looked at my watch and realized that we had been talking for four hours. It seemed like ten minutes. I rose, and tried to thank him for an extraordinary time. He got up and gave me a big hug. "We're going to work wonderfully together!" And he walked me to the door.

Out in the corridor my head was swimming with the whole day and evening. I was exhilarated and exhausted and when I reached my room I threw myself down on the bed and was asleep instantly, sprawled out and fully clothed. I was awakened what seemed like seconds later but was, in reality, 9:00 AM, by the ringing of the telephone. McClure was calling from New York. "We're all set here," he said. "The engineers will be in Boston tomorrow and we'll test the hall as soon as we can get set up." "Test the hall?" I asked. "What do we have to do that for? The Boston Symphony has made records there for years." "I know," he replied, "but they've never licked the sound problem. I think we can. I think I know what to do." "Is it going to be expensive?" I asked reluctantly. "Oh, no," he replied. "Not really." "What do you mean by 'not really'?" I said. "Don't worry," was his answer. And he rang off. "But I do worry," I said into a dead instrument. And I put the phone down. I pulled off my tie and took off my pants. I'll just lie here for a few more minutes, I said to myself, stretching out properly on the bed. And within seconds I was dead to the world.

When I awoke it was past noon, and the Bernsteins were due to leave Washington in an hour. I slapped some cold water on my face, brushed my teeth, combed my hair, and went down the hall to their suite. It was opened to reveal what was for all the world a levee. People were everywhere, sprawled on couches, over chairs, on table edges. The air was blue with smoke. In one corner, seated at a table having breakfast, was Felicia and for one wild moment I thought I was on the set for Act I of a modern-dress *Der Rosenkavalier.* "Hi there!" she said cheerfully. "Have some coffee." And she poured a cup. "No thank you," I replied. "I can't drink coffee in the morning. I like tea." "We must order some straight away!" And she went to the phone. "Please!" I said, startled, "Let me do that. You finish your break-fast." And I reached for the phone.

"While you're there order me some eggs and toast. I'm *starving!*" It was the maestro, making his entrance looking and sounding fresh and animated. "What a *wonderful* morning! It's so fresh out!" And he took a deep breath. He said it with such excitement that other people in the room began to look out the window. I did the same thing. What was there about him that made people respond so strongly? I think if he had asked me to jump in the pond around the Lincoln Memorial I would have done it in an instant. No wonder he touched so many people. His appearance started a veritable tidal wave of conversation and to each person in the room he seemed to give his undivided attention, including the waiter who brought his breakfast. His excitement and sense of joy in living was contagious.

Presently people began drifting away, with hugs and kisses and ex-clamations of love, and the phone stopped ringing and the smoke set-tled and the bellboys came for the bags and they were off for that night's concert. I went to the lobby to say good-bye and before climb-ing in their car they both embraced me. I almost cried at seeing them depart.

I took the next shuttle plane back to New York and when I arrived at the office I found that McClure had already left for Boston and that all was in order for the recording of the Shostakovitch. I turned my atten-tion to trying to figure out where we stood on the matter of Bernstein's contract.

From official papers I found that he had a lawyer named Abraham Friedman and I was told by the law department at Columbia that he was a very tough negotiator indeed. That didn't surprise me: Bernstein would need a tough representative if his business affairs were to be handled properly. Even in our brief acquaintance I sensed his lack of interest in the details of business matters but not any lack of common sense in these areas. Friedman was very courteous to me when I reached him and we made a date.

When he came to my office he looked like any small businessman who'd had a moderate success in life and was preparing to spend the rest of it in warmer climes. When he smiled, his face took on a beatific look, a cross between a leprechaun and a Jewish Santa Claus. He used that smile as a punctuation point and over the years I would recognize it as the closing point of any argument. Friedman had been Bernstein's lawyer for some little time.

The other people in Bernstein's life included an accountant named Gordon Freeman and his former piano teacher, now secretary, Helen Coates. Miss Coates was the direct antithesis of Friedman and Freeman and even Bernstein himself. A spinster living in New England, she had early on recognized Bernstein's potential when he came to her as a fourteen-year-old to take piano lessons. As he grew and his talent developed she made it her mission in life to guard and protect him. The team of Freidman, Freeman, and Coates was formidable; they were to be joined a few years later by the shrewd and charming well-known New York theater and literary agent Robert Lantz.

When Friedman had settled himself opposite me I began our talk by pointing out that Bernstein had been recording with Columbia all his professional life and that I couldn't see any advantage in his not continuing to do so at this time. I pointed out that the New York Philharmonic was also on the Columbia label and that it would be a little difficult for the orchestra to have one affiliation and its music director to have another. He nodded and I went on to point out the many virtues of my extraordinary company, including the long friendship between Lieberson and Bernstein. When I'd finished Friedman leaned back and said, "Of course, of course, but we have to look very carefully into details." And he proceeded to tell me what was acceptable: a twenty-year contract with minimum guarantees against maximum royalties and the right to record anything he pleased at any time he desired to do so. There would be no more repertoire selection by the company. And he sat back and smiled. As he was doing so he reminded me that there were other companies prepared to meet these terms with larger monetary guarantees than he was asking from us and even to send him a blank contract to be filled in as Bernstein desired. And his smile widened.

I replied that I didn't think we would have a major problem, although as I said this my heart was racing. I had no idea what my colleagues' reaction would be, especially Lieberson, who was very careful with dollar guarantees, but I wanted time to think and not have the feeling that a gun was at my temple. "You think this over," Friedman said, reading my mind, "and I'll be in touch in three days. We must let the other companies know where we stand." And he rose, shook hands, and left.

I called Lieberson's office and asked for an appointment and when I saw him I relayed my conversation and asked what he felt we ought to do. I reminded him that we had the New York Philharmonic contract expiring and that it was entirely possible that both Bernstein and the orchestra might move to another label, particularly RCA Victor, where Alan Kayes and George Marek would like nothing better than to have the latest hot combination in the classical music field. Lieberson was not happy with the thought of such a blow to the company and was quick to realize that they held a very strong hand indeed. "What do you think?" he asked. "After all, it will be your responsibility to make the new contracts work." I told him that I thought we ought to go ahead with the twenty-year proposal and with the guarantees. I said that I felt neither would be a problem: that Bernstein's public was growing by leaps and bounds as his regular appearances on television were opening up the audiences for good music and his televised *Young People's Concerts* were reaching crucial numbers of families in an area that was of tremendous importance: education and culture. I pointed out that with the advent of stereo and the changeover from monaural to stereo equipment we would have to be redoing almost our entire classical catalogue and what better way of doing this than using all our resources—Ormandy and the Philadelphia, Szell and the Cleveland Orchestra, Bruno Walter and our group in Los Angeles, and as the capper, Bernstein and the New York Philharmonic.

The only part of their request that bothered me was the choice of repertoire and I said I thought this was probably more of a key to a new contract than any other point. I said I thought we'd have to take a chance here on establishing a new relationship between Bernstein and the company that would make this clause possible to live with. Lieberson listened to my points, asked me some pithy questions, and finally said that I should make the decision I thought best. I left his office realizing that I had come upon one of the secrets of his success: an ability to let people stand on their own, make decisions, and back them up. I was glowing.

I called Friedman the next day and said we had a deal and suggested we meet with the business affairs department of the company to work out the details. I then called Bernstein in Boston and told him that I thought we were on our way to completing his contract even before he went into the sessions in Symphony Hall. I was feeling fine until my door opened and in walked the head of the business affairs department, white with rage. "What have you done?" he said. "You have in one stroke broken all the precedents we've worked so hard to maintain. You'll cost the company a bundle and it won't look too good on your corporate record." He was glaring with such rage that I had a panic moment of my own. "I know it's unusual and that I'm new here but I'm not about to lose Bernstein in my first weeks and I think we can live with these terms and make money with them." "I'll have to see Lieberson about this," he replied, and went out the door. Minutes later Lieberson called me back to his office. "Are you sure you want to go ahead with this?" he asked, with the business affairs person standing at his elbow. "Absolutely," I replied. "Okay," he said, "the decision is yours." And he turned to the other fellow. "Help him in any way that you can." We left the room.

My next attack on the problem had to be the New York Philharmonic. The Philharmonic by itself was not a very attractive proposition, as far as recordings were concerned. Its success depended entirely on who was conducting and with Bernstein on the podium it would do well. I hoped the management would be realistic when we opened our talks.

Indeed they were. Philharmonic manager George E. Judd, Jr., was quick to realize that with Bernstein the Philharmonic had a ticket to record success, just as it was enjoying television performances for the same reasons, and he was not about to strain too far. Our talk, plus a few meetings with the Columbia and Philharmonic lawyers, led to a deal that was reached without any problem. We signed the contracts, both the Philharmonic and Bernstein, in November 1959 and we were off and running.

Our first order of business was to establish the repertoire to be recorded over the next five years. I had spoken briefly with Bernstein on this subject but wanted to delay detailed plans until all the papers were signed and until the Shostakovitch was safely recorded. I wanted to prove Columbia's new classical management meant what it said, hopefully with a minimum of fuss and fanfare. The Symphony Hall sessions went well and we were able to release the album as a special recording for the Christmas business and it sold extremely well. It was also praised by the critics, who made special note of the high quality of the recorded sound. Nowhere on the album was there any note about where the album had been made but many seemed to guess that it had to have been done while the orchestra was on its post-European tour and most probably in Boston. This did not endear me to Charles Munch, who, during the next summer at a party following a Tanglewood performance, came up to me, eyes flaring, and, putting his finger under my nose, opened our conversation with "*A bas* Columbia!"

As it became evident that our business affairs with the maestro were going to be in order I telephoned Miss Coates to make an appointment for a planning meeting. Miss Coates kept telling me how impossible his schedule was and how, in effect, I would have to stand in line. I told her that while she did not know me, she would before we were through and that I hated long meetings and wanted to get on with the job. In truth I was anxious for just as long a meeting as possible for I was mesmerized by the Bernstein charm and enthusiasm and found great pleasure in his company.

An appropriate appointment was made to meet in the maestro's study at The Osborne, a wonderful old apartment building on the corner of 57th Street and 7th Avenue that houses a fair collection of the city's active artists and writers. The building, with its long corridors and high ceilings and wide spaces, gives one the feeling of leisure and time. The Bernsteins lived in a large, comfortable apartment furnished with impeccable casual taste. He had a separate study on the second floor, with a small office attached for Miss Coates with plenty of space for scores and books, a concert grand piano, sofas, and comfortable chairs facing a good-sized fireplace and the rugs deep and inviting. The walls were covered with pictures and testimonials of all kinds. While I waited for the maestro to appear Miss Coates explained that she kept the walls up to date with his honors and that the rooms were, in a sense, a living library. When Bernstein entered she left and I sat down alone within him to concentrate on a very important subject to both of us.

At the desk he pulled a large yellow legal pad toward him. He was tan, dressed in elegantly causal clothes, a small scarf around his neck. His face was relaxed, his hair loosely brushed and, I noticed, beginning to turn gray at the temples. He was handsome and compelling and I felt immediately at ease, as if I were meeting an old friend of years standing.

"Now that you've got the right to record anything you want, what do you want to start with?" I asked to get the conversation rolling. He turned and fixed his eyes on me. "I wanted that right because I was tired of being told what I could and could not do," he answered, "and I want to make a plan with you that will make us both happy. You tell me what you need, I'll tell you what I would like to do and together we'll develop a good catalogue. How's that for a start?" "Couldn't be better from my standpoint," I said. "Good," he replied, "and we have to start immediately with the Mahler symphonies. I plan to play all of them over the next few seasons and I want to record them all. The public is ready to respond to Mahler. His time has come.''

As he went on outlining his reasoning about this composer, his eyes lit up and he was talking to me in the communicative and exciting manner that was so effective on television. I sat spellbound while he traced Mahler's life story. I was particularly fascinated by what he had to say because my own feelings about this composer had been tempered many years before by comments made about him in the old Victor Record catalogue. I remember reading as a child that not one crashing chord of Mahlerian sound could equal a cadence of Beethoven, and since in those days anything the Victor catalogue said was gospel to me, I turned my back. I did this for many years, until a Sunday in the late 1940s when we were at a concert of the Philharmonic conducted by Mitropoulos and the last piece on the program was to be the Mahler First Symphony. As the time came for the symphony to begin I leaned over to my host, our friend Skitch Henderson, and thanked him for a pleasant afternoon. He looked around at me in horror. "Where do you think you're going?" he asked. "I don't like Mahler," I replied. "You sit down." he said, getting up from his chair and going to close the box door firmly. "But I don't like Mahler," I said, quite intently. "Do you know this piece?" he asked. "No," I said truthfully, "but I don't want to." "Oh yes you do," he replied. "Sit down!" And for some reason I did and before I knew it I was caught up in the spell of this overpowering work. At the end I was on my feet shouting bravo after bravo. I've been a convert ever since.

By the time Bernstein got through with his presentation I knew there was no way out and felt in my gut that he was right. Then and there we started to lay out a schedule of the symphonies and the other major works. Since the Bernstein Columbia catalogue at that time was extremely slim we also had plenty of room for the standard repertoire. It seemed to me we had an exciting time ahead.

I left his study after our first meeting refreshed and exhilarated but realizing that I also had to cope with several other maestri at the same time—Ormandy, Szell, and Walter in particular— and I wanted to be careful not to upset them by seeming to give the plums to Bernstein. Szell was a relatively easy problem because Columbia had established a second label called Epic and Szell was its classical star. The problem was really with Ormandy and Bruno Walter, especially when it came to the Mahler symphonies. Bruno Walter had been almost the lone Mahler pioneer until Bernstein came along and he was now an old man, not well, but still with the missionary zeal about Mahler who had been his former teacher and guide. Walter was anxious to remake the First Symphony in stereo, having made the Second, the Resurrection Symphony, with the Philharmonic on his most recent visit to that orchestra as guest conductor. The First was also on Bernstein's list and I thought that we could get both of them on tape and release the Walter immediately, saving the Bernstein until the initial market for the Walter version had passed its peak. Actually, I would have scratched the First from Bernstein's schedule but he did have that special clause in his contract and I knew that he was determined to go ahead no matter what Columbia's problems.

The Bruno Walter recording was completed first in California. John McClure was the recording producer for all our west coast work and had a very close relationship with Walter. He was not entirely convinced that it was a good idea to go ahead with Walter's desire to record Mahler's First but I persuaded him to give it a try and said that we'd cope with the Bernstein problem later on. McClure went to California in early January 1960.

One afternoon in February he appeared in my office carrying acetate record dubbings of the Mahler tapes and looked at me long and hard before speaking. "I suggest you listen to these with nothing else to do," he stated. "And you better be prepared." I put the records on my turntable and settled down to listen. Out poured the most unbelievably beautiful sounds, measured and polished and serene yet filled with tension and passion; a reading of the work by a great old master doing final homage to his hero. When the symphony was finished I couldn't move from my chair. I sat staring at the wall, touched beyond measure. When I did pull myself together I knew I had to call Bernstein, contract or no contract, and ask him to put off his plans. When he came to the phone I told him that we had just finished a Mahler First with Bruno Walter and that I thought he might want to postpone his plans for the piece. We talked about this for a few minutes and finally he said, "Let me hear what you're raving about." I sent the dubs to him that afternoon.

About five days later the phone rang and it was Bernstein. "Oh my God," he said, "That is unbelievable, that is one of the most beautiful performances I've ever heard. Forget it for me this year. We'll wait forever if necessary. Nothing must interfere with what you've got there!" "That's very generous of you," I replied. "Generous, nothing!" he answered. "I couldn't bear the thought of trying to do the work now. It is his." And he rang off. And indeed it was many years until Bernstein got around to recording the First and even then was not satisfied with what he did with it. Such is the measure of the man and his wide-open love of his art and the great ones who practice it. Jealousy is not part of his nature.

Shortly after the Mahler episode we met in Carnegie Hall during a rehearsal break to discuss the Liszt Faust Symphony, a work he wanted to record and we had absolutely no interest in having in the catalogue. This time Bernstein was all determination and wanted more than anything else to convince me that he was right. We sat on the stage smoking cigarettes during a rehearsal break and he poured out his reasons in his usually compelling way. I turned as deaf an ear as possible. The work would be expensive to record, would never sell enough to justify doing it, and, at least in my opinion, was not of such overwhelming importance as to ride roughshod over business logic. The discussion ended with my agreeing to "think it over" and he went back to his rehearsal.

The next day I called him and said that I had thought it over and still felt that it would not be a good idea to do. At this point he said, very quietly, that he wanted to record it and was going to record it as he was allowed to do under the terms of his new contract. Shortly afterward Lieberson called and asked me what was going on. He had just heard from Bernstein, who was upset that he had to do something against our wishes. I explained and he sounded sympathetic. "Well, let's hope he's right and you're wrong," he said.

We did record the work, very well, too, with the Choral Arts Society and tenor Charles Bressler, and the critics called it a "masterpiece" long overdue in the catalogues, praised Bernstein's interpretation and generally applauded the foresightedness of Columbia. The album was a sales disaster. Later that year a package arrived at my office containing a picture of Bernstein and myself taken in Carnegie Hall the day we were discussing the symphony: the supplicant and the one being supplicated. I cherish it to this day.

During these years we recorded some splendid performances: Eileen Farrell singing the Wesendonck Songs and the *Götterdämmerung* Immolation Scene, Mahler's Symphonies 3, 4, 5, Beethoven Concerto #1 with Bernstein as soloist, Ravel's Shéhérazade with Jennie Tourel, the Missa Solemnis, the Bach Magnificat, the Beethoven symphonies, the Schumann symphonies, the Brahms symphonies, and a recording of his own music for the film *On the Waterfront* and a symphonic suite drawn from the songs and dances from *West Side Story*. We also did a remake, including all the dance music, of the score of *On the Town*.

Betty Comden and Adolph Green, the show's authors as well as its stars when it initially opened in 1944, were on hand to recreate their original roles, and with Bernstein conducting, it turned out to be a lively package.

The *Waterfront* and *West Side Story* recording, however, was enormously complicated. The suites were orchestrated by Irwin Kostel and Sid Ramin and were intended for live performances. When we decided to record them we had to pay the arrangers all over again for their work and this was expensive. On top of everything else the two suites were to have their debut at a special concert of the New York Philharmonic honoring Bernstein, who was to be in the audience. The concert went off as scheduled and at the last minute Bernstein decided to conduct the recording himself. I thought that was fine but pleaded with him to be careful about recording time rehearsals. "But they don't need much rehearsal," said he. "We'll just touch up a few things in the studio. Don't you worry." But I did worry; I knew what Bernstein's ideas of "touching up" might be and I kept saying to him at every possible opportunity that the recording was going to be horribly expensive and please be careful. The day came for the recording and about halfway through the allotted time I called John McClure and asked how everything was going. "Oh fine," he replied. "He's rehearsing away. We haven't recorded a thing." "What?" I yelled. And slammed down the receiver and raced out of the building toward the studio.

I arrived as everyone was having a break and sought out the maestro. "Listen," I said, "you promised me that you didn't need to rehearse and so far that's all you've done. I don't want to be difficult but this recording is going to end up as the most expensive classical recording ever made if we don't get on with it." "Don't worry, dear Schuy," he said with a charming smile, "it will be fine." And he went back into the studio.

The afternoon dragged on endlessly and the money kept being spent. It was too late to pull back now. The investment was made and we might just as well push ahead and complete the project. We did just that and when the calculations were made the disc cost $25,000 a side, something of a grim benchmark for the industry at that time. To his credit Bernstein was horrified when I told him the figures and suggested that he delay receiving royalties until the costs were recuperated. I said I'd take him up on that if I needed to and suggested that he pray with me that the recording be a success. It was. By the end of 1962 it had completely recovered its costs and was making money for all of us. But it was touch and go in the beginning and I learned a permanent letter of the law for Bernstein: never accept the phrase "don't worry." Start worrying when you hear it.

During this time we had gradually become dear friends with both Lenny and Felicia and spent many a happy hour in their home with the entire family. Our relationship grew, starting with after-concert supper parties where close friends would gather for post mortems or, more likely, discussions of what was going on in the theater or politics. Usually the parties lasted into the small hours, with people drifting away as their energies waned or their morning appointments loomed too near. Occasionally Felicia would give up and retire but not until overseeing the supper itself. We never stayed long, at least not at first, because our four boys and Betty herself had to be ready early for the Dalton School. The boys were students; Betty worked in the admissions office. The Bernstein children, Jamie and Alexander, were also at school but Alexander was a frail youngster given to severe respiratory infections and there was much worry about his bad health. Felicia talked to us about this problem and as the winter of 1960 wore on it became increasingly evident that he needed to be in a warm climate. She decided to take him out of school and they journeyed together to Arizona. This didn't work and they gradually made their way south to Chile, where the two spent the balance of the winter and most of the spring.

Jamie and the maestro missed them badly but the household continued to function smoothly under the hands of Julia Vega, a soft, small-voiced Chilean who kept things running then and still does.

When Alexander returned he was brown and healthy and had put on needed weight. He had also forgotten how to speak English and had brought home with him a small crucifix in a box, a gift from one of his Chilean relatives. Bernstein paled at this and began introducing the boy to his Jewish faith. They had to talk together in Spanish until Alexander's English returned.

The relationship between parents and children was always close, and when Nina was born in 1962 she was warmly welcomed by both her parents and her siblings.

Every once in a while Felicia would decide to give a formal dinner party. One such evening bears recalling because besides being funny, in a socially disastrous sort of way, it brought out the best in all the guests assembled, to prevent what might have been a true social Armageddon.

Felicia decided to give a party celebrating her redesigned dining room. "And let's be a little formal," she said. "Black tie." There were quite a number of other guests and the dining room was fitted out with three tables, one of which was for four people, one for six, and a third for eight. Most of the guests were old friends, and during cocktails we settled down in anticipation of a pleasant, relaxed evening.

When dinner was announced I saw that I was placed at the table for four, with Carmen Weisel, Jennie Tourel, and Herman Shumlin, one of the best producers and directors in the American theater. As we sat down, I introduced him to the two ladies, who smiled at him and began talking to each other. Herman looked over at me and asked, in a stage whisper that could be heard across the room, who they were. I quickly explained that Jennie Tourel was a world-famous singer and that Carmen Weisel's husband was important at the New York Philharmonic.

At this point Jennie turned to me and in her wonderful Russian-Paris-New York accent asked if I knew of her latest triumph in Chicago. I loved Jennie Tourel but she was totally humorless, particularly when it came to her career, and consequently I replied very seriously that I did not. She then proceeded to tell us about it in some detail, much to the amusement of Herman, who would, every now and then, interject a sly comment.

The Bernstein servants were all in formal black uniforms and white aprons and the tables glistened with sparkling silver and crystal, all at their best in glowing candlelight. The first course was a Chilean dish, pastelde choclo, a rich gummy stew with ears of corn scattered throughout. We had just been served at our table and the maid had moved away when Herman, adjusting his plate and barely touching the table, overturned the whole thing into his lap. Plates and glasses slid toward him and in a moment he had a great pile of everyone's first course. There were cries of consternation and we all tried to help. Fortunately, despite the cascade of utensils, he escaped relatively unmarred, and in short order we had the table readjusted and were served another portion of pastelde choclo and settled down to our interrupted conversation. Herman was a bit shaken by the accident but seemed to recover in good measure and was soon joining us in general talk.

The plates were changed for the second course, a claret was poured in preparation for the roast beef that appeared in all its splendor shortly thereafter. We all helped ourselves liberally and by this time Herman and Carmen Wiesel were enjoying each other's company and I was busy listening to the continuing triumphs of Jennie Tourel. As we began to pick up our forks Herman laughed gently at some remark of Carmen's and as he put his head back the table collapsed again and this time the tilt was so violent that everything, plates, glasses, cutlery, and candles ended up in his lap.

"What *is* this?" he asked in an angry voice, and began slowly rising from his chair, dripping everything the while. Both Felicia and Lenny leapt over to our table with anguished cries, Lenny knelt alongside Jennie, picking up dishes and glassware and Jennie, barely breaking the rhythm of her talk with me, turned her head to him. "Lenny," she said, did you read my wonderful notices in Chicago?" Ignoring everything, she went on to explain what a success she had had. Herman, in the meantime, was standing up, dripping beef and claret and candle grease, as well as some choclo remains from the first accident. Felicia tried to persuade him to come away from the mess and down to Lenny's dressing room, where he could be outfitted in a complete change of clothes. Fortunately both men were a similar size. Everyone in the room was trying to be sympathetic but most knew something about Herman that I did not, namely, that he had a fierce temper. Although he rarely lost his temper, it was apparent that when he did, it was not advisable for others to be around. Felicia knew this and was doing everything in her power to prevent the explosion which, from the look on his face, was not too far away. She finally got him by the arm and led him out of the room. Meantime, Lenny, with our help, was trying to pick up the pieces, while Jenny continued to tell him about her triumphs in Chicago.

Presently Herman returned, his pants sponged and wearing a new shirt, tie, and coat. We had found the problem with the table, which had a loose catch on one of the wings, and we shifted it around so that the dangerous part was now in my area. With some suspicion and not a little hesitation Herman sat down. We were served again and ate well, even though Herman looked very somber and skeptical about the whole thing.

The next day Betty and I sent Felicia a plant with a card reading: "To Felicia Bernstein: the first annual Herman Shumlin Award for the Hostess of the year." Herman, Lenny, Felicia, and all of us chuckled about this for some time afterwards; Jennie, as far as I knew, finally got Lenny to read her reviews from Chicago, which were, in fact, remarkably good. It was not an evening to forget.

After my departure from Columbia Records in 1964 I did not see much of Bernstein professionally until 1968, when after ten years as music director of the New York Philharmonic he decided to step down from the post, much to the sorrow of the Philharmonic's trustees and the music public. He was appointed Laureate Conductor, a title specially created for him, and began making plans to compose and guest-conduct around the world. At the same time my Lincoln Center activities were drawing to a close, and one day over dinner we talked about the possibility of working together again. One of the thoughts that evolved was the idea of making films and videotapes, as well as phonograph records, of his performances to have material on hand when the home videocassette market developed. We knew that there was already a tremendous market for this kind of material in Europe, where television networks presented good music as a regular part of prime-time programming.

Our discussions got more into focus as the year progressed and climaxed one night in November when Bernstein, in an almost offhand way, mentioned a telephone conversation he had had that afternoon with William S. Paley, chairman of CBS. While discussing another matter entirely he had asked what CBS was planning to do about the 1970 Beethoven Bicentenary. Paley had replied that he didn't know and asked if Bernstein had any ideas. Bernstein did, of course, and ended the talk by saying that he would get back to Paley.

"What do you think?" he said to me. "What kind of a show do you have in mind?" I asked. "I don't have all the ideas," he said, "but one work must be featured and that's *Fidelio*. I've been invited by the Vienna State Opera to do the official production of the work in the Theatre an der Wien where Beethoven composed it and where he conducted the premier. We must get this on film, It's an opera that people neglect and that can be wonderful, thrilling, and deeply moving if it's done right."

I had no argument on that point, remembering Bruno Walter's performances at the Metropolitan, but I did not think that a film on Beethoven could be built just around *Fidelio*. "Who should we think about to direct the film and work with us?" I asked, realizing that I had just committed myself to being the producer. "I like Humphrey Burton's work," came the reply. "Do you know him?" Curiously I'd never met Burton but I knew a great deal about him from other artists who thought his work on the BBC and on London Weekend Television to be almost the best visual presentations of music anywhere in the world. "No, I don't," I replied," but I feel as if I do." "Good. Let's get him to come over here and talk this over. "

Burton flew to New York and the three of us, sometimes joined by Lenny's agent Robert Lantz, discussed the Beethoven project and began to draw up some ideas. In the middle of one of the discussions Burton asked what was being planned for television regarding Bernstein's scheduled performance of the Verdi Requiem in Albert Hall in February of 1970. "Oh, we must film that too," he exlaimed, "but in St. Paul's Cathedral. What an unbelievably beautiful place to perform that glorious work!"

With my parents and younger brother, John Griswold Chapin, in Mt. Kisco, 1925.

At NBC, 1946, in the only available civilian suit.

In the Air Force, 1945. Complete with helmet, goggles and white scarf, one childhood ambition fulfilled.

Karsh of Ottawa

"To Schuyler (G. Chapin)—In pleasant remembrance of the
one night 'stands'—Cordially—Jascha Heifetz—March
1954."

Costa Manos/Magnum

Van Cliburn at the piano, Ted and Hank Chapin studying his
technique. 1958.

With Stravinsky. The photograph is signed "To you dear Schuyler (Chapin) my very best greetings—I. Stravinsky—Hollywood, July 6 '63."

At the signing of Horowitz's contract to record for Columbia Masterworks, with Goddard Lieberson and Mr. and Mrs. Horowitz, 1961. My right leg was in a cast for I had just broken it skiing with Leonard Bernstein.

With Horowitz, arriving at Carnegie Hall for his historic return concert, May 9, 1965.

With Sol Hurok, 1971.

Henry Grossman

With Oliver Smith and Leonard Bernstein at St. Paul's in London, during the taping of the

Signing Bernstein for the Metropolitan Opera recording of *Carmen*, 1972. The laugh is over our sudden reversal of roles.

Photograph by R. T. Kahn

Goeran Gentele

Wide World Photos

September 19, 1972—opening night of *Carmen* and the '72–'73 season at the Met. At the master control board with Osie Hawkins, the executive stage manager, and Stanley Levine, the stage manager (back to camera). (*above*) Backstage the same night—with James McCracken, still made up as Don José; Ted Chapin; and Betty. (*below*)

Henry Grossman

With Marit Gentele and Danny Kaye, immediately after the first *Look-In,* April 1972.

Photograph © 1977 Helen Marcus

With Lucine Amara, at the Library of Performing Arts reception given in honor of the Chapins, 1974. (*above*) With William Steinberg, James Levine (then principal conductor) and Danny Kaye, during rehearsals for *Parsifal*, 1974. (*below*)

With Galina Vishnevskaya, costumed as Tosca, 1975.   *J. Heffernan*

Photograph © 1977 Jill Krementz
With Beverly Sills, after *La Traviata*, February 5, 1976. "To
Schuyler—with my love—which you have forever—Beverly
XXX."

With Birgit Nilsson, after the *Götterdämmerung* matinee on March 29, 1975, her last performance at the Met.

Bill Mark

With Licia Albanese, Dorothy Kirsten, Joseph Gimma (Albanese's husband) and Bidu Sayao—spring 1974.

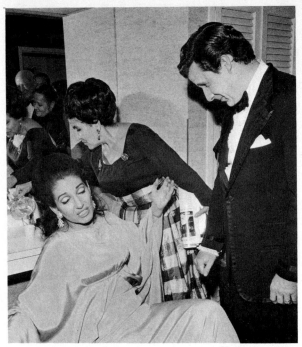

Henry Grossman

With Maria Callas and Licia Albanese, with Francis Robinson and Bidu Sayao reflected in the mirror, after Callas' Carnegie Hall recital, 1974.

Camera One/Joe Cordo

With Isaac Stern, planning the Carnegie Hall Concert of the Century, 1976.

Betty Chapin

The Metropolitan Opera Company in Japan, costumed for the *Carmen* dress rehearsal at the NHK Theatre in Tokyo. Left to right, front row: Adriana Maliponte, Kazuko Hillyer, Marilyn Horne, Paul Franke, Christine Weidinger, Shirley Love; back row, Schuyler Chapin, James McCracken (hidden by Maliponte) Guillermo Sarabia, Andrea Velis, William Lewis, Russell Christopher, Richard Best.

A tempura lunch in Japan, with Betty, Richard Bonynge and Joan Sutherland, 1975.

The Chapin family at Hank's wedding—September 1975. Left to right, Miles, Sam, Ted, Hank, his wife, Amy (Darley), Betty and myself.

July 1, 1975. Before announcing the Opera in the Park, my last duty as general manager. With Miles, Betty and Ted.

We all agreed and I realized that we now had two major film projects ahead. The time had come to pull ourselves together, form a little company, and get properly organized. Bernstein's lawyers and agent agreed and I accepted the post of executive producer in Amberson Productions, a brand-new television and film-making company. The name Amberson is derived from Amberson Enterprises, Inc., Bernstein's publishing and holding company, and came, in part, from the name he used as a youngster in the popular music field, Lenny Amber. This, in turn, was derived from the fact that the German word *Bernstein* means *amber.*

From the standpoint of the calendar, the Verdi Requiem was first on the schedule and financing it became my first order of business. I went to Roger L. Stevens and Robert Whitehead, who had produced the original *West Side Story,* and told them what we were planning to do. "Who's singing in the Requiem?" Stevens asked. "Arroyo, Veasey, Corelli, and Ruggero Raimondi," I replied. "That's good enough for me," he said. "How much do you think it will cost?" I'd worked hard with Humphrey on developing a budget and I replied, without hesitation, between eighty-five and ninety thousand dollars. He thought a moment. "You have a deal," he said. "Any film of the Requiem with Bernstein, St. Paul's Cathedral, and such a cast is bound to work. And let's not go to lawyers over this or we'll never get it done." And he took a piece of paper and began roughing out an agreement. He gave it to me, I went over it with Lantz, and two days later we met in Lantz's office to sign. The entire agreement was a page and a half and clear in language and intent. Stevens signed and I signed and Bernstein signed and we were off and running with our first project.

While the Requiem plans were going on I began an assault on CBS regarding the Beethoven project. I called Mike Dann, then the senior vice-president in charge of television programming for the network. Dann had a tremendous track record at CBS and had survived several administrations, always pushing for what he believed would deliver top ratings and not totally assault the senses of the viewing public. I had known Mike ever since he came to the NBC publicity department from the New Haven Railroad back in the 1940s and watched his career with interest. I knew him well enough to know that he harbored secret desires in music, opera, and dance, and I thought we might have a chance of organizing a Beethoven celebration if he seemed interested.

Dann was interested. He had just sent Howard Taubman, the retired chief music critic for the New York *Times,* to Vienna to try to work out a Beethoven show with the Vienna Philharmonic and the Vienna State Opera. He said that they had just about settled on a telecast of the

Ninth Symphony from the opera house which was going to be the CBS Beethoven homage. I told him that Bernstein planned to do *Fidelio* for the State Opera and concerts with the Vienna Philharmonic and that we wanted to develop a ninety-minute special that would be a proper Beethoven television biography. Dann asked who would be working with us, and when I mentioned Humphrey Burton's name he pointed melodramatically to the telephone. "Call him," he said. "Get him over here today." Fortunately I reached Humphrey at home. Explaining that I was talking from Mike Dann's office, I asked if he could possibly fly over again immediately for conferences on our Beethoven project. Humphrey detected the urgency in my voice and caught the next plane. On his arrival we sat down with Bernstein to make an outline of what we were going to do. After some discussion we finally did agree that the show would contain parts of *Fidelio*, parts of the Ninth Symphony, parts of the First Piano Concerto, and some biographical material.

With this Humphrey and I had a meeting with Dann, who proceeded to talk to us in a manner that reminded one of a combination of David Belasco, Billy Rose, Mike Todd, and Louis B. Mayer. He finally authorized us to fly to Vienna and see what we could put together as a package.

On arrival in Vienna we began a round of talks that were exhausting. We had scheduled meetings the next afternoon with the head of music for the Austrian State Television, the head of the Vienna Festival, the orchestra committee of the Vienna Philharmonic, and the intendant of the Vienna State Opera. The Viennese are charming people, the city is a delight, but they have their own particular way of doing business and nothing is apparently going to change them. We sat in meetings and after lengthy discussions would think we had arrived at an understanding. Just as we were ready to go I usually summed up what we'd discussed for a final nod from everyone and then would step out of the room to put the key points into a memo for everyone's initials. All this would be done and we would just be leaving when someone would say, "Oh, Mr. Chapin. What a pity! Please forgive me; I don't know what I was thinking about. Of course you cannot do that on Thursday. And Friday is impossible too!" We would sit down again and find out what the problem was and it usually was money. We would shake our heads and try to match them in politeness but eventually had to give all or part of what they had suddenly discovered they wanted. Sometimes these talks took place on the street outside the building we'd just been in, as we were getting into a taxi. Sometimes they took place in the lobby of the Hotel Sacher, where we were staying; one such took place at the airport just as we were leaving and literally as we were at the departure lounge. One thing we learned in a hurry: wherever we were and whatever contract we had agreed upon it was bound to be changed and we had better be prepared for it.

Basically, however, we accomplished a great deal in twenty-four hours and I was able to return to New York with enough information to put together a pretty secure budget. I did this, together with an outline of what we planned to do, and took the papers over to Mike Dann's office. I told him that I was leaving again for Europe in exactly ten days and asked him if CBS could possibly decide yes or no on the project before that time. I realized I was asking a lot; most producers have to wait for all the committees and committees within committees to make up their minds. I reminded Mike of the initial conversation between Paley and Bernstein but knew full well that this could be used only in an emergency. Bernstein loathed the idea of doing anything that might smack of selling himself but I figured that if worse came to worst I could figure out a way for him to do it that would be dignified and proper.

The next days were filled with the details of the Requiem project. I had a hunch that Franco Corelli might cancel at the last moment. He is world famous for doing this, and I wanted to protect us with another world-class tenor. I sought out Placido Domingo. Julius Rudel had discovered Domingo in Israel and brought him to the New York City Opera. Almost immediately the Metropolitan signed him as well and he was enjoying a huge success. Domingo had replaced Corelli that year at the openings of La Scala and Covent Garden. He was becoming known as the stand-by for Corelli and this was beginning to rankle.

Domingo was at that time living in New Jersey and in the middle of his Metropolitan season. I explained our problem and could see his sensitive eyes react with sadness when he heard the name Corelli. "Listen, Mr. Domingo," I said, "I believe in telling the truth. I think Corelli will back out of this and I think the film and recording will be yours. And at this stage in your career it would not hurt you in any way to be associated with Bernstein." "Oh, no, of course not!" he rejoined. "Nothing would please me more. I have such admiration for the maestro!" And he smiled in a way that left no doubt in my mind that he meant exactly what he said. "It's just that I don't want to stand by for Corelli any more." I said that I understood his point and asked if there wasn't a way that we could work out an arrangement that did not put him into a compromising position. We finally agreed that I would call him from London at 5:00 PM on the Friday before his Saturday

Metropolitan broadcast and two full days before our filming was scheduled to begin. He would come if we asked him then.

His agent and I reached agreement on his fee and, almost as an afterthought, I asked whether or not he would be in Europe in April when we might be filming the Ninth Symphony. It happened that he was and so I offered him the tenor part on his own and this pleased him very much. We were now ready to go ahead.

The day for departure neared and still no word from CBS on the fate of our Beethoven project. I kept calling Dann and his deputy Jim Krayer but nothing was happening. I finally talked it out with Krayer and we agreed that if Bernstein could speak to Paley once more something would surely happen. I broached the subject of Paley to the maestro and he glared at me: "You know I *hate* doing that," he said. "It's cheap and vulgar and pushy." I explained that he didn't have to do anything in bad taste. I asked him to call Paley on some pretext or other and close out the conversation with a casual reference to the fact that his producer had submitted a proposal for a Beethoven program to his television program people and that he, Bernstein, hoped it would all work out. He scowled at the idea but he did it and Paley said he'd have a look. And have a look he did, for within a couple of days Dann called me. We met and he told me the project had tentative approval subject to completion of a contract and an acceptable budget. I turned everything over to Abe Friedman, asked him to keep in touch, and flew off to London with the Bernsteins and Oliver Smith, who was to be co-producer and designer for the Verdi Requiem film.

The morning after our arrival Oliver and I met with Humphrey Burton, who was concerned about the lack of agreement to do the film from the British musicians' union. This was supposed to have been handled by the management of the London Symphony but had not been done. Oliver was concerned about lighting St. Paul's and other production problems and we adjourned our discussions to the cathedral itself. "I'm going to cost you a lot of money," he hissed in my ear as we entered the building, "but it's going to be beautiful. I studied this cathedral inside and out during my student architecture days and I know every inch of it. You see up there?" And he pointed to the arches in the transept. I looked, but other than the arches themselves could see nothing. "There are beautiful frescoes hidden up there," he said, "and we're going to light them so they can be seen. The only thing is that it may take every spare theater light in London to do it." "Go ahead," I said. "You're my co-producer and whatever you spend will have to be justified not only to me but also to yourself!" He gave me a hug.

From the cathedral I returned to the Savoy Hotel, where I had set my room up as a production office. I had a lot of work ahead; we were scheduled to shoot the film exactly five days later and had to do the whole production in one night. Ordinarily this would have been a joke but the filming was to be preceded by a live concert in Albert Hall and numerous rehearsals before that. A recording was also to be made by Columbia Records, which did not want to risk using the soundtrack of our film. Arrangements had been made for production assistance from London Weekend Television, where we received the facilities and a fee for exclusive use of the production in Britain. The video cassette market was just beginning to rear its head at this time and we wanted video cassette rights from all the artists involved, including the musicians, and this was to prove sticky going. No one wanted to set what they felt might be a precedent and as a result each negotiation was endless. I raced around London tying up all the pieces in a hired car with driver, at the insistence of Oliver Smith, who told me to drop my New England sense of thrift and spend the necessary money. It was good advice and saved a lot of time.

Despite all my efforts, however, the musicians' union was proving stubborn; it would not grant us the cassette rights and my principals were rightly insisting on this point. Humphrey Burton was especially helpful here and introduced me to the labor expert from London Weekend who took over for me and somehow or other got an agreement that was both fair and proper. It was clearly understood that our contract was not setting any precedent and any other ideas involving cassettes would have to be handled on an individual basis.

The afternoon of this victory I returned to the hotel for a meeting and a cup of tea with Felicia and as we sat in her sitting room I heard the most painful bleating coming from the living room of their suite. It was obviously the Verdi score but the singer sounded as if he had swallowed a peach pit and was about to leap out the window. I looked at her questioningly and she shrugged. "It's been going on all afternoon," she said. "It's Corelli. He doesn't feel well." I listened for a moment more and then buried my head in my teacup. Presently the maestro entered and poured himself a cup. "Did you hear that?" he said, looking sad and concerned. "I did," I replied, "and I think we're going to have to do something about it." "We'll wait until after tonight's rehearsal with the chorus and other soloists and see," he replied, "but we better be ready with Placido just in case."

The rehearsal that night was with piano, soloists, and chorus and it was obvious that Corelli was not himself. He was pale and perspiring and terrified. At a break we all agreed that we had to let him go. I ex-

cused myself and went tearing back to the hotel to complete my telephone rendezvous with Domingo. He had been waiting exactly as we
had agreed, and I asked him to come. Although he could not arrive in
time for the Sunday concert, he agreed to come right after his Metropolitan broadcast and be ready to work on the following Monday,
but not Sunday night. We agreed to his schedule and I booked him a
room at the Savoy. The next problem was telling Corelli that we were
not going to use him for the film or the recording but hoped we could
patch him together sufficiently for the Albert Hall performance. I went
to bed that night trying to figure out what I would say to his agent.

I was awakened the next morning very early by the phone ringing in
my ear. It was Loretta Corelli, hysterical and crying, telling me that
Corelli was sick and had to cancel the whole Requiem package. I sat
bolt upright in bed. "You mean he's cancelling everything now?" I
asked. "Si, Signor Chapin, everything. We go back to Italy. Franco
has such beautiful memories of the *Cavalleria Rusticana* with the maestro he don't want anything to disturb this. [Corelli had sung *Cavalleria*
with Bernstein earlier that season at the Metropolitan.] Goodbye."
And she hung up.

My first reaction was relief. With his withdrawal we had no obligations to pay off his contract and I could save money. But then I thought
about Sunday and Albert Hall. It was, after all, Saturday morning and
this did not leave much time to find a substitute. I began a round of
calls to various agents but it seemed at first that everyone was either
singing that night or out of town. We struck paydirt halfway through
the morning when the English tenor Robert Tear agreed to perform,
and to rehearse on Saturday night. He was superb, Bernstein was happy, and he had an enormous success with the audience.

The next day rehearsals began again for the filming and recording.
Our soloists guarded themselves carefully since they were going to be
required to sing steadily over the next few days. We all had our fingers
crossed, what with the London winter weather and vocal fatigue, but
they all made it. Only Raimondi seemed unperturbed. He would finish
every session and leave either Albert Hall, where the recording was
taking place, or St. Paul's Cathedral looking impassive. There was always a beautiful girl with him, as near as I could tell a different one
each time, and he would return for the next session looking calm and
satisfied. Martina Arroyo, not known for robust health, stood up wonderfully well, as did the mezzo Josephine Veasey. Domingo was fine.
He, too, did not lack for feminine company. He never does.

Our only real problem was that we had very little rehearsal time in the cathedral itself and everything had to go like clockwork. We were to be allowed into the building at noontime and the filming performance was to start at 7:30 PM. Our invitation to the public to attend had resulted in double lines outside that began forming early in the morning. They lent an air of anticipatory tension to the day.

I arrived at 8:00 AM and watched as electricians crawled all over the ceiling installing lights. What seemed to me endless rolls of wire were playing out and disappearing into the vastness. Eight cameras were being placed around, carpenters were putting the finishing touches on the orchestra platform and covering the sides and floor; the usual sights and sounds of preparation for an event of great theatricality were everywhere about. In the middle of the chaos Oliver Smith stood, overcoat draped over his shoulders, looking like a battlefield general as his troops are advancing against heavy fire. Humphrey Burton was there as well. Usually unflappable, this morning he looked a little harassed. "I'm having camera trouble," he said as I approached. "One is dead and another is dying and I've sent away for replacements but I don't think we can find them. We may have to make do with six." And he smiled wanly. Just then I was approached by the verger. "I beg your pardon, Mr. Chapin," he said, pronouncing my name "Shypin," as it frequently is pronounced in England. "Could you have a word with the dean?" "Certainly," I said, and went along after him. The dean greeted me with a certain reserve and I took the moment to thank him for all the cooperation we were receiving and to assure him that he would not be displeased with the results. He smiled coldly and said, "Our problem at the moment is that there is smoking in the cathedral and this is absolutely forbidden. It must stop immediately or we may be forced to cancel the entire project." I immediately thought of Bernstein, who is a heavy smoker and with the extra tensions of these sessions would be driven crazy without tobacco. "I do not wish to be unreasonable; there are other than ecclesiastical reasons for this, particularly fire prevention and we must enforce the rule without exception." I told him I would pass the word and thanked him again for his help. This time he thawed a little and we discussed the opening of the program and the procession that would enter the cathedral to get things under way. He seemed very pleased and I sent for Humphrey to join us and explain what he had in mind. Things thawed considerably after that 'but there was no question about the smoking problem and I had to figure out what to do about it, at least as far as Bernstein was concerned.

At noon the orchestra and soloists arrived followed immediately by the maestro, who was shown into a small office that was to serve as both his dressing room and a command headquarters. It was a round room, fiercely damp, with a small w.c. and washbasin located far up a dark, frigid spiral staircase. There was an electric heater near the desk. I opened one of the several mystery doors in the rear to discover a passage leading to additional stairs that evidently went up to the roof. The wind was whistling and it was cold. When I stepped back in the office Bernstein was just lighting a cigarette. "Hold it," I said, walking forward to take it away from him. "We cannot smoke anywhere in the cathedral. I was told this in no uncertain terms. Unless we behave the whole project will be cancelled." "But what am I going to do?" he wailed. "I think I've found a solution," I said in an even voice. "Follow me." And I led him into the staircase passage. It seemed even colder the second time but the wind did seem to carry the smoke away and I felt that he could puff up a storm in the w.c. and no one need know. He took a few puffs gratefully and we returned to the room.

The rehearsal got under way around 4:00. Humphrey had preplanned almost all his camera shots and had worked closely with Oliver Smith on what corners he was going to explore and how they would be lit. I tried to have a look at the monitors but was repeatedly called away with the kind of details that plague the life of a producer, and therefore I didn't have a chance to see much. Musically, matters were in secure shape. The big problem was stationing the trumpets for the Dies Irae entrance. We were making the soundtrack in stereo but since most televison sets are monaural and have bad sound equipment we wanted to try for the illusion of antiphonal sound, the effect of sound coming from both sides of the building and having the viewer feel absolutely certain that he was hearing that way. This was a question of creating a picture on the screen that made you think you were hearing antiphonally.

A great many so-called acoustic problems are really problems of vision.* With the Requiem we wanted to give the visual allusion that the music was coming from all over the cathedral. In the main, I think we succeeded.

---

*No better example of this existed than the original Philharmonic Hall in Lincoln Center, New York, when it opened in 1962. The critics, particularly the New York *Times*, screamed about the acoustics, which, indeed, were not totally satisfactory but were never as bad as was constantly being reported. What was bad was the design of the hall itself, which gave the audience the feeling they were looking at the stage through the wrong end of a telescope. Not know-

The filming started almost exactly on time. Every available inch in the cathedral was taken up by the audience and there was an air of high anticipation. As the dean, the verger, and Bernstein began their procession toward the podium, with the cameras tracking them. I realized we were now finally under way.

The performance went quite smoothly. The antiphonal trumpets sounded fine, the chorus and soloists in good voice, and the orchestra on its toes. There were two terrible musical bloopers, however, that I knew were going to have to be corrected. One was the unison entrance of the soprano and mezzo in the Agnus Dei, a section that always gives trouble, and the other was Arroyo's opening phrase in the Libera Me, which was punctuated by the cathedral chimes ringing out ten o'clock. Also, I became aware that Humphrey was having troubles with his cameras and I went around to the vans containing the monitors to have a look. All was quiet in the various places but one sensed an air of great tension. There was nothing I could do at this point and I walked around to the front of the cathedral to have a look at the proceedings from the front door. The effect was deeply moving. The lights around the orchestra, chorus, and soloists and the lights over the ceiling, around the nave and transept, and over the heads of the audience gave you the feeling that you were entirely in another world.

Finally, at a little after ll:00 PM, the work was completed and the same group of dean, verger, and conductor walked solemnly back to the dean's office. Once they were away from the podium Humphrey came out to announce that there would be some necessary retakes which would begin in about thirty minutes. He then joined me in the dean's office.

Bernstein was huddled at a table, an overcoat over his shoulders and two heavy bath towels around his neck, sweating hard, his hair matted against his forehead. He had the score in front of him and was busy marking points that needed to be done over. The dean and verger were off on the side watching in awe as people came and went with cups of tea, books of music, light lines, and other impedimenta of television filming. When Humphrey and I arrived he grabbed us both. "We have *lots* of problems," he said, "we really should do the whole piece over." Humphrey spoke quietly and assured him that such was not the

ing what was disturbing them, they automatically thought it had to be the sound and joined in the chorus of lament. After it became Avery Fisher Hall, after that generous and caring music-lover donated the funds to redo it, the acoustic problems disappeared and so did the visual ones.

case. He pulled out his notes and the two began making a list of imperative retakes. Bernstein was obviously dying for a cigarette and kept looking over at me and at the cathedral officials. "I'd give anything for a cigarette," he moaned loudly, "anything." The dean looked at the verger and both approached the table. The dean cleared his throat. "Mr. Bernstein," he began, "after what you've given us tonight, the unbelievable beauty of it that I shall never, never forget . . . please, smoke as much as you want!" And he reached in his pants pocket and took out a lighter. Bernstein leapt for his cigarettes and was soon puffing away to his heart's content. There might have been problems yet to face with the film but it was obvious that the performance itself had reached out and touched the Church of England.

The retakes went slowly. Everyone was tired and some of the tension of the performance was off so that more mistakes were made and the more that were made the more irritated everyone became. Roger Stevens and Robert Whitehead had flown over for the filming and were now sitting in the audience looking at their watches. We had organized a small supper party at the Savoy for the key people on the project and I knew we were running later and later and that this was going to add to the costs. I began to get nervous.

Finally, at about 1:30 AM, we were finished and dismissed the company and crew. Hardly any of the audience had left during the retake process, which seemed a good omen for our work. We got to the party a little after 2:00 AM and everyone was very subdued. A drink and a bit of supper was all I could take and before leaving I confirmed with Humphrey that we would look at our raw tapes at 9:30 in the morning. I thought it only fair to invite Stevens and Whitehead to have a look as well, although I was unsure what we were going to see and how good it would be. My feelings were not buoyed by Humphrey, who looked extremely tired and discouraged, and as I said good night to him and his lovely girl I had the feeling he too was apprehensive.

I was overcome with the possibility that our first Amberson production project might end up a total disaster and that in the morning we would look at a lot of imperfect tape that had cost us a considerable sum. In my room were several messages all stacked neatly. One of them contained the joyous news that Mia and André Previn had just become the parents of twin sons and that I was expected to be godfather to them both. Another was from CBS in New York and another from our lawyer. I called André Previn, even at that hour, and made a date for lunch the following day and with a whirling of kaleidoscoping colors and shapes I put my head back on the pillow and was asleep in twenty seconds.

Five hours later I staggered out of bed, and taxied to a Dean Street studio, where I was joined by Whitehead and Stevens, Humphrey and Christina, Oliver Smith, and a couple of other people who had been involved in the production. Whitehead had recently remarried the lovely Zöe Caldwell after his first wife's death, and Zöe, too, was in the little screening room. Bernstein was not there. I had persuaded him to stay away, because I knew that we would tell him the problems soon enough. It was also early in the morning after a strenuous night and it was better for all that he be absent. "Let's go," I said to the tape room engineer as the lights were lowered and I sank further and further down in my seat.

What came on the screen was the raw master tape of the performance and the sound track in monaural just as it unfolded in the cathedral. With the opening titles I surreptitiously glanced around the room and saw Humphrey scrunched way down, his eyes barely looking over the back of the seat in front of him. Stevens and Whitehead were both sitting professionally straight staring at the screen. Oliver was slumped in front of me and the few others were looking in a noncommittal way. The titles rolled on and presently we were caught up in the dignified and moving procession to the podium, the simple bow of Bernstein to the dean just before raising his hands to begin, the lowering of lights in the cathedral as the quiet, opening strains of "Requiem aeternam dona eis, Domine" floated upward; then the raising of light with "Te decet hymnus, Deus, in Sion"; and the blaze of wrath and anger with the opening strains of "Dies Irae."

As the tape moved along we were all caught up in the power and beauty of the work and of the setting in which it was being performed. The artists were inspired. The cathedral fairly breathed with the piece. At those moments when the intensity became almost too much the cameras would break away for a glance at a statue or a look at a ceiling fresco. Every work of art shown matched the spirit and mood of the music. It gave one the feeling that·it was all spontaneous and inspirational. It flowed freely and with Verdi.

I was deeply moved and tears came to my eyes, partly emotion at witnessing the beautiful tape and partly relief that we had something priceless here that should be around for a long time. I reached into my pocket for a handkerchief to blow my nose as discreetly as possible. A hand came toward me from out of the darkness. A voice that I recognized as Oliver Smith asked if I had another. I did and I gave it to him. He blew his nose a little less discreetly. Soon another hand tapped me on the shoulder. I raised my right arm and the handkerchief was removed and used by someone else. Humphrey slipped over and asked to borrow one. Suddenly I was aware that everyone in the room was weeping but I seemed to have the only handkerchiefs. Eventually someone slipped out and returned with a package of tissues. It was passed around as the rest of the performance unfolded before us.

The lights went up at the end and no one spoke. Finally Oliver rose and turned to Humphrey and me and said, "I think this is the proudest moment of my professional life." He hugged us both. Humphrey dissolved. In a quiet voice he explained that when he left the party he was absolutely certain that he had failed and simply had not been able to get a good performance. Bob Whitehead and Roger Stevens, both with tears coming down their cheeks, felt that every penny invested was worth it. I sat stunned.

Presently I got up and found a telephone to call Bernstein. He came on after a short delay and I tried to tell him how moving it was and how very pleased he should be. My voice cracked in the process.

There was a lot of work to be done on the tapes before we would have a finished product to show to the maestro for final approval but it was obvious that the material was there and it would only be a matter of settling down in an editing cubicle and going to work. What emerged is a Requiem for a long time to come, with artists, chorus, and orchestra at the absolute peak of their form. The Requiem itself is Verdi's tribute to the great Italian patriot, poet, and literary influence Alessandro Manzoni, and it was appropriate that Bernstein would see the tapes of his performance for the first time while in Italy some six weeks later. He was not displeased and neither have been audiences in England, Germany, France, eastern Europe, and Africa. The Japanese purchased the tapes and showed them on the thirtieth anniversary of V.J. Day over the full NHK, the state network. London Weekend entered into an arrangement with us whereby it will be used as a standby for showing in the event of grave national emergencies. One day it will be seen widely in the United States. It is ironic that the piece is honored everywhere except in the country that produced it.

With the completion of the Requiem all attention now turned to Beethoven. Bernstein had concerts in Paris for two weeks and I flew back to New York to gather the pieces for the final contract details with CBS. Betty and I were also planning a quick ten days in Jamaica with our old friends the Guettels before I pushed off for Vienna. While there the final details of the Beethoven project were hammered out with a series of wild telephone calls that always found me standing in the middle of our bedroom dripping wet from the pool. I felt like a hero in an MGM musical of the thirties!

Bernstein, Humphrey, Burton, and I met in Vienna to discuss again what we were going to include in this special. We all realized that it was unusual for one of the three major networks to commit itself to a prime-time special on so noncommercial a subject as Beethoven. We felt, and I articulated this point more than the rest, that we had to produce a program honoring Beethoven in a manner that was authentic and acceptable to music lovers and scholars and yet accessible to the general public who might be curious about the man and go on afterward to explore his life and music. We had to tread a fine line and I thought we could do it considering the talents involved, to say nothing of the power of Beethoven himself.

Bernstein was principally concerned about *Fidelio*: he believed that the message of Beethoven's creative genius was wrapped up in this opera and that it should be the focal point. Humphrey and I agreed on its importance but were not certain how to handle it.

Opera on television is a cantankerous subject. The NBC Opera Company in the 1950s had made innovative strides in trying to translate the medium onto the small screen and had supplemented this with two national tours of the NBC Opera across the United States. Public television was doing an occasional production and opera films were being made by the gross in Europe. None, however, were really satisfactory. The technique of video translation was eluding everyone and I felt we were heading into the same morass with *Fidelio*. We discussed these and other points and ended up with a format roughly dividing the program into three parts: a biography of Beethoven, *Fidelio*, and the Ninth Symphony. Bernstein and Burton began work on the script. I chased around Vienna completing contract assignments.

The first act of business was to establish command headquarters in the Hotel Sacher, where the *portiers* and staff were in awe of the maestro and ready to lean over backwards to help him with anything. The next was to call upon the Vienna Philharmonic, the Vienna State Opera, the Festwochen, the opera chorus representatives, the various theater unions—stagehands, wardrobe, makeup—the management of the Theater an der Wien, the ministry of education and culture, and the officials of the Schoeller bank to firm up all details. The major organizations had agreed in principle and in some cases to specific fees during my earlier rush through the city in January but now these oral understandings had to be translated onto paper. With the Viennese this turned out to be a constant lesson in elusiveness. I always felt I had my hands around a bowl of ectoplasm. At one point when I thought I had everything set the phone rang one morning and the cheerful voice of the *portier* greeted me with the news that representatives from the orchestra, the opera chorus, and the Festwochen had all arrived to see me. I said I hadn't any appointments with any of them but it soon became evident they wanted to see me because of certain difficulties. "I'll put the orchestra in the Blue Room," he went on, "and the chorus in the Coffee Room, and the Festwochen in the Red Room. Which do you wish to see first?" I sighed and said the chorus. Why not start out with singing?

The chorus wanted more money and guarantees of payments in the event of reruns and assorted other matters that had been thrashed out in long meetings before. Humphrey glared at them from across the table and finally brought his hand down sharply on the table's edge. "No more!" he shouted. "No more, do you hear?" And he became very red in the face. We hadn't discussed strategy and I was surprised at this uncharacteristic outburst. The leader looked startled. Humphrey went on, "You think that just because this project is American and CBS that there is a bottomless well. There isn't, and if you want to work with us, fine. If not, stop wasting all of our time." And he picked up his coffee cup, took a sip, and banged it down into the saucer. I caught the message and added that I was shamed and shocked by their lack of ability to make an agreement and stick to it. The chorus representatives conferred among themselves in German with occasional glances at Humphrey and myself and finally turned and said, "You take care of us if the film is shown in theaters. We make a formula. Then we agree to everything. We sign the papers right now." "I've heard all this before," I said, rising to the moment. "How do we know that you will not find one more new difficulty after we agree on these points?" "You have our word for this," the leader replied, looking very solemn. Humphrey and I exchanged glances. "We'll have these points put to paper and you return here tomorrow morning at eight-thirty AM to sign." They bowed, *auf wiedersehned*, and left. We moved on to the Festwochen in the Red Room.

Here we walked into great agitation. Ulrich Baumgartner, the Festwochen director, was pale and angry. "There will be no more filming in the Theater an der Wien," he stated. "You are causing too much trouble. It is all *unmöglich.* I am ordering your cameras and crew out of the building." And he paused to light a cigarette. We both knew what had brought on this outburst. On the second day of filming a stagehand had brought the house curtain down directly in front of our huge, hot lights and the material had passed close enough to the lights to burst into flames. Instant work on the part of everyone got the fire under control in seconds; the rehearsal we were filming went on without interruption while stagehands and Vienna City firemen wandered around the stage looking for sabotage. It admittedly had been a close call and I was concerned about the general fireproofing of the curtain regardless of this incident. It would have been impossible to leave the theater at this point and Baumgartner knew this as well as I, but he was putting on a good show for the officials from the city that he had brought with him. After his outburst I said that we were all deeply sorry about the accident but that it had not been our fault. The stagehand made a mistake and it was not fair of them to turn us out for something we did not do. I looked at him and spoke in my hesitant German, throwing in the English word when I could not think of the German. Our talk went on for some little time until finally Baumgartner agreed that if we could regain the permission of the theater management we might continue doing what we had under way. We shook hands on this and I assured him that his name and that of the Vienna Festwochen would appear prominently on the credits for the film both in Austria and in America. He nodded at this suggestion and left.

Humphrey went on to deal with the orchestra problems, in the Blue Room, and I went to the Theater an der Wien to see if we could placate the manager and continue. I was greeted with stony silence and negative looks. There were four or five people at the meeting and finally I asked to see the manager alone. The minute we were together his whole attitude changed. "We must agree to let you continue," he said, "but my colleagues, well, they feel that perhaps you might do something to help us all over the, what shall I say, strain of these last days." I reminded him that it was his stagehand that had made the mistake, to which point he merely shrugged and looked helpless. "Well, let us say that the accident wouldn't have happened at all if your special lights had not been there." And he smiled. I looked at him long and hard and after struggling with my conscience and my temper replied that I thought some details might be worked out to everyone's satisfaction and that I would consult my lawyer, who would be in touch. We shook hands warmly and the matter was under control.

Despite these problems, we moved ahead on the project, filming endless Beethoven houses, the stage and room rehearsals of *Fidelio*, the Vienna Philharmonic in the Musikverein with Bernstein playing and conducting the First Piano Concerto, and the full Ninth Symphony, played in a special set designed by Oliver Smith, in the Konzerthaus. We took helicopter shots of the city and the surrounding area, of the woods and parks where Beethoven walked; we absorbed as much as we could to have plenty of raw material to shape our final version.

Winter blended into spring and 1970 was a particularly lovely spring in that area of the world. Bernstein was living in the suburb of Grinzing in a house with a lovely pool and garden. The sun poured in and gave the place a feeling of the beauty of the Vienna woods. Visitors came and went, seeking out the maestro for other projects around the world. Wolfgang Wagner arrived one day to try to persuade Bernstein to come to Bayreuth the following season to conduct a new *Tristan und Isolde*. Wagner looked like all the pictures of his grandfather come to life and he spoke in a tight, controlled voice about what a joy it would be for Bayreuth if Bernstein were to come. It was Dr. Strangelove coming to life. With considerable effort, and as subtly as possible, he moved his left hand over to control the other. Elliott Kastner and Topol came, the former one of the smartest of the new crop of movie producers and the latter the Israeli actor with masculine energy, sex appeal, humor and charm, to persuade the maestro to do the score for a new film in which they were both interested. Bogianckino came from La Scala. We walked one overcast afternoon in the Schoenbrun gardens while discussing what Bernstein might do at La Scala. "Anything he likes," Bogianckino kept saying over and over, "anything he likes. He must come. The public demands it!" Zeffirelli sent writers and designers and assistant directors to keep up a relentless attack about *Brother Sun, Sister Moon*, a giant film planned by the Italian, who was determined that only Bernstein should do the score. The two had been talking about the idea for over two years but nothing much was happening. UNICEF sent a representative in the person of Leon Davico, who was anxious for the maestro to open the Austrian UNICEF drive. Marcel Prawy, the Viennese musicologist and artistic director of the Volksoper, Peter Weiser, the director of the Konzerthaus, Rudolf Gamsjaeger of the Musikverein, Rolf Gintel of the Staatsoper, various representatives from the ministry of education and culture, from the Foreign Office, from the chancellor himself, as well as just friends were at the doors almost every day and night. The levee never stopped.

Princess Lily Schoenburg, a beautiful and bright and funny friend to us all, would look at the goings-on and wink. We would run away from it every once in a while to her family castle, a mid-eighteenth-early nineteenth-century schloss on the Rainergassestrasse, falling down, desperately in need of repairs, presided over by Lily's mother the Gräfin Schoenburg whose posture and firmness gave no doubt of her aristocratic position. Lily and her mother lived in the castle virtually penniless with whatever they had going toward the most desperately needed repairs. Lily was unmarried largely, I think, because there were no properly eligible Austrian princes left. Her passion was music and she is an accomplished pianist. Chamber music was often performed at the schloss by some of the best players in Vienna with Lily taking part. The gardens and parks of the estate were frequented by members of the Vienna Philharmonic, the opera, the symphony, all stages and stations of the musical life of the city. Lily and I, sometimes under the watchful eye of her mother and sometimes not, would sup by candlelight and she would fill me in on all the gossip.

Bernstein was a big figure in Viennese life, not only the musical side. He had become something of a folk hero, a dashing free figure representing the energy, kindness, and drive of Americans. When he appeared on the streets he invariably collected a crowd of people asking for his autograph, or just standing back and applauding. It was all exhilarating, touching, exciting, moving, exhausting. I couldn't keep up with it all and Lily sensed this and extended quiet and peace and friendship.

Others who did the same were the Schoeller family, Fritz and Anne and their assorted children. Fritz von Schoeller runs the Schoeller bank, in which I kept our company's considerable money on deposit. He was a friend of Bernstein and in the middle of the Beethoven filming invited him for a few days' skiing in San Anton. Arrangements were made for the maestro to take the evening train into the Austrian mountains. He would stay in the same hotel as the Schoellers, ski and socialize with them, and return to Vienna at the end of five days. We planned to work around him, shooting scenes and backgrounds that did not demand his presence, and take a closer look at the footage we already had. Bernstein had promised to let me know what train he planned to take back, but by the morning of the fifth day there was no word whatsoever.

About noon I called the hotel in San Anton to be told that he had just left that morning and was flying back to Vienna. Indeed he did; he arrived at the Sacher about 4:00 PM after a nearly five-hour trip in a chartered helicopter. He looked fit and rested, reporting that the train ride had been a rough and tumble affair where he hadn't closed his eyes and that he was determined to avoid a repeat. My New England background came to the fore. "Chartered a helicopter?" I asked. "How much is it going to cost?" He looked at me. "I've no idea. I didn't ask."

He gave me the charter papers and I went to the phone to call the company. When I reached someone who spoke English I asked about the charter. "Ah yes," said the voice, "Maestro Bernstein this morning from San Anton. Wonderful! A great honor for us!" "To be sure," I said, "but how much is all this going to cost?" "Let's see," came the reply, "San Anton to Vienna and back to San Anton again. That's almost ten hours flying for the machine and ten hours for the pilot." "They usually go together," I commented. "Oh, no, of course," he murmured, "but it does add to the expense. Let me see . . . I must double-check with San Anton but I think our bill will be in area of $5,000." I thanked him and hung up, reaching for the nearest chair.

I must have looked pale because Bernstein was over to me in an instant. "How much was it?" he asked, with a slight catch in his voice. His New England background was coming forward as well. "$5,000, at least," I replied. "My God!" he exclaimed. "$5,000? I had no idea." And by this time he was paler than I. "What are we going to do?" "Pay it," I said. "I'll have a check for them in the morning. I don't suppose you thought about Beethoven while you were on the slopes." "Oh yes I did," came the reply. "I even had a chance to write some script." And he indicated his briefcase. "May I see?" I inquired and he nodded. I opened the case and took out a large handful of yellow legal-size pages crammed with his handwriting. Indeed he had been working. The material was rich in descriptions and outlines of Beethoveniana, including a first draft of the crucial denouement of the film. "With this I think we might be able to put the helicopter down as a production expense. I don't know whether or not CBS will accept it but it certainly is worth a try. After all, rest and recreation has produced some specific results!" He looked a little relieved. "Well, that's your decision," he said. "Next time I think I'll ask the price first."

A few days later Fritz Schoeller's secretary called on me at the Sacher and presented a few bills in connection with the maestro's trip. I paid them, as they all seemed to be in order, but was amused at the precision with which they were ticked off. Schoeller wasn't a banker for nothing. Later Fritz and Anne invited me to a country weekend at Reichenau, the country seat of the Schoeller family some 50 miles south of Vienna in the Schwarzwald. Reichenau is a comfortable hunting lodge, with streams and pools and gardens and incredible mountain walks and drives. Fritz has responsibility for thousands of acres of mountains and valleys. The house itself is pure Hapsburg;

stags and roe buck and deer and antelope stare down from the walls, antlers gleaming. Stuffed birds and fish are interspersed with pictures of hunters and their catches, everyone standing in lederhosen and feathered cap and loden coat. My bedroom was large and comfortable with high ceiling, a fireplace with a low fire going, a nightstand with basin and bowl and eiderdown quilts. I flung open the window, letting in the fresh, vigorous mountain air and fell asleep that first night almost instantly. Some weeks later, when Betty had joined me for two weeks, we were asked again to Reichenau and I was able to show her some of its beauties.

Fritz spent most of his time there coping with ecology and animal preservation, rather than hunting. We journeyed up the mountain one day with his gamekeeper, Anne and I in the back of the Land Rover, Fritz and the gamekeeper up front. A rifle was tucked away but the chief armaments were powerful field glasses. We were stalking to see what was there. Halfway up one high hill pass, Anne was ordered out of the car. "But why?" I asked. "Tradition," came back the answer. "Women do not go any higher on these trips." Anne seemed to take it philosophically enough. I thought it was absurd, but then again, lots of Austrian traditions seemed rooted in their imperial past.

We did see some striking animals standing on the slopes, great graceful figures with heads high, necks arched and antlers straight and tall. I was glad to see them where they belonged, being appreciated by our little group with glass and camera.

The Schoellers and Lily Schoenburg were wonderful divertissements but our task was to concentrate on Beethoven and we were rarely away from this. By mid-April we had filmed pretty much everything we wanted except the completion of *Fidelio*. After long conferences and much thought we decided to film the entire dress rehearsal from start to finish and film the actual opening night only if we ran into disaster. For the dress rehearsal, we asked permission to request that the audience come in evening dress. The Opera authorities were delighted to cooperate and word went out that no one would be admitted without formal clothes. We stationed people outside the theater doors to tell the audience that they were going to be photographed and turn any away that didn't like the idea. Since the rehearsal was by invitation only, we were free to do this. No one refused. A Bernstein rehearsal is big enough on its own but when it is also the rehearsal for the official opening of the Beethoven Bicentenary season it has extra dimension.

At 8:00 PM we started and the minute Bernstein entered the pit it was obviously going to be a special night. The tension normally present at a dress rehearsal was there together with a special eagerness. Our technical people knew the theater well by this time; Humphrey knew exactly what he wanted to get and we were as prepared as we could be. The rest was up to the artists and they came through. By the end of the opera as the chorus rang out with "Heil sei dem Tag, heil sei der Stunde" we had captured a rare performance. As the backstage cameras took over to cover the curtain calls chorus members were embracing each other, stagehands were shaking hands, and the maestro, clothes soaking wet and hair matted on his forehead, was gently chastising Gwyneth Jones, the Leonora, for not looking at him carefully enough. They went out to bow and the house rose. The ovation was overwhelming. It was a powerful experience and I'm happy we have it all for posterity.

There remained one more part to complete before the maestro was due to take off for Israel. None of us was satisfied with the text he had written to precede the last movement of the Ninth Symphony. While it was perfectly acceptable it wasn't what it could be and no one was more concerned about this than Bernstein himself.

A film crew was scheduled to be at his house to make the final wrapup and lead into the symphony. As we started the script still wasn't right and after a couple of takes he called a halt and, taking his legal pad and pencils, went upstairs and closed the bedroom door. About an hour later he re-emerged and handed me a bunch of paper. I read through what he had written and it was brilliant. He had given a mood and thrust to our entire project. One line caught my eye particularly. In describing Beethoven's music he wrote that it is "accessible without being ordinary." A perfect description of Bernstein himself, I thought, as I gave him back the papers and signaled that I thought it was okay. Humphrey read through his remarks, looked over at me and winked, gave the script back, turned to the cameraman and lighting man, said, "let's go" and in a few minutes Bernstein was pouring out his thoughts to the camera.

When he was finished we all had a glass of champagne and celebrated the fact that the principal photography of Beethoven's Birthday was completed.

Within the next few days Bernstein flew off to concerts in Israel and with his departure Humphrey and I settled down to look at all our material. Our partners in the venture, Austrian State Television, were anxious to know how we were coming along and were not the least shy about expressing their opinions. I was basically concerned with the American audiences because I knew we had one of those rare opportunities of presenting a prime-time commercial television program about music. Europeans, and for that matter many of our own countrymen as well, do not understand that American television is, as advertised, a commercial medium appealing to the widest possible mass audience. Music, dance, and classical drama do not appeal to the mass market; they appeal to a small segment but that segment is not the one that makes or breaks a product or a show. When CBS, or any of the other commercial networks or stations, puts an art program into prime time it knows it is going to lose the ratings battle for that particular time segment. Often people in my profession, both administrators and trustees alike, think that commercial television is the answer to all the economic problems of the arts. It isn't and it never will be. The most that we can hope for is the involvement of some kind of programming on cable and box office TV that can be sold to the viewer who wants it and a continuation of exposure on public television. I do not believe that either will solve the economic problems but both can be helpful in assuring a portion of income. So might the video cassette market if that lumbering giant ever gets into action. Commercial TV will always be a visiting spot for the arts.

After a few days with the Austrian technicians it became evident that we were not getting good rushes of our material. We also had not resolved our most perplexing problem: what to do with *Fidelio*. Humphrey and I talked over and over again but couldn't resolve the problem. Finally I suggested we let it drop for a moment and decide exactly how we wanted to handle the first section of the program, a pictorial and narrative biography of Beethoven. Humphrey had an answer for that one. We would use part of the First Piano Concerto as the musical bridge to take the viewer on a tour of Beethoven's Vienna, its parks and woods, and especially the thirty-seven houses he lived in during his ten-year residence. To get over Beethoven's restlessness, his domestic chaos, and personal boorishness we toured the streets, looked at the drawings and caricatures of the period, and then, to the relentless rhythms of the second movement of the Ninth Symphony, showed house after house after house. The effect was galvanizing; in a matter of just over twelve minutes the viewer had a feeling about Beethoven the man and a tantalizing glimpse of Beethoven the genius.

With this and the last movement of the Ninth Symphony we had a brilliant beginning and ending to the program but no acceptable middle part. *Fidelio* was becoming not only a weight around our necks but a serious problem in producing a good film. We needed some outside help and fast. Humphrey reluctantly agreed and we decided to pack up

everything and move to London, where we could get at people and
equipment as needed. Humphrey had a thought about a film editor we
might turn to. "You'll like Michael Bradsell, you'll see," he said.
"He's quiet and imaginative and mad about music. If he doesn't work
we'll find someone else." "Okay," I agreed. "Let's see if Mr. Bradsell's interested. We haven't all that much time to find a solution."

Michael Bradsell, who worked often with Ken Russell, was interested in having a look and we made a date.

Bradsell appeared right on time, a short, roly-poly man with sprout-
ing red hair and a fierce red beard. He looked like a mad prophet as he
sat looking at the screen with no expression whatever on his face. After about thirty minutes of looking he said that he'd seen enough and
we stopped the film and brought up the lights. He looked at me and
then at Humphrey, no expression on his face, and finally, in a quiet
voice barely audible, said he thought he might have a few ideas and
would like to take the material with him for a couple of days. He'd let
us know when he was ready for us to see what he had done. We explained that we had time problems and he smiled, nodding, and said
that he'd be in touch. As we left the room Humphrey and I looked at
each other and crossed our fingers.

I had two free days and called the Glendevons to see if I could come
to Greys and unwind. Humphrey drove me down to Henley on a sparkling late spring afternoon and said he would call as soon as he had
heard from Bradsell. In the meanwhile, I bathed in the luxury of
Greys, the perfect English house. Liza's immaculate taste provided a
home that had the best comforts of American plumbing and the graciousness of English country life. The food was delicious, the talk interesting, and the countryside ideal for walking. I relaxed completely
for two days, and right on schedule Humphrey called to say that Bradsell had something to show us that afternoon. I took the train to London and met Humphrey at the room. We took our seats and even the
always collected Humphrey Burton looked frazzled. "Are you
ready?" Bradsell asked considerately. The lights went down.

On the screen came a shot of Bernstein rehearsing the principals in a
rehearsal room. The atmosphere was light and cheery but thoroughly
professional. He was talking about the piece to his cast, explaining
how this tempo should move and that rhythm be accented. He spoke
about the black and white characters, either all good or all bad, and
how they had to be given dramatic human qualities to take away from
the cardboard images expressed in the libretto. He gave a lot of his attention to Theo Adam, the Pizarro of the production, and said that he

thought Pizarro had the worst time of all because he was so unrelentingly villainous. He had to be given some human characteristics, some sign that he was a disturbed man. Adam listened to this with polite attention and the camera caught the interplay between the two of them.

Next we saw a stage rehearsal with piano and Bernstein and Otto Schenck, the director, talking about the Pizarro problem. Bernstein was explaining his theories and Schenck nodded in agreement. "Let's have him wear glasses when he reads the message about Don Fernando's impending arrival," says Bernstein. "*Wunderbar*," exclaims Schenck and goes up onto the stage, taking off his glasses and handing them to Adam. "And be paranoid!" exclaims Bernstein. "He should tug at his collar; he should sweat with fear and look around to see if his weaknesses are observed." "Right, right!" says Schenck, and in German and pantomime shows Adam what he wants. Adam shakes his head and in German says that he's played this role all over the world and never been asked to do things like this before. "He's afraid he will mar his good looks!" exclaims Bernstein, and he laughs. The camera catches Bernstein and Schenck watching Adam rehearsing the new business.

The next shot on the screen is Adam in actual performance, putting on the glasses and tugging at his collar. The effect is powerful. The audience has seen the evolution of a dramatic idea through conception, rehearsal, and final results.

The lights were raised and Bradsell turned to us. "I've looked through all the material and you've got enough to carry this idea through the whole production. You will make the segment be *about Fidelio* and not just *Fidelio* itself." Humphrey and I looked at each other and shook hands. We knew we were in business.

Over the next weeks Humphrey worked with Bradsell in assembling a rough cut of the entire ninety minutes while I returned to New York to other Amberson business, including complicated talks with Joseph E. Levine and his company, about a series of co-productions. The talks dragged out for weeks, with batteries of lawyers representing both sides trying to draw up a contract. Levine stayed out of the meetings and I found that the wrangling began to get on my nerves.

One afternoon I left a session to get a glass of cold water and chanced down a corridor that led to Levine's office. "How's it going in there?" he asked as he saw me pass his office door. "Not too well, I'm afraid," I replied. "The lawyers are so busy protecting the lawyers that I think they're losing sight of what we're here to do." I looked in the room and he was reading a letter. Next to his desk was an Andrew

Wyeth painting. I looked hard at it, prompting Joe Levine to say, "Are you interested in Wyeth?" "Very much so," I replied. "I think he is my favorite American painter." "Come in, come in!" he said. "You're a man after my own heart." I came in and saw around the room some beautiful examples of the painter's work. "Most of my collection is at home. You must come see it." I said I'd love to. "You must see it even if we don't do business together." And he put his arm on my shoulders. I did go to his apartment, met his sparky wife, saw his collection. It is beautiful. But we never did business together.

That summer we put the final touches on the Beethoven film. Humphrey criss-crossed the Atlantic several times and we wrestled with decisions on final takes and sound balances. One hot July night we were ready to have Bernstein see the biographical first part and consider what kind of text he wanted. That night will go down in history: New York was in the grip of a midsummer heat wave. The temperature was hovering in the nineties, the humidity around eighty-five percent. Sidewalks had been baked with the heat for at least three days. There was no wind. Our viewing room was in midtown Manhattan and about an hour into our work the air-conditioning broke down. The room had windows but these were sealed and could not be opened unless broken. All our material was spread over the room; it would have taken a couple of hours to pack it up and move somewhere else, if indeed we could find another room at 9:00 PM at night. There was nothing to do but strip down to the fewest possible clothes, drink endless glasses of iced tea, wrap one's head in towels and hope for the best.

In the middle of the night, around 1:00 AM, Bernstein tore up all the script he had written and flung it against the wall. "Not good, not good," he murmured. "Let's look at that opening again." And once again the projector started up and the images flicked across the little screen.

He said nothing, just stared. Humphrey sat back, a hand across his forehead, his glasses fogged in the hot dampness. I sat looking at them both and suddenly thought of the Indian jungle and World War II. Not since then had I felt such oppressive heat and humidity. Suddenly Bernstein looked at us. "I've got an idea," he said. "Go away for half an hour and let me think it out." And he turned his back to us and began writing.

We took the moment to step outside the room for what passed as fresh air. The night was sticky and uncomfortable. The buildings were giving off heat: having absorbed it during the daytime, at night they play it back so that the streets and the people never have a chance to cool off. "What do you suppose he'll come up with?" I asked, really just to make conversation. "Something rather marvelous, I should suppose," replied Humphrey, rubbing his hands over his irritated eyes.

We went back in half an hour and Bernstein looked as if he'd just conducted a full program. He was sweating from every pore but didn't seem to be paying much attention to it. "Let's look again," he said, "and I'll read what I've done here and see how it times out with the film."

The machine began and he, with one eye glued on the screen and the other on his script, read through a narrative that gave the salient points of Beethoven's life with passion, humor, and directness. He'd found the key.

It was now about 3:00 AM . "I'm sorry," I said, feeling quite nauseated, "but another five minutes and I'll be sick all over everything. I'll see you in the morning." I staggered out and home, wondering why I was willingly going through all the agonies of heat and frustration to work on some fool film.

Our bedroom was air-conditioned. It felt like the inside of an icebox and I fell asleep as soon as I got into bed. I dreamt of Beethoven shaking his head at the three of us trying to reconstruct him. I'd reach out to touch him and he'd shrink away. Strains of music came and went; horses and carriages clopped past half-finished buildings. Napoleon appeared, tears in his eyes because the dedication to the Eroica Symphony had been destroyed. I felt myself turning, restlessly, from side to side. I awoke at eight, splashed water on my face, and went back to the studio.

The scene was just as I'd left it; Humphrey was blue-lined with fatigue and the need of a shave, Bernstein looked matted but unlined. "We've got it!" said Bernstein as I walked in. "Let's show it to him." The machine whirred again, Bernstein's voice sang out with his words, and the music clues were clearly indicated.

Indeed they did have it. From that night and morning in the hot-box editing studio to the final process and the final product itself very little was changed. The three parts were spliced together accompanied by a connecting narrative, the music was edited, color balanced, titles added, and three weeks ahead of schedule I called the CBS television people and invited them for a screening of their program. They came, Bernstein, Humphrey, and I each spoke briefly, then we put the program on the screen. At the end there was no comment whatever; they all came to us and shook our hands. "We'll win an Emmy with this," one commented. "It's beautiful. Thank you."

We were all encouraged and a few days later I volunteered to help the CBS sales department if they felt I could be useful. The days and weeks dragged by and nothing happened. I asked when the program was to be shown and never got a straight answer. I kept up a barrage of calls; the more I asked the less I was told. When I came into the CBS office to finish up the accounting for the production, and actually handed them a refund of $2,500, I was told over and over what a beautiful "product" we had and how proud they all were to have it for their network. But no word as to when it would be shown. Finally in late November I got a call that said it would not be scheduled in 1970 at all because they had been unable to find sponsors. "How can you do this?" I pleaded. "The whole project was developed for the Beethoven Bicentenary. Don't tell me you can't find sponsors for something as good as this. There must be other reasons." "Sorry," came the reply, "we won't be using it this year." And the conversation ended. So did the argument. The program was finally aired in the United States on Christmas Eve 1971. It was shown in Austria, Germany, and England as an official program to mark the anniversary and elsewhere in the world as well, but in our own country we had to wait for a whole year. It did indeed win an Emmy in 1971 and was favorably received by the critics. It was a shame, however, that it was not seen at the right time for its purpose.

XIII

Bernstein—Japan, Berlin, Kennedy Center

With the completion of Beethoven's Birthday we now had two potent films in the Amberson catalogue, four actually, if you broke up the Beethoven project into three separate films. We did exactly that and put them on the education market immediately, where they began a still intensely satisfactory life.

In the summer of 1970 Bernstein was invited to take the New York Philharmonic on a tour of Japan. I was reluctant at first to go with them. Memories of World War II came flooding back and I felt uncomfortable. On our arrival in Osaka, where I was sitting with the pilot of our chartered 707 helping him find the runway through the dense smog, the group of people assembled to greet us as we disembarked reminded me of Nanking right after the surrender in 1945.

These feelings were soon overshadowed by the excitement and color of Japan itself. Our daily activities included not only concerts but frequent visits to Kabuki, No theater, temples, gardens, receptions, and meetings with Japanese artists. Among these, Bernstein had a letter to Yukio Mishima, the controversial but brilliant writer whose works were causing quite a stir in the West. The two men talked on the phone from Osaka and arranged to meet in Tokyo. I had just read *Temple of the Golden Pavilion* and *The Sailor Who Fell from Grace with the Sea* and was anxious to meet him as well. Bernstein and I agreed that I would come for a few minutes after he arrived and leave at the appropriate time so that the two of them might see whether or not there would be any possibility of some kind of artistic collaboration.

The day arrived for their meeting and at the right moment I tapped on the door of the Bernstein suite and entered the room. There sitting on the couch was Mishima, clothed in what looked like an old Roman gladiator outfit, with leather straps criss-crossing his body. His voice was deep and sonorous and he gripped my hand with strong muscles. His eyes were hypnotic and as we sat down I saw that his pants hugged his body, showing every muscle possible but, I would have thought, making any movement impossible. I told him how much I'd enjoyed the books I'd read and he seemed pleased with this. We all had a drink and after ten minutes or so I rose to leave. "So soon?" he said. "We've barely begun to talk." "I must," I replied. "I've got to attend to business matters. I leave you and the maestro in peace." And we shook hands.

The next day Bernstein was strangely silent about their visit. He told me that Mishima wanted him to see a film and was sending someone to fetch him at three o'clock that afternoon. I said I would go too and precisely on time three young men arrived, all with shaved heads and white uniforms and swords at their sides. I introduced myself and they bowed solemnly. They were members of Mishima's private army, part of a group that had stirred up considerable controversy in Japan by espousing the old warrior civilization and the code of the samurai. I introduced Bernstein and their bows were accompanied by a murmur of recognition.

We crossed the street from the hotel to a side door of a movie theater and walked up some small, steep steps. At the top was Mishima waiting to greet us, dressed this time in a uniform similar to his young troops. "I made this film quite a while ago," he said by way of introduction. "I think it is one of my best works." We took seats and the lights were lowered. What came up on the screen was the story of a 1936 scandal involving a young warrior and the imperial household that led to the young man's hara-kiri. The young man was played by Mishima himself and the hara-kiri was dragged out to revolting lengths. I slipped lower and lower into my seat, covering my eyes as much as possible. Bernstein sat bolt upright watching but not making a sound, unusual for him at any theater where he is not shy about passing his comments in stage whispers that can be heard all over the auditorium. The soundtrack of the film was a passionate rendition of portions of *Tristan und Isolde*. It was altogether gruesome.

When the film was finished we got up and walked toward the back of the projection room. There stood Mishima, arms akimbo, staring at us as we approached. "Well," he said, after a long pause, "what do you think?" There was silence. Bernstein looked at him and said nothing. To break the silence and say something I made some comment or other about the soundtrack. "It seemed to give an added dimension to what you were doing," I said, somewhat timorously. "Of course," he replied, as if I were some kind of class idiot. He was staring at Bernstein. "Well," he said again. "What do you think?" Bernstein looked hard at him and said, "I need time to think." We started out of the room. I made a stab at saying goodbye but Mishima was interested only in Bernstein and stared at the back of his head as we were going down the stairs. When we reached the street Bernstein turned around and looked back. He didn't say a word, just waved and crossed the street. The two men obviously did not get along and planned no further meetings. I was bothered by Mishima but at the same time curious to know more about him. I never got the chance; later that year, in a final outburst of his version of patriotism, he committed hara-kiri.

During the previous spring I had been discussing a contract with Unitel of Munich for a series of films with Bernstein conducting. This was settled, oddly enough, one morning over breakfast in Tokyo's Imperial Hotel coffee shop. Contracts had to be written and I knew this was going to be a lengthy process with assorted lawyers, but in the meantime we had to begin production plans for our first film, Mahler's Symphony Number 9, with the Vienna Philharmonic to be filmed at the Philharmonie in Berlin, while Bernstein and the orchestra were on a European tour. We were to use a new technique, that of 35mm cameras tied into a group of television monitors that allowed them to be used with the flexibility of videotape. It sounded awkward to me but I could see the advantage of film from an editing standpoint. Videotape is expensive and difficult to handle in the editing room; film is relatively easy and for music might even be preferable. We would soon see.

With the signing of the Unitel contract Amberson was now obliged to film all nine Mahler symphonies and the four Brahms symphonies with the Vienna Philharmonic. In addition Unitel had first call on any other television projects that might come along. For this they put up 100 percent of all production monies, paying advances and fees to the company in an arrangement that suited us just fine. The first Mahler filming, the Ninth Symphony, was scheduled for the week of March 8, 1971.

We also agreed to create a film about *Der Rosenkavalier*, which

Bernstein was reviving at the Vienna State Opera in the spring of 1971. The film was to be based on the formula we had evolved for *Fidelio*. The Unitel authorities were very much impressed with what we had done in creating a film about the opera rather than of the piece itself and they wanted the same kind of treatment for *Der Rosenkavalier*. Bernstein was very enthusiastic about this idea; he was scheduled to record the opera for Columbia Records and the idea of also having a film made him very happy. But first we had to get permission.

Der Rosenkavalier is very thoroughly protected by copyright, and that is guarded over with fierce devotion by Strauss's publisher in London, Boosey and Hawkes, and one particular officer of that company, the redoubtable Belle Ampenhoff. Miss Ampenhoff had to agree and set terms. She was known to be tough but I also knew that she was anxious to obtain the Bernstein catalogue from the American publisher G. Schirmer and I hoped this might make her more tractable.

In London on a cold, Dickensian February morning, I had my first meeting with Miss Ampenhoff. She sat behind her large desk listening impassively to what I had to say and seemed not the least impressed. I told her exactly what we had in mind and asked her if she knew of any of Bernstein's television activity. She replied that she did but that she had not seen *Fidelio*. I asked her if she would allow me to set up a screening and she nodded assent. The whole interview was rather teacher-pupil and I was beginning to get a little put out by her attitude. That was not going to help the cause, however, so I swallowed my annoyance and arranged a screening for the next morning through the offices of Amberson's European sales representatives. I also asked them to be present, hoping to show Miss Ampenhoff the extent of our organization.

To the screening Miss Ampenhoff brought an ancient Hungarian gentleman complete with sideburns, a pipe, and hair sticking out his ears. He was introduced as the house musicologist, and nodded continuously while extracting a pair of iron-rimmed glasses from a rusty metal glasses case. His suit was rumpled and stained, his fingers yellow with nicotine, his shirt cuffs ragged and dirty. Central casting could not have improved on the classical absentminded professor. We all settled down and the film began. I kept looking over at the professor, who sat bolt upright in his chair once the film began, and I could catch enough of his face to see that he didn't approve at all.

When the screening was completed the lights came up and the professor and Miss Ampenhoff began an animated conversation in Russian. Finally she turned to me and said that she would like me to come to her office later that same afternoon and she would have word for me. The professor looked over, shaking his head, and said that he didn't understand what we were trying to do and didn't like Bernstein's tempi for the opera. We obviously had not picked up a friend.

Later that afternoon I appeared in Miss Ampenhoff's office and was calmly told that we could do our *Rosenkavalier* project if we used no more than fifteen minutes of music and paid a 30,000 royalty. "Thirty thousand pounds," I said, why that's almost [and I tried a quick calculation] that's almost eighty-five thousand dollars. There must be some mistake." "No, there is no mistake," she retorted. "I've been in touch with Franz Strauss [Richard Strauss's son and heir] and that's what he wants." "But does Herr Strauss realize that what he is asking for is outrageous? I'm told that he admires Bernstein's *Rosenkavalier* very much indeed and in fact made a special point of seeking him out after the premiere of his production to tell him so. This seems like a strange way of showing his interest." Miss Ampenhoff sat staring, making no further comment. "Perhaps the maestro might like to consider filming some of Stravinsky's ballets," she finally said. "I'll take the Strauss terms to my principals," I replied curtly, "and be in touch with you tomorrow." I walked out furious.

The next morning I called to say that the deal was off and that Herr Strauss and Boosey and Hawkes could take their £30,000 and stuff it. Scratch a good idea.

A few days later I flew off to Paris to join Bernstein, who was conducting l'Orchestre de Paris and for meetings with the French television people who were negotiating with us for Amberson products. While there I received a phone call early one morning from Stockholm. As I put the instrument to my ear a cheery voice came on the line. It was my friend Goeran Gentele, whom I had not seen since 1967, when we had discussed the possibilities of the Stockholm Opera visiting New York as part of the Lincoln Center summer festivals. I had kept track of him through Isaac Stern and other friends who would bring me greetings and funny messages when they returned from Swedish visits and I had suggested his name to Lowell Wadmond, chairman of the board of the Metropolitan Opera Association, as that organization began its search to find a successor to Rudolf Bing as general manager, but I had not had any direct contact for four years.

"What are you doing?" he asked cheerily. "Sleeping until a few moments ago," I replied, "particularly since I didn't get to bed until almost dawn." "That's too bad," he went on, "such a lazy life. I want to change that." "Change what?" I said. "I'm working with Leonard

Bernstein, we have a wonderful little production company with enough projects to keep us busy for the next ten years, we work happily together. What's there to change?" "Well," he said, "can you keep a secret?" "It depends," I replied. "What's this all about?" His voice now became conspiratorial. "I think I am going to the Metropolitan," he said. "I'm meeting with George Moore, the president, this week in Spain and then I go to New York to meet with the board. If it all works out I will be the new general manager and I want you to come with me as the assistant general manager."

"You must be kidding," I replied, now fully awake. "I'll do anything in the world to help you if your appointment goes through. It's exciting and marvelous that the Met board is really considering you. It means great things for the future but I don't think you want me. I've tangled with a few of the board before and I don't think my name will be unanimously applauded. In any event, I'm up to my elbows now. But I'll do whatever you want to help." There was a pause. "We'll see about all this later on," he finally said. "I'm very stubborn!" "Okay," I said, "fair enough. When are you going to New York?" "Next week," he said. "Everything must get settled at that time. Love from Marit. I'll be in touch." And he rang off.

As I got out of bed I realized that it was my forty-eighth birthday. So did Bernstein, for when I picked him up for the scheduled 10 AM concert he gave me a big hug and a beautiful yellow Lanvin sweater that we had both admired in a shop a few days before. That night Sam Spiegel, the last of the major independent film producers, had flown in from Spain to meet with us about the possibility of Bernstein writing the music for his film *Nicholas and Alexandra*. He took us to dinner at Chez Garin. Chez Garin, alas, no longer exists but in its day was one of the great restaurants of the world and that night we dined in perfect style. Sam Spiegel brought his current Paris girlfriend, who didn't say much and didn't have to. She just ate everything in sight and looked slinky and provocative. I tried not to stare; Sam wouldn't like it and he was the host. I couldn't help it, though, and the lady and I exchanged a few nostril-dilating glances. It was a lovely birthday dinner, but the deal never came off.

The final concert of the series took place on February 15 at the Great Hall of the University of Paris. Every seat in the hall was filled and students were jammed into all the aisles and exits. The hall itself is harmless modern and when filled with people looks like a Wedgwood saucer. The enthusiasm was contagious and by the end of the evening the applause and cheering almost hurt the ears. As a final gesture Bernstein, after countless cheerful curtain calls, threw his baton into the crowd and ran off the stage. He was promptly herded into a large open area near the stage and began signing autographs and talking with the students as they came to him. We were there for hours; his patience and interest in young people know no bounds and he was prepared to stay all night if they wanted him. The only way we escaped was when the university guards finally made everyone leave the hall and closed down all the lights. Too elated by the evening, Bernstein was in no mood to sleep. We gathered up a group of friends and made our way through Les Halles, with onion soup and *oursins*, until 6:00 in the morning. I kept reminding him that we had to leave for Vienna the following day but he paid no attention. Finally I gave up and decided to move along with the group and let tomorrow take care of iteself.

When tomorrow came we were delivered to the airport and arrived at the gate to find it closed and some very smug Air France personnel telling us that we had missed the flight. I looked out and saw that the plane was still on the ground; the boarding procedures had just finished. "We must get on that plane," I said to the leader. "There is a large group of people meeting us in Vienna and rehearsals scheduled for Maestro Bernstein in the late afternoon." "The flight is closed, monsieur," came the terse reply. "But there must be someone who will help us," I pleaded. Suddenly Bernstein looked at me. "You stay here and see what you can do. I'll find a manager." And he bounded off, overcoat flapping. In a minute he was back with an official who clapped his hands, gates were opened, and a car was brought to the door. The official herded us on board and piled in our considerable hand luggage. From out of nowhere a pretty stewardess appeared and jumped in after us. The car lurched away from the door and sped down the tarmac, coming to a halt about 100 yards from the rear door of our plane. I noticed that there were gendarmes standing about. "We have a hijack alert," the official said, "that's why all the security. Now you two get out of the car behind the stewardess. She will distract the gendarme, I will talk to him too, and you both run for the open tail door. But hurry." And we did, walking up the last steps as the ramp was folding up into the plane. We pushed our way forward to our seats and sat down, exhausted. Outside, the stewardess, the official, and the gendarmes waved at us. We saluted back.

Arrival in Vienna meant immediate work on the revival of *Der Rosenkavalier* and production planning for the Mahler Ninth. It also meant the Opern Ball, high point of Vienna's social season. The Opern Ball is held in the State Opera House, which closes down for two days before to take out all the orchestra seats and surface the floor for dancing. White tie is required, and decorations as well. We were both asked to be the guests of the Israeli Ambassador in his box. I ran around Vienna trying to rent tails but so did a lot of other people and I was unable to find any. At the last minute Herbert Kloiber, Karajan's godson and sales manager for Unitel, lent me his. They were elegant and fit me surprisingly well. They were also made out of durable thick material and could practically stand in the corner of their own accord. Lily Schoenburg was our date and we swept into the opera house. From the ambassador's box we looked down on the dancers swirling below and it was a nineteenth-century engraving come to life. Lily and I danced and with each step my borrowed clothes became a vise, squeezing in the heat. We waltzed, always in the same direction—I was told that any other way is not Viennese—and I concentrated on not becoming seasick. Lily remained cool and collected throughout. I kept a good facade but it was a classic example of mind over matter. Bernstein got on the floor and people made way for him. He danced conservatively and bowed a lot. The women, on the whole, were not very elegant; the men, in their tails and decorations, looked much grander. Here and there one could spot a Parisian dress or someone wearing clothes with a touch of style but on the whole this was not easy to find. Bernstein took his leave early; Lily and I stayed until the wee hours and I took her home in a horse and carriage. It was romantic all the way.

Der Rosenkavalier proceeded apace as did rehearsals with the Vienna Philharmonic for the film and the spring tour. We began filming Mahler Ninth rehearsals with hand-held 16mm cameras to prepare a separate film on the rehearsal process itself. With both projects moving along at the same time there was very little time to spare.

The Mahler dress rehearsal was held at 4:00 PM in the Musikverein. The cameras caught the communication between conductor and players, especially as the orchestra had, by this time, become immersed in the music and to a man felt Bernstein's particular intensity about this symphony. The Ninth Symphony was composed during the first of Mahler's two seasons as conductor of the New York Philharmonic. It was completed on April 1, 1910, and the score reflects the complex emotions of a sensitive artist who knew he had little time to live—that he was, in fact, killing himself. All of Mahler's creative life was about conflict, conflict, as Bernstein himself put it, between "Mahler the creator versus Mahler the performer; the Jew versus the Christian; the Believer versus the Doubter; the Naif versus the Sophisticate; the provincial Bohemian versus the Viennese *homme du monde;* the Faustian philosopher versus the Oriental mystic; the Operatic Symphonist who never wrote an opera—but mainly the battle raged between Western man at the turn of the century and the life of the spirit.''

All these points, in one form or another, apply directly to Bernstein himself, a man trapped by the political and scientific horrors of our age and the potential strength and beauty in mankind. These inner ragings have few moments of artistic translation for him but one such is in performing the Mahler symphonies, although physically and mentally they drain him. This is especially true of the Ninth, which is a summing up of Mahlerian thought and a welcome of death. By the time the performance reaches the last measures of the final movement one feels that Bernstein has become Mahler and awaits death with calm and tranquillity. However overpowering and moving this is I am always glad to see him come off the podium in one piece. The Vienna Philharmonic caught the fierce kinship between Mahler and Bernstein at the same time as they were playing Mahler's music intensively almost for the first time since the end of the Second World War. In the Hitler days his music was banned and while there was still a broad sprinkling of older men in the orchestra who remembered Bruno Walter's performances before the Anschluss most of the personnel were younger and had never heard any of Mahler's music at all, let alone played him. We wanted to capture as much of this sense of discovery as possible because it was a three-way adventure between the composer, the orchestra, and the conductor. That afternoon in the Musikverein we began our odyssey.

The next days were spent in rehearsals for a second program to be taken on tour, including the Ravel G Major Piano Concerto, in which Bernstein was to be the soloist. The Ravel, and the other works on the program, were a direct contrast in every respect to the Mahler and provided a wonderful antidote to intensity. There was only one problem: Bernstein had not played the concerto in some time and was out of practice. This meant sessions at the keyboard in his suite at the Sacher and lots of groans and moans as to whether or not he should change the program at the last minute or find another pianist or just sit down and cover his head until the whole problem went away. I kept agreeing to everything on the theory that he had no real intention of changing anything and he would, from time to time, smile at me with the air of a martyr.

The tour began in Munich on February 27, 1971, and I flew ahead to Berlin to work on details of filming. We were going to take a gamble; one of the three scheduled performances in Berlin was cancelled and replaced by a day of filming the Mahler with an invited audience. Musically this was sound as the work was being played every other night on the tour, but from the standpoint of a film production many things might go wrong, even if we were prepared shot by shot in what we wanted pictorially. Tons of equipment, including cameras, batteries of lights and generators, crates of film, massive stereo sound consol systems, grips, gaffers, assistant directors, timekeepers, and wardrobe personnel, all filed into the Philharmonie, one of the newest buildings in Berlin's cultural rebirth but already showing signs of wear and tear and crumbling masonry. The Philharmonie is normally the home of the Berlin Philharmonic and from a design standpoint is one of the truly innovative concert halls. The performers are surrounded by the audience but not in the sense of being intermingled without definition. Intimacy is there without shoulder rubbing and it creates a warm atmosphere for everyone. It also provides problems in photography and lighting that had been carefully studied in Munich beforehand by Humphrey Burton, who was to direct, and Fritz Buttenstedt, the technical production overlord of Unitel. The three of us met in Berlin a week before the filming to iron out last-minute details and for me to deal with whatever problems might arise between our production and the management of both the Philharmonie and the Berlin Philharmonic.

Curiously, there was only one area where problems might develop. Herbert von Karajan, the conductor of the Berlin Philharmonic, also had a contract with Unitel but always insisted on dubbing his films, that is, having the orchestra record the soundtrack before the photography and having the sound played back while the cameras were in action. I wanted to avoid this at all costs, for to me the results of this method were stilted and fake and gave none of the feeling of the concentration and emotional impact of a live performance. The Unitel authorities were skeptical of our approach and I spent long hours in discussions with them, finally coming to the point where I had to make it an "and/ or" situation before we could get started. I knew that the Berlin management was going to watch our method carefully. I also knew there was an unspoken competition between the two conductors and that we were in Karajan's home territory ready to try a new method. I wanted to avoid any emotional problems.

On March 10, 1971, we began our one-day shooting schedule with a rehearsal for the cameras from 11:00 AM to 1:00 PM, to be followed by filming sessions with audience from 5:00 PM to 7:00 PM and 8:00 PM to 10:00 PM. From the beginning we were blasted with problems. Twenty minutes before we were to begin the young assistant director had a heart seizure, brought on, I suspect, by around-the-clock work and excitement. He insisted on carrying on his responsibilities but the doctors forbade him to do so. Since he was the only one who fully understood the intricate mysteries of the filming system it left Humphrey in the awkward spot of having to ad-lib his way with camera magazines instead of having someone at his elbow who could warn him when film was running out. Since we wanted no interruptions in the shooting each camera had a film boy crouched alongside ready to replace each magazine as needed. The assistant director was the straw boss of this group and the boys now had to learn a new system under pressure. In addition, the sound equipment had problems with stereo spread and miking, a third of the big lights kept blowing out, and the temperature in the hall was arctic. Outside a blizzard raged and to top everything else Bernstein had caught intestinal flu and had been up half the night before. I looked around at our careful plans crumbling by the second and wondered what on earth I was doing in the midst of what was surely to be disaster.

But as is often the case talented heads prevailed and when 5:00 PM rolled around we were prepared, tense and on edge but that is not a bad mood for the Mahler Ninth. As the performance unfolded it was musically gripping and I could look out at the audience and see the attention they were giving to what they were hearing. I spent some of the night in the sound booth helping in any way I could but mostly I stayed out of the way while the experts did their job. By 11:30 PM they had done it well, and an exhausted but exhilarated Bernstein was ready for supper at the home of the American Minister to Berlin, Brewster Morris, and his wife.

We drove to the Morrises in the teeth of a winter storm that had been howling and swirling all day, arriving after midnight. I had warned our host and hostess that we probably wouldn't arrive until very late and they didn't care. As a result we were welcomed with open arms and greeted by fellow guests, mostly the cream of Berlin artistic and cultural life, as if we were settling down for a party starting at a more civilized hour. Lorin Maazel, then music director of the Berlin Opera, and his wife, were people I was particularly glad to see and settled into a corner with them and a plate piled high with cold roast beef, bean salad, potato dumplings, and cheese and a glass of German red wine. I was tired but certain that we had actually filmed a magical performance and that our gamble had paid off.

The next day we flew off to Hamburg for a continuation of the tour. Bernstein was still feeling rotten and in midday began to run a high fever. He went to bed the minute we arrived at the Vier Jahreszeiten Hotel and I sent for a doctor. The doctor, after careful examination, decreed exhaustion, the grippe, and intestinal upset. He ordered that the concert be cancelled but Bernstein would have none of this. The doctor then bowed and stated that he would have no responsibility for the consequences. He clicked his heels and presented me with a bill. That night the maestro was practically carried to the concert hall but the minute he put his foot on the stage his illness disappeared. It returned with a vengeance when the concert was over and we carried him home and put him to bed, looking more dead than alive and for the first time alarming me. I decided to spend the night on the sofa in the living room of his suite, just in case something happened. At about 4:30 AM he awoke, hungry, and I could hear him ordering some food from room service. "Order some for me, too," I croaked from the couch. "Breakfast!" We sat down together at 5:00 AM and he looked almost completely recovered.

The next morning, having completed the tour, we returned to Vienna, and that night, as I was climbing out of the bathtub the phone rang and it was Goeran Gentele, this time from London. "Good afternoon," he said with great friendliness. "I've just returned from New York and I want to see you immediately. I am prepared to fly to Vienna tonight if you can see me in the morning. I bring you love and greetings from Betty." I took a deep breath.

A few days before I'd received a letter from her in which she urged me to pay attention to what Gentele wanted. It was most unusual for Betty to make any comment about my jobs unless specifically asked. She always had opinions but reserved them until they were sought out. This time she was gently but firmly pointing out that I should not be so cavalier to Goeran "She's written me about your talks," I said. "I must say you are a very stubborn man." "Good," came the reply. "I'll see you tomorrow." "Oh no, you won't," I rejoined, pulling myself together. "I'll come to you. It is not right for the general manager-elect of the Metropolitan Opera to call on possible staff members. I'll come to see you. I've a little cleanup work here for the next three days and then I could make myself free to come to Stockholm. I will miss the high point of my year if I do this because I will have to pass up the Queen Mother and a party at 10 Downing Street, but for you I'll make the sacrifice!" He laughed. "I'll see you four days from now in Stockholm. Come to the Grand Hotel. A room will be waiting. Let me know the time of your arrival. We have lots to talk about. Marit sends her love. Come fast!" And he hung up.

That night the Bernsteins and I had dinner at the Viennese restaurant that in the past had been a favorite hangout of Herman Goering and the Nazi bigwigs but now belonged to an Israeli couple. Over dinner I broke the news that Gentele was going to be appointed general manager of the Metropolitan and had asked me to come as his assistant general manager. I said I was going to pass up England and the royal family to go to Stockholm on March 18 to meet with him. They both seemed sad at the thought of my leaving them but were encouraging about the opportunity that might be opening up. "Besides," said Bernstein, "for some crazy reason you have always wanted to be general manager of the Met and maybe someday it will happen. Why you want this I've never understood but since you do you better look into what Gentele is talking about." "Thank you," I said softly. "You do understand this crazy compulsion of mine. But in talking with Gentele I must put out of my mind any possibility of the top job. That is beautifully filled with his appointment and I must rest satisfied, if I go, with the number two spot. But I haven't decided anything yet. I'll talk with him and then see." They agreed this made sense.

On March 17, I checked into my Stockholm hotel and went across the square to the Royal Opera House. I knew the house well from my visits in the sixties and I went up to Gentele's elegant office. He was sitting behind his writing table surrounded by various Metropolitan Opera documents, financial statements, board minutes, artistic planning books, and piles of correspondence. He greeted me warmly and looked just as I remembered. We talked briefly and I picked up some of the material from his desk. "These things look to me as if they demand some quick answers," I said, after looking at the Artistic Administration folder. "Yes, they do," came the reply, "but certain decisions have to be made before casting can begin. And one of those decisions revolves around you." I looked at him warily. "Will you meet Marit and me at the Opernkeller for dinner at seven-thirty?" "Of course," I replied. "It's now six PM. I'll stroll around Stockholm and think a little."

I went outside into the early spring night. It was still cold but the air was clear and dry and good for walking. I went to the harbor and sat looking out at the boats. I didn't know what to do.

At 7:30 I joined the Genteles at the Opernkeller. Marit was ravishing, her beautiful features set off by a touch of makeup and a dress that gave softness and femininity to her every gesture. We were seated on an enclosed piazza overlooking the canal and opposite the royal palace, the lights playing on the water and the water reflecting on the walls behind us. We ordered crayfish and veal and spring salad. I was hungry and curious, exactly in the mood to be wooed.

Gentele opened the conversation by asking what I thought about Raphael Kubelik. I told him that I had nothing but admiration for Kubelik, based on his Chicago days and his American tour with the Concertgebouw in my early days in the concert business. "I've asked him to be my music director at the Met," he said, "and I think he will do it. I told him I was asking you to come and he seemed pleased by this." I looked at him. "You do keep these surprises for the right moments," I said. "What else do you have in mind?" "I will take care of the stage, Kubelik will be in charge of the music, and you will take care of everything else! That's what I have in mind!" He took a sip of wine. "But you know that there are many on the Met board who do not like me," I replied. "They might want to make it difficult for you if I'm around." "I'll worry about the board," he replied. "You worry about the house."

I looked at him carefully and took a bite of veal. "What do you know about that board?" I asked. "I've not talked to any of them for a while but I cannot believe that you are coming there with 100 percent of them in favor of the idea." "I don't know," he replied, "but George Moore is in charge and as long as he's there I will be supported." And he proceeded to give an analysis of some of the others that struck me as being extremely perceptive. "But forget about the board for a moment," he went on, "they are not the main point. The main point is the great Metropolitan Opera Company and what it can do in the future. There is no limit to the excitement that we can create! I see a new look at the standard repertoire. I see operas being done that the Met has never touched, like Berlioz's *Les Troyens* that I want to do in my second season. I've got the okay for a new *Carmen* to open my first season and I want to go back to the original. And I want Bernstein to conduct. He must conduct. He's the only one who would understand the reasons for the return to what Bizet wrote. I must meet him and must talk to him. We would make a wonderful team!" And he took another forkful of food.

His enthusiasm and belief in what could be done were contagious. "But stop all this talk," I finally cried. "How can I possibly stay away? It sounds up my alley but you can't afford me." "How much do you want?" I told him. "Done," he said, and we shook hands. Before I knew it, dazed and bedazzled, I had agreed to come. "We will plan this summer with Kubelik in Switzerland for our first three seasons. Can you be with us?" I whipped out my date book. "Yes, if you meet in

July. I'm co-producing the opening of the John F. Kennedy Center in Washington, D.C., in September and from mid-July on until we finish I cannot think about anything else. You may remember that Bernstein was commissioned by Jacqueline Onassis to write the opening work in memory of her late husband and so far he has only sketches and a very rough idea of how he wants to proceed. There's a lot of work ahead." We agreed on a schedule, including spring meetings in New York, and also agreed that we would keep our arrangements secret until such time as the opera board voted approval and we could use my coming in the most effective way possible.

I returned to Vienna the next day in time to greet the Bernsteins, who had just come back from London and a special Albert Hall gala in honor of the Atlantic College scheme of Lord Louis Mountbatten. The concert was taped for television and Prime Minister Edward Heath gave a party at 10 Downing Street afterwards which was graced by the presence of the Queen Mother, a great rarity since the royal family do not often attend any functions in the Prime Minister's house. Felicia described the evening in great detail. The day of the concert also happened to be the day that Henry Ford had announced he was not building any more factories in Britain because of continuing labor union problems; the pound took a beating on the international money markets; and a general strike was being discussed by the largest union in the country. As Bernstein arrived late at the party he had greeted the prime minister at the door with a big embrace and the question: "Well, Ted, and how is your tottering government tonight?" There is no record of his reply but I would love to have seen what must been the expression on his face!

I told the Bernsteins of my talk in Stockholm and that I had agreed to go provided the Met board approved and that until such time I was still the executive producer of Amberson. I said that I anticipated going to Switzerland in July to confer with Kubelik and Gentele but that in any event I wouldn't actually move to the Metropolitan until early 1972. "We still have the Kennedy Center to face," I said. "And how are you coming along with this project?" "I'm not," came the reply. "I am desperate. I've so much to do. I've lots of music, but we must settle on a director who will work with me in shaping the piece. That's our first order of business when we finish up here. We must do this tomorrow morning! But first we have *Der Rosenkavalier*. I wish it was over. I can't conduct and compose. Now Richard Strauss must be in my head and heart." And he moved around the room pushing his hands through his hair. "What am I going to do?" he pleaded, looking at both of us.

What he did, of course, was to prepare a *Der Rosenkavalier* of such beauty that even Lily Schoenburg, Viennese to the marrow and as fussy as all Viennese about Strauss and particularly *Der Rosenkavalier*, turned at the end of the first act and said, "It is not possible for it to be more beautiful." Her eyes were brimming with tears. The maestro was full of doubts, as usual, and insisted that the performance was not up to his expectations. This time Lily, Felicia, and I just laughed at him. I'm not certain he liked this.

With *Der Rosenkavalier* set for its performances and recording I began serious work on the *Mass*, which had to be ready on September 8 to open the John F. Kennedy Center for the Performing Arts in Washington, D.C. Postponement would be a national embarrassment and unthinkable. Bernstein had been working on the piece off and on for almost three years but did not have a very clear idea as to how it should be put on the stage. He felt there must be dance and marching bands and soloists and street people and supplicants. He wanted a collaborator-lyricist to help with the text, particularly those parts that were not drawn directly from the liturgy of the Mass itself. I felt that the first order of business was a director who might be able to take what had already been done and begin to make some theatrical plan from it. Hal Prince was one of the first people who came to mind and he agreed to fly to Vienna to talk about it. He did, meeting with Bernstein in the middle of the *Rosenkavalier* recording sessions, but their talks were not fruitful. Roger Stevens, Robert Lantz, and I drew up a list of possibilities and we all felt that the director had to be someone whose creative juices would blend with Bernstein and help push him on to complete the work.

It was hard to solve this problem over the very long distance of the Atlantic Ocean and we waited patiently until the recording sessions were finished and the maestro returned home. In the meantime I had to work out my own schedule in order to be ready to go to Switzerland for meetings with Gentele and Kubelik in mid-July and to combine that trip with a screening of the first rough cut of the Mahler Ninth film in Munich. The days and nights were full.

By early May, Gordon Davidson was asked to become director and after long talks with Bernstein agreed to do so. Roger Stevens and I let out one long sigh of relief and with Gordon's acceptance work moved into high gear. Alvin Ailey was tapped for the choreography and brought his brilliant company into the cast. Auditions were started for the leading roles, particularly the Celebrant of the Mass, who had to be a young, intense, attractive, compelling, and sympathetic young man representing goodness, curiousity, spirituality, independence, and toughness. Several days went past with people coming into the auditions who had some of the qualities needed but just did not seem right.

Late one hot early June afternoon a young man walked in with his guitar, sat down, and began to sing in a rich baritone. His sound made us all look up and his strength and ability to communicate from the stage were startling. When he finished we asked him to come down from the platform and talk with us. Within minutes we all knew that we'd found exactly the right person. He had heard about the audition from a friend and had wandered over just to see what was happening. It was a good afternoon's wandering. His experience had been mostly operatic outside New York, although he was a member of the New York City Opera. Prior to music he had worked in a mental hospital and while there had married a fellow worker, both of them touched and tortured by the problems of the mentally ill. He had lived, for a young man, an unusual life and his experiences showed in his work. His name was Alan Titus and I had a feeling a lot of people would know about him if the *Mass* project was a success.

During May and June Bernstein kept turning out material, Gordon Davidson and Alvin Ailey worked to shape it all for the stage, Oliver Smith began work on the sets, Gilbert Hemsley, Jr., on lighting, and Diana Shumlin took on the next to impossible job of coordinating the whole production. We never had a formal production budget and Diana and I would meet at the end of a day and try to figure out what that particular day's efforts would cost. Stephen Schwartz, fresh from his triumphs in *Godspell*, had been signed as Bernstein's collaborator-lyricist. Schwartz was somewhat caught up with his own success, which was indeed formidable for a twenty-four-year-old, and had rather grandiose ideas of his own importance to the project. Nevertheless he was doing good work and worth the trouble. Roger Stevens had his hands full with the enormous other problems of getting the Center ready on time and that left most of the producer's role to me. Diana Shumlin and I became life-long friends in the process.

Right in the middle of everything I had to take off for my meetings with Gentele and Kubelik. I flew to Zurich, rented a car, and drove to Lucerne, where the Kubeliks have their home, and had three days of intense meetings where, together with Francis Robinson and Herman Krawitz of the old Metropolitan staff, we hammered out a three-year plan for repertory, beginning with the 1973–74 season and going through 1975–76. For 1972–73 we knew we would have to take pretty much what Bing had planned three years back, for such is the time schedule that all opera houses must act upon if they hope to get th'e world's recognized star singers. Our planning was not going to be solely dependent on the star system but we needed a fair share of them to please the basic Metropolitan subscription audiences. At the end of our three days together I felt good about the possibilities for the future and left Switzerland with high spirits.

While I'd been away much had been done to shape the show. Maurice Peress had been engaged as music director and shortly after my return I went to a rough run-through one afternoon and began to feel, for the first time, that a very exciting theatrical event was being created. It was much too long, in my opinion, and after the run-through I asked Gordon Davidson to dinner and told him my feelings. He indicated that he agreed completely but that Bernstein was touchy on the subject and not in the least interested in discussing it. "You and Roger will have to help," he said. "I'll do all I can and so will Alvin and everyone else. But you and Roger must keep after him." I promised we would.

Rehearsals continued in New York until we packed up the whole troup and moved to Washington in late August. At the Kennedy Center a very tight opening week schedule limited everyone's rehearsal time in the opera house. It was imperative that we have every moment possible and that meant asking Julius Rudel, the Center's music director, to move around his dates and hours to fit into ours. Rudel was obliging but could only do so much. The machinery in the theater was new, the stagehands and technical personnel were new as well, and we were all tense. Progress was being made but the closer we came to the opening the more stubborn Bernstein became about cuts. Nothing Gordon or Roger or I could do seemed to help. We kept saying that we felt a strong and vibrant piece here but that it would not work to his satisfaction if anything were overstated. Bernstein's arguments against this position were compelling and reasoned. They were just not very theatrical.

We had decided to have very few performances before the formal opening, with just one public dress rehearsal and a formal preview. After the dress rehearsal all of us again landed on Bernstein, who by this time was exhausted, and finally, at some ungodly hour in the morning he agreed to Gordon's cuts for the preview, with the understanding that they would all be restored for the opening. We agreed but in my heart I was counting on Felicia's help. She was coming down to the preview and had not seen any of the work during rehearsals. She would be a pair of new eyes, new eyes that would see and hear and give her opinions to the maestro without any hestiation. And from past experience I knew he listened carefully to what she had to say. I was also counting on the audience reaction to be of such strength that he would not want to change anything.

Gordon and Alvin and Maurice Peress went to work on the cuts and I approached the preview performance with high heart. Indeed, I had every right to, and my feelings were borne out by the thirty-minute ovation that greeted the work at the end of the evening. We were all deeply moved, no one more so than Bernstein himself, and we returned to the hotel feeling elated. We should have known better. Bernstein arrived and looked at all of us. "Now you've all had your fun," he said. "Everything goes back in tomorrow."

And it did, despite Felicia's pleas, which were added to ours. The opening night arrived and while the work had a marked success it never was quite the triumph it might have been if the cuts and trimming had been allowed to stay. I've thought often about this, not only with Bernstein but with other creative friends as well, and come to the conclusion that frequently the creative person is the worst possible judge of his or her own material. They lose objectivity and often forget that they are creating something to be shared by other people. That's why there will always be room for the impresario or producer whose prime job it is to keep that objectivity always in front.

The *Mass* was the last big non-Metropolitan Opera project we worked on together. During the summer Bernstein had met Gentele, studied the Bärenreiter edition of *Carmen* and agreed to do it to open the 1972–73 season. He liked Gentele, who was to direct the work, and wanted to give us both a solid send-off in the post-Bing years. Before leaving Amberson I started arrangements with Harvard University for the 1973 Norton Lectures that were to bring Bernstein back to his alma mater for a semester as a visiting professor, and gradually turned over the affairs to my successor, Harry Kraut.

While I indeed did leave the actual day-to-day chores of our relationship, I never really left at all. One doesn't leave Bernstein; he becomes a permanent part of the psyche, a constantly fascinating force of excitement, challenge, adventure, love, irritation, at once frighteningly vulnerable and perceptively accurate. He is music; he is larger than life. He is what we would all like to be if the gods spread out the creative gifts. He is the past; he is now; he is the future. And he makes one want to stand in it eager for what might happen.

XIV

The Metropolitan:

Prelude

The new general manager of the Metropolitan Opera, Goeran Gentele, departed on July 1, 1972, for a few weeks holiday before tackling his new duties as head of one of the world's greatest opera companies and had left me, his new assistant general manager, in charge of the company. We were deep into labor negotiations; all the union contracts at the Metropolitan expired at the same time and there were some fourteen different talks going on all at once. Before Gentele's departure we had settled with the orchestra, one of the toughest contracts, in an atmosphere of discussion that boded well for the future. We had been authorized by the board to settle three-year contracts with no more than a 15 percent increase in costs over the thirty-six months. We had succeeded with the orchestra and the day Gentele left we had met in the board room to initial the understanding and celebrate with a glass of champagne. The toasts were warm and friendly, in marked contrast, I gathered, to the last round of talks in 1969, when the negotiations had broken down and the entire company went on strike in an atmosphere of bitterness and hate. The season's opening was delayed three and a half months and the end of that strike didn't really settle anything. The bitterness remained and something even more disastrous happened.

Until that time the Metropolitan's subscription rate ran at something close to 75 percent of capacity. With the strike New Yorkers began to realize they might be able to live without going to the Metropolitan Opera and began deserting. On top of this, the board, in a hasty and ill-considered move, decided to refund without question all subscription money for the missed performances. It apparently never occurred to any of them to ask the subscribers to help by donating their missed performances to the general operating expenses of the house. By the time the truncated 1969–70 season got under way the damage had been done and by the end of the subscription campaign for the following season the slippage was alarming. At the end of Sir Rudolf Bing's last season the subscription rate was down to under 59 percent. This was part of the problem the new management inherited and we were determined to complete our labor arrangements as swiftly and effectively as possible.

Gentele had taken his family to Sardinia for three weeks. His family included his wife Marit and their two daughters plus his older daughter from his first marriage. It was to be their only chance for a holiday before plunging into work on the new season, a season scheduled to open with a new production of *Carmen*, conducted by Leonard Bernstein and directed by Gentele himself. Gentele's background, apart from his years as director of the Royal Opera, was theater and films. He made his first operatic splash when he directed a production of Verdi's *Un Ballo in Maschera*. He had stirred up Sweden's opera audiences with contemporary repertoire, exciting productions of the standard works, and the rebuilding of the Royal Swedish Ballet. He persuaded his friend Ingmar Bergman to direct a new production of Stravinsky's *The Rake's Progress* that the composer felt was one of the finest the work had yet received. He was a man of many talents wrapped in a personality of great charm and his advent onto the New York scene promised excitement and flair.

On the night his appointment was made public, December 9, 1970, we had been invited to join the Genteles at the home of Isaac and Vera Stern. The Sterns were old friends of the Genteles, going back to the days before their marriage when Vera lived in Stockholm, and they had been instrumental in arranging for us to meet. We all sat around the Sterns' library watching various television newscasters handle the story in their individual ways and toasting each other to the good days ahead. New York City was in the heavy grip of a taxi strike and a municipal transportation slowdown, but despite these inconveniences, and the damp, cold weather, the Genteles exploded with optimism about the future. Being a basic optimist myself I shared their feelings. At one point Vera disappeared for a moment and returned with a scrapbook, opened to a blank page. "Here, everybody, we must sign and

date this night. It's a special one!'' We all signed with appropriate comments, Gentele writing "General Manager, Metropolitan Opera" with
a special flair. It looked good.

Later that night we left the Stern apartment together. They were
staying at the residence of the Swedish Consul General on East 64th
Street and we had to find our way across town. There was not a taxi or
bus and there was nothing to do but walk home across Central Park. It
was well past midnight and we all had the usual fear of venturing into
the park after dark. "I know how we'll do this," I said. "Follow me."
And we started out walking in the middle of the traffic transverse.
"How would it look for the papers to have a headline about the new
manager of the Metropolitan mugged in the park after midnight?" Gentele asked as we entered the road. "Not too good," I rejoined, "so
let's stay in the middle under the lights." We linked arms and walked
swiftly. The emptiness of the park, that special silence that screams
loudly, infected our gaiety and we found ourselves singing at the top of
our lungs and laughing and marching in step. We reached Fifth Avenue
safely, a little winded but happy. "This is good!" Gentele said.
"We've overcome our first crisis."

All these thoughts came flooding back to me on the evening of July
18, 1972, when, at about 6:30 PM, I was summoned from a restaurant
by a telephone call from the opera house asking me to return immediately, that "something had happened to Mr. Gentele." I was having an
early dinner with a friend and had planned to return to the opera house
for the performance of Bernstein's *Mass* that was currently playing
there under the management of Sol Hurok. A new cast member was to
take the principal part and I wanted to see what he would do with it. I
never got the chance.

When I returned to the opera house I found a group gathered outside
my office. It was there I learned that Gentele had been killed in an auto-
mobile accident in Sardinia, the news relayed to us by NBC, who had
called asking me to make a comment.

Friends, artists, members of the company had to be told, and fast.
Most particularly I needed to reach George Moore, then president of
the Metropolitan Opera Association, who was en route from his home
in Spain for the regular July meeting of the board. Quick cooperation
from Olympic Airlines enabled me to reach him as he was about to
drive into the city from the JFK Airport. When I broke the news to him
on the phone, he let out a groan—I thought instantly of a maimed wild
animal—and within the few words, the few seconds, his and the
board's plans for the Met's future were smashed. There was no time
for private grief.

The next day Moore was fabulous: he grasped the importance of leadership and moved fast. I especially remember a meeting at his office a few days later. Bill Hadley, then our director of finance, had been in the meeting, but, after a few minutes, Moore asked him to leave us alone. He then proceeded to give me an extremely interesting history lesson on his bank. When he came to it, he explained, one man's shadow dominated the business. Now, at his own retirement, Moore said, it was a public institution capable of being run without regard to who was in charge. The needs of the Metropolitan were somewhat the same, he indicated. There was something in diversified authority, I agreed, even though the Met was not a bank. I thought then that we could work together, and I was determined to give it a try.

The fact that Gentele had brought me there in the first place, over my great reluctance, was in itself a triumph of persuasion over logic. I had not wanted to join him because I still bore scars from my Lincoln Center days in trying to cope with the continuing opposition of Anthony Bliss (then the president of the Met board) to the importation of any foreign opera companies visiting New York for the Lincoln Center summer festivals. His opposition had been tricky, devious, and firm, and in the course of figuring out how to get around it both Bill Schuman and I had acquired bad tastes in our mouths. The visiting companies had come, of course, and the Met survived and his opposition was ridiculous, but I felt that if at all possible I did not want to get myself into a position of having any further professional relationship with him. Bliss, though, had lost his board presidency by the time of the Gentele appointment, and I thought, all things being equal, that I would join the new group on the off-chance that some new thinking and clean winds might be sweeping the board room.

Three years later, almost to the day, I left the Metropolitan Opera— my post, that of general manager, having been declared obsolete. Perhaps the story of my experiences there may reveal something of the inner workings of America's leading opera house and of its responsibilities to the public it serves.

XV

End of a Dream

The first few hours after Gentele's death were spent in trying to find out how badly Marit Gentele had been injured and exactly where she'd been taken after the accident. I decided to send Charles Riecker and his wife Wally to Sardinia that night. Wally Riecker, the daughter of the long-time Metropolitan maestro Fausto Cleva, spoke fluent Italian, as did her husband, the new artistic administrator of the house. I felt that the Rieckers could ferret out all the necessary information and see that Marit was properly cared for. George Moore, after recovering from his first shock, provided all necessary credit and the Rieckers took off at 1:00 AM.

At the opera house the phones never stopped ringing. The world press wanted every detail and one had the feeling, as the night progressed, that the story had struck a human interest chord in everyone. Between the press calls, which we distributed among various staff members who had been hastily assembled, I tried to reach various artist friends of the Genteles as well as other board members. I was particularly anxious to reach Lincoln Kirstein, the prickly genius who together with George Balanchine created the New York City Ballet. Gentele was one of the few people who understood Kirstein and who shared his obsession about quality. The two men had known each other slightly in Europe but had become fast friends during Gentele's first months as general manager-elect. I reached Kirstein in Saratoga, New York, and his scream when I told him the news was earth shaking.

I telephoned the Goddard Liebersons in Sante Fe, leaving them both in a state of shock. Finally I called Bernstein, knowing that this was going to be perhaps the toughest call of all. I reached him in Tanglewood and first broke the news to Felicia. When Bernstein came on the phone I said that I could not find any other way of telling him except straight out and after a few moments to catch his breath he said that we owed Gentele a brilliant *Carmen* and should begin working on pulling it together immediately. He was absolutely right, of course. The best answer to a senseless death of a brilliant artist is to carry on in his mold and I agreed to get back to him either later that night or early in the morning.

At about 12:30 AM Grant Simmons, Jr., then a vice-president of the board, called to ask whether I would accept appointment as acting general manager. He said that an informal canvass was being made and this seemed to be what most board members hoped would happen. I told him that I would.

During the early morning hours the phones kept humming. Mayor John Lindsay, a childhood friend of mine, wanted to be kept up to date and made any service we might need available on demand. Representatives of the governor, Senator Javits, diplomats, and artists all kept the wires humming. Television and radio were pouring out the story and the first pictures of the accident began to come in by wirephoto. They showed a four-door Fiat crumpled like a used coffee can alongside a huge Mercedes-Benz truck.

At about 2:30 AM I called a halt, sending home the remaining staff and closing up the administrative offices. I walked out through the empty theater and stood onstage for a moment looking out into the house that was suddenly, inexplicably, tragically, and melodramatically going to become my responsibility. In the midst of the shock and pain I realized quietly that my old childhood fantasy had been brought to life. I thought of Oscar Wilde: "When the Gods wish to punish us they grant us our wishes." I remembered a party, three years before, when a fortune-teller had looked at my hand and told me that great beauty was coming into my life, a dazzling experience was about to happen in a totally unexpected manner. The fortune-teller and Oscar Wilde. Maybe they were both going to be right.

When I got home I found our son Ted sitting in the kitchen. He was reading a magazine over a cup of coffee. When I walked in he came over to me, sensing something was wrong. He had not turned on the radio or the television and did not know the news. I told him and as I did so the enormity of the situation overcame me and my eyes filled with tears. Just then the phone rang and Ted answered it. It was John Lindsay, to tell me that the plane to Sardinia on which I had sent the Rieckers had just taken off and that his office would keep me advised on their progress. I thanked him and said that I was going to try to get a little sleep.

Sleep wouldn't come, of course, although I suppose I did doze a little from time to time. At 7:00 AM, though, I was wide awake and took a shower. Moore called and we agreed to meet later in the morning. ''I want a complete report on the Gentele family and up-to-date news of Marit by the board meeting this afternoon,'' he said, all business, now that the first wave of shock had worn off. I told him I would get what I could. My chief concern at that moment was reaching our new music director Rafael Kubelik, whom I couldn't find anywhere the night before. By 8:00 AM I'd found out where he was, conducting in a little town in south Germany, and after about ten minutes of international telephonic ups and downs he came on the phone. He had just, moments before, heard the news and was trying to reach me at the opera house. ''I will come to you tonight,'' he said, ''as quickly as I can arrange a flight. We must be together now. We started as three; now we are two.'' His voice was strong but sad. ''Let me know when you have your plans made,'' I replied. ''I'll meet you.'' ''I will be there as soon as I can,'' he said.

That afternoon the board met and I was able to give them a report on the accident and explain exactly what we'd done during the course of the last hours. The board members stared at me while I spoke, their faces reflecting disbelief, horror, skepticism, and compassion. This was particularly true of the chairman, Lowell Wadmond, who had championed Gentele. Wadmond's business interests took him a great deal to Sweden, and being a careful international lawyer, he had checked out Gentele's character and reputation in great detail before recommending him for the post. His eyes were filled with tears and he nodded his head back and forth in shock as I spoke. Moore asked me to step out of the room for a few minutes after my report. I was soon called back and with great solemnity asked by the chairman whether I would take on the responsibility of becoming acting general manager of the company and assuring a season. I looked at all the faces and sensed their eagerness to have me accept. I did so and Wadmond, Moore, and I shook hands.

When the meeting ended, a press conference got under way. Moore, Wadmond, and I faced a battery of international press, some having to do with the arts and others reporters of a general nature following up on a human interest story. It was my first experience with the press en masse with myself as the center of interest. I stood with Moore and Wadmond answering questions as well as I could while countless flash-bulbs went off and I was conscious of the low-pitch whirring of television cameras. When the general discussion was finished CBS and NBC wanted to interview me separately, as did the AP and the New York *Times.* I glanced over at Wadmond and Moore, thinking they should be included as well. They were in conversation with some other reporter, and when I failed to catch their eyes I suddenly realized that they were not the ones charged with the responsibility of running the theater; I was and I had better start acting as the general manager. It was a conscious decision, the crossing of a psychological barrier. Up to this point my entire professional life had been as a second man. As a second man I had undertaken marvelous projects and become involved with extraordinary people, but until this moment I had never been in command, never been at the top, never been the one to bear the ultimate responsibility for the decision-making process. I watched Moore and Wadmond, each successful in his own field. They had just handed me a mandate, one that was unthinkable forty-eight hours before. I'd better start using it.

The press conference drew to a close. I did separate interviews with the major networks and posed for a special picture alone taken by the AP photographer. I stated my thoughts about Gentele, about the house and its traditions, and vowed to carry on what the three of us—Gentele, Kubelik, and I—had planned during our weeks together. I meant every word and I think my sincerity got across to the reporters because over the next days the newspapers, magazines, television, and radio were all extremely supportive. The AP picture appeared all over the country and resulted in quite a bit of mail, some of it from old World War II friends with whom I'd lost touch. The attention was not unpleasant and the obvious feeling that I as the underdog should be supported and encouraged was a great help to my morale.

On July 21, I received a brief note from Wadmond. In it he enclosed a copy of a cable received from Rudolf Bing and his reply. "Deeply shocked tragic disaster. If you feel my temporary help useful naturally at your disposal in this terrible emergency. Rudolf Bing." Wadmond's reply was: "Appreciate greatly your cable and generous offer of assistance. Board appointed Schuyler Chapin acting general manager who is grateful to you and will be in touch in event necessary. Regards Wadmond." One era was, at least, definitely at an end.

The tasks to be taken up were now on my desk and I called a meeting of the administrative staff on July 20 to review our assorted problems and begin rearranging administrative responsibilities. My three key aides were artistic administrator Charles Riecker, technical and business administrator Michael Bronson, and director of finance William Hadley. They were joined by Henry Lauterstein, general counsel for the Metropolitan, and Francis Robinson, press and tour director. These men became my "cabinet." We had to make decisions about the continuing labor negotiations. Only the musicians had agreed to a contract and there were thirteen unions remaining. Usually the musicians were the most difficult and dragged their talks on right to the deadline. This time, perhaps because of a new atmosphere and administration and perhaps because they had hired for themselves a first-rate tough, shrewd, and honest lawyer, they had signed first and this created a good atmosphere for the remaining talks. I did not want to return personally to the negotiating team. I felt it better to sit on the sidelines and let our lawyer and appropriate administrative department heads carry the day-to-day responsibility. I was always available when needed but I felt it would be better to have the acting general manager as a court of last resort. I did, however, go to the first meeting of each group that took place after Gentele's death, not only because I wanted to speak about him but also because I wanted to show the members of the house that leadership was in place and that we were going ahead with the season as planned and with the management team that had been created. I told Francis Robinson that I wanted to see the music and arts press one by one over the remaining part of the summer as I wanted to reach the public with the same kind of message. I knew that the Gentele tragedy had touched many thousands of people, whether they were connected with the arts or not, and I thought this might be advantageous for the Met if handled properly.

Our meeting was moving along with these and other decisions when there came an agitated knocking on the board room door. I had left orders that we were not to be disturbed unless there was a grave emergency and I turned with some impatience and called out to the intruder to "Come in." The door opened and a member of Bronson's staff stood in the doorway, pale and shaking, his eyes seeking out Michael. "There's been an accident," he said, "an accident on the stage." "What happened?" I asked, as calmly as possible. "A stagehand has fallen through a trap and been killed." I stared at him. "Let's go," I said, turning to Michael. I looked at the other faces around the table, each reflecting the same horrified disbelief. "You all please stay here and continue talking. We have a lot to cover." I held up my hand to still the protest. "Remember, we are all in the theater and no one ever said that ours was a safe profession. Now please get on with our plans."

On our way down to the stage I began to wonder what kind of a House of Atreus I'd inherited. As this thought passed through my mind another came along and took its place. If the news of this accident should become public in any big way it could lead to all kinds of rumors and stories and reviving of theatrical superstitions. It would put the spotlight on the Metropolitan in exactly the wrong way at the precise wrong moment.

On reaching the stage I went immediately to a small group standing around a roped-off stage traphole. "What happened?" I asked the crew chief, in as soft and sympathetic a manner as possible. "He broke the rules," came the reply. "No one is allowed to handle the trapdoors alone. We were doing some maintenance work and this kid just picked up the door by himself, lost his balance, and fell through the opening." I looked down through the hole to the understage, twenty-seven feet below. "Does his family know?" I asked. "Yes," came the reply. "He has a wife and a small child just born a few months ago." I took a deep breath and asked Michael if he knew the man. "Yes, I did," replied Bronson. I said, "I would like to see his widow, if she is up to it, and if not, I would like to talk to her. I hope the man's benefits and insurance are in order." "I believe so," Bronson said. I then turned to the New York City policemen who were filling out their reports. "Gentlemen," I said, "you may or may not be aware that this opera house lost its general manager three days ago in an accident in Sardinia. Not only did we lose the general manager but two of his three children were killed as well. Now we have this tragedy to face. The theater, and opera houses especially, are very superstitious places. We will do everything in our power to protect his widow and family. His union will do the same thing. We would all be grateful if the incident could be kept out of the press. The stories would be painful for everyone." Some of the man's colleagues had drawn around us in a circle and seemed to agree with what I said. "The front page isn't going to bring him back," one of them commented. The police agreed to keep their reports in official channels. Bronson and I returned to our meeting, reported the details to our colleagues, and told them of our request to the police. I asked

Francis to do whatever he could with his friends of the press to help us.

When our meeting was done I returned to my office with Riecker and brought in the other members of the artistic administration. "I want a report on where we are with all the artists signed for the first part of the season," I said. "I want everyone contacted and reassured that we are going ahead. Kubelik will be arriving in a day or so and I want the reports on my desk to pass on to him. I also want to know what problems we have, aside from the obvious one of *Carmen* and the need to find another director for it. We've got a lot to do and working together we'll get it all done. You'll find me very easy to work with. I trust people and when a project is assigned I don't look over your shoulder to see that it gets done. That's your responsibility. But if you lie to me or duck out of your responsibilities then we will have difficulties. I don't think there will be problems in these areas. Let's go to work."

I then started in on the problem of *Carmen*. Before Gentele's trip to Sardinia he had had one long meeting with Bernstein where he'd discussed his concepts and gone over the Josef Svoboda designs. These designs had already been translated into sets, just now coming out of the shops. Svoboda was due in New York two weeks hence. The costumes, too, had been approved and were in the shops being made. The production was, at least physically, frozen into the mode created for Gentele's ideas and there was not time or money to start afresh. Rumor had it that a series of production notes existed in a logbook that Gentele had in his apartment. I went up one afternoon to have a look but found nothing.

I was in constant touch with Bernstein and we both thought that the ideal replacement might be Jerome Robbins. I called Jerry and he agreed to come down and have a look at the models but was not encouraging about his personal participation. He went over the production with a painstaking eye and after doing so came to my office and said, "You have nothing to worry about. The production is already a success." He elaborated his views that the whole concept and physical realization of it was daring and brilliant and that almost anyone could follow through. "What about you?" I asked. "No, Schuyler, I cannot, much as I would like to help you. I simply am not physically up to it and if I ever did an opera I would want to start from scratch anyway. Later on we might talk about *Salome*. I've some ideas for this piece combining singing, mime, and dance but I'm afraid I must sit this one out." And he rose to go. "Remember what I've said, though. It is already a success." And he went out the door. Later he wrote me an affectionate letter expressing the same thoughts, but for the moment I was back to square one.

I called Bernstein and began discussing a series of other names. In the process I kept referring to Gentele's assistant, Bodo Igesz, and as we talked Bernstein remembered working with Igesz when he was conducting *Falstaff* in 1964. "What about him?" I asked. "He conferred with Gentele, he knows the piece, you like him, and I think the two of you could work together." "Let me think about it," came the reply. "It may be the right answer. I'll call you back."

I checked our rehearsal department to find Igesz's schedule and found that he was, at that moment, at the Santa Fe Opera. I called Santa Fe and got him on the phone. After the first sentences of sympathy I brought the conversation around to *Carmen.* "How much work did the two of you do together before Gentele went off," I asked. "Not too much," came the reply. "We just got started. We were to develop details when he returned. You know he went off to think through the problems and complete his own planning. And if there were notebooks he took them with him." "Thank you, that's very helpful," I stated. "When do you finish up in Sante Fe?" "In another week or two," he replied. "I'll be in touch," I said.

Bernstein called me the next morning and said that he would be happy with Igesz and if possible he would like to meet with him in the next few days. "I happen to know he's in Santa Fe at the moment," I replied, "but I'll see what I can do." I put in another call to New Mexico and asked Igesz if he would like the assignment. For a long moment there was silence on the line. "Are you there?" I asked finally. "Oh, yes," came the answer. "I'm just trying to think about my answer." "It's a wonderful opportunity for you," I stated, "and it gives me a chance to offer a staff artist a chance when the opportunity arises. And this is one of those opportunities." There was another pause and finally, quietly, and almost solemnly, Igesz agreed. He asked that I talk with John Crosby , the head of the Santa Fe Opera, to arrange an adjustment in his commitments and free him to fly back and forth between New Mexico and New York. Crosby was understanding and cooperative and details were quickly ironed out. I relayed the good news to Bernstein.

The *Carmen* problem may have been out of the way but there was no time for a breath. Five operas were being produced for the first week, including *Carmen—Madama Butterfly, Un Ballo in Maschera, Die Zauberflöte,* and *Roméo et Juliette.* Each had its problems requiring careful decisions. From the first rehearsal with the orchestra it was obvious that the wrong conductor had been engaged for *Butterfly.* Somehow or other he was confusing Puccini with Wagner and the result was a hodgepodge. Raina Kabaivanska and Sándor Kónya, the Butterfly and Pinkerton, were at a loss to follow his tempi, the orchestral sounds constantly covered the singers; it was an error in judgment that had to be corrected. I also felt it important to take a decision on this matter to show the company that mistakes could be rectified and firm decisions made. After consultations with Riecker and attending a second rehearsal I invited the conductor to my office and asked if he was pleased with the way *Butterfly* had been going. He looked unhappy at my question and gave me a convoluted answer that seemed to say both yes and no. I told him that I thought he would be badly received by both the public and the critics and since he had responsibility for *Roméo* as well, why not give up *Butterfly* and concentrate on repertoire that he would find more to his liking. I think he welcomed the suggestion, judging from the look that came into his eyes when I spoke, but he put on a hurt face and made routine protests. I eased him out the door with a handshake and the promise to handle the matter publicly in a way that would not embarrass either of us. I then asked Jan Behr to come and see me. Behr had been a part of the opera's musical staff ever since his arrival in this country as a refugee from Hitler's Germany. I knew his work from my years in the audience and I knew the respect his colleagues had for him as a first-rate opera conductor, musical and dependable. When he arrived I asked him if he would like to take over *Butterfly* for the season. His eyes filled with tears. He bowed and thanked me and said that he would do a good job. And he did, bringing distinction to himself and the Metropolitan.

The worst problem involved Franco Corelli. The tall, tempestuous tenor had not been heard from all summer. He was scheduled to be in New York for *Roméo* rehearsals right after Labor Day and was nowhere to be found. We tried telephoning Italy to all his known haunts but he was not there and no one seemed to know where he was staying. The *Roméo et Juliette* production had been created for him and was being revived because of its success and as a concession to him. *Roméo* without a Roméo is a bit tricky and either we canceled the production and substituted a last-minute replacement opera utilizing the other singers already contracted or we tried to find another Roméo quickly with the hope that we could reach Corelli before the season began. We decided on the latter course and asked George Shirley if he would like to take over, at least for the first performances. Shirley, a bright man, had been going through vocal difficulties over the recent months and I knew that he would decide about the role taking into account his condition and artistic instincts. He accepted, largely, I believe, because he knew we had a severe problem, and to be on the safe side we asked

William Lewis to be his cover. Lewis is the kind of singer no house can be without. His repertoire is wide and his voice musical. He's a good actor and thoroughly reliable. Lewis agreed and rehearsals could now get under way.

Two conductors were making their Metropolitan Opera debuts the first week. These were the veteran Peter Herman Adler for *Un Ballo in Maschera* and the Dutch conductor Peter Maag for *Die Zauberflöte*. Adler had been the musical director of the NBC Opera, during that organization's television days and two seasons of touring. He had never been asked to the Metropolitan before but had discussions with Bing from time to time about repertoire and production ideas. Gentele knew of his work here and in Europe and as one of his first gestures asked him to take over *Ballo*. Peter Maag enjoyed a brisk reputation in both the symphonic and operatic fields and had accepted *Zauberflöte* for his first production. Both maestri were dealing with splendid casts. *Ballo* had Martina Arroyo, Placido Domingo, Sherrill Milnes, Lili Chookasian, and Gail Robinson; *Zauberflöte* included Edda Moser, Nicolai Gedda, Fernando Corena, Theodor Uppman, Rosalind Elias, Ruggero Raimondi, and John Macurdy.

For every problem solved another rose immediately to take its place. Before the first rehearsals of *Carmen* got under way I received a cable from the Micaela, Teresa Stratas, cancelling her appearances because of illness; the conductor Michael Tilson Thomas, who was scheduled to work with Bernstein and take over the production the second half of the season, cancelled. We were fortunate to get Adriana Maliponte to step in for Stratas; the conductor problem was not so easily solved and we decided to wait on that one until we saw how the production progressed.

While all these—and, indeed, many more problems of various nature—came and went, my relationship with Moore and the executive committee was beginning to take shape. It was a queer and uneasy shape because Moore was not around very much and in his absence formal meetings of the group were often cancelled. I turned to Wadmond when I needed help or advice, not knowing the others, and Moore resented this. "I am the president," he would say, after hearing of my talks. "He's the chairman. You talk to me."

The three of us were drawn together, however, when Moore, Wadmond, Betty and I, and Francis Robinson flew to Sweden for Gentele's funeral on August 13. I was dreading our meeting with Marit but knew it had to come sometime. What was I going to say to this incredible woman who had lost her entire family in one blinding moment? Under normal circumstances the meeting would be difficult enough, but here I was, brought to the Metropolitan by her husband, and now his successor, calling upon someone whose dreams and plans had vanished.

Betty and I decided that we wanted to see her alone and on reaching the Grand Hotel I called and arranged a date right away. We walked from the hotel to her apartment, a walk and route that I knew fairly well from my visits in the past. The door was opened by Jeanette, Gentele's daughter by his first marriage. Marit came down the hall to greet us and while her eyes filled with tears she seemed remarkably in control of the situation. We went into the living room and within a few moments both were telling us what happened to them after the accident at the Sardinian hospital. They wanted to talk and we were a receptive audience. One could feel the tension slowing down. Presently we were joined by Robinson, Moore, and Wadmond and shortly thereafter by Erik Bruhn. About an hour later a buffet was brought into the room and Marit asked to speak to me alone. We went into their kitchen and stood for a moment staring at each other. "You must carry out the plans," she said. "I want to help in any way I can. I plan to come to New York as soon as the doctors will allow. We will work together." I took her in my arms for a silent embrace.

The funeral for all three of the Genteles was held in Forsamling, in a tiny church fifty miles south of Stockholm, where the family had all enjoyed the pleasures of country living. Birgit Nilsson and Ingvar Wixell sang and the church was packed with people. Outside the press waited a proper distance away. When the service was over we all came out emotionally exhausted and living the pain all over again. The questions were polite, the picture taking discreet, and we got into cars to take us to a country villa for refreshments. It was raining as we drove into the hills and the whole setting reminded me of a Bergman film. It was even more Bergmanesque when we arrived at the villa itself. It was pouring rain when we pulled up to the entrance and gloomy inside, with candles and faint electric light trying to cheer things up. I sat at a table with Gentele's mother and sister, who unsmilingly drank their tea and every once in a while stared over at me. Finally his sister came over to my side of the table and sat down next to me. "My brother is dead," she said, lifting back the black veil she was wearing. "He is dead. You must do what you want to do. Do not try to carry out his ideas. Carry out your own!" Before I could say a thing she had replaced the veil and gone to the other side of the table.

When we rose to return to Stockholm his mother embraced me and his brothers shook my hand firmly. Another who did so was his first wife. As we left, the rain was still coming down but not as hard as it had earlier and we all drove silently back to the city.

At our hotel I flung myself down on the bed, exhausted and drained. After a time I turned to Betty and said that we were going to have a good dinner. I called Francis Robinson and asked him to join us. I then called the Opernkeller. I made a reservation for three and when we arrived the maître d' recognized me from previous visits. He shook hands slowly and nodded his head and brought us to a lovely table overlooking the canal. We ordered a drink and the menus and as we were looking at them my eyes wandered across the room.

Suddenly I stopped looking: there, sitting in the corner at a table for two, was Dr. Willard Gaylin, the New York psychiatrist who had been so helpful in the late sixties and early seventies when I went through analysis following a hospital stay for bleeding ulcers. He was dining with his wife and I must have looked startled because Betty turned to me and asked if I was all right. I said I was but got up and moved toward the Gaylins. I tapped him on the shoulder and he looked up. "My God!" he started. "We've been thinking of you." "And I of you," I replied. "What are you doing here?" And there came an explanation about visiting Europe to see a daughter and having ended their trip in Stockholm. After these preliminary words they joined us for a drink and their compassion and friendliness helped us all through a difficult evening.

The day after the funeral I had lunch with Moore and Wadmond. They were both nervous and ill at ease and deeply worried about the Met's future. They interrupted each other constantly and neither seemed to notice that I was with them. I finally took the threads of their talk and made an attempt to put some order into the things they wanted done. We arranged a program for Marit at the house. I thought she should take over a project that had been planned but not implemented for Gentele's first season, a special series of performances for children called "Look-Ins." The "Look-In" was just what the name implied, a look at the mechanics and details that go into an operatic presentation blended together by a skilled host and introducing highlights from several operas. The total package was designed to tantalize children into curiosity about opera and the lyric theater. Gentele himself planned to be the host, as he had been when the idea was first tried out at the Stockholm Opera. I thought this project might keep Marit involved and more than that play an important service in getting the idea translated into action at the Metropolitan. The biggest problem was going to be finding the right host and I told Moore and Wadmond that I would think about this and let them know the possibilities later on.

During the talk it became obvious that both men wanted to be certain that there would never again be a dictatorial dominating single voice at the house. Moore reminded me of our talk about the management of the bank and once again I stated that I agreed with the principle but that it had to be adapted for the special conditions that separated an opera house from the running of a commercial business. Wadmond was full of suspicion about every key employee. I had the feeling he thought that the nightly box office receipts and petty cash accounts of the various departments were regularly pilfered by the general manager and his staff. I tried to reassure him on these points but he didn't seem to want to be reassured. The two men were tired and depressed, I suspected, not only about the Metropolitan but the world in general and as lunch progressed our talk became less and less focused. At the end both men insisted that a particular secretary in the organization be fired because she had been around the organization for many, many years and had wide knowledge of various activities of the past. The lady in question was indepensable to me, having retired from full-time employment some years ago and now doing a tiresome but necessary task to insure the smooth running of the general manager's box. I had no intention whatever of firing her and let the two men finish out their reasoning without making any response. She remained at her job and fulfilled it magnificently all the time I was general manager. When we were through the meal I felt a bit discouraged and sad myself. The job was going to have a lot more problems than I had thought about.

XVI

Getting Started:
Carmen, *the Mini Met, Look-Ins*

We returned from Stockholm on August 16 and one week later I had my first meeting with J. William Fisher, a vice-president of the board and head of the Gramma Fisher Foundation of Marshalltown, Iowa. Fisher and his sisters had been generous supporters of the Metropolitan and he had given the money for the Gentele *Carmen.* He and Gentele got on well together. I found Fisher likable and straightforward in a solid American way but I sensed instability, perhaps an insecurity and frustration in the New York Metropolitan Opera social whirl and an underlying feeling that he thought he knew more than anyone else how affairs at the house should be handled. He was saddened by Gentele's death and, I think, felt that I was not the right person to succeed him. At our lunch he said as much to me, which was at least honest, and I replied that I intended, insofar as possible, to follow up on the plans that Gentele, Kubelik, and I had worked out the year before. I told him that I thought some changes and modifications were going to be inevitable and that I intended to work as closely as possible with the board and executive committee in developing new artistic and administrative procedures. Fisher consumed several martinis during our talk and by the end of lunch I had a difficult time following his train of thought. I sensed he thought me a nice fellow but for reasons that were totally submerged felt that I was not the man for the Met. I didn't realize that he thought of himself as the ideal person for the post. We left the lunch table taking careful measure of each other.

Throughout the remainder of the summer we all moved ahead to put the last details of the season in order. The new *Carmen* as the opening night presented extra problems, in addition to the director and Micaela. With five other operas to bring up at the same time the normal rehearsal schedule for a new production had to be cramped. The sets themselves were stark, dramatic, and plain, depending for the most part on careful and brilliant lighting. Special lighting equipment had to be bought and installed, a kind that was foreign to these shores and both expensive and difficult to handle. The sets themselves were massive and required careful handling. On top of everything else Bernstein was feeling poorly, with an intestinal infection that was stubbornly resisting all treatment. Josef Svoboda, the designer, and the Metropolitan Opera's chief electrician, Rudolph Kuntner, were at odds, the cast was nervous about the dialogue and feared that the rug covering the stage floor was going to absorb the voice. The rug was necessary as an absorber of light and the focus area for special visual effects. Tests had shown that the material did not absorb sound but none of the leads would believe it, particularly Marilyn Horne, the Carmen, who is not shy about expressing her views. Word came to my office that either the rug went or she did and we had to devise some way of proving that the rug would not interfere with her work. Finally James McCracken, the Don José, also not known for reticence, threw himself down on the floor and let fly with a few well-chosen vocal phrases. Marilyn Horne was in the auditorium and heard him. The subject never came up again.

Just as this problem was settled a howl went up about the removal of the prompter's box. The prompter's box, a holdover from the nineteenth century, has become a crutch on which many artists depend for cues and entrances and indications of stage business. It serves a role, to be sure, when an artist is a last-minute replacement and does not know his or her way around a particular set but it is greatly over used by artists who know their roles well and simply lean on the prompter rather than their own memories. Early on Gentele had decided his *Carmen* was doing away with the device and that his cast would have to commit to memory all the music, dialogue, and stage business. The sets were designed without places for the box and when Horne saw that it was lacking she let it be known that either it was restored or, again, out she'd go. Others joined her on this point, making it clear that with the many changes from a conventional *Carmen* we needed to be certain that no mistakes were made. I had to give in: *Carmen* was going to get on the stage in a daring and exciting manner and I felt that the prompter's box problem was one to be argued another day. Svoboda wasn't happy about this, and the resulting cuts in the carpet meant a bit of relighting but he took it in good grace and the work was done.

As the dress rehearsal and opening night approached interest in the Met grew to almost unprecedented size. The normal media trappings for any opening were greatly enlarged by world television, radio, and magazines that ordinarily did not feature the performing arts as one of their major interests. The Gentele story had gripped the hearts of people all over the world and the opening night of September 19, 1972, came to be a symbol of whether or not the understudy could pull it off. I was bombarded with requests for TV appearances and interviews. Reporters sought out Betty and the boys; we found ourselves kind of instant celebrities. Strangers would stop me on the bus or subway or while I was crossing the street and wish me well. The phone never stopped ringing, often with people whom we knew ever so slightly asking us to dinner or the theater or to little Sunday brunches in the country. All of the panoply of success dropped on our shoulders and fortunately, having spent most of our lives in and around the creative and performing world, none of this changed our perspectives. The Met season was the first order of business and divertissements were not going to get in the way.

The *Carmen* dress rehearsal was scheduled for Friday, September 11, at 1:00 PM and was to be closed to any audience. On the Wednesday before, Bernstein came to me and asked to have the house filled. He wanted an audience to see how the whole production played and Igesz agreed with him. I consulted with the Metropolitan Opera Guild, whose director, Dario Soria, was an old and cherished friend of many years. We realized we had the hottest ticket in town but could not find our way around the various union regulations to sell them and raise a little money. The house was, therefore, filled with people who were invited at the last minute and a lot who had, as usual, found their way in without an invitation.

About an hour before the rehearsal was to begin Moore called me, all agitated, and insisted that he come. He had heard rumors that all hell was breaking loose at the house and that the production itself was in deep trouble. This was the first of many times when I realized that not everyone in the world was hoping the new administration would be a success. I asked him what specifically he was talking about and he grew vague. "Come on up," I finally said, "you're always welcome at any rehearsal. You're the president!" "I'll meet you in your office.

Charon [his wife] and some of the family want to come too.'' ''We'll take care of them,'' I assured him.

When they turned up I saw that his family were seated in various places throughout the auditorium. I wanted Moore to enter the theater with me, to show a solidarity to the packed house and help put down the rumors that we were already at odds. We walked down the left aisle of the orchestra and took seats in the roped-off area reserved for people connected with the production itself. As soon as we were seated he began talking about various other problems at a machine-gun clip and I finally had to turn to him and ask that we postpone such talk until after the rehearsal. I pointed out that I had a few immediate responsibilities and turned to talk with Svoboda and Igesz and have a word with Rudy Kuntner. Svoboda and Kuntner may have not gotten along too well but Svoboda would be gone in a few days and Kuntner was a permanent part of the house and had to establish a working relationship with the acting general manager. There were also some production points that I had been called in to adjudicate and I wanted to see if all was well.

At about 12:55 PM Osie Hawkins, the executive stage manager of this production, came to me and said they were ready to start. I told him to go ahead but to be certain he came in front of the curtain and explained to the audience that we expected them to behave at what was really a working rehearsal and to refrain from expressing themselves until it was over. The version we were doing was long and I didn't want any overtime problems. Hawkins came before the curtain and laid down the rules and then, in a dramatic and grand manner, introduced Bernstein, as he was making his way into the pit. The audience rose and cheered. Bernstein turned around and waved and then, baton firmly in his right hand, gave the downbeat for the overture.

Within the first notes it was obvious that this was to be a *Carmen* of special variety. When the curtain rose before the first statement of the ''fate'' theme in the overture, revealing a darkened Seville and one lone figure silhouetted against a shaft of light, people knew they were in for something unusual. When, with the last crashing, questioning chords of the overture, the full, hot lights of the city burst forth there was a gasp. The lone figure, Don José, walked slowly off into the crowd and the audience was suddenly made to realize that he was something more than Carmen's passionate, disappointed lover. It was, as critic and musicologist Harvey E. Phillips later wrote, ''an indication not only that the tenor was intended to emerge as a more central character in the work—a protagonist whose downfall we would watch with as much interest as Carmen's own journey to death—but also that the idea of fate in all its mythic dimensions would be the basis on which the production would succeed or fail." I stole a glance at Moore, whose face was firmly toward the stage, his mouth opened slightly as if taken by absolute surprise.

Rushing through my mind were the myriad problems we had overcome in the production to arrive at this moment: the change of Micaelas; Tom Krause, the Escamillo, forced to arrive late because of prior commitments to a *Le Nozze di Figaro* at Salzburg; the spoken French proving a high hurdle for the non-French cast; the on-again-off-again negotiations with Deutsche Grammophon about a recording, forcing that company to hire an outside chorus because the Metropolitan group would not accept the terms offered, some of the soloists objecting strongly to the sets and costumes. Up to this dress rehearsal an impartial observer might have felt that everything was pulling away from the center and, if he surveyed the long faces and frayed nerves, might have concluded that fate was in charge, if not doom itself. But he would have reckoned without the theater itself and the realization that an opera house is a place of miracles.

Final dress rehearsals of new productions at the Metropolitan are actually very much like performances. In theory a dress rehearsal can be stopped for corrections, and occasionally is, but for the most part this rarely happens. There was only one interruption that Saturday afternoon—during the rather busy dialogue scene between Carmen and Don José that precedes her dance in Act II. McCracken, as Don José, while protesting his overwhelming desire to make love to his gypsy, was unable to loosen his scabbard and get himself into position. In faultless American, Marilyn Horne interjected, "Sure, as soon as you take the sword off." The house went wild with laughter, but it was the laughter of an audience thoroughly captured by what it was seeing and hearing. The house was *with* the artists. *Carmen* was working.

Moore, by this time, was mesmerized. He kept asking me who was singing what and looking around to see if he could spot friends. By the end of Act II he was beaming from ear to ear. During the intermission various people came up to congratulate him and he took all the compliments that came his way. I stood back and watched his performance with some misgivings but largely with relief that he had found something to please him and, perhaps, counter the hearsay that the house was falling apart at the seams.

Act III, was the most difficult and controversial part of the production. Svoboda, who had conferred many times with Gentele, had underlined the harshness of the whole story everywhere except in Act

III, where a stygian abstractness took over almost as if the darkest powers needed this black crucible to develop into their final form. In Act I it was all uncompromising, brilliant light throwing into stark relief the superpassions of Carmen and José. Act II, Lillas Pastia's tavern, was at first inviting in its subdued colors, but gradually, with the fierce, sexy dancing created out of Alvin Ailey's talented inspiration, and smugglers plotting, turned into a background for hopeless seduction. For Act IV Svoboda constructed the exterior of a bullring that in itself was an arena of death, but Act III was the most subtle and difficult. The problems were compounded by the chorus, who at one point in the earlier rehearsals had refused to go on unless additional light was supplied for sure footing on the sharply raked platforms. The fight between Don José and Escamillo resisted easy working out, despite the efforts of the Kolombolovitches, the Metropolitan's father and son team who specialized in stage fights and stage weaponry.

In addition to everything else the physical set itself was giving real trouble to the stagehands. The mountain pass was constructed entirely out of one giant piece of carpet, very tricky to handle, suspended as it was from a series of guidelines that were stretched taut almost to the breaking point. At one stage rehearsal a couple of them had broken, causing a long delay. There was an extra measure of caution as well, no one wanting to repeat the fatal backstage accident of earlier that summer. I was extremely tense and anxious as the lights were lowered for the act to begin and Moore chose that moment to lean over and begin talking about budgets. He was pushing his points in an insistent way, jabbing my arm to keep my attention. I turned to him in disbelief. "Not now, George, please," I said. "I must concentrate on the stage. This is a very dangerous moment and I have to keep my mind on the show." I turned away but he kept on talking. I didn't hear a word of what he was saying and finally, after seeing that I could not be diverted, he shut up and turned his own attention to what was happening onstage. When Micaela made her entrance and sang her aria *"Je dis, que rien ne m'épouvante"* Moore asked me for at least the fourth time who the artist was. I told him for the fourth time it was Adriana Maliponte, who had stepped in to replace Stratas. "She's good," he whispered. "Good, Good, Good." And he stared ahead.

That afternoon, when the curtain came down on Act IV, an audience that had gasped at the realism of the murder united in a cascade of bravos. All the effort had paid off. The question had been answered: Goeran Gentele's *Carmen* was going to be a hit.

On September 19, the opening night performance surpassed all hopes. The critics went into ecstasy: "Daring and provocative . . . a thrilling testimonial to Goeran Gentele," wrote the New York *Times*; "a triumph of continuity," said the *Post*; *Time* praised Bernstein for his "crackingly taut performance"; *New York Magazine* termed Marilyn Horne's Carmen "one of the most remarkable minglings of endowments and intelligence I have witnessed on any stage;" and *Newsweek* commented, "As Don José James McCracken gave one of his most spectacular performances." What New York saw that season was a *Carmen* without spitcurls, and as Harvey Phillips wrote, "A *Carmen* that rid itself of all the local trappings of operetta, all its prettiness and with it the post-Bizet Guiraud recitatives. This was a *Carmen* that went back to the original blood and brutality of Mérimée, a *Carmen* that Gentele had seen as a stylized tale of the collision between a man's barely suppressed instinct for violence and the woman who cannot resist it." It was quite a night.

At the end of it Betty and I went across town, tired but pleased that the season had gotten off to a good start. It was only when I got into bed that I realized that this was the first of some 275 performances of 22 different operas that had to get on that stage during the year. I pulled the covers over my head.

With the season under way, my next step was to sort out the problems we faced and establish some kind of priority in trying to solve them. Rafael Kubelik had flown to New York for the opening and he and I spent some hours together sorting out the pieces. I wanted him to have charge of all musical matters and to supervise the artistic administration. We agreed that the concept that had brought us together in the first place, a "troika" of responsibility shared by music, stage, and administration, should be continued. The stage director was the big artistic missing link. Administratively we needed help in both the artistic and technical and business side. In addition, the whole subscription, promotion, press, and touring system had to be re-examined and the relationship between the professional management and the board of directors had to be repaired. The deterioration of this side of the house had been going on for years. Bing, a forceful personality, had, in large measure, held most of the board tightly in his hands. He had established an atmosphere of crisis and had kept it up until it became part of his modus operandi. As assistant manager-elect I had attended several meetings as an observer and I sensed that there was strong tension and relief in the feeling that an autocratic regime was drawing to a close.

One of our immediate artistic problems concerned the 1973–74 season. Gentele, Kubelik, and I had chosen the new productions for that year back in 1971. These included Berlioz's *Les Troyens*, to be done for the first time at the Metropolitan, Rossini's *L'Italiana in Algeri*, Offenbach's *Les Contes d'Hoffmann*, Wagner's *Götterdämmerung*, and Verdi's *Un Ballo in Maschera*.

Un Ballo was to be a production directed by Gentele based on his presentation of the piece in Stockholm. It was a thoroughly valid concept, depicting Gustav III, King of Sweden as a homosexual. History shows us that this was true. It also tells us that Gustav III was mainly responsible for creating Sweden's European cultural life. When Verdi wrote the work it was too close to the political situation in Italy, and could not be produced until the locale and characters had been changed. Gentele had returned to the original setting and scored a brilliant success. He intended to produce the work in the same manner at the Metropolitan and had assembled a first-rate cast to do it, including Monserrrat Caballé, Nicolai Gedda, and Sherrill Milnes. I felt very strongly that we should not do the piece without Gentele to direct it. A carbon copy of what he intended might be all right somewhere else but not in New York. I remembered the basic failure of Wieland Wagner's *Lohengrin* production that was completed by Klaus Lehmann after Wagner's sudden death. Gentele's ideas were fresh and original, but if he was not around to carry them out I felt the whole project should be dropped and something else found.

I expressed these thoughts that first week to Kubelik and James Levine, the newly appointed conductor of the house, and they agreed. The problem was what to substitute. We talked over various ideas and at one point Levine said, almost casually, that he was recording Verdi's *I Vespri Siciliani* the following summer with a cast that was almost the same as the ones engaged for the Met's *Ballo*. "When are you doing this?" I asked. "In August," came the reply, "in London for RCA." "Well, then," I said, "maybe we have our answer. I'm sure you both know the enormous success the work had in Hamburg in a production directed by John Dexter. If Dexter's free we might do the work here. Think of all the musical preparation that will have been done courtesy of RCA. It sounds to me like exactly the right thing to do." Both my colleagues agreed and I immediately put in a call to Dexter in London.

Dexter and I had first met in 1967 when he came to Lincoln Center to direct Peter Ustinov's play *The Unknown Soldier and His Wife* as part of the first Lincoln Center summer festival. Ted Chapin, seventeen at the time and determined on a career in the theater, served as Dexter's assistant in that production and through him we shared an occasional free evening with Dexter and discussed various artistic matters. That same season Rolf Liebermann had brought the Hamburg State Opera to the Metropolitan Opera House. Liebermann, a great admirer of Dexter's work at the National Theater in London and elsewhere, had wanted to meet him to discuss a possible production. I arranged their rendezvous and this had led to Dexter's being engaged by the Hamburg company to produce *Vespri*. This success prompted Liebermann to invite him back for several seasons and he had done, among other things, *Billy Budd* and *Boris Godunov*. Kubelik had worked with Dexter in Hamburg as well; they had done an impressive production of *The House of the Dead*. Kubelik had been impressed not only with his stage talents but his sensitivity to musical problems.

I reached Dexter in London and proposed the idea. He was interested but only if I could get Svoboda and Jan Skalicky. I told him we wanted to premier the work on January 31, 1974, and he said his commitment would depend entirely on the availability of Svoboda and Skalicky. I put a call in to Svoboda in Prague and to my great pleasure found he was both willing and free. I called Dexter back and before the afternoon was over the pieces were in place. Dexter was concerned about Caballé and how she would respond to strong stage direction but I felt the two could work well and told him so. He remained skeptical and made it plain that he expected her full cooperation. I told him that he would not have any trouble but I kept my fingers crossed.

There were two other projects that had been planned by Gentele that I was anxious to get into action. One was the creation of a "mini" Met, to perform repertoire unsuitable for the main stage of the house, and the other was a program to introduce children to opera and the musical theater, the "Look-In." The Mini-Met idea grew out of a series of productions done on an attic stage within the confines of the Royal Opera House in Stockholm and encouraged contemporary composers to experiment with the operatic art. It was a kind of operatic musical laboratory that re-examined older scores as well and brought an added dimension of artistic expression to the activities of the Royal Opera. When the idea was first discussed with Kubelik and me, I thought it was of prime importance for the Metropolitan to take an important position in this area and even aim to become a leader in operatic exploration. I felt it would stamp the new administration as artistically progressive and attract an audience that was largely turned away from the standard operatic productions that are the hallmarks of the company. We talked at great length about the idea and how it should be structured. I felt a musical or artistic adviser should be appointed to work on developing projects and I kept reminding Gentele that he was going to have his hands full with other matters, particularly his first few seasons. With the right person he could participate in the basic artistic decisions but leave the execution of them to a separate staff. I had also pointed out that we would have to find outside funding for the project even before discussing it with the board.

In the spring of 1972 Betty and I and the Genteles found ourselves, on a wet Sunday, at lunch in Connecticut with Philip Johnson. The other guests included Richard and Zaide Dufallo. The Genteles and the Dufallos got along famously. Dufallo, as a conductor and former clarinetist, had a deserved reputation for interpreting contemporary music, but I knew he also harbored ambitions for the opera house and was an excellent administrator. After lunch, as we were walking through Johnson's picture gallery, Gentele asked me about him. I said that I thought he should definitely be one of our candidates for the Mini-Met post. With that Gentele sought him out for further talks and before leaving for his Sardinian vacation had pretty much decided that Dufallo was our man.

Gentele had one bothersome habit: he hated making final decisions. He always delayed until the very last moment and sometimes lost out on artists because of this tendency. I was determined that in this case a decision was going to be made before the end of the summer as we had found someone who was willing to finance the first three years, a period which would give the Mini-Met a chance to grow and establish roots. The donor insisted on absolute anonymity but did want a sense that the project was developing. Gentele promised me a final decision as soon as he returned from Europe.

With his death it looked as if the Mini-Met project might have to be postponed indefinitely but I was determined that this was not to be the case. I presented the idea to the board at an early fall meeting after first discussing it with Moore, who was adamant that the whole idea be abandoned. He spoke loudly and uninterruptedly about the Met's financial crisis and said that he and the board would not tolerate anything that might in any way add to the deficit. I told him over and over that we had financing from the outside and that we were going to produce whatever we did on a break-even basis. I reminded him that it was time the Metropolitan reached out to new audiences, not only for the sake of the big house but for the general good of the operatic arts. He didn't listen; he kept on saying no. Finally he asked me who the anonymous donor was. I told him that I was not at liberty to reveal the name. "Well, he'll make over the gift to the general funds." he stated. "You tell him to." I said that was impossible; this gift was for one purpose and I doubted very much that the donor could be persuaded. And before he could say anything more I told him that I wasn't fool enough, or that poor an administrator, to want to add extra programs that were unfunded or would become a permanent part of the general administrative responsibilities. "This project will be self-contained, run by a special group that will be hired for the purpose and separately funded. It makes sense from many standpoints—artistic, audience development, and public relations to start it up in our first season, particularly after Gentele's death. We've stated over and over that we plan to carry on those ideas of his that can be done and I feel this is one of them." Moore stared at me, his eyes narrowed and fiery. "That money can be brought into our general funds. Get it." I made no answer.

Shortly after our talk I approached our patron and led into a discussion following Moore's instructions. I had barely opened my mouth when a restraining hand was put on my arm. "If you've come to ask me to transfer my gift to the general funds, please do not. I won't do this. I want the money to go to create the Mini-Met or otherwise I will use it elsewhere." And from the manner of the statement I knew I could proceed no further. Within the next day or so I told Moore of the talk, and he, I guess having reflected on our previous conversation, decided that he would go along on the basis that I had outlined. We went to the board meeting together and he supported my position. Some others of the group were pleased; some were hostile. The measure passed, however, and I was given permission to go ahead.

I called Dufallo and asked him to come to see me. I also called Marit Gentele, who had been active with her husband in creating the project in Stockholm. When the two of them were in my office I told them that we were going ahead and that I hoped Marit and Richard would work together.

During the summer a lot of thought had been given to the first Mini-Met season's repertoire. Thought and work had also been given to finding a place to play and we all felt the ideal solution would be to develop the program jointly with the Juilliard School, which would give Juilliard operatic students a chance to work professionally with the Met and us the opportunity of performing in the jewel-like Juilliard Theater. Several meetings had been held about this idea with Juilliard president Peter Mennin, first by Kubelik, Gentele, and me and then by me alone. Mennin was elusive and we finally broke off talks when it became obvious that he was not anxious for us to work with him.

My next thought was the little Forum, now the Mitzi E. Newhouse

Theater, housed in the basement of the Vivan Beaumont Theater. The Forum, a theater in the round without a proscenium, seated 299 people in an atmosphere of intimacy and could be made to work for a small operatic production. At the moment it was under the care of Jules Irving, the artistic director of the Lincoln Center Repertory Company. Irving was enthusiastic about collaborating and in short order we had blocked out a schedule for rehearsals and playing time. We now had a place to work, at least for the first season, and I was hopeful that over the year we might be able to get Peter Mennin to change his mind.

I also knew at this point that I was going to have to appoint an administrative coordinator for this project and I decided upon William Nix, a young man who had been brought to the Metropolitan to oversee the operations of the Metropolitan Opera Studio. The Studio was one of the progressive developments that took place in the later years of the Bing administration. It was made up of young singers, who were coached musically and dramatically and developed their talents under careful and tough professional supervision. The Studio was, as the Mini-Met hoped to be, an independent unit under Metropolitan aegis, financed from the outside. Because of the seasonal nature of its activities, Nix could undertake both assignments without neglecting either. I now had the basic structure and could proceed.

The next step was to bring Marit, Dufallo, and Nix together with the units of the main company that would have to coordinate their work within the house and, most important of all, to decide on the repertory that could be mounted with the funds in hand. Dufallo and I had discussed this aspect often throughout the summer and I had also talked it over with Marit. She had plenty of thoughts and ideas that had been discussed with her husband in the past. I felt strongly that we should do one classical chamber opera and one modern work. I did not want this to be too modern or outside the mainstream because I felt we had to woo our audience to trusting that the Metropolitan was not going to give them an excess of new thinking right at the outset. There would be time for this later and we had strong thoughts about future years. I was hoping that we could set up a commissioning program and a real atmosphere of laboratory experimentation, but I knew this had to come after we established the fact that we were really in business for the long run.

After considerable discussion we settled on Purcell's *Dido and Aeneas* for the classical work and Virgil Thomson's *Four Saints in Three Acts* for the contemporary offering. Both seemed right as important works and both were possible to do imaginatively in a theater in the round. We also decided to add an absolutely contemporary curtain raiser before the Purcell, more for expressing an artistic philosophy than any other purpose. This was Maurice Ohana's *Syllabaire pour Phèdre*. Richard Duffalo was largely responsible for the idea that seemed to us all to make a broad arch from the classics to general modern to contemporary.

With the repertoire set my next step was to contact Virgil Thomson and see whether he would agree to our doing his piece. We met on October 12 and I broached the idea to him. "Why of course," he said, "of course. Gentele had talked to me before he died and we'd already agreed. Didn't you know this?" "No, I didn't," I replied, "and I'm delighted we came to the same decision." Thomson smiled and then said, "You let me take care of the musical matters and you can take care of the stage. I won't interfere with you and you won't interfere with me. That way we'll have the perfect collaboration." "Agreed," I said, "except that Nix will be looking over your shoulder on budget matters." "Agreed," replied Thomson, "and we won't come to you unless we have a problem that we can't solve together." He rose and we shook hands.

I had mentioned to Thomson that I planned to ask Alvin Ailey to direct. We had all been impressed by the imaginative work he did on Bernstein's *Mass* and in creating the dances for the new *Carmen*. During the course of both projects I had come to know, respect, and admire him as a human being and a glorious talent. Thomson was intrigued with the idea and asked me to tell Ailey that he hoped to work with him. Alvin came to see me one afternoon a few days later and I put the suggestion to him. At first he held up his hands with a show of horror but as we talked I could see that the idea appealed to him. I told him that he would have complete artistic freedom within the constraints of the budget and that I thought he would enjoy working with Thomson. He decided to consult with Virgil and get back to me with an answer. This he did in quick time, accepting with the understanding that he had overall authority, subject only to Thomson's choices in the matter of casting, conducting, and tempi. Thomson wanted Roland Gagnon to conduct and we all agreed on Ming Cho Lee to design the sets and Jane Greenwood the costumes for all three works. For the Purcell and Ohana double bill Richard Dufallo took up the musical responsibilities and suggested that we try to get Paul-Emile Deiber to direct. Deiber was due to be at the Met during the same time period as the Mini-Met productions to restage *Norma* for Caballé and Fiorenza Cossotto at the big house. I reached him in Chicago, where he was staging for Carol Fox and the Lyric Opera, and he agreed to think it over. We met a few weeks later and after discussions with all of us he accepted the assignment.

We were now all set for the Mini-Met's initial season. For the Ohana and Purcell double bill, Richard Dufallo and Paul-Emile Deiber; for the Thomson, Roland Gagnon and Alvin Ailey. For the Mini-Met organization itself, Dufallo as artistic adviser, Marit Gentele as consultant, and William Nix as administrative coordinator. I called this group together in my office, after the repertoire and artists were all arranged, and said that it was up to them to make it work. I was available to help with problems but it was essentially their show.

On February 17, 1973, the first season opened with a Guild benefit of the Ohana and Purcell works followed on February 20 by a benefit preview of the Thomson. Both evenings were well received by the critics and public and when we came to the end of the first season and balanced the books we came out $275 in the black. Our anonymous donor was delighted; the Metropolitan Opera board made no comment at all. As far as it was concerned the project passed almost unnoticed.

The other Gentele plan, in which it did show some interest, was the children's Look-In. At several meetings they asked me what I planned to do and I said that I was anxious to start this activity, in cooperation with the Guild and as a supplementary program to the already well-established student performances, if I could come up with the right person to develop the program with us. I had talked about this with Marit but we had not reached any conclusions.

One afternoon shortly after the board discussion I was having a drink at the home of Goddard and Brigitta Lieberson. The Liebersons had taken Marit under their wing after she returned to the United States and the idea of the Look-In had been discussed around their house. Brigitta turned to me at one point in our talk and said, "Why don't you ask Danny Kaye?" "Why not indeed," I remember replying, "that's a terrific idea. I really don't know him very well. We've met only once in Washington when he came down for a performance of *Mass* but it's certainly worth a try. Do you have his address and telephone number?" "Right here," she replied. "He's in New York for the next few days. Good luck!"

That night I called Kaye and he was polite and sympathetic. I gave him a rough idea of what we had in mind and he suggested that I come see him the next afternoon. "Are you one of those people who make a date for three PM and show up ten minutes late?" he asked. "In no way," I replied. "I hate to be late for anything, in fact I'm almost paranoid on the subject." "Well, I *am* paranoid," he replied, "and I look forward to seeing you tomorrow afternoon at three. We'll talk more."

The next day at 3:00 PM I presented myself at the door of his apartment. In fact, I arrived in front of his building at 2:55 and waited until exactly 3:00 to go up. The door opened promptly and Danny Kaye stood there, a welcoming grin on his face, an eye cocked to his watch. "I checked the time before I came here!" I said as an introductory sentence. "So you did!" he replied. "Come in."

We went into the cheerful living room and sat opposite each other on two couches. I proceeded to elaborate on what we had discussed the night before but before I got very far he held up his hand. "Don't say any more," he said. "I simply can't do what you ask. I've booked myself all over the world between UNICEF and the symphonies and I mustn't take on another commitment. I didn't want to turn you down over the telephone considering all the problems you face but I just can't do it. Of course if I were to do it we might take your ideas and play around with them a little." And he got up and began pacing around the room. "We could get some singers to show what vocal technique is all about. We could show the kids that opera is great theater and not just some remote stuffed-shirt experience. We could get them excited." He went on talking about what might be done. I sat back and listened while he developed thoughts from our original outline. After about ten minutes he stopped talking and looked hard at me. "You know what I'm doing?" he said, almost belligerently. "I'm talking myself into it." "Keep right on going," was my reply. "You're doing just fine." I looked at my watch and realized we'd been together for almost an hour. "You must forgive me," I said, "but at four-fifteen I must see a lady about some money for next season's production of *Les Troyens*. Now you will take over the Look-Ins, won't you?" And I tried to look my most pleading. He smiled. "You bastard," he replied. "Before I make up my mind I want to see the theater and the people with whom I might be working." "Can you come tomorrow at three PM?" I asked. He looked straight at me. "Tomorrow at three. Okay." We walked out to the hall. "You have to raise money too?" he asked. "Oh, yes," I said, "particularly for the new productions. If I don't, the board will force me to cancel them and this is impossible, since they all must be planned at least three years in advance. The most difficult about this problem is our president George Moore. Rather than argue with him I'm out raising the money myself." We shook hands and I left, confirming that we'd meet the next day.

I left his apartment pondering the money problem. From the very be-

ginning Moore had been unrelenting in his demands that new productions, already planned and agreed to by the board for Gentele's first
three seasons, be cancelled for lack of money. Some of them already
had financing, such as *Carmen* from the Gramma Fisher Foundation,
Siegfried and *Götterdämmerung* from Eastern Airlines, as part of its
1967 commitment to complete a new *Ring* cycle, and a new *Don Giovanni* promised from Francis Goelet, a bright, cultivated, and interested member of the board, and one of the few who knew the real need
for the board's responsibility in raising funds.

Prior to 1972 the overall fund-raising activities had been under the
direction of the dynamic Mrs. Lewis Douglas, one of the few women
on the board, who told the men where to head in. She was tough and
determined and brought organization to the Met's fund-raising efforts
that had been lacking for some little time. She was relentless in her pur-
suit of what she viewed as the Met's due, calling on heads of big corporations and rich individuals with equal determination and persistence.
Peggy Douglas believed in the Metropolitan and translated her beliefs
into action. In 1972, however, she felt she had had enough. Her husband was sick with an illness that eventually led to his death and needed to be in a drier climate. Judy Laughlin was Peggy Douglas's choice
as successor, but Judy was scared out of her wits with the responsibilities she faced. As is often the case when a strong leader is replaced, the
replacement inevitably gets caught in the shadow of the original and it
takes quite a while for the new person to develop a character of his or
her own. Judy Laughlin was right at the start of such a period of transi-
tion when Gentele and I arrived on the scene and I realized quickly that
she had considerable confidence to gain before she could develop her
own style. This made the whole funding question uncertain, including
the new productions. Over the years Bing had developed some close
friendships that helped him finance his, but the biggest contributor,
Mrs. John D. Rockefeller, Jr., had died. On her death she left the Metropolitan five million dollars which was used to set up an endowment
fund. Nothing had been done further about increasing this fund beyond
the occasional gifts that came from old friends and the deaths of others
who remembered the Met in their wills. Nothing seemed planned for
the future either, except a lot of talk about the need for a capital drive
and a lot of shaking of heads about expenses. Before too long I sensed
that the artistic commitments given to Gentele didn't mean a thing to
Moore and that if I was going to be able to carry on I had better find the
funds myself.

Some board members were enormously sympathetic to my problems, particularly Mrs. Ogden Phipps, who was in touch with me every few days to see how things were going.

When I realized the totality of my financial responsibility I called on her to help finance *Les Troyens*. We lunched together in her charming New York apartment but she was unable to pledge the money herself. As we were talking she came up with the suggestion that I ask Mrs. Charles Payson, the redoubtable owner of the New York Mets, sister of John Hay Whitney and joint owner with him of Greentree Stables. Joan Payson had been going to Met performances for years and loved opera. I said that this sounded like a good idea but that I did not know Mrs. Payson. "I'll arrange that," Lil Phipps replied. "She should do this and you tell her so."

The next day Mrs. Phipps called and told me that Joan Payson would see me. I telephoned for an appointment and was asked to come on October 26, the same day, it turned out, that I approached Danny Kaye for the Look-Ins. I left the Kaye apartment to go to my very first attempt at raising money. On my way uptown the thought went through my mind that if one has to have a first time at such an activity it's just as well to start at the top.

Mrs. Payson received me graciously in her library. I sat opposite her and looked into an inviting face with smiling but wary eyes. I spoke about *Les Troyens* and about the necessity for the Metropolitan to produce this masterwork. I spoke about its grandeur and scope and also about its size. I warmed up to my subject and Mrs. Payson seemed interested in everything I had to say. At what I thought might be the right moment I brought out the Colin Davis recording of the work and presented it to her. The album is large in itself and when she took it from me she almost dropped it. "My goodness," she said, "it is heavy, isn't it?" "The records may be but the opera is not!" I replied. "I'm going to the country tomorrow for a long weekend," she said, "and I must do all my Christmas lists. Perhaps I can listen to it then, but I don't know on what. You see, I have no Victrola." I looked at her. "I guess that word is not used much these days," she said, smiling. "Anyway, I'll see what I can do. How much will the production cost?" I took a deep breath and said "Four hundred thousand dollars." She nodded and rose. I shook hands with her, thanked her for listening, and asked when I might have her decision. She said she would think it over on the weekend and be in touch with me the following week. As I was leaving I said something to her about being asked for money and that she must be heartily sick of such requests. "Oh, I don't mind," she responded. "I've learned to give an answer quickly." And she laughed gently. I took my leave.

I telephoned Mrs. Phipps and reported on my visit. "I'll keep in touch with her over the weekend," she volunteered, "and let you know how things are progressing." I said I would be keeping my fingers tightly crossed.

The next day, promptly at 3:00 PM, Danny Kaye arrived at the opera house and any anxiety I had about Joan Payson's decision was put in abeyance. Danny swept through the company at a breathtaking pace, interrupting rehearsals on the stage and in various rehearsal rooms. Everywhere he was greeted with affectionate enthusiasm and my only concern was that he would cost us overtime by interrupting too long. He didn't, though; Danny has an impeccable sense of timing.

After looking over the house we settled into my office. "Let's look at a schedule," he suggested. "When did you want to do the Look-Ins?" "We thought in the spring of 1973," I replied. "I think it will take us that long to get everything organized." "That's okay with me," he said, "as far as I know, but my life changes all the time and I'm never quite sure where I'll be from one moment to the next." "We have to plan so far ahead," I said, "that I can tell you now what will be on the stage three years from now." "I'd hate that," he replied. Just at that moment my secretary announced that Marit Gentele was outside. "Ask her to come in," I said, and turning to Danny, I explained who she was and that I would like her to work with him in developing the Look-Ins for the Met. Marit walked in and moments later Danny had her in a great bear hug. She looked a little startled but not displeased and I felt that a good team was in the making. Danny started telling stories and within seconds we were all laughing long and loud.

"I'll do this project," he said. "Come on, Marit. We'll go where it's less noisy and talk it over." And they swept out of my office. Nothing had been discussed about fees and while I was delighted that Danny had agreed, I was fearful of what it was going to cost. I had no idea who to talk to about this, as we'd never discussed anything about agents or contracts.

The next morning I called Danny and asked him how everything had gone. "Just fine," he replied. "Well, I guess there's nothing left except to talk fees. Who is your agent these days?" There was a long pause. "I'm very, very expensive," he said slowly, "and I'm not sure whether you can afford me." "How much is expensive?" I asked, with the vision of his participation fading rapidly. "Expensive is expensive," he said. "What do you pay Nilsson?" "A lot," I replied, "and she deserves every cent." "And what about Corelli?" he asked. "A lot, too," I said, "when I can find him." I went on about the fact that these were to be student performances sponsored by the Guild and that the admission charges were nominal. I spoke about the Met's long tradition of children's performances and worked my way up to a passionate speech about our obligations to prepare a future generation of opera lovers.

When I paused to take a breath he said, "I'm going to be your most expensive performer." I said that this was not possible. "Oh yes it is," he replied. "Oh yes. You see, my fee is no dollars per performance." I asked him to repeat that. He did. "But you can't work for nothing," I said. "Oh, you'll pay all right," he laughed, "but I cannot charge for this. However, you'll tell people if they ask that I'm the highest paid artist at the Met. Maybe it will help you in your other negotiations!" "I sure hope so," I said, "and thanks. For someone who asked me to come to see him face to face in order to say no you've come a long way!" "It will be fun. See you in a few weeks and we'll discuss details. Marit and I are working already. Goodbye." I was delighted to know that the Look-Ins would be joining the Mini-Met as two major new projects that had been planned for the new Metropolitan and both were going to see the light of day.

XVII

On-the-Job Training

That weekend I resisted the temptation to find out how Joan Payson's decision was coming along but on Sunday night Mrs. Phipps called to say that she had heard from Mrs. Payson's secretary that it was all off. "Why?" I asked. "She seemed interested." "I think she is, but I think she feels that the work is too long." "I'll telephone her tomorrow," I said. "Thanks for the tip."

The next day I called and reached Mrs. Payson on Long Island. "I wonder if you've had a chance to think over our talk," I said. "Have you come to a decision?" "Yes, I think I have," she said. "It is beautiful, as you said, but it's much too long. I couldn't possibly sit through the whole evening." I felt my support slipping away. I thought quickly. "But it's really two operas, you know," I went on, "and we plan to start the first one at seven PM. It lasts an hour and a half and you can stay for it and still get home in time for dinner. You can come back another time and see part two. Why don't you give me the first opera?" I held my breath. She laughed. "Oh, that's a good idea," she finally answered. "I'll do that!" I mopped my brow with my handkerchief and thanked her. "That's quite all right," she said. "I look forward to it."

That left me with part two to finance, as well as the remaining new productions for the 1973-74 season, but I felt that I was on my way. I reported my success to George Moore, who seemed only vaguely interested, and to Frank Goelet, who was then chairman of the production committee. Frank was delighted and congratulated me warmly. He was just as concerned as I was in finding production funds.

When I reported my success with Mrs. Payson to Bill Hadley, our director of finance, he too congratulated me and said that he thought it was now time for me to learn the real depth of the Met's financial situation. He asked for an appointment and came to my office bearing two charts, each in its own file folder. He came around my desk and spread the first one out in front of me. "What's this?" I asked, my eyes running down a long column of figures, ending up with a red-circled one of $2,500,000. "That's the cost of this building," he said, "for heat, light, air-conditioning, maintenance, and security. That has nothing whatever to do with the company or its performances. That is what we pay each year to live here." "Who pays for this?" I asked. "You do," he replied. "How long has this been going on?" I asked. "Ever since we moved here from the old house. It's gotten worse every year. Not a damn thing was done to anticipate this when the house was built and it's going to get worse. Now have a look at this." And he opened the second folder. Out came a chart showing a financial projection for the Metropolitan from 1968 to 1978. "I drew this up in 1968 to show the board where we were heading," he said, "and to get them thinking about a major fund drive. Nothing has happened so far." He took out another piece of paper. "We're now in late October 1972. See how accurate this damn thing is." I looked and saw that it was not off by more than somewhere between $75,000 and $100,000. "Not bad forecasting on a long-range budget," I said. "Yes, replied Hadley, "and it's going to get worse. We are heading into the worst crisis in the history of the company and almost no one is doing anything about it. You've got your work cut out for you." We finished our conversation and Hadley went off, leaving both charts behind. I stared at them gloomily.

During my early weeks the magnitude of the Met's financial difficulties began to be more and more a part of my thinking. There was an attitude throughout the company, though, that no matter how difficult the problem might be, there would always be an answer, a saving angel or series of them, and that somehow the Day of Judgment would never come. There had been close calls throughout the years but we'd always squeaked through. This time the problems seemed to grow with greater intensity. The 1969 strike had been a near disaster for everyone, and had led to a much lower subscription rate. The labor contracts included expensive work rule clauses insisted upon, I believe, as an insurance policy against a management that seemed out of touch with the needs of its workers. Perhaps everyone had been around too long; in any event the attitude of the rank and file of the company was not good and the advent of a new management was awaited with pleasure. Gentele's presence seemed to inspire; his death was not just a shock but a cataclysm. There were great fears that the board would turn back to the old hands. When it did not there was a sense of relief but this relief itself put a tremendous responsibility on our shoulders and it was imperative that I deal with everyone on a candid and honest basis. Real or imagined, the company felt it had been fooled too often and I wanted to eradicate this feeling as quickly as possible. These feelings, plus normal professional administrative procedures, compelled me to seek out as quickly as possible the true state of financial affairs and everywhere I turned the signs were awful.

I studied Hadley's charts with great care and consulted with the staff, particularly Michael Bronson, the business and technical administrator and Charles Riecker, the artistic administrator. I searched out Jim Jaffray, then treasurer of the association, a vice-president of the First National City Bank and close business associate of George Moore. Jaffray was the direct opposite of Moore in personality, but equally tough in fiscal matters. He underscored the problems and in endorsing Hadley's charts pointed out that there were basic administrative procedures, such as advertising and promotion, that in his opinion had never been used properly to expand the subscription base. He was impressed by management's concerns about fiscal matters and frank to admit that the board had been negligent in establishing a major capital fund drive.

During my first months Jaffray was a big help in understanding the depths of the problems. Another helpful source was the study of the 1969 labor settlements that committed the Metropolitan board to large increases in salaries for three of the four basic elements of the house: orchestra, chorus, and ballet. These amounted to an 80 percent increase in the salary of a dancer, from an average of $6,700 a year for 1968-69 to $12,000 for 1971-72; a 47 percent increase for members of the chorus from $10,200 in 1968-69 to $15,000 in 1971-72; and a 28 percent increase for the orchestra from a 1968-69 average of $16,400 to a 1971-72 average of $21,000. The fourth large group, the stagehands, received comparable increases but not with the same overall financial impact on the association, as the off-season rentals of the house called for the renters to pay the full stagehand expenses.

In addition there were substantial reductions in rehearsal times for all groups with an adjustment in starting and finishing hours for rehearsals that reduced the working day for all performers. It was agreed that the chorus and principal artists would have one free day other than Sunday in every two-week period. For the principals there was a reduction in services from four performances per week to three and a half; the chorus salaries were to cover performances only, with extra compensation for all rehearsals, and the number of actual performances reduced from seven to five a week. For the ballet the hours worked per week for which they received base pay was reduced from thirty hours to twenty-five in the last year of the contract.

The settlement of the 1969 strike made the performers of the Metropolitan the highest paid in the world with percentage increases far exceeding the then prevailing settlements throughout the industry. The total economic settlement resulted in an expected operating deficit of six to seven million dollars in the 1971-72 season, described in a report on the negotiations as "burdensome to finance."

Curiously the new Metropolitan contracts in 1969 finally recognized that the burden of supporting artistic institutions could no longer be borne by the artists themselves in the form of substandard wages that were in effect subsidizing the organizations. The results of the 1969 negotiations, however unpleasant they were to carry out, did accomplish a great deal, but also made it incumbent on the association to seek out new sources of revenue to support what it had agreed to do. When I faced the 1972 talks everyone on both sides of the table realized that the giant steps had been taken in 1969 and our discussions were in a much easier frame. But the association, for whatever reasons, had done relatively little about assuring its ability to increase income. The time was rapidly approaching when the fiscal crisis would be total. Hadley's charts forecast 1978. According to my reading of them, it would be even sooner.

But life in the general manager's office, even as acting general manager, was not devoted solely to finance. I was learning rapidly about the daily crises that face every opera company manager in the world. Illnesses and cancellations seemed to be the order of the day and I thanked God for the Metropolitan's "cover" system that at least assured that we probably would get the curtain up every night.

The "cover" artist is one who is ready to step into a major role on a moment's notice. He or she is paid well for this service but it is always a touchy business because to be a "cover" one has to have vocal excellence and usually that excellence is seeking a career on its own. The problem is further complicated by the Metropolitan's relative isolation from other centers of major operatic activity. For the months when

Chicago, San Francisco, and the New York City Opera are in season it's a little easier to find last-minute replacements, but when the Met is all alone in the middle of the winter the finding of a major artist for a replacement is a great problem. That is why the "cover" system is so important and why I was anxious to give "cover" artists the chance to perform when the opportunities arose. Kubelik shared these feelings and also wanted to upgrade the artists on cover contracts.

I have marked November 18, 1972, as the day of the light, the light being my recognition of just what it was to run the Metropolitan Opera as its acting general manager. In the weeks before, the excitement of the opening of the season, the completion of labor contracts, and my growing familiarity with the house and its people, to say nothing of my increasing knowledge of the financial mess, made each day rush by. I used weekends to study background material and to prepare myself for onrushing problems of all kinds. Since the Met plays two performances on Saturday and most of the administrative offices except artistic and technical are closed it is usually a good day to get things done.

On this particular Saturday in November I arrived at the theater to find Mr. and Mrs. Tito Gobbi sitting outside waiting to see me. They both looked extremely solemn and upset. I greeted them and took them down the corridor into my inner sanctum. "What's wrong?" I asked. "You both look anxious and sad. It can't be that bad." "Oh yes it is," replied Tilde Gobbi. "Tito is not well. He has not been well all season in Chicago and now he has a fever and the doctor tells him he must go home." "Now?" I queried, my eyebrows rising. Gobbi was due to start rehearsals for *Otello* on Monday, in a revival of the Zeffirelli production. It was going to be extremely difficult anyway because Jon Vickers was scheduled to sing *Otello* and had never sung the role in New York before and had made it very plain to me that he loathed the production and was going to insist on numerous changes. Gobbi was to be his Iago and the two of them together promised operatic fireworks. "Yes, now," replied Tilde, and Tito agreed, nodding his head sadly. "Then this means you're cancelling *Otello* at this late date?" I asked, stunned. "We're afraid so," came Tilde's reply. Both rose from the sofa. "Come, my dear," Tito said. "We go back to Italy." "But what about the rest of the season?" I asked. "We'll see how quickly Tito gets better," came Tilde's reply. "Tito loves the Metropolitan but he is no good for it if he is not well." I wished them a quick return to good health, and they went out the side door on their way back to Italy. That meant no Iago for *Otello*, unless I could find a suitable replacement in a hurry. The "cover" artist for this part was just that and not someone who could match Vickers's temperament either artistically or personally.

I had barely a moment to digest this news when my secretary came into the office with a cable. It was from Mirella Freni, announcing the cancellation of her entire 1972-73 Metropolitan season, "with regrets." The "regrets" were pinpointed by the Internal Revenue Service, which had been at odds with her for some years over back taxes. Apparently she decided to leave well enough alone and stay out of the country.

I was just digesting this news when I heard the unmistakable footsteps of Erich Leinsdorf striding down the hall. He walked unceremoniously into my office and announced, "I want another Wotan by Monday." *Die Walküre* was at that moment in the last of its rehearsals and Leinsdorf was, as usual, grumbling about rotten planning and the lack of attention to his needs. The week before he conducted our new production of *Siegfried* with Birgit Nilsson, Judith Blegen, Lili Chookasian, Gerhard Stolze, Thomas Stewart, Jess Thomas, and Gustav Neidlinger making his debut as the despicable Alberich, and it had been a great success. This was the first of the so-called Karajan Ring productions to be directed by Wolfgang Weber. Karajan had dropped the whole project in the last years of the Bing administration due, in large part, to the strike of 1969. Leinsdorf had agreed to take over the musical responsibilities after Karajan, but he was not going to be asked to undertake *Die Götterdämmerung* the following season. This plum was going to our new musical director, Kubelik, and Leinsdorf was particularly unhappy about this. His feelings made all his problems worse and he was not in what one might call a good humor. "Why?" I asked. "Because Adam cannot sing a dress rehearsal on Wednesday and a premiere on Friday, And Stewart is committed to *Siegfried*. And the situation is not to my satisfaction. Adam will sing the premiere but there must be an artist of equal stature to rehearse on Monday." And he turned and walked out the door.

Somewhat breathless I sat down to contemplate the problems. Here were three juicy ones for a Saturday morning. Earlier that week Jon Vickers had arrived for his *Otello* rehearsals and created towering scenes on the stage showing his displeasure with the production. He had been in and out of my office during the week threatening to quit and had given both Levine, the conductor, and Fabrizio Melano, the stage director, a very hard time. Now Gobbi, for whom he had great respect, had been forced to withdraw because of health and I had to dig up from somewhere a first-rate Iago who was available right this moment. Freni had been scheduled for quite a number of *Bohèmes* and *Fausts*, for she is a big favorite in New York with good reason. She is one of the great sopranos of our day and a splendid actress to boot and the public would not understand or appreciate her absence. As for Wotan, the great scarcity of Wagnerian singers all over the world was not going to help with this problem. Most of the world-class singers of this repertoire were already under contract to us and scheduled precisely to both sing and cover. Our "in house" Wagnerian expert was assistant artistic administrator Paul Jaretski who watched over these matters with a fierce dedication equaled only by the watchdogs of Bayreuth itself. He reminded me that we had an untried young German Wotan cover named Hans Sotin, who had first come to this country with the Hamburg State Opera and scored a resounding success in its concert version of *Der Freischütz*. Sotin was a big talent, had sung the role in provincial houses but never on a major stage.

The matinee that afternoon was *Orfeo ed Euridice* with Marilyn Horne, Adriana Maliponte, and Colette Boky, conducted by Charles Mackerras. After checking backstage that all was well I called a meeting with Riecker and Jaretski to tackle the problems. We agreed that Maliponte would be asked to undertake Freni's Marguerites in *Faust* and that I would ask Renata Scotto if she were free to do some of her *Bohèmes*. The only problem was that at that time Scotto was mad at us and had recently granted an interview to the New York *Times* complaining that while the new management said they loved her all they offered her was Butterfly. Maliponte was Freni's *Bohème* cover and would not be pleased to lose the role in favor of Marguerite. This was going to be a tricky switch.

The Iago matter had a glimmer of hope in the person of Louis Quilico, a French Canadian baritone who was at that moment on the west coast with the New York City Opera. Quilico knew the part and had sung it with success in Canada and Europe. He was strong enough vocally to match well with Vickers. We also thought of Milnes, who was scheduled to sing the part later in the season; Spiro Malas, the Greek baritone who was supposed to be excellent in the role; and several others. We started trying them, one by one, but no one was available. Finally I called Quilico, assuming that he, too, would not be free, and as I was doing so I realized that if I bombed out here I might be forced to cancel the production. I was totally unprepared, therefore, for a cheery voice saying yes, he could make himself free in time to sing the dress rehearsal on December 1 and the first five performances, beginning December 5 and ending December 23. I couldn't believe my luck and the relief that emanated from all of us was almost visible.

By this time it was late in the afternoon and I adjourned the meeting. We decided to postpone the Freni problem until Monday but knew that both *Bohème* and *Walküre* had to be solved over the weekend. *Otello* looked to be in order but *Bohème* and *Walküre* were still way up in the air.

I went home for dinner and decided not to return to the house but to try working out the problems at my own desk. I reached Hans Sotin during the course of the evening and asked him if he would be prepared to sing the dress rehearsal as well as the rehearsal of Acts I and II on Monday and Tuesday. As a cover Sotin was obliged to be in the theater and to sing rehearsals if his principal was sick but he immediately smelled that something else was in the air. "What about Adam?" he asked. "Adam's fine," I replied, "but we just want to make sure that he doesn't strain himself." "Good," said Sotin. "I will do the rehearsals but only those as a cover unless you promise me a performance in the role before the season is over. You must promise me an assigned performance with publicity and critics even if I have to go on before that." He said all this in a thick German accent and meant every word. "Otherwise," he continued, "I might find the New York weather dangerous to my health." There was a long pause. "I'll call you back in an hour," I said and hung up. I was now facing operatic blackmail for the first time and I had to decide how to cope with it. I telephoned Leinsdorf and told him the story. "He's very young," the maestro replied, "and while he has a good voice I think he'll wear himself out during a performance and not know how to pace the role. I worry about the last act." And then he paused. "But it is your decision," he went on and I could hear the sarcasm in his voice. I called Sotin back and accepted his terms. There was really little else I could do and in the back of my mind I knew he was going to be a fabulous Wotan and his "official" performance might be a special night in Metropolitan history.

On Monday, when I went into the theater, things were reasonably quiet and remained so throughout the week. The *Walküre* premiere with Theo Adam, Birgit Nilsson, the debut of Gwyneth Jones, Jon Vickers, Mignon Dunn, and John Macurdy went off well and I knew the next big hurdle was going to be the stage rehearsals of *Otello*. Vickers erupted when he learned that Louis Quilico was to sing Iago. Quilico and Vickers were on the outs, and fireworks threatened. They continued to threaten right up to the dress rehearsal on December 1 and it was with some tension that I sat down in the auditorium that morning hoping that things would go smoothly. And they did, on the stage at least, and I was beginning to think that we were going to have a great show when I felt a slight tug at my sleeve.

My secretary, Peggy Tueller, was there with the news that Nicholai
Gedda, scheduled to sing Rodolfo that night, was ill and had to cancel.
This was the performance that was to have been Freni's first of the season and we had persuaded Renata Scotto to step in for her. Now the
tenor was gone as well. I turned to Charles Riecker, sitting alongside
me, and asked who Gedda's cover was. Without comment he pointed
to the stage where William Lewis was singing an impassioned Cassio.
"He is," Riecker said. "Do you want to interrupt the rehearsal?" "Oh
God, no," I replied. "Who else do we have?" "No one we could put in
tonight," came the answer. "All our other major tenors who sing the
part are either ill or unavailable." I told Peggy to go back upstairs and I
stared ahead at the stage. I'll think of this later, I told myself. I'll think
of it later. Right now we have *Otello* and it must stay on the track. I
found I was able to divide the problems and concentrate on one issue at
a time. It made me feel like the infantry soldier who has survived his
first run through no-man's-land.

Upon the completion of *Otello* I went up to my office and summoned
the artistic administrative staff. "What do you suggest?" I asked as
they came into my office. "I don't know. We're stuck with this one,"
one of them said and looked me straight in the eye. We were silent for a
moment and then Riecker asked if anyone had seen the squib in the paper that Pavarotti had arrived in the country the night before. I said I
had not and buzzed Peggy. "Can you call around and find out where
Pavarotti is staying and let me know immediately?" I asked. "I've never met him," I said, "and since he isn't due here for a few months he
must be on his way to Chicago or San Francisco. If we can find him I'll
ask if he'll sing tonight." I remembered suddenly the great maxim
taught me by Tex McCrary in the agitated days of the past: "The most
that people can say is no." This, if ever, was the moment to give such a
philosophy a try.

Peggy buzzed back with the name of his hotel and I placed the call.
Within a few minutes he was on the phone. "Mr. Pavarotti?" I said.
"We haven't met. My name is Schuyler Chapin and I'm the new acting
general manager of the Metropolitan." "Oh, Mr. Chapin," came the
reply, with the name being pronounced Chappeen. "I'm so glad to hear
you. I look forward to meeting you." "Mr. Pavarotti," I replied, "so
do I and very soon indeed. Tonight, in fact, if you would be gracious
enough to help us out. We have a big problem. Gedda is ill and can't
sing Rodolfo. Freni has canceled her entire season and Scotto is singing for her tonight. Would you come in and replace Gedda?" "I'm so
sorry to hear about my friend Gedda. Is anything serious?" "I think

not," I replied. "He's got a touch of the current flu bug but it has knocked him out." "Oh sure, I'll come," he said, "but you tell the public." "Damn right I will!" I replied. "And thank you. I'll see you tonight." I put down the phone and looked at the staff. "He'll do it," I said, and couldn't repress a grin.

With this news the theater sprang into action. The rehearsal department was alerted, the costume department, wigs, makeup, and publicity. The machinery that makes the Metropolitan one of the best-organized theaters in the world began to hum and by curtain time that night everything was in order for this last-minute substitution.

Everything was in order all right, except my nerves, for this was to be my debut before the curtain announcing major cast changes. I thought of the times through the years when I had heard Osie Hawkins announce such events in rolling tones. I had even been present on some of those times when Bing came before the curtain.

At dinner that night I took two vodka martinis as a precaution. They were going to either kill me or steady me and fortunately they did the latter. As 8:00 PM approached I took my place behind the curtain and waited for the house lights to go down, the spotlight to be turned on, and the cue from the stage manager to walk out. As the lights went down and the spot came up I could hear groans from the house. Everyone knew that some change was in order and I could feel the slight hostility that greeted me when I came out.

However, I was in for a surprise. As soon as I stepped into the light the audience began to applaud and I stood looking at them with a somewhat bewildered expression on my face until I held up my hands for silence. "Thank you very much," I began, "I appreciate your greeting and so does the whole house." And the applause began again. This time I held up my hands quickly. "Please," I said, "I've come out front tonight to tell you that unfortunately Madame Freni has been forced to cancel her entire Metropolitan season this year." The groans started. I held up my hand again. "We are most fortunate that Miss Maliponte is here to take on Madame Freni's roles but that means that she has to prepare *Faust* and therefore cannot sing Mimi tonight." There were more groans. I held up my hand again. "But we're most fortunate that Renata Scotto has agreed to appear tonight." And there was a rising sound of oh's and ah's of pleasure. I went on. "Unfortunately the vagaries of operatic life are such that at eleven AM this morning Mr. Gedda was forced to cancel because of a bout of the flu." The groans started in earnest. I let them go on for a moment and at what seemed like the right time I held up my hand again. "Replacing

Mr. Gedda tonight will be,'' and I paused a second, ''Luciano Pavarotti.'' The house went wild. I stepped behind the curtain and Pavarotti was seated at the battered table in the first act garret scene waiting for the curtain to rise. The sound of the roar outside could be plainly heard onstage and I went over to him. ''Was that all right?'' I asked. And he listened for a few seconds and broke into a grin. ''That's nice!'' he said, rising from his chair and giving me a big bear hug. I thought that was nice too!

At the end of the performance I went to thank him. ''It's okay, Mr. Chappeen,'' he said, ''I love the Metropolitan. I'll help anytime I can.'' And then he said, ''You know, no other theater in the world could replace a Freni with a Scotto and a Gedda with a Pavarotti! I wish for you the best.'' And we embraced again. I now felt blooded. A Wotan, an Iago, a Mimi and a Rodolfo, one on top of the other, to say nothing of *Carmen*. At long last I was beginning to feel that I was leading the job, not the other way around.

XVIII

Becoming General Manager

On December 5 the tension-ridden *Otello* had its first performance of the season and Vickers sang one of the great interpretations of his career. Teresa Zylis-Gara was the Desdemona and matched perfectly with Vickers so that the great duet at the end of Act I, *Gia nella notte densa,* melted one's heart. Quilico was a more than adequate Iago although his acting was not his strongest point. He did make it up with superior vocalism and the total effect was strong and dramatic. By the end of the opera I knew that we were home free. During the curtain calls, Vickers's tension eased for the first time that season, helped by the public who tore up programs and showered them down at him as an extra measure of thanks.

The next day he came to see me and the smiles were gone again. He had been scheduled to sing three operas that year, *Die Walküre, Otello,* and *Pique Dame. Pique Dame* was just beginning rehearsals. "I've too much to do," he said, "too much, too many problems. I'm dropping *Pique Dame.* I just can't do it this year." I knew better than to argue. "I'm sorry, Jon," I replied. "We'll all be disappointed, especially the public, but I understand and will try to make other arrangements." He looked at me mysteriously, as if he hadn't expected my reaction to be quite what it was. "I'm so happy for all of us about *Walküre* and *Otello,*" I went on, "and we so look forward to next season's *Tristan und*

317

Isolde with you and Ligendza and Nilsson. I want you to be happy here and we'll do anything we can to make you so." He sat back for a moment and looked sharply at me. My expression did not change. "Well, we'll see about all that," he said after a few moments, "and in the meantime no *Pique Dame.*" "I understand what you're saying," I added, rising from my chair and putting out my hand. He took it, shook it hard, nodded his head, and left the room.

I called Riecker. "Vickers has just said he won't do *Pique Dame.*" "Don't worry," came the quick reply. "We're all set there. Gedda does the first ones, as you know, and Bill Lewis is his cover. It's a perfect role for him and he'll do the second run beautifully. We'll have to get another cover who can learn it in Russian but basically Vickers's leaving does not present a problem." I breathed a sigh of relief.

There were no sighs of relief elsewhere, though. We were now well into the season and there was no sign from Moore or the board as to what they intended to do about a leader for the theater. Moore had been good about improving my assistant manager's salary to something approaching a reasonable fee for my present responsibilities but beyond that he had made no decision about appointing a general manager. I kept reminding him that we could not postpone the decision indefinitely, that the very nature of opera demanded decisions being made now for three years down the road and that willy-nilly I had to commit the company even if I did not have proper authority. He bristled at this and told me not to make any firm plans. I told him I had to if there was to be a Metropolitan season in 1975-76, to say nothing of final details for 1973-74 and 1974-75.

He insisted I stop. I had to appeal to other members of the executive committee to get him to realize that I had to go ahead. Kubelik took up the cudgels and between us we finally got him to agree. But we lost a lot of time and our lack of decision-making was beginning to hurt. Artists who could not get commitments beyond those already made were beginning to turn away from the Met. Agents were getting frantic; the profession began to feel a lack of confidence in what was happening at the house. The atmosphere was getting tense and I wanted to put it to rights.

One day during this period I received an unusually cheerful call from Moore. "I've just had a great idea," he began. "We need an overall artistic director for the house and I've got just the person." "Oh, who?" I replied with some curiosity. "You sound very excited!" "I am, I am," he said. "Maria Callas." "Maria Callas?" I queried. "Maria Callas as artistic director?" "That's right," he said. "She'll be great and maybe she'd even sing a few performances herself. That would be good for the box office." "But, George," I said, "you're talking about one of the great artists of our time whose singing days are restricted and I have a feeling that the details of running an opera house might be a little exasperating for her." "Oh, no," Moore answered. "I know her very well. I see her all the time. She would be great, great. I think you should do something about it. I'll tell her to be in touch with you."

He wasn't fooling. Shortly thereafter I came back to my office one afternoon to find a message that Callas had arrived in New York and was expecting my call. I telephoned back and we made a date for lunch the next day, 1:00 PM at the Oak Room of the Plaza. I selected the Oak Room, which had recently changed its timeless luncheon policy to admit women, because I'd often seen her there in her halycon days, surrounded by admirers, friends, and opera groupies. I arrived a little early and asked for a table in the back of the room. The Oak Room was a rendezvous point for people in the musical and theatrical world and I did not want us too visible to curious eyes.

A little after 1:00 PM she arrived, looking, to me, far more attractive in person than she did on the stage. She was wearing a very becoming outfit of reddish-brown tweed and on the fourth finger of her right hand was a ruby and diamond ring of splendid magnificence. She smiled at me as I rose to greet her. "We must become such good friends," she said, seating herself as I pulled the table away from the banquette. "We must work closely together. There are so many changes to make." She looked up as a waiter approached. "I will have tartar steak," she said, "and a glass of red wine." I gave my order and we returned to business.

Over the course of the next hour she never stopped talking. I had planned to ask a few questions but decided that silence on my part might be the better part of valor. She went on and on about the dreadful state of opera houses and opera managers, of how she had been so badly handled over the years and how her successes were largely due to her own outstanding abilities plus a little help now and then from understanding colleagues. As she talked I noticed that she looked at me in an odd way and it wasn't until she paused in her narrative long enough to put on glasses that I realized she had not really been able to see me. The glasses gave her face an oddly attractive soft look and I became aware of what a compelling, feminine, and sexy woman she was.

We finished our lunch and she rushed out of the room on her way to some other appointment. We had agreed that she must come to *Otello* the following Saturday and start with this opera as a base for her theories of reorganization.

The night of the performance arrived. Earlier that day (December

29) she called me asking to have a limousine sent for her. The *Otello*
she was to see and hear had McCracken, Milnes, and Zylis-Gava. As
8:00 PM drew near there was no Callas and we put the curtain up on
time regardless. She finally arrived just as the second act was about to
begin. She came into our box and smiled sweetly at Betty and acknowledged the stares of surrounding boxholders with a slight bow of her
head. The act began and she alternated between watching the stage and
giving me sideways knowing glances, with an occasional nod of her
head. I was not sure what all these gestures meant but I gathered we
were sharing a conspiracy about how awful everything was up on the
stage.

At the intermission we went back to my office and were joined by
guests she had brought with her to our box, Mr. and Mrs. Guiseppe di
Stefano and, I believe, one of their daughters. They all settled themselves onto my sofa and chairs and were delighted to be offered a glass
of champagne.

Early on in my acting general mangerial days Mrs. Phipps, realizing
that Betty and I planned to do a lot of entertaining of VIPs, sent us several cases of Dom Pérignon to help things along. I always kept a couple
of bottles on ice just in case and this night was definitely one of those
moments.

The champagne was consumed quickly, and Callas turned to me
midway through her glass and said, "Of course, you know the whole
production is dreadful. No one on the stage sings or acts with any authority. The set is really awful and we're going to have to do something
about all this." I was about to make a response when she looked at her
watch. "Oh my goodness, we must go!" she said, rising from the
couch and sweeping the di Stefanos along with her. "It's Pepo's birthday, you know," she added, "and we must all be at his birthday dinner." "Aren't you going to see the rest of the performance?" I asked
with some incredulity. "We have a lot to do together and you seem to
feel that what you've seen so far is bad. Shouldn't you stay to the end
for a proper critique?" "Some other time, of course, my dear," she replied, "but right now we must be off." And she came over to kiss me.

I let them out through a special side door in my office and she went
on to her dinner. Betty and I looked at one another and shrugged our
shoulders.

A few days later Callas called again and asked to see me. It happened that I had a very busy day ahead but I made room at 6:00 PM,
canceled our dinner plans, and prepared to spend the whole evening
with her.

She arrived on schedule, in a second limousine, and settled down in a chair opposite me. She was wearing another attractive outfit, with what looked like a sable coat thrown back loosely from her shoulders.

I decided the time had come for me to make a few comments and I started by saying how our friend George Moore had suggested her for this new post and how happy I was to have a chance to talk it all over with her in some detail. I went on about the opera house itself, about the fourteen unions, the over two million dollars in building maintenance costs, the board, the shops, the scheduling complications, and after about a fifteen-minute narration suggested that we tour the building, starting at the very top of the house. "You know the dressing rooms, the stage, and the rehearsal halls," I said, "and I think we can skip these for the moment. What you don't know are the shops and the sewing rooms and the administrative offices, the accountants, the artistic staff, both musical and administrative, the house directors, the chorus master, the chorus, the orchestra personnel manager, and the orchestra committee. We'll have to have you meet all of the key people involved." She paled visibly. I got up and offered her my arm. She shook her head. "Not now, please," she murmured. "There will be time for all that later. We must talk about that dreadful *Otello*. We must not have things like that on our stage." I tried to tell her that there were some who had different thoughts about that particular production but got nowhere at all. "Did you come back and see the first and last acts?" I asked. "No. I couldn't find the time," was her rejoinder, "but I know what it's like. And we must change it."

With that she rose and, draping her fur coat over her very attractive shoulders, held out her hand. "Goodbye," she said, "I'm leaving for Spain tonight and will tell George of our fascinating conversations. Have you any special message for him?" "No, just give him my best. When do we see each other again?" "Oh, I don't know, perhaps in a few months when I return to New York. I'll let you know." And with that she swept out with all the glamor and magic that had been her hallmark on the stage.

A few minutes after she left I placed a call to Moore in Spain and gave him details of our meetings, suggesting that perhaps Madame Callas had other things to do that she might find less taxing. Moore was silent, unusual for him, and the subject never came up again until the spring, when one day I asked what had happened when Callas reported to him about her visits. "Nothing at all," he said, "in fact, come to think of it, she never mentioned a word. Very strange, very strange. Not like her." I made no comment.

About the time of Callas's visits I was facing a much more important artistic problem which Kubelik and I were trying to resolve. In 1971, during our planning talks at Lucerne, we had all discussed the likelihood of obtaining the American premiere rights to Benjamin Britten's newest opera, *Death in Venice*. I knew something about this work, not musically, but from the standpoint of obtaining the rights from the Thomas Mann estate to do the work in the first place. Abraham Friedman, Bernstein and Amberson's lawyer, also represented Britten's interests in America and kept me advised as to how negotiations were moving. I knew at that time that the thought was to give the opera to the New York City Opera for its American debut. Gentele, Kubelik, and I were all anxious to get it for the Metropolitan, even though it was supposed to be a piece for a much smaller theater. At the time we all talked the work was still being written, consequently none of us had the remotest idea what it would actually turn out to be. All we did know was that the principal role of Aschenbach was being tailored to Peter Pears and that the Tadzio was to be danced. We wanted it for the Metropolitan and made plans to pursue obtaining the rights.

In early 1973 we were approached by Hans Heinsheimer, senior editor of G. Schirmer, Inc., and by Donald Mitchell of Boosey and Hawkes, Britten's English publisher. We arranged a meeting of the four of us and the whole matter was settled in less than fifteen minutes. Both the American and English group were delighted with our interest and when they asked what our plans might be we told them that we planned the premiere for October 18, 1974, and that Kubelik was to conduct. They agreed immediately and we all shook hands. Heinsheimer kept shaking his head. He and I were old friends, going back many years on many different projects, the last of which was Bernstein and Amberson. "It is so different now," he said, "so different. A few years ago such a conversation would have been unlikely. Now it is all set. Extraordinary!"

After they had all gone, I thought to myself that it was all very well to plan exciting things for the future but would I be around to help carry them out? During the winter and early spring the stage was active with a lot of excitement. *Pique Dame*, even without Vickers, was a great success, made so in no small part by the young Polish conductor we introduced to this country named Kazimierz Kord. *Macbeth* with Grace Bumbry and Sherrill Milnes brought new life to this not very strong score. Vickers's towering achievement in *Peter Grimes* with Sixten Ehrling conducting and a splendid revival of *La Fille du Régiment* with Sutherland and Pavarotti also helped keep the box office active. I was reminded of Gatti-Casazza's talk with Verdi, when as a young man, prior to coming to the Metropolitan, he had just taken over direction of La Scala in Milan. "Always keep your eye on the box office,'' the venerable composer had told him. ''When the house is full you are a success. When it is empty you are not!'' We were most fortunate that our houses were very full indeed.

But in the board room there was another story. Moore flew in and out of the country from his house in Spain and one never knew from one minute to the next what he might have to suggest. The executive committee, at that time the prime governing body, had more meetings canceled than kept, and from individual members of that group I would hear from time to time that they were dissatisfied with the way things were going. No one ever said as much to me except Bill Fisher, vice-president of the Association, who made it plain that he did not think I was handling things in the right manner. We squared off on several occasions but even these times he never got specific. He was one of the few, however, who sensed the need for permanent leadership, even though he was convinced that that leader should be someone other than myself. To that end he rushed back and forth across the country and in and out of Europe hoping to find a leader. In Italy he stopped. He met Massimo Bogianckino, then the artistic director of La Scala, and in Fisher's mind he was to be the lifesaver of the Met.

Bogianckino is an old friend of mine, dating back to the mid-sixties when we worked together to bring the Rome Opera, of which he was then artistic leader, to the Lincoln Center Festival of 1968. He had been educated in America after World War II and had attended Columbia University in New York. He is a bright, sensitive, capable, and charming man with a distinguished career in music and the theater but not someone to cope with the Metropolitan's problems and I told him so when the board invited him over to talk. We spent a long afternoon in my office and I'm afraid Massimo felt that I didn't want him around in any kind of teamship way. I didn't, really, but I felt that if the board were to have confidence in him I would stay around as his administrative partner, assuming of course, that he would get along with Kubelik. The whole business seemed distasteful to me and not well thought out. It was bound to lead to extra unneeded clashes all around and I was very glad when the board decided on its own that Bogianckino was not the man.

All this took many long hours and weeks, and meantime plans had to move ahead and I had to take the attitude that I was the leader. But the ''acting'' position could not go on for much longer. The financial crisis was at hand, the unions began to grow restive, the stars suspicious, and the attitude increasingly negative.

Kubelik and I had a midwinter meeting in Paris to discuss the situation and he agreed to keep after Moore to make some resolution. We knew that we both were in a very exposed position without a true mandate to continue and we both knew there were severe problems within the house administration itself that really could not be resolved without leadership fully supported by the board.

By mid-March nothing except the Bogianckino visit had been accomplished and my patience was at an end. I called Moore and said that we should have a talk, that he and I had gone over this ground time and time again and nothing was being done. I reminded him of Kubelik's feelings and urged him to have any private meetings he wanted as long as a decision was forthcoming to appoint someone to lead the company. I was very quiet on the phone but very firm and said that as far as I was concerned I had brought the subject up for the last time and didn't wish to discuss it any more.

As I put down the phone I glanced up at my window to find the face of Sir Rudolf Bing looking in at me. I motioned for him to come around to the entrance and went out to admit him. "Forgive me," he said as he sat down. "I was passing by and wondered if you had a moment." "Certainly," I said, "it is nice to see you. Is there anything I can do for you?" "Yes, there is," came the reply. "I have one question. Is Corelli returning next year?" I thought this a bit odd since he surely knew of all the Corelli problems we had been having that season. "Yes, he is, as far as I know," I replied, "and he's supposed to have a good season." "Ah good," he said. "I think he is one of our greatest artists. And what about the post of general manager. Is anything happening about it?" I told him that it was odd that he turned up this particular day because I'd just gotten off the phone talking to Moore on the same subject and telling him that I had no more to say about it. "But who are they going to take if they don't take you?" he asked, his eyebrows rising. "I don't know," I said, "but they better decide on someone. The company cannot be leaderless much longer."

The next morning the phone rang at home about 6:45. It was Moore. "Perhaps we better talk face to face about all this," he said. "Meet me for lunch at the Racquet Club at one. I'm going to see Kubelik at eleven." I already had a date that I was not anxious to break but I agreed and put down the phone. Betty turned to me. "Now don't get mad and don't lose your temper," she said. "Be patient and listen to what he has to say." I said I'd try to behave myself.

At the appointed hour I met him at the Racquet Club and we went to the bar. I ordered a drink, something that I do not often do in the middle of the day. Moore prattled on about various ideas, shooting from the hip, so to speak, with each one. Finally I asked him if he'd had a good talk with Kubelik. "Oh yes, oh yes," he said somewhat impatiently, "and I showed him my plan." "You have a plan?" I asked. "I would love to see it." He pulled out a crumpled piece of paper and pushed it toward me. "See, this is how it can work," he said. I couldn't make head or tail out of what he proposed. There seemed to be a lot of names and crossing lines of authority. The whole business looked as if it had been made up on the spur of the moment. "May I say something now?" I asked, politely. "And will you do me the favor of not talking until I have finished?" "Of course, of course," he bristled. "What do you have to say?" I took a deep breath and started.

I explained carefully that regardless of the problems, or maybe especially because of them, the Metropolitan Opera needed a leader at this point as badly as it ever had in its history. I reviewed the reasons for my coming in the first place, to backstop Gentele and Kubelik and form the third line of the "troika," and I outlined what I felt to be the right steps to carry that original idea out. I said that Kubelik and I could work well together and that we would jointly search for the right stage producer to join us and re-glue the troika. I spoke moderately, choosing my words carefully and trying to make each sentence as unambiguous as possible. When I was finished I took a sip of my drink and waited for his reaction. It wasn't long in coming. During my narrative I could see his jaw clenching and unclenching and when it was obvious that I'd had my say he leaned over toward me and barked, "Well, that's just unacceptable!"

I grew deathly quiet within myself. The word "unacceptable" was one he used often and with rampant carelessness. I had now heard it one time too many. I could feel my bile and temper rising and before I knew it I found myself tense as a steel rod and, leaning over toward him, my head quite close to his, I replied, "I've got some news for you, George. You're not acceptable to *me*." And I illustrated my point by jabbing my index finger at him. "I've had enough. We've been struggling these months against unbelievable odds and you have behaved inconsistently and often burst forth with ideas that had obviously never been thought out. Now I've had it, and I give the opera house back to you today, right now. And good luck."

I rose from my chair and started toward the door. "Sit down," he barked peremptorily. I looked at him. "I have no intention of doing any such thing and I cannot see any reason for us to continue this ridiculous conversation." By this time my voice had risen and I could see heads at other tables turning around to see what was happening. Two waiters were more or less frozen in their tracks. Ordinarily I would have been hideously embarrassed by such a display but this time I couldn't have cared less. "Sit down," he said again, this time a little less bombastically. I looked at him and started out of the room. *"Please* sit down," he said, now acutely aware for the first time that our words were being heard all around the room.

I stared at him for a moment and sat down abruptly. My hands were shaking, my mouth dry, my head light, and I recognized all the symptoms of losing my temper as a child. I felt a quick blush of shame but it went away fast. I took the glass in both my hands to steady it and drained every drop. The vodka felt like water. I looked straight ahead at Moore. I was in agony.

"Shall we go to lunch?" he said, rising. I nodded and followed him out of the room. We went upstairs to the dining room, were ushered to a window table, and ordered. My stomach was on a rampage but I was determined to spend the rest of our time together in as civilized a way as I could muster.

Presently we were finished. I had hardly spoken a word during the meal. He had talked on about various matters as if our set-to had never happened and I nodded from time to time without hearing a word that was spoken. When we reached the street his car was waiting and I shook his hand briefly and walked away.

When I reached the opera house I told Peggy that I was going home and was not to be disturbed unless there was an unsolvable crisis connected with that night's performance. She looked at me oddly. I must have shown signs of the strain but she was discreet enough not to ask me any questions. I walked across town but by the time I reached our apartment I was steaming mad all over again and blew up at Betty. She, too, was the soul of discretion and let me get it all out.

After an hour of stalking up and down and getting everything off my chest I went to the bedroom, stretched out on my bed, and was fast asleep in a few minutes. Betty let me sleep for almost two hours and when I awoke I felt relaxed and fresher than I had for many weeks. Even Moore began to be seen in better perspective.

The next morning early Moore telephoned. "You got rather mad at me yesterday," he said, to begin the conversation. "No, George," I replied. "I got *very* mad at you." "You think I don't listen to what you have to say," he went on. "No, George," I said, "I *know* you don't listen to what I have to say." "Well, I do, I do!" he barked. "And you don't know how I've been fighting to save your skin. There are lots who don't want you around." "Fine," I replied, "I'll leave now." "Oh no you won't," he shot back. "Now, George," I went on, "don't you think enough is enough? This company needs a leader. For whatever reasons, there seem to be some who don't want me. Fine. But get someone because this betwixt and between can't go on any longer." "I know, I know," he concluded, "and I'm going to do something about it." I sighed and rang off.

By the time I reached the theater the news of our fight must have gotten around because various staff members made excuses to drop into my office and see how I was. I told my top people, Michael, Charlie, and Francis, what had happened and said that I didn't know whether or not I'd be there much longer. But I said that while I was there decisions were going to be made and plans continued and I expected everyone to go about their tasks in good spirits.

Fortunately I had a major diversionary problem that kept my attention away from the board and on the business at hand. Monserrat Caballé had arrived for her performances of *Norma* and made it clear that she was not about to do our *Vespri Siciliani* if the set was to be similar to Hamburg. "There are too many steps," she said in her attractive Spanish-accented English. "I'm afraid it will be difficult for me. Before I agree I must see a model of the sets and meet Dexter and talk with him."

I knew this was impossible. Dexter was heavily involved with theater commitments in London, but Svoboda's models had arrived at our scenery shops and we could show them to her. I didn't want to do this without some aid and assistance and I called James Levine and asked him to talk with her about the musical side. I told him that after I'd been in touch with Dexter I would arrange a meeting and wanted him to be there to back me up.

I reached Dexter on the phone and he gave me the ideas he wanted put across. He said he would draft them in a letter and get it off posthaste. Fortunately Caballé was very busy with *Norma* but every time I saw her she reminded me that we had to discuss the *Vespri*.

Dexter's letter arrived in a week and was indeed explicit as to what he expected her to do. I sent a copy to Levine and when he was ready I asked Caballé for a meeting. I had the models brought down to my office and went through the various changes with David Reppa, the head of our scenery department, who had worked carefully with Svoboda in creating them. I also called Bill Fisher, who had agreed to pay for the production through the Gramma Fisher Foundation with the understanding that the work would be done both at the Metropolitan and the San Francisco operas. Fisher was dead set on opera houses sharing productions and I was all for this when it came to the unusual repertoire. *I Vespri Siciliani* seemed to me to fit into that category. Fisher was puzzled but basically pleased with what he saw and the stage was now set for Caballé herself.

The lady arrived on the morning of the appointment accompanied by her manager and press agent. They all took places on my sofa, sat staring straight ahead at the model stage, and at the appropriate moment I went over and began explaining how everything was going to work. I had tucked Dexter's letter behind the small stage but within easy reading distance and referred to it as I went through scene after scene. Whenever I paused Levine was ready with a musical comment and after thirty minutes of this we had gone through the entire opera and reached the end. Caballé struggled to her feet, came over to both of us, and enveloped us in a huge embrace. "It is beautiful!" she said. "It almost makes me cry. Of course I will do your lovely production. I know Mr. Dexter will take care of me." She hugged once again, put on her enormous mink, and left. Levine and I looked at each other and solemnly shook hands. It had been a good morning.

Norma, with Caballé, Fiorenza Cossotto, and Carlo Cossutta, opened on February 12, the twenty-second week of the season and the twenty-second week of one of the worst years for flu and respiratory disease in modern New York operatic history. Almost every night there were substitutions and I thanked God for the cover system. The big trick was to make certain that the curtain rose every night, hopefully with the advertised work. If an opera had to be substituted at the last moment it caused enormous havoc with subscriptions as well as those people who had bought single tickets especially for a specific performance. We had to refund money if the opera changed: if it stayed the same we were not obliged to do so, and I wanted to avoid refunds at all costs. All costs sometimes meant a performance on the stage that was below the usual Metropolitan standards, especially if we were forced to ask second covers to go on when first covers as well as the particular stars in question were sick themselves. Nevertheless we succeeded in getting the curtain up every night with a lot of brave people in a lot of tough roles and we learned firsthand about the need to strengthen our house artists.

We had several house artists signed for the full season that were on their way to stardom. Among these were the tenor William Lewis and the bass James Morris.

Lewis is the kind of artist that no opera house can be without. His repertoire is wide. He is a good actor and solid musician and there were times that year when he sang almost every other night. Morris, a big strapping young man, was a pupil of Rosa Ponselle and had been well taught. He has a big, solid voice, extremely musical with a wide range, and I felt we were not going to have him under yearly contract for too long a time. It is impossible to estimate the number of performances saved by soprano Lucine Amaras, who could have had a major career on her own if she had not elected to stay as an almost exclusive Met artist. The Amaras, the Lewises and Morrises, and the Shirley Loves, Christine Weidingers, the Jean Krafts, the Velises, Dobrianskys, the Paul Frankes, and the like are the backbone of the company. They give the Met its ensemble spirit and frequently keep the curtain up. I got to know them well as they moved in and out of their own performances plus those of stricken colleagues.

After my big blow-up with Moore things quieted down for a while. No decision was forthcoming but I decided to forge ahead with things that had to be done and figured that whether I was appointed or not Kubelik and I were going to plan the future as if we were both going to be there. Looking ahead to the next season I realized that only *Les Troyens, I Vespri Siciliani*, and *Don Giovanni* had actually been financed and that I had better get a move on to assure the other new productions that had been promised back in 1971. These included *L'Italiana in Algeri* and *Les Contes d'Hoffmann*.

During the course of the winter Betty and I met a great many people who were committed to the Metropolitan and might be in a position to help. Through another board member, William Mayo Sullivan, I was introduced to a delightful eccentric opera lover named Thomas Brush. Tom Brush looks like a portrait of a young Kaiser William II, with a fierce moustache and pointed beard. He carries himself ramrod straight and at first glance seems a trifle offputting. But that is only at first glance; he is a man of great taste and sensitivity and this was borne out at our first meeting, a small dinner at the opera house with the Brushes, the William Mayo Sullivans, and ourselves.

At dinner we talked about Kubelik and I told him the story of Kubelik's escape from Czechoslovakia after the Communist takeover in 1948. On the proscribed list for his outspoken disapproval of the coup d'etat, he picked up his wife and son and enough clothing to last them through the Edinburgh Festival, which had invited him as a guest conductor. As their plane took off from Prague he turned to them both and told them to look out the window at the homeland which they were not going to see again. He left behind all his worldly goods, including the great library of scores and music books that had been started many years ago by his father Jan Kubelik, a violin virtuoso of the early part of the century. It is a story of great courage and determination and when I was finished telling it, Brush's eyes were filled with tears. He obviously cared about people as well as art.

A few days later I called him for lunch and he ended up inviting me to the Quo Vadis, where we had a splendid meal and I found myself telling him about our upcoming *L'Italiana in Algeri*. He listened with interest but his heart was obviously set on something else. "Aren't you planning a new *Boris Godunov*?" he asked. "Yes," I replied, "but that's not until 1974–75 season and right now I've got to be sure we can do what we've planned for 1973–74."

Then, emboldened, I went on to tell him some of the problems I was having with Moore and how the threat of cancellation of all new productions was hanging over my head unless I could find financing. He listened carefully but we went back to talking about *Boris*. I told him that we were planning to use the second Lamm edition of that score, which would return the work to something close to what the composer had in mind. I told him that we hoped to beat out the problem that always plagued *Boris* productions, the endless waits between scene changes, and how I was confident that the team of August Everding and Thomas Schippers was going to find a solution.

I ended the *Boris* description by returning to *Italiana* and describing in some detail this absurdly delightful comedy which depends entirely on having the right cast. This is particularly important for the role of the heroine, Isabella, a mezzo-soprano role that calls for vocal acrobatics and a talent for comedy. Marilyn Horne was to sing this in a production to be designed and directed by Jean-Pierre Ponnelle in his Metropolitan debut. Brush listened with interest but I didn't want to overstate my case and switched the conversation to general matters. After a few moments he looked at me intently. "How much will *Italiana* cost?" he asked. "One hundred and seventy-five thousand dollars," I replied, taking a swallow of coffee. He looked at me for another moment. "You have it," he finally said, "but I don't want my name listed in the house program. I don't want any public credit. If I do, every Harry, Dick, and who knows what will be writing me asking for money and I don't want to be in that position. I'll tell my friends. I'll tell all those I want to know but we'll skip the public!" I thought this was definite enough and tried to find the words to thank him. "Nonsense, nonsense," he replied, looking embarrassed but also, I thought, immensely pleased.

Frank Goelet was delighted with the news when I called him a few hours later and that now meant only the *Hoffmann* was uncovered.

This particular *Les Contes d'Hoffmann* had an unusual history as far as the Met was concerned. It originated in Seattle, created by the Seattle Opera for Joan Sutherland, who sang the four main parts. I was anxious that nothing go wrong in carrying out the plans for this event because I felt that Miss Sutherland already viewed me with grave suspicion as the man who was bringing Beverly Sills to the house. Sills and Sutherland, of course, sing basically the same repertoire and each has dominated her particular New York theater in those operas. Early on, both Gentele and I felt it imperative that Sills be invited to the Met and we had discussed repertoire for her. She was delighted to come but felt that her first Met apperance should be in a production especially set up for her. We agreed and together with her capable adviser, Edgar Vincent, had selected *I Puritani* as the right vehicle.

Alas, we did not know that this was a work that Sutherland had been asking Bing to produce for her for over ten years. When the rumor got around that Sills was going to be invited to sing it, I received a call from Sutherland's manager, who made it very plain that if, indeed, Sills was to get *I Puritani*, Sutherland would never set foot in the Metropolitan again. We discussed this with Sills, whose attitude was splendid. She said that if Sutherland had come into her theater, the New York State Theater, and been offered a work she had been waiting for, she, too, would never darken her theater's doors again. We then decided to think about the right work and keep in touch with each other.

One day, while visiting Thomas Schippers on matters connected with *Boris Godunov*, he casually asked what we were planning for Sills's debut. When I told him that we had no idea he produced an Italian radio recording of *L'Assedio di Corinto* that had been made with Sills and Horne at the time of Sills's La Scala debut. I then remembered all the publicity that had broken after the event and I dimly recalled favorable comments about the opera itself. "Why don't you and Gentele listen to this?" he suggested. "If you like it I'd love to conduct it again since I did most of the work reconstructing the score." I told him we would listen carefully, which indeed we did, and it wasn't long afterward that we decided to settle on this piece. When it had been performed at La Scala, Marilyn Horne had sung the mezzo role but did not wish to repeat it at the Metropolitan. We offered the part to Shirley Verrett, who accepted it with pleasure, and we scheduled the premiere for April 7, 1975, some three years away. We were all delighted and decided to keep any official announcement out of the press until the right moment.

All of this made the Sutherland situation especially sensitive. Another area of sensitivity was that nothing appropriate was settled on for the 1974–75 season and that meant she would be absent from the Met stage for the first time in over twelve years. I sensed a certain wariness in our early talks, both from Joan and her husband, Richard Bonynge, and I wanted nothing to go wrong with *Les Contes d'Hoffmann*. And nothing would, I hoped, as long as I could find the production money. We had surrounded Joan with a superb cast, including Placido Domingo as Hoffmann and Thomas Stewart as all the villains and Huguette

Tourangeau as Nicklausse. The production was by Allen Charles Klein, direction by Bliss Hebert, and it was to be conducted by Bonynge. Since the production had originated in Seattle we had only the costs for transportation and adaptation to the Met stage, as well as remaking the costumes for the chorus and dancers. All told this came to $110,000 and I was looking for a patron.

Fortunately one, or I should say two, appeared in the form of Mr. and Mrs. Samuel Tedlow. The Tedlows are opera buffs supreme and I had met them when I was guest of honor at the Opera Club's 1972 fall dinner. Later we asked them to dine with us before a performance and during our conversation I mentioned that this was my first job as the boss, that I had spent all of my career so far as a "second banana" and that I was beginning to enjoy the number one spot even with all the problems. Tedlow smiled at that comment and looked knowingly at his wife but nothing further was mentioned. We talked about opera house matters and I mentioned that we needed a new *La Bohème* somewhere along the line and that I was seeking funds for Sutherland's *Les Contes d'Hoffmann.*

About two weeks later Tedlow called me and asked if he and his wife, Lillian, could see me. We made an appointment for 6:00 PM one evening and they came to my office in evening clothes. They sat on the sofa and I pulled up a chair. They were very quiet, looking back and forth at one another, and finally he began to speak. He had been drawn to me by my tale of "second banana" and he felt that the time had come for both of them to help out the new regime. He brought up the possibility of a new *La Bohème* but I explained that our needs were greater for *Hoffmann.* They asked how much it would cost and I told them.

By now I was getting used to quoting large amounts of money and I did it without batting an eye. They looked at one another, took each other's hands, and then looked at me. "All right," they said. "We will give it to you. We want to help you in any way we can." They rose. I kissed Lillian, shook him firmly by the hand, and my eyes were not entirely dry.

Later that night I phoned Frank Goelet and told him the news. He was delighted. This meant that all the new productions for the first real season of the new management were now financed and this problem was out of the way for another year. I also telephoned Moore, who seemed impressed by the news.

The 1972–73 season was now coming to its last weeks and I felt reasonably safe in honoring commitments I'd made to the Metropolitan Opera National Council to take a swing through the western part of the country on behalf of its auditions program. I had always been impressed with the Metropolitan auditions ever since I used to hear them broadcast on the radio when I was a young boy. At first they were sponsored on the air by Sherwin-Williams paints, whose motto was "We cover the earth." I've always thought the Met auditions are something like that. While they may not cover the earth, they cover a great deal of territory, including the Hawaiian Islands and Australia, and are the one actual program that truly reaches out all over the country, which adds to Met's claim for national position.

In my view the national council was under used, despite the auditions zations that are part of the Met family, the national council might be the one to save the company in the 1970s, as the creation of the Metropolitan Opera Guild did in the thirties. Oddly, both organizations had been started by the same person, Mrs. August Belmont, who perhaps more than any individual since Otto Kahn has been responsible for keeping the Met alive.

In my view the national council was under used, despite the auditions program and the Central Opera Service that it began. Each member was a person of importance in his or her particular community and if inspired could be made into a national lobby for the Metropolitan, useful in countless ways. I was particularly keen to make my spring trip to meet as many members as possible and to have them meet us. Moore was bored by the council; it should give money, or get out, was his general feeling. A belief echoed, in large part, by the officers. It was another area where we did not see eye to eye and I was not surprised to get a phone call one day before we were scheduled to leave suggesting that I cancel the trip.

"It won't be good for you to be away now," he said. "You need to be here to defend yourself. Besides, I've been meeting with Kubelik and we feel that the leadership should be divided into a troika with Bogianckino as artistic chief, Kubelik as music director, and you as the responsible administrator. The job of general manager is too big for one man." And before I could respond he went on to tell me that he had been visiting the Ford Foundation and been complimented about the new look and feel at the Met. Once again my head was spinning. I had thought the Bogianckino matter had been put to rest and here it was obviously very much alive in a new scheme drawn up by Kubelik and Moore.

I did not lose my temper this time, merely said that I intended to carry out my trip as I thought it important and that I'd just have to take my chances with the board. I was calm and deliberate on the outside. On the inside I was seething. No one had discussed this new idea with me in any way and I felt that whatever ground I had gained during the past months was slipping away. I thought I ought to express myself on the subject to Moore in writing and the next day, while we were flying across the country, I composed and sent the following letter:

March 1, 1973

DEAR GEORGE:

Forgive the bad paper but it is all I have in my briefcase and I am writing en route to California.

As you must realize by now, I am extremely upset by the news you've given me over the last 24 hours. Most of all I'm shocked and indeed stunned that your plans should have been discussed with Kubelik completely behind my back. The feeling I have is that obviously neither you nor the other members of your selection committee have any confidence in my artistic judgment, let alone the capacity to lead the company. And all this just hours after your meeting at the Ford Foundation where they complimented you for the new look and feel at the Met. Who's responsible for this look and feel. Bing? And to top everything off there is now Lowell Wadmond's [chairman of the board] carrying-on about my traveling, as if I was doing it as a lark. Boggles the mind, it does!

In any event now that I do know what's going on I must make clear my own feelings.

1. A "troika" will not work. Someone has to be the boss, despite any lawyer's theories to the contrary. Kubelik's here no more than 6 months a year, Bogianckino probably not much more. What happens when they're not around? Kubelik, for all of his fine musicianship, is not that experienced in day-to-day problems of repertory opera. Bogianckino, who did fine work as artistic director of the Rome Opera in the late fifties and early sixties, is also accustomed to the *stagione* system, quite different from ours, and has little knowledge of American theatrical or operatic life. Everything can be learned, of course, but why this move when we are trying to make more and better use of our own talent? Above all, isn't this a matter that should ultimately be decided by the management of the house rather than the board?

2. *You* were the one that took the bold step of giving me the authority to run the company at a time when swift and decisive action was needed. Your courage and strength at a dark moment was what made it possible for us to take an almost impossible situation and make it work and work damn well. We've not spent long hours together talking about every problem. You trusted me and I responded to that trust and the institution has emerged stronger for it. Just as the tide is moving right it would seem that this is not good enough and decisions that should be made between Kubelik and myself—we do work well together—are going to be imposed from without rather than developed from within.

I am a professional in this field, have been for almost 20 years, and despite the fact that I've never run an opera company before we're doing pretty well. And the institution is *not* too big to have one person in charge. General Motors has a chief, your bank does, and there's even rumor that someone occupies a White House on Pennsylvania Avenue in Washington, D.C.

I must say I wish I was embarking on this trip for the Metropolitan with a little more confidence about my part in its future.

I hope to see you before you return to Europe.

Sincerely,
SCHUYLER

I mailed the letter when we landed in Los Angeles and we went about our speechmaking and audition judging for two days, then flew off, before going on to Hawaii, for three days in Baja California with our friends Hank and Mary Guettel, to catch our breath. We stayed at Cabo San Lucas, a charming spot with communication limited to a ship-to-shore two-way radio. Moore called me there, evidently upset by my letter, and tried to reassure me that he had not been dealing behind my back. I made no comment. He went on to report that there were a lot of people who wanted me out and that he was fighting for me to retain the job.

Perhaps all this was the usual political maneuvering that seems to go with anyone in any kind of top position. I knew I had enemies just as I knew I had friends and I realized that, while the whole situation of being the man on top was a totally new experience for me, I was being exposed to executive manipulation just as if I had been the boss at any large company. I also was aware that my career was not the conventional one for a Met general manager. If I were to be appointed it would be an appointment where in a very large sense the board would be taking a chance. I tried to keep all this in my mind but with all the emotional and professional pulls this was not an easy thing to do.

We went on to Hawaii as scheduled and felt once again the potential power of the national council. Many of the most important people on the islands, in business, law, government, and education were a part of the Hawaiian group, and as we met them and attended various dinners and cocktail parties I sensed the latent power that could be drawn upon to help the Metropolitan in various ways.

We returned to New York heartened by what we'd seen and were greeted by an irate Moore, who had discovered that the director of finance, his own appointee and a first-class administrator, had, because of illness and a painful operation, overlooked recent changes in the social security laws and the Met was going to owe the federal government an additional $300,000 in withholding taxes by the end of the fiscal year.

As is frequently the case in any progressing crisis the movement toward crisis continues straight along until some one thing or action causes the whole situation to blow up. Such was the case with the $300,000, for now Moore really began to see in alarming proportions the real extent of the money problems and at the same time the need for leadership. He called for extra meetings of the executive committee to force a decision of my status and finally, on May 8, with great reluctance, they appointed me general manager for three years.

When I went into the board room to be given my formal notification the applause was polite but brief; very few came up to me afterward to wish me well. I did not have what might be called an overwhelming mandate but, tattered or not, the months of indecision were over and I was to be allowed to carry on what had already been started.

Later that same afternoon we held a press conference and I announced, among other things, that the rumors of Beverly Sills's upcoming debut at the Metropolitan were true. I said that this was my first formal release of future information and that we all were delighted that matters for this important event were now in order.

Right after the conference we left for Atlanta, Georgia, to catch up with the company's spring tour. On the night of my formal appointment the fact had been announced to the Atlanta audience and had been greeted with warm applause. The company had caused a huge cake to be baked with appropriate slogans and good wishes and we cut this backstage with enough for almost everyone on hand.

XIX

The Season's Under Way

With my formal appointment as general manager I again turned my attentions to the very real problems that were daily facing the institution. We ended the 1972–73 season with a $7.8 million gross deficit, which added on to our accumulated deficit of $5.5 million meant that the Met, for all practical purposes, had used up its few endowment resources, and was in a very tight cash position. We would have to take some drastic decisions if we were to get through the season.

The first of these involved reaching out to broaden our subscription base. The subscription had grown steadily over the years and by 1969 had reached over 70 percent of capacity. After the 1969 strike the figure slipped badly as people began to realize that they might be able to get along without the opera. We had to make a major effort to recover our losses and hopefully reach out for many newcomers. Second, we had to trim the operations of the company to the bone, reorganizing and consolidating responsibilities to get along with fewer people. Third, we had to mount a major emergency fund drive, not only for the immediate problems but to bring home to the public the seriousness of our situation and hopefully to prepare the board for the long-neglected capital fund push.

We needed to take some dramatic steps to spotlight our situation and two such seemed appropriate right at the outset. I decided to cancel the new production of *Don Giovanni*. This was a practical thing to do as well, since the designs were still in the planning stage, nothing had been committed to the carpentry shops, and the money might be transferred to general funds. I knew this was going to raise havoc with the artists involved, particularly Leontyne Price and Karl Böhm. Price had been very wary of the Met ever since *Antony and Cleopatra*, Samuel Barber's opera that opened the new opera house in 1966, and the new *Don Giovanni* had been especially earmarked for her. Böhm had been a favorite in the house for many seasons and this new *Don* was to mark his eightieth birthday. The production itself was needed to replace the 1957 one designed by Eugene Berman and generally regarded as one of his masterpeices. During the 1971 planning days in Lucerne I had questioned the wisdom of doing away with it. However, when I saw it in the June festival of 1972 I realized it had fallen on evil days and looked as if it was one step away from the ash heap. Francis Goelet had agreed to underwrite the costs of a new one and I'd asked Jo Mielziner to design it. Mielziner had not worked at the Metropolitan since his 1933 production of *Emperor Jones* and as one of the country's senior designers and major artistic figures I felt he might have some ideas about the work that would be fresh and inspiring. He also knew how to work within a tight budget and had begun his thinking in close collaboration with Günther Rennert, who was scheduled to direct. All these people would have to be told and hopefully in such a way as to continue their interests in Metropolitan affairs.

The first one I approached was Price. I called her and asked to see her at her home. She replied that she would come to see me and did within a day of our talk. When she was seated I broke the news to her about the fiscal problems and why I had picked *Don Giovanni* to cancel. She was enormously understanding but wanted to be released from her last two contracted performances if we were going to use the old production. I told her that it was my intention to treat the revival as if it were a new production in terms of rehearsal and stage preparation but agreed to her request.

Next I telephoned Karl Böhm in Europe and, as ill luck would have it, I called on his eightieth birthday. We chatted for a moment and I sent on to him messages from his friends at the Met but then had to come to the real purpose of my call. He was, to put it mildly, not pleased by what I had to tell him. "If you have to cancel all new productions that is one thing," he said in high indignation, "but to cancel mine on my eightieth birthday, this is too much. I will not come at all." And he rang off with a crash.

This was bad news indeed, for in addition to *Don Giovanni* he was scheduled to conduct *Der Rosenkavalier* and I was not anxious to lose either of them. I called him back the next day and he wouldn't talk to me, putting his son on the phone instead. His son told me in no uncertain terms how upset his father was and how badly he thought he was being treated after his many long years at the Metropolitan. I tried to explain the reasons but they fell on deaf ears. Finally I reminded him that we had a signed contract that called for a considerable amount of money and his reply to this was that we would have to pay the full fees because we were in breach. I told him I'd look into this and promptly called our lawyer, who replied that we were not. I called the Böhms again and stated our position. I suggested a compromise; Böhm come for *Der Rosenkavalier* and I'd find another conductor for *Don Giovanni*. This was agreed to. Not happily, but agreed to.

Kubelik and I discussed the problem and tried to fit it into his already overcrowded schedule but this simply did not make any sense. Finally we decided to ask Levine, who agreed provided we stuck to new production rehearsal schedules and he could juggle around his other commitments.

About the time all this was going on the board appointed a new treasurer, to replace Jim Jaffray, who was retiring from the Citibank and settling into a life in Maine. For this post Moore selected a younger man, son of old friends and a senior vice-president of Peat Marwick Mitchell & Company, public accountants and management advisers, named James S. Smith. Mr. Smith was in his early forties, a 1945 graduate of Harvard and a music lover, trained in the new corporate system of decentralization of authority and government by committee. As an expert in this area he immediately had an audience since few of the board members were familiar with his kind of work. Mr. Smith was quietly ruthless with his theories that he believed applied to theaters and opera houses as well as giant conglomerates. It wasn't long before we had teams of efficiency experts pouring all over the theater, pads and pencils in hand, looking at everyone as if they were so many ergs. He came to see me, unsmiling, with his impersonal blue eyes staring out, and asked me how I proposed to cope with the crisis. He behaved as if I had personally created it and I decided to answer him word for word and attitude for attitude.

I traced the history since the move into Lincoln Center, both as an outsider and an insider, and told him that I thought we did have to examine everything we were doing but that I doubted very much if we were going to have vast savings in our operations. I explained the

workings of a repertory system, the need to plan so far ahead, and the
problems I already faced for the 1975–76 and 1976–77 seasons due to
the board's vacillation. I pointed out, among other things, that I was
still, despite my appointment, working without a formal contract. I
spoke about the importance of our spring tour, the possibility of developing a national constituency out of the various elements that made up
the sum total of the Metropolitan's assets, the necessity for the long-
delayed fund drive, the need for board reorganization, the need for administrative reorganization within the company; in short, many of the
problems as I had seen them develop during my brief time at the helm.
He listened without changing expression. "You must do something to
show the board and the public that you mean business," he finally
commented. "You must take some action."

I outlined what I had done about *Don Giovanni* and then, as we
talked, an idea formed in my mind. "Perhaps one way of being dramatic about our problems would be to ask our tour cities to help," I mused
out loud. Smith seized on the idea. "That sounds excellent," he said.
"Why don't you do something about it?" "I will right now," I replied,
staring at him and fascinated by his machinelike coldness, "right
now." And I went to the phone and put in a call to Lulu Humphreys in
Cleveland.

Lulu Humphreys, or more properly Mrs. George Humphreys, was
the informal chairwoman of the tour cities, a loyal supporter of the
Met, and someone who had become a quick and good friend to both
Betty and me. I told her what we were trying to do and how important
it would be for the tour cities to help us dramatically at this crucial
time. She understood and reminded me that there was a tour cities
meeting scheduled in Chicago in early fall and that we might come to
that gathering and spell out the problems in as much detail as appropriate. In the meantime she urged me to call each individual city and see
what I could work out.

Since I wanted one dramatic result of my talk with Smith I called two
other cities, Detroit and Atlanta, and they both agreed to help. I asked
each of them for $50,000 over and above their tour fees and both in-
dicated if the need was as real as I described they'd see to it that the
money was forthcoming. It wasn't as easy as all this seems in retro-
spect but most important was the attitude of our friends and the ac-
knowledgment that something had to be done to assure continuation of
the Metropolitan.

After the calls I told Smith that I thought he as treasurer should attend the Chicago meeting and lay out the problems in detail. He looked

startled at this suggestion and even a little nervous at the thought. I was glad to see a very human reaction. We then discussed a new system for keeping a closer watch on our expenses and he asked me to assure everyone that his efficiency people were here to help and that they should receive full cooperation. I assured him that both Bronson and Riecker had been fully alerted and that I anticipated full cooperation.

When our meeting broke up he left my office with the same impersonal attitude he had when he came in. I sensed a new and potentially dangerous adversary. Administrative efficiency and cost control are essential in the theater as in any business; how you achieve these goals and with what attitudes can be either helpful or destructive. I wasn't certain which thrust would apply here.

With the cancellation of *Don Giovanni* I asked for a meeting with Frank Goelet. I had assumed that his gift for the production could be moved over to general operating funds and intended to ask him for permission to do so. Before we could have the meeting, however, word came to me that another donor, the one responsible for Part II of *Les Troyens*, had withdrawn due to complications in settling her husband's estate.

This gave Moore the opportunity of banging away at the cancellation of the whole production and toward this end he called a special board meeting with me in the witness chair. I was, in effect, attending star chamber proceedings, with Moore as the self-appointed judge and accuser and the rest as a rubber-stamping jury. When I'd taken my seat he started in on my reasons for wanting to go ahead. I went over familiar ground yet one more time: the commitment made in 1971, the need for the house to do commanding works in a major way, the costs of canceling a production at this stage, with scenery and costumes almost completed and an expensive international cast assembled, the high anticipation for this work on the part of the public.

I reminded him that I had the money for Part I and that despite the current difficulties about Part II I was confident the balance could be found. More and more I was on the defensive, a position that I had no business to be in and as he hammered away the rest of the group remained silent. Finally Mrs. John Barry Ryan, daughter of Otto Kahn and long-time Met supporter and board member, spoke up for the work. Moore paid little attention, he turned to me and said, "You'll have a box office disaster. No one will come. This will cost us millions." Nin Ryan countered with the history of the work at Covent Garden and one other person spoke out about the success of the recent recording. Someone mentioned the previous year's concert performance at Carnegie Hall, but Moore, this time with the help of the chairman Lowell Wadmond, kept saying over and over, "No one will come. It will be our biggest disaster." I thought quickly of *Antony and Cleopatra* but said nothing.

The talk grew hotter and I could see that the board was heavily divided on the question. As calmly as possible I made it clear that I was not going to do the canceling and the meeting broke up with no formal resolution, just a lot of shaking heads and tut-tutting. I had firmed up my thinking, however: no cancellation from the general manager's office. If there was to be one it would come from the president of the Metropolitan Opera Association.

When Goelet and I met to discuss *Don Giovanni* the new problem about *Les Troyens* had come out and rather than ask that his money be applied to general funds I asked if he'd be willing to apply it toward the missing Part II. Frank Goelet is a quiet man, one born to money and position who has taken time to become one of the most cultivated and educated of patrons. He is shy, abhors the spotlight, and gives the impression of someone who is easily swayed. Such is not the case. He knows precisely what his interests are and where his feelings lie. He dislikes fights and showdowns and power plays and retires from such scenes with alacrity, although so quietly that you hardly notice he's gone. But take him for granted or cross him and you find a backbone of tempered steel.

As I asked my question I could see his hand tighten around his fork and his gaze fix on the wall straight ahead. With great calmness he put his fork on his plate and turned to me: "If you cancel *Les Troyens* I shall never give another penny to the Metropolitan. You may have the *Don Giovanni* money for Part II but only for Part II. It is Mr. Moore's job to look after the general funds. I give money for productions, or perhaps I should say for the purposes of the Metropolitan." He looked carefully at me. I replied, "I have no intention of canceling *Les Troyens* and if I am ordered to I shall resign. I mean it." "I have no doubt you do," he replied after looking at me carefully. He picked up his fork and resumed eating. By this time our fish was cold, the vegetables soggy, the iced tea lukewarm. But Goelet and I understood each other.

Financial crisis notwithstanding, the eighty-ninth season of the Metropolitan opened on September 17, 1973, with *Il Trovatore* starring Martina Arroyo, Placido Domingo, Cornell MacNeill, John Macurdy, and Mignon Dunn, conducted by James Levine. It was the first season planned by the post-Bing management and the official first season with Rafael Kubelik as music director. In addition to the new productions we had scheduled a repeat of last season's successful *Carmen*, as well as *Salomé, L'Elisir d'Amore, Die Zauberflöte, Madama Butterfly, Rigoletto, La Traviata, Simon Boccanegra, La Bohème, Manon Lescaut, Il Barbiere di Siviglia, Otello, Der Rosenkavalier, Don Giovanni* (in the old Berman production), *Parsifal,* and *Tristan und Isolde.* The *Tristan* production, originated in Bing's last season, was, as one critic put it, "achingly beautiful," and we were repeating it with Catarina Ligendza and Birgit Nilsson alternating as Isolde with Jon Vickers and Jess Thomas as the Tristans. This was to become one of the artistic causes célèbres before the season was out, but on that shiny September evening such thoughts were far away.

Our first new production of the year was to be the much-discussed *Les Troyens* on October 22. *Les Troyens* is a gigantic work in every respect. As I had told Joan Payson, it is really two operas combined in one: The Trojans in Troy and the Trojans in Carthage. It remained dormant for many years until Kubelik revived it in London in 1957. Until that time it was considered almost unplayable. The forces required are huge: an orchestra of 120, at least 110 in the chorus, 22 principal parts, a large corps de ballet, acrobats, and numerous supers.

Berlioz composed the work in two years, between 1856 and 1858. Ill and sorely pressed financially he had failed to make his way as a composer and had been forced to earn his living as a music critic and librarian of the Paris Conservatory from 1838 until his death in 1869, at age sixty-six. As a boy Berlioz had fallen under the spell of Virgil when his father tutored him in the classics. His libretto is a model of clarity and concise epic-making and often comes directly from the Latin (Books I, II and IV of the *Aeneid*). He made one major change: in Virgil, Aeneas tells of the fall of Troy as a flashback at a feast given by Dido; Berlioz dramatizes it in the first act of his opera, with Cassandra as the major figure.

Notes and letters from the period of its composition show Berlioz's exhilaration and joy as well as fear for the success of the piece. The Paris Opera would not accept the work; in those days it was interested only in less serious matters, and it wasn't until after 1862 that he tried to interest the smaller Théâtre Lyrique in Paris. Worried that he might never see any of the work performed, he agreed to cut it in two and only the second half was done on November 4, 1863, and it, too, was severely cut. No absolutely complete score was published until 1969, 101 years after its inception.

In large measure its modern success was directly attributable to Kubelik, who brought the work in abridged form, and in English, to the

Royal Opera House, Covent Garden, in 1957. Its success made public and critics alike view Berlioz as a force in opera. Boris Goldovsky staged it once in Boston in 1955 and it later appeared in truncated form at the San Francisco Opera in 1966. On September 17, 1969, again at Covent Garden, *Les Troyens* was finally given in its entirety with Colin Davis conducting. This was followed by the same version in Paris and by Sarah Caldwell's Opera Company of Boston in 1971.

For our production first-class forces had been assembled. Dido was to be sung by Christa Ludwig, Cassandra by Shirley Verrett, and Aeneas by Jon Vickers. Aeneas was the part that had brought Vickers to international fame in 1957 and he was anxious to repeat his triumph in New York. Peter Wexler, the talented young American, had been assigned as set and costume designer, and the entire production was in the hands of Nathaniel Merrill, whose work had been steadily successful at the Metropolitan. For the chorus we had engaged John Nelson, who also was to serve as associate conductor. Nelson had performed *Les Troyens* at Carnegie Hall in a concert version the year before and Kubelik had been highly impressed with his work.

Rehearsals for the October 22 premiere began in August, immediately after the company reassembled from the summer break. This in itself was almost unprecedented but Kubelik insisted on a long rehearsal period to acquaint everyone concerned with the opera's problems. The cast, chorus, orchestra, director, designer, and conductor were hard at it until Labor Day, when the main stage had to be cleared for the repertory scheduled for the opening week. They continued in rehearsal rooms up to three weeks before the first performance, when they returned to the stage.

Discussions on the work had begun in March, 1972, when Gentele, Kubelik, and I looked at the first experimental designs resulting from our meetings earlier that year with Peter Wexler, Nathaniel Merrill, and Michael Bronson. The first ideas that Wexler and Merrill evolved were not right and some lively talk went on among us all. This led to another full-scale meeting in November, only by that time Gentele was dead and we had to begin thinking again.

It wasn't too long before Wexler and Merrill hit upon an idea that appealed to all of us. Basically it was that the opera is the story of the founding of Rome, the bringing of Greek culture to Italy. They decided that dramatically *Les Troyens* needed flow, with scene changes and intermissions kept to a minimum. Since the work is constantly in motion they felt that all the scene changes should, of course, be integral to the action and made in front of the audience. It was to be a bare production but monumental in scale. Two basic playing areas were created, one for Troy and one for Carthage. For Part I there were seven towers moving on the turntable; for Part II platforms and ramps were added and throughout the whole production were numerous backdrops and curtains and things that changed. To keep expenses down and take into account that *Les Troyens* would have to play in repertory every principal had one costume and every chorus member one basic gown. The "look" changed with accessories—hats, wigs, capes. There were approximately 250 to 350 costumes, 280 hats, 250 wigs and 200 tabards, allowing for some 500 to 800 variations of looks for Trojans, warriors, temple virgins, Carthaginians, and others. The production was strong and masculine, in line with the period of ancient history.

In an interview in *Opera News*, Wexler described Troy as a place where "the sun is setting and the atmosphere claustrophobic," while Carthage finds "the sun rising, the feeling more open and colorful." In Troy the colors were to be red and gold, with the Greeks dressed in black; in Carthage he emphasized orange and yellow. "A sense of gold is important," he said, "because it was the metal of the period." The armor was to be stony and bulky; hats and wigs tall with emphasis on the shoulders to keep a sense of the heroic. He employed all techniques—film, slides, projections—to clarify events and make them magical at the same time.

Nathaniel Merrill, noting that the period of the opera is one of barbarism, sees the destruction of Troy in 1200 BC as one of the great savageries of history, following which the Trojans sail for Italy to be killed and "Ulysses has a terrible ten-year journey home." The work is complicated because of the number of scene changes with no curtain and no real entrances and exits. As Merrill says in an interview in that same *Opera News*, "It is not a plot of A-B-C but a series of events, with a large cast and significant characters who relate to Aeneas." Part I he finds exciting because it has no rest; it "goes and goes in a flow of scenes." Then there is an "act of trying to show the inactivity of Aeneas, with long lulls when nothing happens. Ennui, a very French thing, sets in—boredom, inactivity. The period of the love affair is passive until Mercury intervenes to tell him, 'Enough dawdling.' Act III is again active as Aeneas prepares to go and Dido kills herself." In a very real sense Wexler and Merrill created their own myth to tell the story of *Les Troyens*.

The final dress rehearsal took place on October 19 and the usual operatic gremlins were hard at work. Christa Ludwig had become ill a few days before and by the time of the dress rehearsal was forbidden by her doctors to set foot on the stage. Nell Rankin had been engaged to cover her part of Dido but we were faced with the fact that Shirley Verrett, the Cassandra, had also sung Dido elsewhere and knew the part intimately. She was anxious to sing both roles on the opening night if Christa Ludwig was unable to appear. Miss Rankin was naturally anxious to show her stuff if the opportunity came and made this abundantly clear. We decided to ask Shirley Verrett to sing both roles at the rehearsal, not only because there was a very real possibility that Christa Ludwig would be out of the picture but because with a proper rehearsal she might be able to sing both roles opening night and make a special kind of Metropolitan history.

Miss Rankin did not take too kindly to this idea and we were forced to walk a very diplomatic tightrope with her in order to assure that she would be available if Shirley Verrett found the double-header too much.

Verrett loved the double-header and we made the decision to give the Dido to her, at least for the opening, with the hope that Miss Ludwig would be all right by the second performance. If that was the case her appearance would be all the more dramatic and we would see that the spotlight stayed on her.

On the morning of October 22 Miss Ludwig did notify us that she thought she might be able to make it after all but we told her that without the dress rehearsal she would be risking too much, as would all of us, and that we were going ahead with Miss Verrett. I sent her flowers and a letter saying that when she was well we would see that her first performance was given special critical and promotional attention. She was not happy.

At 5:30 PM Betty and I met in the Grand Tier restaurant for a bite of supper. We had asked Joan Payson and Frank Goelet to join us and as an escort for Mrs. Payson we had asked our youngest son, Miles, who had known her slightly when he was a child and had gone from time to time with a nephew of hers to Shea Stadium to watch the New York Mets. Mrs. Payson owned the Mets and was a rabid baseball fan as well. Her team had just missed winning the World Series the afternoon before and we were prepared to deal with a lady filled with disappointment. Such was not the case at all, she, being pleased that they'd gotten as far as they did that season, was all smiles and charm. Frank Goelet added to the pleasure of the occasion and between them all I was kept busy enough to hide my nervousness.

I had plenty of good reason to be nervous. *Les Troyens* is perhaps the biggest opera ever conceived and we were doing it at a time when the Met's finances were in deep trouble. Although the expenses for the production were completely underwritten I knew it was going to be costly to keep it in the repertory system but nonetheless I felt it was imperative that the Metropolitan take a major, bold step to inaugurate its real first season under a new management. I felt that if we were successful people who had turned away from the house in the past might have their interest reawakened. I felt that it was daring, provocative, and theatrical; I also felt that it was marvelous public relations at a time when we needed all the help we could get.

Another box guest that night was Leonard Bernstein. Felicia Bernstein, née Montealegre, was playing the mime part of Andromache in her first appearance on a New York stage in some years. Her scene was the kind that every actress dreams about: one woman and a small boy alone on a stage surrounded by two hundred people, all of whom are looking at her as she goes through her very moving action. The orchestra is playing music that heightens her scene and other than that there is not a sound anywhere. Four thousand people out front, two hundred people onstage; a great moment and Lenny wanted to be there to share it with her.

At 6:30 I left the group and went backstage, as I did almost every night of the season, to wish the artists well. I made an effort to cover my nerves and I think I succeeded. I had an affectionate embrace with Kubelik and we kissed emotionally on both cheeks to symbolize the formal beginning of our new relationship. Promptly at 7:00 PM he entered the pit and the performance got under way.

I slipped into our box and sat in the rear. Everything was going smoothly. Miles was up front following the libretto with a small flashlight and turning every once in a while to whisper various points to Mrs. Payson. Frank Goelet was sitting calmly with his eyes on the stage and so was Betty. Every once in a while Lenny would lean over and ask Miles some point in a loud whisper. I kept thinking how much I loved the man but how I wished he was anywhere but in my box at this moment. Going to the theater, concert hall, or opera house with him as a member of the audience is a mixed blessing. He is very inclined to forget about the fact that there are others around him and makes whatever comments he has in a fairly loud voice and quite frequently. There is usually a good deal of "sh-shing" from neighbors that he proceeds to ignore and soon one is apt to be squeezing down in one's seat to avoid having to look at disapproving faces. No amount of remonstrating does any good; he promises to behave himself and the minute the lights go down he's off and running. I sat in the box that night determined to hit him if he got too loud and the thoughts about this acted as a tonic to my nerves.

Part I proceeded beautifully and audience response, even though it was a Guild benefit, was remarkable. Shirley Verrett was lovely on the stage and Vickers was in splendid looks and voice. The chorus was superb; a whole new sound and they were acting with passion and belief. The performance was going well and I left my seat to walk around the theater, trying to get a good look at people's faces as they watched the opera. I started at a favorite spot in the top balcony and worked my way down the sides of the theater. Everywhere I went I saw faces riveted to the stage, the best possible sign.

When I re-entered the box I did so just in time to see Miles turn to Mrs. Payson and whisper something into her ear that caused her to begin to laugh. She nodded her head in what looked like agreement but had to cover her face with a handkerchief to prevent laughing out loud. I glared at the back of his neck, determined to wring it the first moment I had. Presently she calmed down and the dramatic last scene of the first part, the killing of the Trojan women, got under way.

As the turntable brought the ladies into view, slowly revolving while blue and silver lights shimmered on lacy gowns and scarfs, the audience burst into applause and at the end, with the abrupt and brutal entrance of the Greek soldiers, I could see backs visibly stiffen. When the lights went down and the special act curtain descended the whole house rose in a standing ovation.

We left the box and made our way to my office, where Mrs. Payson's driver was waiting. I had promised her that she could go home after Part I and she did so; she would return to a later performance to see the rest of the opera. She embraced us both, thought that what she had seen was wonderful, and hugged Miles. As she left the room, others came in and I could not find the moment I wanted to find out what had made her laugh.

Finally, as the intermission was drawing to a close, I found a moment to speak to Miles, and with some suppressed anger in my voice I asked what in the world he had been talking about with her. "Oh, I just asked her if she thought you'd spent her money wisely!" came the reply. I didn't say anything.

Part II began on schedule, and after Narbal's incredible aria Bernstein rose from his seat, announcing in a loud whisper that everything from here on was downhill, and took his leave. As he passed me he leaned down and said quietly in my ear, "It's a winner!" Just at that moment I was beginning to think so myself.

When the opera was over the audience stayed standing for almost twenty minutes. The artists were recalled time and again and well within any overtime limits I finally ordered the house lights raised. I went down to Kubelik's room, directly under the press department's performance office, and he was collapsed with exhaustion, his face gray and pale. Elsie, his wife, seemed concerned and I asked whether or not we should call for the house doctor. He did not want this but for the first time I realized that there was something to the rumors that I had heard concerning his health. The man looked the picture of vigor and energy and yet it was obvious, even to the most untrained eye, that the performance had taken more out of him than it should. I stayed a few moments and then suggested that everybody leave to give him time to rest.

Upstairs Merrill and Wexler were ecstatic, as well they might be, and were congratulating the executive stage manager for the production, Chris Mahan, for the incredible job he had done in coordinating and running the whole production. The artists' dressing rooms were filled with happy people, especially Shirley Verrett, who had carried off both assignments with great success, and was basking in her deserved glory. I knew that this was going to make problems with Miss Ludwig and probably also with Miss Rankin but at that moment I felt the problems, whatever they might be, could wait until the morning.

I ran into George Moore backstage and he pumped my hand. "It was glorious, glorious," he said. "If we have to go broke we might as well do so with our best flags flying!" Perhaps we had scored a point or two at that.

However, other than Moore and Frank Goelet, not another officer board member said a word. It was almost as if the production had never taken place. A few, such as Nin Ryan and Peggy Douglas, went out of their way to comment but not the executive committee. There, all was silence. Even though I did not want to think so at the time I must have subconsciously begun to realize that the battle was on.

A few performances later Bill Fisher came on an evening when I was not in the house and passed the word to my staff that he thought the production was monstrous and should be canceled immediately. He did want to know who designed it and asked to be introduced to Wexler, which he was, some weeks later, and proceeded to hire him for a special project of his own. But he was a declared enemy of *Les Troyens* on the stage of the Metropolitan.

The executive committee might have been displeased but the public was the opposite. Within a day of the premiere all the tickets for the remaining eight performances were gone and I began to realize that I had ever so many friends on the outside who just had to get into Troy and Carthage! The success was real and immediate; it started the new management off artistically at a high peak.

At about the time of *Les Troyens* I received a call one morning from Kazuko Hillyer, an alert and petite Japanese woman who had, shortly after her marriage to violist Rafael Hillyer, set herself up in business as Pacific World Artists and begun importing from and exporting to Japan various artists and ensembles. The stated purpose for her visit was to inquire whether or not we would be interested in having the Metropolitan Opera tour Japan. Some years back, in the Bing days, there had been many ruffles and flourishes about such a tour; various administrators were flying back and forth to Tokyo and Washington and there was an atmosphere of great busyness about the project. It came to naught but I remembered all the fuss and thought it would be wonderful to pull such an event off without excessive *Sturm und Drang.*

I told Mrs. Hillyer that we'd be delighted to go and that I'd be delighted to talk about it in detail when she returned with a sponsor who was able to put up at least $2.5 million dollars and not to bother me further until this was arranged. She understood and left my office.

About three weeks later she phoned again and reported that she had someone who was interested. I asked her who it was and when she replied, "The Chibbu-Nippon Company in Nagoya" I was immediately impressed.

I had come to know the Chibbu-Nippon Company officials during my trip to Japan with Bernstein and the New York Philharmonic at the time of the Osaka World's Fair in 1970 and if they were indeed interested I knew we would not be dealing with any fly-by-night outfit. I also knew that they had imported many Western musical attractions over the years, including most of the major world orchestras and instrumental ensembles, as well as many individual virtuosi. "Two and a half million dollars is a lot of money," I said to Mrs. Hillyer, thinking to myself that I better find out whether that figure, which I really pulled out of the air, would stand up under close examination. "Why would they want to consider such an expensive adventure?" I asked. "Because they wish to celebrate their twenty-fifth anniversary as a company with something unique and unusual. The Metropolitan Opera fits that category, provided, of course, that you are able to bring many of your stars."

As she said this I reflected back on the Metropolitan's overseas history and found it, to put it mildly, wanting. There had been only two trips in ninety years—Paris in 1910 and Paris again in 1966. Both were disasters. In 1966 the company had been booked into the Odéon, with a tiny stage, an even tinier orchestra pit. The preferred Metropolitan repertoire of *Aida* and *Rigoletto* had to be abandoned in favor of *Le Nozze di Figaro* and *Il Barbiere di Siviglia* to squeeze into the Odéon quarters. Even then the orchestra had to be reduced to about thirty-five players and altogether the effect was less than happy. I did not want to repeat these mistakes and told Mrs. Hillyer at the outset that we would want to take at least three of our major productions, possibly four if the money could be found.

Immediately after she left I called Michael Bronson and Charlie Riecker and asked them if the $2.5 million I had been so blithely quoting was valid. We drew up figures based on *Carmen, La Bohème,* and *La Traviata,* took into account every contingency we could think of, and the arithmetic worked out to just about what I'd quoted. I then sought out the best advice I could about negotiating with the Japanese and went right to John McKinley, the president of Texaco.

Texaco has sponsored the Metropolitan Opera broadcasts since 1940 and the current president is a good friend of the house and a good friend of mine. He had befriended me at a crucial moment in my life and I was grateful to him as well as smart enough to know that he had vast experience in the Orient and could give me valuable hints and advice. This he proceeded to do and I drew up a list of particulars that I strapped to my knee, much like the navigation maps in my cockpit over India, and checked off points as we covered them in negotiation.

I reported to the board that we had opened discussions about a proposed trip to Japan and they received the news matter-of-factly. Perhaps they had run through this gauntlet before and would believe it when it actually happened. I assumed this might be their attitude and soft-pedaled the whole project until it was further along.

Onstage *Les Troyens* had joined *Il Trovatore, Carmen, L'Elisir d'Amore, Madama Butterfly,* and *Salomé,* among others, as a big hit. The surprise, and an extremely pleasant one, was to see the charming Merrill–O'Hearn *Elisir* production become a best seller. This was no doubt due in large measure to the Nemorino sung by Luciano Pavarotti, who was on his way to becoming an operatic superstar.

Immediately after the *Les Troyens* premiere the stage was occupied with our second new production of the season, Rossini's *L'Italiana in Algeri,* which had not been heard or seen at the Metropolitan except for four performances in the 1919-1920 season. *L'Italiana* requires above everything else a mezzo who can command the role of Isabella, rule it, as it were, with a voice of velvet and iron. She should also be an actress with an ability to play comedy, not the garden-variety operatic camp version of same, but play with an almost perfect sense of timing and an ability to understate a situation for effective results. Marilyn Horne met all these qualities, particularly as her interpretation was shaped by Jean-Pierre Ponnelle, the greatly gifted Frenchman who was both director and designer. Horne was surrounded with a strong supporting cast including the great Swiss buffo Fernando Corena as Mustafà and the lithe Luigi Alva as Lindoro. The group was rounded out by Theodor Uppman as Taddeo, Shirley Love as Zulma, Christine Weidinger as Elvira, and Gene Boucher as Haly. The conductor was Gabor Ötvös, Kubelik's choice over some of our very strong objections, and the work had its premiere on November 10, 1973.

L'Italiana tells the story of Isabella and her trials and tribulations with the Bey of Algeria. Marilyn Horne described Isabella as "warm and loving but at the same time combining Joan of Arc, Florence Nightingale and Susan B. Anthony—the original women's liberation!" Ponnelle designed a production of lightness and grace, mostly browns in various hues and whites, creams, and at the right moment blues, both light and dark. The ensemble spirit of the opera was joined strongly and the fresh, breezy costumes and lighting added greatly to the lightness and airiness required for the piece. Curiously enough, L'Italiana was written in twenty-seven days (some say as few as eighteen) by a composer who was almost at the peak of his success.

Our production was a success, although not the success we were all hoping for. The critics, particularly the New York Times, thought the production vulgar and while praising Horne's vocal achievements felt that her acting was not what the part required. New York Magazine took directly the opposite view; and the audiences enjoyed what they saw and heard. Since the public was unfamiliar with the piece, as indeed they were with Les Troyens, they came to sample and for the most part liked what they saw and heard. One of the chief problems was Ötvös, who was simply not the right conductor for this type of music. Kubelik felt very strongly that he was and I bowed to his judgment.

The excitement and activity surrounding the new productions did not in any way ease the problems of finance. During the early part of the season I had been instrumental in organizing a special meeting of the Lincoln Center Council. The council is made up of the professional heads of all the constituents and I called the meeting to examine building expenses. The raw costs for the Metropolitan Opera House were now approaching the $3-million mark; these costs did not include labor, only heat, light, air-conditioning, maintenance, and security. I knew from my past experience that the other buildings were proportionately as costly and I thought the time had come to put the figures all together and see what we could do to get the city to pay some of this upkeep.

Our rationale was simple: the building of Lincoln Center itself brought a slum area out of its rubble and dirt, and created not only a stunning new center for the arts but added immensely to the tax roles. It was estimated that some $32 million a year had been added to the city's tax revenues, not by the Center itself but by the new commercial real estate that had sprung up around it—apartment buildings, office structures, restaurants, shops, and the like. I thought it was time that the city acknowledged this point and began to feel responsible for helping the Center maintain its buildings. Only one receives any city aid at all and that is the New York State Theater. It gets about $300,000 a year toward its operating expenses due to a complicated arrangement among the state, Lincoln Center, and the city that brought the building into existence in the first place. Other than that everyone is on his own.

The meeting resulted in a formal report being prepared on the total amount necessary to maintain the Lincoln Center buildings and it came to a little over $6 million. By far and away the largest was the Metropolitan, which is, among other things, almost a forty-story building turned on its side with enough sophisticated machinery to please the fussiest aircraft carrier commander.

Fortunately for all of us Martin E. Segal, president of the Film Society of Lincoln Center, attended the special meeting. Mr. Segal is a long-time expert in New York City political maneuvering and a confidant and adviser of the then comptroller of the city, Abraham Beame. Segal knew city finances as well, having been the architect of the basic pension plan adopted for city employees, and he thought our ideas were valid enough to bring to the attention of the appropriate city authorities. He and I went together to call upon Beame on September 24, 1973, and presented him with verbal and written arguments on our collective behalf. Beame and his deputy James Cavanaugh were sympathetic and listened carefully to our arguments. Beame was getting ready to make the political decision to run for mayor and Segal was obviously going to be a help to him. As a consequence Beame wanted to be responsive to our presentation.

After about a half-hour Segal signaled me it was time to go and as we rose Beame shook my hand warmly and promised to study the matter carefully. When we reached the outer corridor I asked Segal how he thought the meeting had gone. "Not too bad," he replied. "Nothing's going to happen right away but Beame has the picture and we'll all keep working on him. He knows what Lincoln Center has done for the city. He'll do what he can." I thought Segal pragmatic and realistic to a point. I didn't feel that our problems were going to get much of a priority.

With the building costs at least out in the open we turned next to a program of reducing our operating expenses and increasing our revenues. Moore was constantly screaming about a balanced budget and during the summer the administrative staff had spent long hours in meetings trying to figure out the best actions to take on a number of fronts. One thing seemed obvious: labor contracts, which had two years to go, were going to have to be frozen at the present levels or, if this were not possible because of inflation alone, whatever changes were made had to be minuscule. We studied carefully the possibilities of freezing wages at the 1973-74 level and in effect ignoring the required increase in the third year of the agreements. This proved out not to be all that effective in curbing costs but as a ceiling for new agreements the third-year fees seemed quite possible and we kept in reserve the possibility of doing just that.

I felt it increasingly important that all the members of the company be given a true picture of our financial problems and we began a series of meetings with the various union officials and delegates to brief them. In addition I called for a general company meeting in early November and prepared a very careful statement laying out the facts. Michael Bronson, Charlie Riecker, Bill Hadley and I spent a lot of weekend time drafting the document which was then shown to Henry Lauterstein, the Met's general counsel. I told the executive committee what I intended to do and they had no objection. On November 15 I called the company together at about 4:00 PM in the afternoon and read them the following:

METROPOLITAN OPERA FINANCIAL REVIEW
NOVEMBER 15, 1973

The Metropolitan Opera is probably in as deep a financial crisis as it has ever been in its history. We have reached the point where even our auditors suggest that "Without substantial increased support or a substantial reduction in expenses it would appear that the Association would have extreme difficulty in continuing at its present level of activity."

The basis for their concern lies in the fact that the Association ended its 1972-73 fiscal year with a record operating loss of $7.8 million, and after contributions of $5 million, had a net loss of $2.8 million, and that this loss increased our working capital deficit to over $5.6 million. What this working capital deficit means is that in order to prepare for the season and open in September, we had to spend the subscription ticket income for the 1973-74 season even before the first performance. If for any reason there were to be an interruption of the season and we had to refund ticket money, we would have to replace it by borrowing from banks.

To pay for our on-going expenses now, we are borrowing from our remaining Ford Foundation grant ($1 million) and from several other smaller special-purpose funds, in addition to the advance ticket money. Before long we will need to borrow from the banks at a rate of almost 10 percent.

We are not yet broke but we are very close to it. Our present estimates for the current year show that we will have another $1 million shortage and that the following year, unless dramatic steps are taken, still another $2 million would be added to our losses. Following this path would bring our working capital loss to over $8.5 million. We simply cannot let this happen.

The reason I can say "We are not yet broke" is that we have two principal assets. One of these is the site of the old Metropolitan Opera House on 39th Street, which has a market value of about $6 million. It is really a fifty-year ground lease to the developer of an office building and is the asset upon which the banks rely in lending us money. The other asset is our endowment trust, with a market value of $7.1 million as of July 31, 1973.

Were our working capital deficit to reach the figure of $8.5 million, we would in effect have spent more than our entire endowment. If we should ever reach the point where our two principal assets have to be converted to cash to pay our debts, the Metropolitan would be left with absolutely nothing to fall back on, and it is not only conceivable but likely that the end of the Metropolitan Opera would follow shortly.

The importance of hanging on to these two assets is obvious. Aside from the fact that we are able to obtain bank loans, because these assets stand as security for a loan, the rental income to us from the building on the old Opera House site and from the investment of the endowment trust brings in about $1 million each year, which is necessary for operating purposes. Without these assets, and therefore without this income, our losses would be a million dollars greater each year.

The concern over the Metropolitan's financial situation expressed by the auditors this summer brought home to us the urgency of reversing the tide. Since the beginning of this fiscal year, we have undertaken a number of steps to bring our expenses and income into better balance for the current season. I believe you already know about most of them. They include cancellation of the new production of *Don Giovanni*, welching on *Les Troyens* and on the parks concerts this summer, and the suspension of the Mini-Met. The administrative staff has been reduced by nearly 20 percent, rehearsal schedules have been modified, and every operation of every department is undergoing the most careful scrutiny to trim costs to the maximum extent possible. These steps are beginning to show results but the day-to-day effort must continue.

In addition to the measures taken for the current year, we are already studying the preliminary budget for 1974-75 to find ways of averting the presently projected loss of $2 million. A reduction of the New York season from 31 to 30 weeks is already planned. In addition we have decided to cancel the June festival in 1975. At the present time there is a possibility that in place of the June festival the company will be invited to perform in Japan. We have made it clear to our potential sponsors that unless every cent of expenditures is paid for, we cannot accept the invitation. Negotiations for this enterprise are in such an early stage that we certainly cannot count on it.

Over the past few years it has become clear that continuation on a 52-week basis is beyond the financial resources of the Metropolitan Opera, and that if the Opera is to survive, some reduction in its activities is necessary.

Looking ahead to 1975-76 therefore, I think it only fair to tell you now that we are planning to further reduce the New York season to 27 weeks, which together with a five- or six-week tour, possible resumption of the parks concerts if financing is available, vacation and pre-season rehearsal weeks will bring the total employment for the year to somewhere between 40 and 44 weeks. It is our hope that such a schedule would make it possible for the Metropolitan to live within its income plus contributions and avoid the danger of having to cash in our last chips.

When you have had a chance to read this memorandum, Mr. Riecker, Mr. Bronson, Mr. Hadley and I are available to discuss with you the substance as it affects each group in this house. We want to begin whatever dialogue is necessary soon so that there will be plenty of time for the many questions that will inevitably arise.

Implied but not stated here, of course, is the need for continuing fund raising efforts by all of us. Beginning with the broadcast on December 7 we will once again mount a major campaign to our radio audience. In addition the development office will be pushing very hard this year, particularly in light of our disastrous fire at the Bronx warehouse. Suggestions that you may have in the fund raising area will be gratefully received. Everyone should feel free to call on me and/or Floyd Landis with specific suggestions.

It is only if we all work together that we can assure the survival of this great institution.

At the conclusion of the meeting everyone filed quietly out of List Hall, their faces for the most part, buried in copies of my talk. Later that night various people sought me out for private meetings and to each I said essentially the same thing: we would have to work together, the problems were solvable but required imaginative thinking on everyone's part. In my heart of hearts I felt that we were sinking steadily under the crushingly dead hands of our board leadership, who were, at that moment, casting around for the knight in shining armor rather than realistically rolling up their collective sleeves and admitting that the problems had to be worked on in a joint management-board mutual trust manner. When in doubt a board can always assume that the management is lousing things up and all can be put to rights if a new group is brought in. At the Met many of the officers of the board felt that the professionals running the theater were not men of business experience and this particularly applied to me. The fact that I had always been involved in the business and administrative side of the arts, as well as taking basic artistic decisions as a manager, record company executive, program officer for Lincoln Center, and executive producer of a film and television music company counted for very little. The clean-the-palette philosophy was beginning to crystallize and I had to make a basic decision. Was I going to try politicking my way into favor or was I going to do the best job possible on the stage and throughout the house and prove by results that we had a good team abuilding. I had long ago decided on the latter course. I saw no reason to change my mind now.

Artistically, Joan Sutherland, Placido Domingo, Thomas Stewart, and Huguette Tourangeau brought new honors to themselves and to the house with the Seattle Opera production of *Les Contes d'Hoffmann*, which premiered on November 29. This oft-battered work had been reorganized musically by Richard Bonynge in preparation for the Seattle premiere in 1971. The conductor was impressed by Arthur Hammond's *Hoffmann* at Sadlers Wells in London and spent hours delving into Offenbach lores and scores. As he told Quaintance Eaton, "I think I saw everything Offenbach wrote!"

For Seattle he had collaborated with designer Allen Charles Klein and director Bliss Hebert and this was essentially the production we had brought to New York. The shift from Seattle's comparatively modest stage to the huge caverns of the Metropolitan meant a rethinking and rebuilding of some of the sets, the adjustment of over a hundred costumes, and the problems of new shoes and stockings. I was continually grateful to the Tedlows for coming forward with the money to make this all possible.

About the time of the *Hoffmann* premiere I lunched one day with my friend Richard Couper, president of the New York Public Library, and discovered that the library was also heading into a financial hurricane. We compared notes and I told him of my visit to Beame and the hope of city funds. "Forget it," he said, "the city's going broke. They're taking money away from us and we may have to close branches down. The only hope is Washington." "But how Washington?" I asked. "There aren't people in the government who will take the libraries or the Metropolitan housekeeping problems seriously." "I don't know," mused Couper, "but we'll never find out unless we try. Maybe we should join forces in a multi-pronged attack."

I thought about this idea after our lunch and the more I thought about it the wiser it seemed. I remembered an earlier conversation with Richard Oldenburg, the director of the Museum of Modern Art; he too planned to attack the city for maintenance funds. I thought a little investigation into the whole area would be helpful so I assigned a member of the staff to research exactly how the city supports those institutions that are on its budget lines, and who, besides us, was left out. I talked with Segal about this. He had, independent of all of us, been doing the same thing.

The immediate results of all this was that Segal went ahead with suggesting to the city that a full-scale investigation be made of city expenditures in the cultural area and a report drawn up with the facts as they now are and recommendations for change.

While this was not going to help the Metropolitan with its immediate problems it certainly was going to lay the groundwork for future aid and I was all for it. On our immediate problems I had a talk one night with the Secretary of Health, Education and Welfare, Casper Weinberger, who as an opera buff had come to New York to attend a performance as a guest in my box. The result of our talk was a visit to Washington to explore further with him whether or not there was a way for the federal government to help the Met, apart from the National Endowment for the Arts. The vice-chairman of our board, Langdon Van Norden, went with me on this visit as he chaired the board's government relations committee.

We were received with great courtesy and explained our problems in detail. Weinberger was sympathetic but there was little he could do except suggest some modifications in our educational programs that might bring them under his department funding. He did suggest that we look into the possibility of some kind of relationship with the Smithsonian Institution along the lines that Dick Couper, Richard Oldenburg, and I had been thinking and said that he would be happy to sit down with us all and see what might be developed. Van Norden and I thought this was a good idea and I decided to proceed with my colleagues at the other institutions as soon as possible.

In the meantime the executive committee kept pressing me for decisions on administrative reorganization. I told them that Kubelik and I were actively seeking a stage producer-director to replace Gentele and that I was trying to find first-class help to bolster the artistic administrative department. I reminded them that this was going on simultaneously with a cutback in administrative personnel and a streamlining of staff work.

My relations with Kubelik were becoming strained. While he was understanding about the financial problems he was impatient with the reorganization of the artistic administrative personnel and the general problems of the theater. In addition his health was not good and he had been forced to cancel the second performance of *Les Troyens*. Fortunately we had John Nelson on tap and he went into the pit and scored a deserved personal success.

Our meetings on future artistic activities such as *Death in Venice*, *Jenufa*, the *Ring*, and *Le Nozze di Figaro* went well but the changes Kubelik wanted to make in the orchestra, comprimari, and in the chorus were slow to materialize. One area did move swiftly. We were desperately in need of a new chorus master and we agreed that David Stivender, the assistant chorus master, was just the person for the job. We decided to make the appointment effective with the 1974-75 season.

On November 15, with many misgivings and worries, Kubelik returned to Europe, where he would be until February 11. We had a last meeting in my office just before he left. I tried to spell out the many problems we faced on all fronts and urged him to be patient with their solutions. I was trying to push him to adopt an attitude that I was increasingly losing myself; namely, that the board and management were coming together with planning and that we had to ride with the punches to see our plans through. I guess, in Kurt Vonnegut's words, I was giving him a dose of bitter-coated sugar pills but I needed him to remain as an ally and work with me. We embraced and seemed to understand.

We were now approaching the Christmas season and Betty and I had planned for a long time to take a week off between Christmas and New Year's up in our house in the country. Our next biggest revival was to be *Tristan und Isolde* with Catarina Ligendza and Jon Vickers in the first performance on January 11, 1974 and Ligendza and Jess Thomas for January 15 and 19, with Vickers and Ligendza together again for

January 26, and Nilsson and Vickers together for two performances, on January 30 and February 4. The last two performances of the season, February 8 and 14, would have Ligendza and Thomas while Nilsson took up *Der Rosenkavalier* and *Götterdämmerung* and Vickers concentrated on *Otello.*

This schedule had been painstakingly worked out in 1971 and 1972 and at the time I expressed doubt to Gentele about Ligendza's health. I recalled two instances where I'd flown to Berlin to hear her only to find that she had canceled. I also remembered various telephone calls and overall I suspected that she was not reliable. Gentele felt that she was basically misunderstood, a fellow Swede who needed only to be handled in a special way and she would come through. He also reminded us all that Nilsson was not getting any younger and that Ligendza was the only major soprano on the horizon who could take up the same repertoire. This made sense but nonetheless I had my misgivings.

To complicate matters further Nilsson was interested in *Der Rosenkavalier* and in order to fit in the role of the Marschallin she had to give up some Isoldes. Leinsdorf, who was conducting the *Tristans,* was also nervous about Miss Ligendza. Remembering the Beethoven bicentennial production of *Fidelio* where she had to be replaced at the last moment, he insisted that an adequate cover artist be provided and recommended Doris Jung. He was insistent upon Miss Jung; he wanted to be prepared.

All was well with *Tristan* until December 24. Around 1:00 PM I was preparing to leave the theater. We had released all the employees who were not needed for that day's operations and I was just closing up shop when I heard the teletype machine outside my office clicking away. The teletype had been installed the previous spring as an easy way to keep in touch with Kubelik when he was in Munich or Lucerne and had proved to be a big help, not only with him but for direct cabling and message receiving. I was about to ignore it when some sixth sense made me go over and lift the lid to see what was coming in. It was a message from Ligendza full of regrets about illness forcing her to cancel her Isoldes and, in fact, her Metropolitan season unless we could put everything off until April. I couldn't believe my eyes but there it was, exactly two days before rehearsals were to begin. And Christmas Eve to boot.

I went back into my office and sat down to think. The family had planned to go to Long Pond the day after Christmas and I could see no reason for canceling that plan. Whatever telephoning needed to be done could be done from Plymouth just as well as New York and if I had to fly anywhere I could do it as easily from Boston as from New York. The big problem was whether or not Doris Jung was ready to take over the Ligendza performances or at least the first two while we chased over the world to find a replacement. Riecker and I met immediately and it was his feeling that she would be unwilling to do the role except in an immediate emergency situation.

To complicate matters further Jon Vickers had been on the phone from his home in Bermuda feeling poorly and asking to delay his arrival for rehearsals until the end of Christmas week. The only major artist who had arrived on schedule, as he always does, was the alternate Tristan, Jess Thomas. We had contacted Leinsdorf in Switzerland and told him of the Vickers problem and he had grudgingly agreed. Now Ligendza was out and this was not going to please him at all.

Rightly or wrongly I went off to the country as scheduled and holed up in my study trying to find an Isolde. I called everyone, everywhere. There was Nilsson in Vienna, who would love to come early if the Vienna Opera management would release her. I talked to Rudolf Gamsjaeger, the intendant, and of course he would not do so, although he was very sympathetic. I talked to Ingrid Bjoner; I talked to Helga Dernesch, who was insulted that she had not been asked in the first place and barely responded on the phone. Riecker was calling from New York; I was calling from Plymouth. We had a coordinated campaign to cover the globe and we did.

Leinsdorf, meanwhile, had arrived for rehearsals to find no Isolde and one Tristan. He prepared the Brangäne, Mignon Dunn, and the Kurwenal, William Dooley, and worked in a limited way with Miss Jung. He haunted Riecker's office every day to see how the search was going.

Then there occurred one of those incidents that happen every once in a while. An agent, one with a reputation, called the office and insisted that he had an artist ready to burst upon the world as an Isolde. If I'd been there I would have turned the whole thing off but I wasn't and an audition was arranged for Leinsdorf to hear the girl.

She was a disaster, not only a disaster but she did not know the role and was, obviously, the victim of her agent's machinations. At this point Leinsdorf blew his temper and announced, to all who would listen, that the Metropolitan was being run by a pack of amateurs who were, at best, commissars of optimism. He all but declared himself out of the running.

At this point, back in New York, I received a cable from Klara Barlow, the American soprano who worked mostly in Europe, saying she had heard about our problems and was ready to fly over to take Ligendza's place. The ironic part was that it was the same Klara Barlow who had rushed in at the last minute and taken over *Fidelio* from Ligendza in 1970, thus saving the Metropolitan's Beethoven celebratory production.

I made a few calls to various European houses to find out about her Isolde and the answers were strongly positive. I cabled her to come and told Leinsdorf that she was on her way. He was not happy.

A few hours later he came to my office, alone, and told me that Barlow was not up to Metropolitan standards. I explained to him as carefully as I could that Miss Barlow was on her way here to help bail us all out of a very sticky situation. I said that I had no intention of canceling the production and I couldn't postpone it because of an already crowded rehearsal schedule that left no room for change. I said that I would go to any measure to keep the work as scheduled in order to assure that Nilsson and Vickers, the greatest Isolde and Tristan of the day, would be heard in these parts in New York City. Our talk was friendly but very firm. "Very well," said Leinsdorf, "if that is how you feel then I want Miss Barlow to sing an audition for me as soon as she arrives. I want to hear the entire first act." I swallowed hard and agreed to ask her.

I explained this to her the next day when she arrived, and she agreed. I asked Richard Woitach of the conducting staff to play the pieces for her and at 4:00 PM that afternoon Miss Barlow walked on the stage and sang the entire first act as Leinsdorf had requested. I sat in the theater looking straight ahead at the stage and I could hear Leinsdorf making comments behind me. I thought Miss Barlow sang splendidly and I went backstage after she'd finished to congratulate her. She was bathed in perspiration and I urged her to bundle up against a chill.

I returned to my office and Leinsdorf came again, this time with his wife and a representative. "I want to be released from my contract," were his opening words. I looked at him. During this *Tristan* difficulty the New York Philharmonic, across the plaza, had lost its guest conductor, Riccardo Muti, to, presumably, the Italian flu. My old friend Carlos Moseley had been as desperate to replace Muti as I was to replace Ligendza and when he called to ask if I would release Leinsdorf to help in his emergency I had agreed immediately, realizing that the Philharmonic and Metropolitan schedules could be made to mesh beautifully. It was one of the reasons I was annoyed at Leinsdorf for making his request at this particular moment.

I said he could not have a release and Mrs. Leinsdorf promptly burst into tears. She told me how much Erich had been looking forward to these *Tristans* and how bitterly disappointed he was that all these problems had arisen. She pleaded with me to agree to Erich's request and the more she pleaded the more I was determined not to give in. Klara Barlow had carried off his request in good order and there was no reason for his withdrawal. Presently the Leinsdorfs looked at one another and rose. "We're leaving now," they said, and swept out of the room.

They had not been gone ten minutes before Jon Vickers came in, his face longer and scowlier than usual. He announced that he had nothing against Barlow but was distraught by all the goings-on and was not going to sing any *Tristans* until Nilsson arrived. I suggested to him that his actions were further complicating an already complicated situation but nothing I said sank in. I sensed that part of his feelings must have come from the maestro but said nothing.

And it is just as well that I didn't say anything because the next afternoon, in the New York *Post*, was a story about Vickers withdrawing because of the desperate tension brought about by Ligendza's cancellation. I was furious, but there was nothing I could do.

The next morning the New York *Times* carried the news and in the afternoon the *Post* kept up the suspense by interviewing Leinsdorf, who made public his remarks about amateurs and commissars of optimism. The whole saga was beginning to take on the flavor of the *Perils of Pauline.*

Immediately after the Leinsdorf interview I called Nilsson to keep her abreast of the goings-on. Above everything else I wanted her arrival in New York to be on schedule and I wanted to be sure that if Leinsdorf walked out we could agree on a replacement conductor. "But you have one right at the Metropolitan now!" she said, "a young man with whom I've sung beautiful Wagner, the *Ring* and Isoldes. He would be fine and you would discover a new star." I knew she must be referring to Leif Segerstam, the Finnish conductor, who was presently in the house in charge of *La Bohème.* "I understand you," I replied, "and thank you very much. I'll see you soon."

The next morning Leinsdorf's agent, one of the truly civilized men in the profession, called me and in a quiet voice asked me officially for Leinsdorf's release. In an equally quiet voice I said no. He then prefaced his next question with the disclaimer that it was really none of his business but if Leinsdorf were to walk out anyway, did I have a replacement?

I told him that it was indeed none of his business and that I was under no obligation to answer his question but the answer was yes. "Is he by any chance a young man?'' the agent asked. "Yes, he is,'' I replied, "about the same age your client was when he took over after Artur Bodanzky's death.''

There was a long silence. "I'll see what I can do," the agent finally said, "and I'll call you back this afternoon.''

I immediately telephoned Segerstam and in as directly indirect a way as possible suggested that he plan to be in the theater for all the *Tristan* rehearsals. He understood and didn't press me further. I did ask him that in case a problem arose was he prepared to step in and he answered a quick and definite yes.

Later that afternoon Leinsdorf's agent called again and said that the maestro would be in the theater the following day for his scheduled stage/orchestra rehearsals. "Good, I'm delighted," I said. "I'll be there to greet him.'' "If I were you I'd stay far away," he suggested. "Just let him get on with his work." "Fine with me," I replied. "I'll be invisible.''

The next day he did come in and worked on the first act with Barlow and Vickers. Vickers had decided to rehearse in order to familiarize himself with the production and the tension on the stage was almost visible. August Everding, who had come over to restage his beautiful work, was going about his business with dispatch but at the end of the day he, too, came to see me and plead that we cancel the performances. I felt that Leinsdorf had put him up to the visit but said nothing. I reminded him that he ran an opera house (Munich), as well as pursuing a separate stage career, and that if he were in my place he would be doing exactly the same thing. I repeated to him that I would go to any lengths to save the Nilsson-Vickers performances, even to singing Isolde myself. He understood.

The next day, during the stage/orchestra rehearsal of Act II, I received a visit from Donal Henahan of the New York *Times*. The *Times* had decided to do a feature piece on the Battle of *Tristan*. This was not what was needed at the moment but I decided to see him and tell him as much of the story as seemed appropriate.

Onstage Act II was being rehearsed with Jess Thomas instead of Vickers and Leinsdorf was driving ahead in a most unpleasant manner, including unnecessary remarks to the executive stage manager and others as they went about their work. No one took offense. I think everyone sensed that one answer or crack of a debate and the whole house of cards could come tumbling down.

The dress rehearsal was scheduled for January 8, two days before the premiere, and it was decided that Klara Barlow should sit this one out and Doris Jung sing it in order to be prepared in case a last-minute emergency developed with Barlow. Vickers, too, decided that he needed to go through the production while Everding was still around and he sang magnificently. By the time he came to the third act he was really involved and his tension came across the stage and out into the auditorium. At one point an aide stopped to whisper something in Leinsdorf's ear and Vickers spotted the intrusion. "What is this, a union meeting?" he shouted from his *Tristan* rugs. "If so, I'm walking out of here right now." And he started to rise. "Sorry, Jon,'" Leinsdorf shouted back. "Shall we start again at the top of the scene?" Vickers glared but slowly returned to his position. The rehearsal went on to the end. As Isolde, Doris Jung sang beautifully and I felt we had a real cover if problems arose.

The next day the New York *Times* piece broke and a lot of people began to wonder what would really happen on Friday, January 11.

On that night, when Leinsdorf made his entrance, the audience cheered him to the rafters and he stood in the pit enjoying every moment of it. The orchestra played the Prelude magnificently and when the curtain rose Klara Barlow was a vision onstage, physically the ideal Isolde and vocally she was outdoing herself. At the end of the first act the audience gave her a standing ovation and at the end of the opera she received at least twenty minutes of curtain calls. Her Tristan, Jess Thomas, was the soul of courtesy and help and she had a deserved triumph.

The next morning the news of her victory was on the front page of the *Times* and all over the television. She had saved the production and had brought glory to herself and to the house.

XX

Kubelik Departs—Alone at the Top

During all these difficulties Kubelik was in Europe, as scheduled, but Leinsdorf made several disparaging comments about his not being around for what was essentially a musical crisis and this, I think, irritated him. He and I talked numerous times during the crisis but his advice was to cancel and replace *Tristan* with *Tosca*. I did not think this helpful and at one point we had quite a set-to on the matter over the transatlantic phone. We are both stubborn.

Barlow sang the Ligendza performances and Vickers, after staying away from the first three, decided he wanted to do the broadcast, which had been scheduled for him. He came to New York and did it but announced that he wasn't going to be around to rehearse with Nilsson the following Monday. Nilsson got wind of this and called me to say that either she rehearsed with Vickers on the scheduled day or she would not sing with him. I passed this on to Jon, who huffed and puffed and threatened all kinds of things but showed up at the theater right on the button to attend the rehearsals.

The first, and as it turned out, only Nilsson-Vickers *Tristan* was on January 30 and those people who attended heard one of the greatest performances of this opera in this century. To me it was worth all the problems and difficulties. It is what, among other things, the Metropolitan Opera is all about. The critics and the public were beside themselves with joy and within hours a pirated recording was being sold at some of New York's best-known record stores.

While all the *Tristan* business was going on we were in the middle of preparing *I Vespri Siciliani* without the leading soprano, Monserrat Caballé. Caballé kept calling from Spain that she was having visa problems or medical problems or family problems and was being delayed. She and I would talk on the phone around noon almost every day and there would always be some problem or other to postpone her appearance. Gedda, Milnes, the chorus, and dancers were all rehearsing their heads off and Caballé's cover, the American soprano Maralin Niska, was standing in.

Dexter and Levine both were getting itchy about Caballé's delay, with good reason, I might add, and I did my best to calm them both and assure them that she would be in New York at any moment. Levine was prepared to work with her musically even at the last minute but Dexter became tighter and tighter about trying to do anything with her dramatically. She missed all the rehearsals up to the final two days before the dress and I'm convinced that she only came then because she realized that I meant to go ahead with the production with Niska if necessary. In fact, I made the mistake of telling Miss Niska that she was going to sing the premiere and then, when Caballé finally appeared, had to tell her that she would not. Things were a bit frosty for a while but she had quite a few opportunities to sing the role during the two seasons we had the work in the repertoire and she carried it off with passion and great authority.

On the opening night of *Vespri* the cast and conductor were warmly received but not so the production. The Metropolitan audience was not prepared to accept Svoboda's starkness and the linear simplicity of the stage and Dexter, when he stepped out to take a reluctant bow (he hates his own openings and rarely is in the theater for them), was treated to a chorus of boos. Those who liked what they'd seen set up a counterdemonstration but Dexter didn't hear it. He came off the stage absolutely seasick green and looked at me with hate in his heart. "I'll never do that again," he said, between clenched teeth, "never again. I've never done it in the theater and there's no reason to do so in the opera. And don't ask me!" And he fled the stage. Moments later, after all the calls, he was back talking to the chorus, thanking them for their superb work. His color was normal but he avoided looking at me.

The next day the press were divided, most of them applauding the singing but stirred up by the production. The exception to this was John Simon, the devastating critic of *New York Magazine*, who, while damning some off-Broadway effort, stated that if people really wanted to see exciting theater they better go, of all places, to the Metropolitan Opera for the new production of *Vespri*. He was the one critic who caught the enormous work that had gone into the dramatic shaping of the characters and the symbolism of the sets and props. The public, too, was divided; they kept coming to the performances, however, and I smiled from time to time when I remembered Verdi's advice to the young Gatti-Casazza: "If your theater is full you are a success. If it is empty, you are not."

Nine days after the *Vespri* premiere we were scheduled to produce a revival of *Otello*. Again, as in the previous season, Vickers would sing *Otello;* Thomas Stewart was to be the Iago, and Teresa Stratas the Desdemona. On the strength of very strong word-of-mouth and articles about her we had engaged the New Zealand soprano Kiri Te Kanawa to cover Desdemona and to sing some performances later during the season. Te Kanawa was an artist who had been projected onto the world stage at Covent Garden. Colin Davis, Covent Garden's music director, and John Tooley, the administrator, were passionately enthusiastic about her and we decided to take their endorsements literally. Te Kanawa had arrived in New York some three weeks before the *Otello* premiere and on first meeting it was evident that we were dealing with a beautiful lady who definitely knew her own mind.

She came into my office within hours of landing in New York and I was not prepared for quite the bombshell she turned out to be. She knew exactly what she would do and what she would not do, the repertoire she wanted to sing over the next several seasons, the directors she wished to work with, the conductors she would tolerate, the costumes she would wear, and the attitude of the theater she wanted when working in it. She said all these things while sitting seductively on the couch, her knees tucked up, her long hair touching her shoulders, her deep-set brown eyes staring out of a café-au-lait face, one of the most totally attractive females I'd ever encountered. I made very few comments; her voice rose and fell in rhythmic cadences and I was seduced. I also knew we had a potential star of the first magnitude on our hands and I was determined that we would bring her to the attention of the New York opera public in a major way.

How major I had, of course, no inkling at that particular moment. She worked hard at the rehearsals and impressed her colleagues with her seriousness and her talent. Even Vickers was impressed, and this boded well for the production.

The premiere was scheduled for Saturday afternoon, February 9, and was to be broadcast. Stratas complained of not feeling well during the preceding week but by Friday afternoon assured us she would be fine for the Saturday matinee. I told Te Kanawa that she would probably not be called to perform Saturday afternoon but I could make no promises and she would have to follow the usual cover procedure and be within ten minutes of the theater all Saturday morning and afternoon.

At about 11:00 AM Saturday morning Stratas rang up to say that she'd been up all night with food poisoning and was flat on her back with a temperature and could not possibly perform. I called Te Kanawa, who was out taking a walk and couldn't be found. I sent Charlie Riecker to her apartment and he found her walking into the apartment house front door the minute he arrived. She called and I told her that she was going to make her Metropolitan Opera debut that afternoon and that the debut would be heard all across the country on the broadcast. I could hear her gulp for a moment and then she said she'd come to the theater immediately.

We notified all the necessary departments—wardrobe, wigs, make-up, as well as the box office, the billboard man, and the ushers. Within an hour notices were up about Stratas's replacement. I also called the New Zealand consul general and the United Nations ambassador and urged them to come to the house, for I was certain it was going to be a very special afternoon. I then called Vickers and told him what had happened and gripped the phone hard, expecting a blast. No blast was forthcoming. "The poor kid," he said. "She's going to need all the help she can get. I'll do everything I can."

And he was as good as his word. He came to her dressing room to give her encouragement and told me not to worry. I went to her dressing room to wish her well and she was sitting calmly being made up. "Toi-toi for this afternoon," I said, "and for many years at the Metropolitan." "Thanks," she replied. "I didn't expect to make my debut so soon but that's life. After all, we're all professional and we better be ready to seize opportunities when they come." And she smiled.

She certainly seized the opportunity that Saturday afternoon. The audience was with her the moment she appeared at the top of the long flight of stone stairs leading down to the water's edge and when she began with Otello the haunting duet *"Già nella notte densa"* she was meltingly beautiful and Vickers responded in kind. The curtain fell on an unforgettable first act and we had a new star. At the end of the opera her *"Ave Maria, piena di grazia"* and subsequent death scene with Otello were stunning and the curtain fell to a standing, howling ovation. Vickers took her out for their curtain calls and on the second put his arms around her, moved her forward, and left the stage to her alone. Standing in the wings, he joined loudly and forcefully with the applause in the auditorium. Te Kanawa came offstage, dragged him back on, and the two of them were pelted with flowers and torn-up programs. Te Kanawa had arrived.

There were further complications to be handled because of the Ligendza cancellation. Nilsson agreed to take on some later Isoldes, but to do so had to be released from *Der Rosenkavalier* because she was simply unable to sing Isoldes and Marschallins, one on top of the other, and prepare for *Götterdämmerung* at the same time. I had to break the news to Karl Böhm, who was mad at us anyway because of the cancellation of the new *Don Giovanni*, and I was afraid he might want to quit again. We suggested Evelyn Lear as Nilsson's replacement and he reluctantly agreed. He was pleased, however, after the first performance and told Lear that she was one of the finest Marschallins he had ever had.

While all these things were going on in the theater there had been an increasing silence from Kubelik. Ever since our difficult conversations about *Tristan* there had been only fitful communication, and I was looking forward to his arrival at the end of February to straighten matters out. I was totally unprepared, therefore, to receive a copy of a cable he sent to George Moore resigning his post. The cable read:

> Dear George—Having tried in vain in the past year to get the administration of the Metropolitan Opera House to work as planned when I signed my contract with you and seeing unfortunate financial situation change the basic conception of my ideals on how to lead musical affairs of the Met and considering the latest attacks on my person from the New York *Times* I see no other way than immediately resign as Musical Director. The situation as developed in the last six months does not allow me to fulfill my promises nor my artistic ambitions for the Met. Please tell press. Will see you next week. Greetings Rafael Kubelik.

I immediately telephoned Moore and urged him to do what he could to prevent such a step. Kubelik, I knew, was angry and disappointed about many things, including the slowness of administrative changes that would have given him what he always wanted, a "computer brain" to carry out his decisions swiftly and decisively without any time lag. I was all for the "computer brain" but the question was finding the right body and this was taking time. Kubelik felt it was taking too long a time and his patience was at an end. He was also disappointed about certain musical changes he wanted to make and, I think, was fettered by union rules concerning the orchestra. What with the financial problems topping everything and the *Tristan* problems bringing totally unfair allegations in the press that he was somehow neglecting his responsibilities he was finding the Met too vexing a place to work and he wanted out. Moore and I agreed that we should do all we could to keep him and I cabled back for Moore a message that read:

Appreciate and understand your feelings considering the multiple problems faced by the Metropolitan but urge you to withhold final decision until your arrival in New York next week and a chance for us to meet. Looking forward to seeing you. Greetings. George Moore.

Kubelik replied:

To avoid further delay in press release which I would like to discuss with you beforehand would appreciate seeing you Monday but please understand that my decision is final. Regards. Kubelik.

During all this time Moore was in Spain and we burned up the transatlantic wires trying to keep in touch. He was due back in New York a day before Kubelik and I was hoping for a meeting with the three of us before any final decision was made. Unfortunately I had a long-standing date to speak at an important lunch in Washington on February 13. The lunch had been planned to announce formally the Metropolitan's return to Washington after an eight-season absence. I had been in negotiation with Kay Shouse, the doyen of Wolf Trap Park Farm, outside Washington, D.C., proper, in Vienna, Virginia, and Mrs. Shouse had agreed to present the Metropolitan as her opening bill in June for one week and this required my making a keynote speech at the campaign luncheon. Kubelik was due in New York on February 11, scheduled to see Moore on February 12. I had to be in Washington on the night of the twelfth to attend a dinner organized by Mrs. Shouse and was unable to be present when Kubelik and Moore met. I knew nothing of the results until the next afternoon, when, just as I'd finished speaking, someone in the audience asked me to comment about Kubelik's resignation. I made some off-the-cuff remark about how I hoped it wouldn't happen but when I stepped down from the podium I was handed a copy of the New York *Times* where the story was on the front page.

There was very little I could say except to express my regrets, which I felt, and I was anxious to talk with him as fast as possible. Paul Hume, the perceptive and sensitive critic of the Washington *Post* spoke with me and the next day wrote a very careful article expressing regrets but taking the position that the Metropolitan must press on with its work and seek out a new music director who would be patient with some of the overwhelming financial problems.

Kubelik is a man who does things in a gigantic manner: his resignation was just such a gesture and he could not be persuaded to change his mind. He was extra sensitive to the press, still bearing scars from his days as music director of the Chicago Symphony when Claudia Cassidy, the all-powerful critic of the Chicago *Tribune*, took a dislike to his work and mounted a campaign to dislodge him. She succeeded. His appointment to the Metropolitan had been generally greeted with favor but the New York *Times* had been critical of his work in *Les Troyens* (wholly unfairly, I might add) and had implied that his contract, providing for specified times away from the house, was not a satisfactory way for the musical affairs of the company to be run. During the *Tristan* crisis Leinsdorf had been publicly critical of the same thing and altogether Kubelik read these comments as a personal attack. At the house itself he was sharply critical and unhappy with me for not re-arranging the artistic administration in a manner that he felt proper and he was impatient with the time necessary before he could reorganize certain parts of the orchestra. Having been music director of Covent Garden in the 1950s he had set ways in his mind that opera houses should run and on top of everything else he was now working not with Goeran Gentele, the man he had agreed to partner, but with his successor and at a time when financial matters were taking the front seat. Rather than try to ride out the several storms he elected to sail away from them.

I was tremendously unhappy about this development. Kubelik had made a major contribution to the artistic life of the Metropolitan during our planning days in 1971. It was he who insisted that we do *Les Troyens* and it was he who held out for the Lamm edition of *Boris Godunov*, which would be one of the great triumphs of my last season, and it was he who brought about the revival of *Jenufa* and reintroduced Janáček into the Metropolitan. We planned three seasons together and as it turned out not one of our new productions was a failure. I was hopeful of his changing his mind but in my heart I knew he would not.

It was agreed between us that he would complete his musical commitments for the 1973-74 season, which included the new production of *Götterdämmerung*. He decided it would be unwise for him to return the following year and that left me with the problem of finding replacements for *Jenufa*, *Death in Venice*, and, above all, the *Ring* cycle, the first one in twelve years and eagerly awaited by a Wagner-starved public. Major conductors are as hard or harder to find than major singers and I knew I was going to have my hands full with these problems.

The press kept up a steady barrage of stories and speculations and we were rarely out of the media. Indeed, just as their interest was beginning to flag, along came a human interest story that was gasoline to the fire. On March 4, during a meeting in my office with staff members, my door burst open around noontime and Peggy Tueller, my secretary, pale and trembling, told me that there had been an accident onstage and that Nilsson had been hurt.

I went with her immediately and as I entered the auditorium the silence was deafening. Act I of *Götterdämmerung* was onstage and cast members were standing around in small knots clutching one another with fear written all over their faces. For the most part they were looking down at the stage floor where Nilsson lay, groaning softly, with her right shoulder blade sticking out at what seemed to be a ninety-degree angle. I went to her side. Our company nurse was there and told me that an ambulance was on its way from Roosevelt Hospital. Nilsson looked up at me and through her makeup I could see that she was in great pain.

I asked what had happened and was shown a small three-step ladder that had been attached to the set for quick exits. One of the steps had given way and she had fallen, in the darkness, to the stage floor. The stagehands and cast were obviously in a state of shock and I thought it wise to say something reassuring. I took Nilsson's left hand in mine and told her that an ambulance was on its way and that everything was going to be all right. I spoke with authority: inside, my heart was pounding, my stomach churning, and my mind trying to figure out what to do next.

Before there was time for my inner feelings to give me away the ambulance arrived at a side door and two husky men were walking onstage carrying a stretcher. I watched as they prepared to lift her onto it and marveled at the firm but positive manner with which they went about their tasks. When the moment came to lift her onto the stretcher itself she let out a cry of pain that ricocheted around the auditorium. Tears streamed down her cheeks, cutting through her Brunhilde make-up, leaving mascara canals on both sides of her face. She started speaking Swedish and shaking her head back and forth. A blanket was wrapped around her and she was carried to the ambulance. I walked alongside until she was safely aboard and then told Peggy Tueller to go with her to the hospital and stay there as long as she was needed. I went back to my office and called the hospital, alerting the admissions office as to who was coming in and asking that every possible care be given. I was assured that matters would be properly handled.

By this time it was about 1:30 PM in the afternoon and I suddenly felt tired. It occurred to me that ever since July, 1972, I had lived facing one crisis after another and there seemed no end in sight. But I was not discouraged; I was grateful for the three years of analysis that I'd undergone that helped me keep everything in proportion. I also loved what I was doing, despite the problems, and I took a second breath, ready to face whatever else was in store.

About 4:00 PM Peggy called from the hospital to report that Nilsson had been given a general anesthetic, her dislocated shoulder had been set, and she was now resting as comfortably as could be expected. I said I would be right over and walked the few blocks between the opera house and the hospital, grateful for a breath of fresh air.

Nilsson was propped up in bed, woozy from the anesthetic but quite clear of mind. Her costume and wig had been removed but she still had the remnants of her makeup, which made her look half human and half goddess. We spoke briefly of the accident and the pain, and I told her that she was not to worry about a thing. She asked me what I was going to do about the premiere, and I said that we ought not to think about that at the moment. She drifted off to sleep and I crept out of the room.

Her nurse told me that she was in considerable pain and probably would be for the next two or three days and that she would have to remain in the hospital for careful examination. Peggy added that the doctors were encouraging but felt she was in for a hard time.

Truth to tell, I had not given much thought to the *Götterdämmerung* premiere since the accident and now my mind had to focus on this quickly. I talked with Kubelik and we agreed that if Nilsson wanted to sing it, and was able to move around the stage, the part should be hers, even if that meant a last-hour decision. Secretly I felt there was very little chance of this, judging from her condition in the hospital, but I decided to bring the matter up with her, if it seemed appropriate, the next day.

Around noon the next day I presented myself at her hospital room. She was sitting up in a chair and looked a hundred percent better than the previous afternoon. Her arm was in a sling, bandaged tightly to her body, but other than that she looked rested and alert. The papers had carried the story, many on the front page, and her phone was ringing off the wall. Flowers were stacked everywhere, and more kept coming in, carried by nurses, doctors, orderlies—anyone who happened to be passing by. She was world news and the big question was whether she would sing her scheduled premiere.

We talked about a lot of things but not about this point. Nilsson is a very self-contained person, extremely sensitive and easily hurt, and not often frank with what might be on her mind. I decided to wait and see if she brought the subject up but she did not. Finally I told her that while this was an awkward moment to discuss such a matter I wanted to know how she felt about singing the premiere if her doctors allowed her to do so. "How do you feel about this?" she answered, looking at me suspiciously. "As far as I'm concerned we'll do it your way," I replied. "And I suggest we don't make any decision this moment. Nothing would be more wonderful than having you on that stage next Friday but let's wait and see." She nodded agreement.

Four days before the premiere she was discharged from the hospital and went home to her hotel. She called me after settling in and asked when I had to have her decision. We agreed that she would call me the day before and let me know her intention. The news media were still at it and by now the big question was will she or won't she.

Back in the theater her understudy, the British soprano Rita Hunter, was taking all the last-minute rehearsals and wanted to know whether she would be going on the opening night. I understood her tension but I was determined to get Nilsson on that stage if humanly possible and told Miss Hunter that I would not be able to tell her until the actual morning of the premiere. She didn't like this at all and sent word that she had to know at least twenty-four hours before in order to be "pitched up" for the performance. Otherwise, as the message went, she might not be in condition to perform at all.

While sympathetic with her and well aware that we would not have a performance at all if she were out of the picture, I nonetheless kept her at bay while waiting for Nilsson's call. And the call came right on schedule, with a quiet and subduded voice saying that if I wanted her to try she was willing to do so. "But you better not let Miss Hunter be in Philadelphia," she added, and with this wry remark I knew everything was going to be all right.

I called wardrobe and told them to get over to Nilsson's hotel and figure out how to costume her to minimize the fact that she had only one arm available. I alerted Wolfgang Weber, the director, who went over to talk modification of his stage movements. The whole house was overjoyed; Nilsson was going to make it.

At her entrance the entire audience burst into applause, something that no *Ring* audience ever does, and Betty and I sat back in our box with tears streaming down our faces. Her first few notes sounded as if she were gargling and I had a moment of panic but this quickly cleared up and she sounded fantastic. She went through the entire opera using all the stage directions she had been given before the accident and carried on as if nothing had happened. At one point I was standing backstage with Weber watching from the wings and he stood looking at her and shaking his head. "I don't believe it, I don't believe it," he kept saying over and over. "She is doing exactly what I told her to do. Exactly. No change. I don't see how she can. But she is." But at curtain calls after Act II, I could see the strain showing, despite her good humor. She was in pain but would have none of it. By the Immolation scene I thought she wouldn't make it but she started almost with a second wind and it sounded as fine as ever. About halfway through she developed pitch problems and the balance was sung on technique and experience alone. At the end she was pale and sweating and for a moment I thought she might faint.

The applause was deafening and seemed to revive her. She came off after her first bows and embraced Jess Thomas, who had been her Siegfried. I heard her thanking him for something and they remained hugging each other for several moments.

When the iron curtain was finally lowered I walked her back to her dressing room and tried to thank her for a great night. She nodded her head and patted my hand. "I'll never forget your entrance," I said. "I've never heard an audience applaud at that spot." "Neither have I," she said, as we were reaching her dressing room, "and it threw me. I was so moved by that greeting that I started to cry. Jess was holding me and I whispered in his ear that I could not go on." For Nilsson to display such emotion on a stage was almost unheard of and explained the gargling sounds with her first notes. "But what happened?" I asked. "You did continue." "That was due to dear Jess," she said, smiling now that it was over. "He squeezed my good left hand hard and kept saying into my ear 'Oh, yes, you can, baby' and brought me back to my senses. He is a wonderful colleague."

As we reached the dressing room door and I bade her good night I felt exactly the same way. Between *Tristan* and *Götterdämmerung* Jess Thomas had proved once again what a great colleague and human being he is. Later that night, when we were safely home, we drank a toast to him, to Nilsson, and to a great night, feelings that were echoed widely the next days in the newspapers and on radio and television. World sympathy had again been drawn to the Metropolitan by the accident and world applause reached us all when everything worked out in a positive way. We were all happy.

Behind the stage, however, our economic problems continued unabated. More and more our new board treasurer, James S. Smith was emerging as the strongman. His management experts were exploring every facet of the house and its operations, and he was in and out of my office, increasingly critical of the way things were being run.

He and I did initiate a new system of cost reporting that gave every department head the real responsibility of administering his individual budget on a daily basis. We tidied up other loose ends and began focusing on areas that needed reorganization, particularly subscription, the artistic administration, and promotion.

With Kubelik's resignation I now felt the need for two strong partners, one for music and the other for the stage. A special subcommittee of the board was formed to advise me on these matters. The committee was chaired by Francis Goelet, and we talked often about the kind of artistic direction the Met needed. Goelet was of the opinion that the Met could have all the good artistic advice it wanted but that the ultimate decisions had to be left up to the general manager and I concurred completely with this view. There were others who kept murmuring about committees and the new way that modern industrial management was being handled. I kept commenting to this faction that the Met was not a factory or a conglomerate and that I wanted good partners who would work together with me as a team. We would make the planning decisions necessary for the seasons ahead, within the budget guidelines approved by the board, and they would, in large measure, carry them out while I spent at least 50 percent of my time like a college president, raising production money and on the road across the country where I felt our ultimate strength had never been tapped. I wanted decentralization, a strong team, and solid board support for the treacherous days ahead. Some members understood my position: most were suspicious of it and growing ever more fearful of the deteriorating financial position. It wasn't that they had any plan; they just began to feel that change, any change, would be for the better. They were desperately looking for the knight on the white charger and finding me instead.

Smith and I did agree on one thing: we needed to seek out stronger government support, both on the national and state level, not only for additional funds but to dramatize our situation and to begin lobbying for the Metropolitan as an organization in need of special attention on a

continuing basis. I felt that we should try to get a major federal grant in
the form of matching funds and mount a campaign on the radio to get
our Saturday audience to participate. Twice before the Metropolitan
had gone to its radio public for help and twice before the help had been
forthcoming. This time I was hoping for at least a million dollars, half
from the government and half from the public. I also thought we
should seek a like amount from the New York State Council on the
Arts, this to be an outright grant without the matching qualifications.
The two million dollars that would result from these efforts would not
by any means solve our problems but it would demonstrate our vital
position in the arts world and would show that the public sector recognized the Metropolitan as a unique institution. The amounts would be
almost the largest ever given to one organization since the creation of
both the federal program and the New York State Council on the Arts
and would also serve notice on our board that there was encouragement for the new leadership.

There was also the problem of city funds. We had been receiving
about $175,000 a year from the Parks and Recreation Department to
help defray the expenses of our free performances in the parks. This
was nowhere near the actual costs but we felt the program itself was of
overwhelming importance to our position in the city and our responsibilities to participate in city activities. The true costs to us were near-
er $250,000 and the city was making noises to indicate that even the
modest subsidy would probably be dropped in light of the city's developing financial problems. I reported this to the executive committe and
reluctantly pointed out that if the city was forced to withdraw I would
seek the money elsewhere but was very much afraid that we could not
afford the program on our own. Under our contracts we were obliged
to pay the fifty-two-week-a-year employees, such as the chorus, ballet,
and stagehands, but that there would be considerable savings with the
orchestra, as they were not guaranteed fifty-two weeks and we would
not have to pay them. This would reduce our expenses for those weeks
considerably.

The executive committee agreed to my proposal and I immediately
called a meeting of the orchestra committee to explain our position and
tell them that unless I was able to find financing the parks season would
be canceled. For our meeting the orchestra group had brought along
their attorneys, Philip Sipser and Leonard Liebowitz, who listened to
my comments without saying anything. At the conclusion of the meeting Sipser took me aside and asked if I would go with him to a special
meeting with the president of the New York City Council, Paul

O'Dwyer, and plead our case for continuing city support. He said that our legal position was correct but our moral posture unconscionable and that O'Dwyer might be able to help if he was filled in on the facts. I, of course, agreed immediately and an appointment was made a few days later.

Paul O'Dwyer is unique in New York City politics. With his thick white hair tumbling down onto his black full eyebrows, his eyes piercing, he looks like a passionate saint clearing out the wicked from the temples. His brogue, soft or flaming as the occasion demands, is used with the skill of an instrumentalist and his background of grinding poverty in Ireland has given him backbone, liberalism, and a life-long determination to better the lot of the less fortunate.

I found myself in O'Dwyer's office on the morning of March 22, 1974, pleading the case of the Metropolitan's performances in the parks. In the meeting I was flanked by Sipser and two members of the orchestra committee, who contributed a thought here and there, but the bulk of the work was up to me. When I'd finished my presentation O'Dwyer asked some pointed questions that I answered as frankly as I could. I explained the Metropolitan's financial situation and how we would have to cancel the performances if city support was not continued. I explained that we would have to take strict advantage of the letter of our contract with the orchestra and pay only those people we were obliged to by contract. I pointed out that the Metropolitan had been carrying the burden of these expenses for years but was now not in the position of continuing if the city withdrew.

O'Dwyer listened carefully and agreed to help. "We'll have to do a lot of work, though," he said. "Are you ready to meet with all the borough presidents and whatever committees they wish?" I told him I was ready for anything and, sure enough, not two days later I found myself closeted with the borough president of Manhattan, Percy Sutton, repeating the same arguments. I went to Brooklyn, Staten Island, and Queens, always early in the morning and always with O'Dwyer himself. We met with citizen groups, with local arts councils, with officials of the various borough presidential offices, with anyone who would listen to our case. I began to get an idea of what political campaigning must be like and throughout all the tours O'Dwyer kept up his argument that the performances were good for the people and must not be allowed to die. We made a good team and I was beginning to feel that the boroughs might support us. The only unknown was the Bronx, where the borough president would not receive us. I was worried about this but O'Dwyer calmed me down. "It's just one of those political things," he finally said. "You leave this one to me. We'll get him in line."

At the same time as the city campaign was under way I was pushing hard at the National Endowment in Washington and the Council on the Arts in Albany. In Washington, Nancy Hanks, chairman of the Endowment, was concerned about our problems and we were reaching agreement on our matching fund proposal. Eric Larrabee, executive director of the State Arts Council, and his music panel colleagues were also working on a proposal with me that would give the Metropolitan one million dollars for general operating expenses and to help cover costs of extra rehearsals that were needed to bring the Met up to the best possible artistic shape. Moore and Smith wanted to be kept abreast of progress and I reported to them how things were moving. They were impatient, particularly Moore, who went out of his way to pass on his opinions to Nancy Hanks in terse terms. Nancy said nothing to me directly but I soon found out that she resented Moore's comments and was beginning to turn away from the kind of help we needed. Early one morning I got word of this from a mutual friend and called her to arrange a visit to straighten matters out. The only free time she had was at 7:30 AM the following day and I wandered the Washington streets at that hour before the sun was up, feeling the way I had so many mornings during the second world war.

We met, ironed out the problems, and a few days later she joined me in a special broadcast announcing the grant and the matching fund requirements. We aired the talk in March and by the end of the broadcast season, on April 20, 1974, we had raised almost the entire amount. Contributions came from every state in the union and every territory except the Canal Zone. I subsequently found out that we were not heard in the Canal Zone even on a delayed basis, and this explained their lack of participation. Often the money was accompanied by letters explaining what the Met broadcasts meant to people and had meant over many, many years. They came by the bagful, swamping our post office. If there was ever any doubt about the Met's position in the United States it was ended once and for all by the heartwarming response.

The state, too, came through with its promised million dollars and O'Dwyer kept the city political forces in line. We remained on the budget line and the parks performances were assured.

But none of this impressed the board. The members were increasingly restive, preferring the open line of operatic gossip. There were difficult administrative problems in the artistic department, principally understaffing and a lack of follow-through that caused a number of artists and agents to complain that the Metropolitan could not make up its mind. These complaints were aired at the constant round of cocktail and dinner parties during the season and in many cases enlarged and embellished to embarrass particular people in the artistic administration.

Word of this would get back to me by several routes, including off-the-cuff visits from various board members who were almost gleeful in reporting the talk. I sensed once again the undercurrent of viciousness and cruelty that seems to be a historic part of the artistic life of the world, the desire to pull down anyone who reaches a certain pinnacle, the unspoken jealousy of desire and envy. This is a human condition, one that applies to any walk of life and activity, but in the arts it seems especially painful as one is essentially dealing in something that is supposed to be beautiful and bring beauty to others and one would hope that the messengers of that beauty might be encouraged in their work. That, sadly, does not seem to be the case at all, and I was learning this fact under the pressure of an extremely demanding job. My idealism was being sorely tried.

Onstage things were moving at a good pace. The old Eugene Berman production of *Don Giovanni* had been extensively repaired and repainted thanks to money given for this purpose by Robert Tobin and his mother. New costumes had been created and the revival was treated from a rehearsal standpoint as if it was a new production. Karl Böhm had withdrawn as conductor, and I had asked Levine if he would take it over. The cast included Leontyne Price as Donna Anna, Teresa Zylis-Gara as Donna Elvira, Stuart Burrows as Don Ottavio, Walter Berry as Leporello, Teresa Stratas as Zerlina, Raymond Michalski as Masetto, James Morris as the Commendatore, and Sherrill Milnes, in his first Metropolitan appearance in the role, as Don Giovanni.

Milnes almost canceled his Don Giovanni when I had to cancel the new production. He is a highly conscientious artist who prepares his roles thoroughly and he was afraid that with the cancellation the production would not be given the proper rehearsal time, both onstage and in studios. I tried to reassure him that this was not to be the case but he was doubtful and worried. He was also worried about proper coaching for the role that he had hoped to receive from Gentele.

I was very anxious that he remain in the production and racked my brains to come up with an idea that might make him comfortable. Betty, Sherrill, and I had breakfast one Saturday morning in San Francisco, where we had flown out for the opening of the San Francisco Opera season, and she suggested that we might ask George London if he would be willing to coach the part. London was one of the most distinguished Don Giovannis of his time and would still be singing the role if nature had not played dirty with his vocal chords, resulting in the paralysis of one of them and the cutting off of his singing career in midflight.

I thought it a wonderful idea, and Milnes was enthusiastic and delighted. I then called London, who was also pleased provided Milnes was really serious and would work steadily with him. I felt the details were better worked out between the two of them and extracted a promise from Milnes that he would meet with London as soon as possible and stay with our production as already advertised. He agreed, provided that he and London got on, and I urged a meeting as soon as possible. This was done, and some two weeks later Milnes called and gave me the green light.

On March 28, when the first performance took place, the production looked shiny new and the artists were obviously happy with it and with themselves. It was a memorable night, Levine's first Mozart opera in the house and a new world-class Don Giovanni in the person of Sherrill Milnes. Price was superb, as were the others, and I was delighted that economy had forced the saving of a beautiful production that had no business being scrapped.

Our last major premiere for the season took place on Good Friday, April 12, with a revival of *Parsifal*. *Parsifal* had not been heard in the house for four years, although in the old days it was practically a Metropolitan tradition at Eastertime. This production had been created in 1970 by the team of Nathaniel Merrill and Robert O'Hearn and was an enormous success when it was first done. We had assembled a fine cast for the revival: Jess Thomas as Parsifal, Janis Martin as Kundry, John Macurdy as Gurnemanz, Thomas Stewart as Amfortas, Morley Meredith as Klingsor. As conductor we had William Steinberg, who had not appeared at the Metropolitan in some time. When last there he and Bing had several disagreements resulting in Steinberg's reluctance to return. He was just stepping down as music director of the Pittsburgh Symphony and had not been in good health. I wanted everything to go well with his production in the hopes that he would want a more active life at the Metropolitan in the years ahead, but it was obvious when he arrived that he was going to be forced into a less strenuous life than that of a vigorous symphonic and operatic conductor. I knew of his fierce reputation for standards and wanted everything to be just right.

During the time that Steinberg was preparing *Parsifal* we had our second season of the Look-Ins with Danny Kaye and the two often met in various rehearsal halls throughout the theater. Each admired the other and when they met went through elaborate rituals of bowing and scraping. Danny was quick to see that Steinberg was not well and did everything he could to jolly him along through the rehearsals.

After he'd been in the house for about a week word was sent to me that Steinberg wanted an appointment to see me. I knew that this meant some trouble somewhere and I brought together the artistic administration to be prepared for any eventuality. Steinberg arrived in my office and addressed himself to me. "I am delighted to be a guest in your house," he said, "and a guest should behave as a guest and not issue complaints." "That depends on the mood of the guest," I replied, "and his welcome from the host. I hope our welcome has been what you wanted." "It has indeed," he replied, "except I have a little problem with one of my fellow guests." And he went on in this vein to outline a situation regarding a cover artist that was not developing the way he wished. I was immensely relieved that it was a minor problem and we soon had the matter put to rights. When our talk was completed, Steinberg rose and moved slowly toward the door. He put out his hand. "A good host means a good guest!" We shook hands.

During April other important plans for the future began to take firm shape. Arrangements for the Japanese tour neared completion; Colin Graham, the director of *Death in Venice*, came for our first meeting on this brilliant but very tricky work scheduled for the next season; Bernstein agreed tentatively to conduct *Porgy and Bess* as the Metropolitan's Bicentennial production; and I had an interesting evening with the Vladimir Horowitzes. I'd not seen them for a long time but we'd kept in touch by phone and I was delighted that he was becoming more and more active on the concert stage.

Our meeting took on an interesting shape. For some time Horowitz had been thinking about giving a recital in the Metropolitan Opera House. No pianist, or indeed instrumentalist or solo singer for that matter, had used the house for a concert. There had been occasional Sunday rentals to outside popular artists as a means of increasing our house revenue but not on any regular basis and not in our field. We talked late into the night and tentatively agreed that we might have such a concert as a benefit for the Metropolitan and as an important gesture from a famous artist that the Met must not be allowed to die. It would be necessary to test the acoustics with a single piano and this meant an expensive gamble. We could do such a test only on a Sunday and would have to call in a minimum stage crew to carry it out. I thought the risk was worth it, particularly after we scaled the house to benefit prices and realized that we really stood to make some money. We settled on a Sunday in early June and arranged to have three pianos brought in. We collectively thought that the best spot on the stage would be dead center just under the proscenium arch, in essentially the same place that the Metropolitan Opera Auditions piano was placed during the spring finals. The three instruments were ordered to be placed in the spot and when Cyril Harris, the major acoustician of the house heard this, he made it plain to me that the test would not work. He told me this while we were on a bus crossing town to the house for the Sunday test and my heart sank. "Let's not hang the crêpe banners yet," I said to him. "Let's see what happens. We'll know soon enough."

As we walked into the auditorium I realized that there had been a confusion of instructions. The pianos were not placed under the pro- scenium but at the very edge of the orchestra pit, which had been raised to stage level. I was furious but there was nothing that could be done at the moment as Horowitz appeared onstage ready to start.

In the auditorium we had a small group of his friends, including Howard Taubman, former music critic of the New York *Times* and now a consultant on artistic matters to one of the major oil companies; David Rubin, concert chief for Steinway & Sons; Wanda Horowitz; and one or two others. Betty and I sat in the back and I was convinced that I'd just poured at least $6,000 down the drain in what was bound to be an abortive test. Horowitz began with the piano on stage right and with the first notes it was obvious that the sound in the house was glori- ous. No one said a word and after a few passages he moved to the pi- ano center stage and the same incredible sound wafted out into the house. He moved over to the third instrument, on stage left, and the same thing happened. He went back to the center instrument, actually his own piano, and started playing Schubert. I crossed the seats to where I could see the back of Cyril Harris's head and came in behind him. I tapped him gently on the shoulder and when he looked around I asked him, very softly, what it was he had told me on the bus. He just looked at me and smiled. "If the pianos had been where you wanted them this would not have worked. But here, there are no problems and there never were!" I patted his shoulder.

We spent almost two hours that afternoon listening to the great man play everything from Scriabin to Bach and Schubert and at the end he was satisfied that the house would work. I was fascinated as the after- noon wore on by the attitude of the stagehands. Bit by bit they gath- ered in small groups just outside the stage area and brought up chairs to sit and listen. One big man came up to me afterwards and said that he didn't know what was being played but "it was goddamn pretty." The highest accolade.

Within days we scheduled the concert for the fall and the announcement of it ended up on the front pages. It was a good boost to our collective managerial morale.

What was very nice for my morale were the two honorary degrees I received that spring, one from Hobart and William Smith College in Geneva, New York, and the other from New York University. I'd always told Betty and the boys that I wanted an honorary degree very much, to make up for my complete lack of regular academic certification, and they were all amused by my wishes coming true. New York University's citation read, in part, that "an academic institution must view with a mixture of unease and grudging admiration the youthful determination and independence of spirit of your school years that has left you, though richly educated, bereft of any sort of traditional diploma. To rectify that oversight, by the authority vested in me, I confer upon you the degree of Doctor of Humane Letters, *honoris causa.*" I was delighted.

XXI

Death in Venice, Jenufa,

Boris Godunov—*The Board Moves*

At the opera house the late spring of 1974 was also a time of continuing vacillation and uncertainty by the board. At the May meeting George Moore had stepped down as president and had been replaced by William Rockefeller, the former chairman of the executive committee with whom I had had various friendly if distant meetings. I felt that Rockefeller was fundamentally sympathetic to the problems and certainly a great deal less volatile than Moore. I hoped we were going to establish a good working relationship but only time would tell about this.

Rockefeller called for a three-day think tank meeting of the executive committe and management away from New York to examine our problems in a more leisurely atmosphere. I asked that the meetings be held in August, rather than July as originally proposed, because I wanted the staff to have an uninterrupted vacation after the close of our parks season. This was finally agreed to, although not with much grace. It was almost as if I were trying to protect the house over and above the convenience of the board.

We did meet, on the old Ruth Pratt estate on Long Island that had been made into a house for business meetings, and right from the outset the sessions turned into a "we versus they" situation. The executive committee and the few other board members who attended were lined up at the table all together, facing the management group on the other side. I had brought Bronson, Riecker, Robinson, Eva Popper, and Bill Hadley and we had come prepared with facts and figures on the state of the house, finances, labor, budgets, and plans for the next three years.

Rockefeller ran the meetings and planned the agenda. We broke up into small groups to discuss specific subjects and prepare recommendations on them to be submitted to larger sessions in the evenings. We went over and over the same ground, coming back to one fundamental issue: money. We talked about various approaches to our 1975 labor negotiations, we talked about cutting expenses, we talked about everything under the sun but no one had the answer to the money question. I pressed for a major capital campaign. All of us stated over and over again that the costs of producing opera were pretty much the same the world over. We showed comparative figures between our costs and those of Chicago and San Francisco (the other two major budget companies in the country) and pointed out that the costs per performance were essentially the same. We stressed that if we were going to produce our repertoire with the right artistic forces our costs were not going to get less. The subject of artists' fees became a big issue and the implication was that we were profligate and careless in this area.

For the entire three days the management was on the defensive and I must take a large share of the blame for not sensing this early enough and calling a halt to the way we were proceeding. The results were not satisfactory to anyone. On the last night I made a final statement in which I said that I thought our gross deficit was bound to be around nine million dollars the next season and was told in no uncertain terms that this was not satisfactory. I returned to the arguments I'd used before but no one was listening. The consensus was that we were doing a bad job and that problems would probably be solved quicker and easier with new leadership. The essential difficulties were swept under Mrs. Pratt's rugs. The three days resulted only in a further freezing of positions and this was not healthy for any of us.

The week after the meeting I asked Rockefeller to dine with me and talk over the result of the conference. He was very guarded and murmured something about the fact that the general manager's job was becoming too big for any one person and that I should think about some kind of a partner. I reminded him that I was seeking a partnership, and building toward one in running the house. John Dexter was about to be appointed director of production and I was hopeful that James Levine and I could work toward his becoming music director. I spoke of some of the administrative problems with which he was familiar and told him that the artistic administration was to be strengthened by the addition of Helga Schmidt, former artistic administrator of the Vienna State Opera and now an agent in London anxious to return to the theater. I had known Helga well during my Bernstein winters in Vienna and admired how she carried out her responsibilities with experience and tenacity. I told him again that I visualized my role as that of the college president, spending at least 50 percent of my time on the road and raising money. I said again that I thought our problems would be solved only by aggressive board leadership selling the organization to the public, to government agencies and to the foundations. I said that the fundamental decision of the worth of the Metropolitan Opera to the national artistic position of the United States had to be brought out into the open and discussed with force and passion. He listened to me but I sensed that he was not hearing anything I said. Toward the end of the evening we talked about our families and other matters while my heart continued to sink in my shoes realizing that none of what we discussed was being absorbed. I began to feel more and more like a character out of Kafka. The more I suggested and spoke the less I was heard. I had a feeling that something had to give and it was only to be a question of time before something did.

I talked over the meeting with Betty and in the talking it out I still couldn't see where we were headed. I had decided back in 1972 that the only thing I could really do was try to run the company as well as possible, get the public reinterested in our activities, reach out to the opera lovers who were in one way or another turned off by the Met, make our work the most compelling and provocative of any in the country. I figured that if we were able to move in these directions the board would feel the new surge of energy and public response and move along with it. I decided that my original thoughts were still correct and I was more determined than ever to prove the point.

During the remainder of the summer we polished our positions toward the new labor talks. Just before the end of the season I had held another company meeting and reported in detail on our finances as they then stood. In my report I had suggested that we were going to have to make some difficult decisions in the fall about many things, not the least of which was whether or not we could continue to guarantee a full year's work. I stated this clearly, and even included it in the copy of my speech that I again gave out after the meeting, but I don't think the truth of my position really sank in. Nevertheless it gave us a starting point for discussions and the preparations of our position. At the suggestion of Irving Mitchell Felt of our executive committee, his friend, Theodore Kheel, the renowned labor negotiator and impartial arbitrator, came to a meeting in my office with Rockefeller, Smith, and

Felt and we reviewed our problems. He seemed to feel that if our finances were indeed as poor as reported we had no other course than to try to rearrange downward the agreements already in hand. He did not think we would have an easy time of it.

A day or so after Kheel's visit Rockefeller called and asked that we have no further meetings on labor matters for the time being. I told him that I thought this a poor idea, that the sooner we let the company know where we stood the better chance we had to tackle the problems candidly. He said that he was "working on something" and would be back to me on the subject soon. I bowed to his wishes and we canceled two meetings already set.

I did hold a pre-season company meeting, however, to bring everyone up to date on what had happened with the financial picture over the summer and reported that with the National Endowment matching grant and the New York state money we had ended the fiscal year with a loss of around $500,000, considerably better than the net (loss) of almost $2 million of the previous year. I stated this was due in large measure to the splendid cooperation everyone had shown in cutting expenses and that we had to do as well or better in the upcoming season. I made no bones about the continuing seriousness of our position but spoke hopefully of the new board leadership and a determination to keep the Metropolitan around for many years to come. One piece of positive news I was able to report was the signing of contracts with the Chibbu-Nippon Company for our trip to Japan, the first of what I hoped would be increasing foreign tours for the company.

The 1974–75 season got officially under way with an experimental week in Cleveland. Our sponsors there had agreed to present us in the fall rather than the traditional spring week to see whether or not it was practical to try splitting the tour between the fall and spring. The idea was to see if we could not free the house at the beginning of the season for outside attractions and give us more flexibility to move in and out of the regular New York season. We presented *Vespri, Butterfly, Don Giovanni, Turandot, Tosca* and *L'Italiana*, all scheduled for our first week in New York. While the performances were not too bad, the public sale was not what we hoped and the terrible differences between our stage in New York and the barn in Cleveland simply made the pre-season preparation period more complicated. Our Cleveland hosts were generous with their help but by the end of the week we knew the fall tour idea was not going to work.

The New York season opened with a brilliant *I Vespri Siciliani* with Christina Deutekom, Sherrill Milnes, Paul Plishka, and William Lewis on Monday, September 17. The preceding Sunday the New York

Times had published an excerpt from a quicky book about the Met by Steven Rubin, which was an extremely unfavorable series of comments about the Metropolitan's problems and my stewardship in particular. It wasn't that the piece was negative; it was cheap and slick and was written more for effect than substance. Curiously it had a reverse effect. I had many phone calls and letters from people, including board members, who thought it in extremely bad taste, including Jon Vickers, who took the trouble to telephone from Bermuda and make it plain that despite our differences he thought the piece rotten. Levine, who was conducting *Vespri*, was also annoyed by it and went into the pit determined to give the audience a *Vespri* they'd never forget. At the end of the first act he called me from his dressing room and asked how we were doing. I said, "Great." "We'll give them something they won't forget tonight," he said. "Just you wait." He already had in the first act but by the time the opera was finished he had the audience standing and cheering their collective lungs out. It was a good start.

The highlight of the first two weeks, however, was *Roméo et Juliette*, which I'd put into the repertory especially for Placido Domingo, who was dying to sing the role in New York. As his Juliette we had the beautiful, petite, and talented Judith Blegen and the two of them swept up the stage with their passion and music-making. The production, designed by Rolf Gérard, was stunning to look at and Henry Lewis, the conductor, was at his best in this repertoire.

We also revived Alban Berg's *Wozzeck* with an excellent cast including Janis Martin, Peter Glossop, and Donald Gramm. Levine conducted and the production was directed by the young Englishman Patrick Libby, who scored a rousing success with the piece the previous season at Covent Garden. The production itself was a classic, having been created by Caspar Neher in 1959. We scheduled only five performances since the box office for the work was not the strongest. Much to our pleasant surprise we did better business than we expected and I thought this boded well for our big contemporary work coming up ten days later. This was, of course, the American premiere of Benjamin Britten's *Death in Venice*.

Death in Venice presented us with some of the most difficult production problems we'd yet faced. In the first place, Kubelik declined to conduct after his resignation, and that meant I had to find someone else who hopefully would be able to do justice to the piece. I was very lucky to get Steuart Bedford, the man who had conducted the premiere for Britten in Aldeburgh the previous spring. The production itself was the same as had been on the Aldeburgh stage, a tiny theater whose facilities would be swallowed by the giant Met. I was afraid that the production would look too small and confided my doubts to Colin Graham, the director, who agreed to sit with me in the balcony when the sets were first put up and also agreed that if it looked too ridiculous we would find a way of canceling the whole project. We had a very nervous hour or two together when the production was being blocked but both of us agreed that it was going to work, perhaps not ideally but in a manner that would present the piece in a proper light.

The casting of the two major parts, Aschenbach and the seven devilish characters, was nicely in the hands of Peter Pears and John Shirley-Quirk, both of whom had been involved with their roles since the premiere. The other parts, including the "hero" Tadzio, a dancing role, numbered 63, divided between singers and dancers, and they had to form an ensemble. It was a formidable undertaking. Fortunately for us the Metropolitan Opera Studio came to our rescue. The studio had a roster of attractive and talented young performers and we turned Colin Graham and Steuart Bedford loose with Bill Nix, the studio director, and they rapidly found exactly the cast they were looking for. The part of Tadzio was more complicated. Sir Frederick Ashton had devised beautiful but highly complex choreography for the part and the dancer had to be a topnotch professional who could look thirteen years old and project strong, boyish masculinity. This quality was essential: the Visconti movie of *Death in Venice* a few years before had turned the Thomas Mann novella into a paean for sensual homosexuality, destroying both the subtlety of the writing and the delicate line of the story about Gustav von Aschenbach and his artistic and intellectual conflict between discipline and passion. Ashton himself did not come to New York but sent his deputy Faith Worth, who, together with Graham and me, set out to find the right person.

I had assigned Florence Guarino of the artistic administration to coordinate the entire *Death in Venice* production and she rounded up a number of dancers from various companies, including the New York City Ballet. Early on in the search I had told all concerned that I would voice an opinion only if an impasse was reached, in which event my decision would have to stick. Everyone understood my position and as a result I was rarely contacted but late one afternoon I was asked to come to the main dance rehearsal hall. The search had been narrowed down to three dancers and all concerned were unsure which one to take. I reminded everyone of the ground rules and then asked to see the three perform. There was not a second's hesitation in my mind as to which of the three should have the role and when I announced my choice there were great sighs and smiles of relief on all sides.

The dancer in question, Bryan Pitts of the New York City Ballet, was sent from heaven. He was small enough to project a thirteen-year-old, danced giving the impression of no effort at all, and was by nature both blond and thoroughly masculine. I asked if anyone had consulted either George Balanchine or Lincoln Kirstein about him and was told that this had not been done. "Then you all better stand by," I said, "because they very well may resent our auditioning one of their people without their permission. I'll go and see what can be done."

I went upstairs and out of the opera house, walking across the Lincoln Center plaza toward the New York State Theater. I got on the stage elevator of the state theater and it stopped a floor below the New York City Ballet offices. When the door opened in walked both Balanchine and Kirstein. "How marvelous," I said, as the elevator door closed. "You're just the people I've come to see. Can you spare me a few minutes? I've a big problem and I need your help." They looked at one another and smiled at me. "Of course. Come on in my office," said Kirstein, "and we'll talk."

The three of us entered his room and closed the door. "I don't know how to begin this," I said, "but I guess without your knowledge we seem to have been auditioning a number of your dancers for the role of Tadzio in *Death in Venice*. Just a few moments ago we found the ideal person, after weeks of searching." "I know about your search," said Kirstein. "I've sent some dancers from the School of American Ballet. Didn't you like any of them?" I explained our system and that I'd not seen any until the final moment. "Who do you want?" Balanchine asked, obviously more than curious. "Bryan Pitts," I replied. "He's ideal." There was a long silence. I broke it by explaining the schedule and the performance requirements. Still silence. Finally they looked at each other and Kirstein turned to me. "All right, you may have him," he said. "We'll put somebody else into his commitments here. He's a good choice; the audiences will love him." Balanchine made no further comment but seemed unsmiling and withdrawn. I thanked them both and returned to the opera house to report my success. I was puzzled by Balanchine's reaction but thought little more about it until someone told me that Pitts was living with one of the great beauties of the company and that Balanchine was probably jealous. I never asked.

Death in Venice had its American premiere on October 18 and was an unqualified success. Peter Pears, onstage as Aschenbach for almost the entire opera, was superb and it was hard to realize that his performance was also his debut at the Metropolitan. John Shirley-Quirk sang and acted the seven personifications of evil with intensity and musical expressiveness, and Bryan Pitts was every bit as good as we'd hoped for in the part of Tadzio. The only shadow over the evening was Britten's illness that prevented his being in New York and nobody felt this as strongly as his life-long friend Peter Pears. Pears was delighted, however, with the audience reception and subsequent critical approval of the piece and this made up, in part, for his special disappointment. I had cabled Britten before the opening and the next morning sent him another, fuller cable explaining the success and wishing him a speedy recovery. His publisher, Donald Mitchell, was in New York for the opening and told us all that the Metropolitan production was the most successful of the work to date. What proved this out from our standpoint was the line of people at the box office. Within hours of the opening we'd sold every ticket for the nine scheduled performances.

Not everyone liked the work. My mail grew heavy with protest notes from subscribers, ranging from gentle rebukes to savage attacks. At the same time there was almost an equal amount of mail thanking us for having produced the work. *Death in Venice* was in every sense controversial, just the kind of artistic whirlpool that gives vitality and life to a theater. We were delighted.

The board was puzzled by the piece itself but generally grateful that it was proving to be a box office success. Most, I think, avoided seeing it but the intelligent and sensitive ones that did seemed to find it stirring. The production had been paid for by the Gramma Fisher Foundation, both in London and New York, and Bill Fisher was rightfully proud of his contribution to the overall success of the work.

Death in Venice was quickly followed by another work unfamiliar to present-day Metropolitan audiences, Leoš Janáček's *Jenufa*. *Jenufa* had its U.S. premiere at the Metropolitan, in 1924, with a cast that included Maria Jeritza, Margaret Matzenauer, and Carl Martin Oehmann. Our production had Teresa Kubiak, Astrid Varnay, and Jon Vickers. It was planned to be conducted by Kubelik. Following his withdrawal, and after careful consultation with Levine, we offered the opera to John Nelson. Both Levine and I felt we had a unique opportunity to boost the career of an American talent who had proved his stuff with the chorus preparation and performances of *Les Troyens*, performances which he had had to take over at the very last minute when Kubelik became ill. The production was designed by Günther Schneider-Siemssen and staged by Günther Rennert and paid for by Mrs. DeWitt Wallace, who also gave me the money for *Boris Godunov*, scheduled to premiere later in the season.

Jenufa was only a qualified success. Schneider-Siemssen's sets were realistic and heavy; Rennert's direction was pedestrian, and the performances never really got off the ground. Perhaps Nelson was not really ready for such a difficult undertaking at this stage in his career. In any event *Jenufa* was acceptable when it should have been brilliant. On the opening night Maria Jeritza attended, covered with jewels, and was acknowledged by the audience. She waved greetings, looking every inch the prima donna she always has been and always will be. It was almost the best part of the evening.

Unbeknownst to me, however, there were plans abrewing in the board room. Things had been generally quiet since the August summit meetings; except for the labor sessions with Theodore Kheel there had not been any follow-up on ideas that had been discussed on Long Island. For a moment I was beginning to think that perhaps my frequent exhortations about a major capital fund drive might be bearing fruit.

There had been a wild, almost Alice-in-Wonderland meeting of the executive committee in late October where I was asked what my plans were for assembling a management team. I was a little puzzled by this question and repeated that I had almost all the team I needed with the exception of the final appointment of John Dexter and a music director, whom I hoped would be James Levine. I reported that Helga Schmidt had backed out at the last moment after signing her employment contract, having been offered the same job at Covent Garden and preferring to live in London, and that I was hopeful of getting Richard Rodzinski to leave the San Francisco Opera and join us as the missing body in the artistic administration. Something about the way I described these things or something about the way I had been dealing with them ever since my appointment as acting general manager rubbed them all the wrong way and they started complaining about everything. I kept asking them to be specific but none were. They kept looking at one another and telling stories about the past. It was almost as if I wasn't there. At one point Rockefeller looked over at me and said something about the fact that he didn't want me to think that they were attacking me personally. I kept asking what they wanted. They kept avoiding the point. Finally one of them said, in stentorian and demanding tones, that it was time I had a plan. "But I do have a plan," I kept repeating, and I went over and over it again. It was the Mad Hatter's Tea Party. I was puzzled, confused, and aware that they were literally not listening to a thing I said. I noticed from time to time they would look at one another and nod their heads, almost as if they were confirming some previously made decision.

Looking back, it is easy to see what was happening. Individually there were, and are, some effective people on that board. Collectively, and with the group of officers that had been elected the previous spring, they were weak, intellectually vapid, leaderless, and, most important of all, victims of a kind of panic that is almost impossible to halt. It was made up of a combination of ingredients: fear, particularly over the money situation that had been growing steadily ever since the move into Lincoln Center in 1966; lack of imagination in viewing the Metropolitan in national and international terms; a strong reaction to the tight and determined era that had ended with the retirement of Rudolf Bing; and, perhaps the frosting on the cake, the untimely and totally unexpected death of Goeran Gentele before that splendid man had had a chance to show what he could do.

Part of all these things might be due to age. At my appointment, the chairman of the board, Lowell Wadmond, while still a partner in the law firm of White and Case, was nonetheless well along in his seventies and had been particularly shocked and affected by Gentele's demise. Moore, also over seventy, is the kind of executive who moves through responsibilities always shooting from the hip and rarely stopping to listen. No doubt effective in the banking world—he is credited with building up the First National City Bank's foreign business—he nonetheless never had the position of chief executive officer with the bank. When he was president the power lay with the chairman; when he was chairman it reverted back to the president. I was told once, probably apocryphally, that a client approached the bank on a business matter and was taken to meet with both the president and chairman. The chairman, not Moore, was a silent type and apparently did not open his mouth at the meeting; Moore talked loudly and incessantly. At the end of the session the client is alleged to have said that it would be hard to do business with this bank where the chairman never talked and the president never stopped. In any event Moore's leadership of the Metropolitan board had its effective phase when he succeeded Anthony Bliss as president. Bliss had been forced to resign his post because of a board sharply divided on the merits and expenses of maintaining a national company of young singers touring the country under the name of the Metropolitan Opera National Company. Moore came into a financial crisis of enormous proportions, a crisis he inheirited from Bliss, and he set about an emergency fund drive that in short order had raised over seven million dollars to bail out the mistakes and errors in judgment that had haunted the organization ever since its move to Lincoln Center. Following this success he and Wadmond were chiefly responsible for zeroing in on Gentele and having his appointment approved. With Gentele's death the fire went out of Wadmond, and Moore, after an initial spurt of leadership in the summer of 1972, spent less and less time on Metropolitan affairs. His enemies on the board were soon joined by others who realized that he was not giving guidance, and board reaction was to turn to new leadership. The only problem was that there was not really any strength to turn to.

One of the louder and more constant talkers was, and still is, as far as I know, J. William Fisher of Gramma Fisher Foundation fame. Bill Fisher prides himself on being a composer and widely knowledgeable on opera, theater, and painting. He is generous to opera companies, giving new productions to both the big ones in America and the regional groups and an occasional foray overseas. His gift of *Death in Venice* to Covent Garden made it possible for us to use their production, and his regional company *Ring* cycle, performing Andrew Porter's new translation into English, has been making a big hit wherever it is done. But Bill Fisher fancies himself a modern Medici and wants to dictate exactly what kind of a production should be done, who should design, direct, conduct, and sing. At the Metropolitan, with its ectoplasmic leadership, he began to get his way out of pure inertia on the part of most of the others.

In the spring of 1974 George Moore was replaced with William Rockefeller, a charming, proper man, cousin to the "other" Rockefellers, with very little imagination and lacking in leadership verve. It was soon evident that he was depending for his views and information on a combination of Fisher and James S. Smith, who was determined on a reorganization that decentralized all authority and set up the Met along the lines of new multinational corporations. Fisher is erratic in his day-to-day dealings with people; Smith is all ice, a perfect product of the new faceless society. More and more I felt the antipathy between this group and myself. Nothing was ever specifically brought out; it was all vague and amorphous, confirming my growing feelings that they had no plans but focused on the need to do something for the sake of doing something and, I suppose, demonstrating to the outside world, particularly the financial one, that they were on top of their problems.

The eeriest part of all was their collective reaction to any success the house might have. With each opera that was well received, either a new production or revival, the silence that descended was monumental. The bigger the success the greater the quiet. Some individuals, such as Francis Goelet, Michael Forrestal, Nin Ryan, Vera Gibbs, and Lil Phipps, would call or write after something particularly exciting but most of them never made any comments. It was almost as if they were hoping for a disaster; fortunately they were to be disappointed.

All the vacillation and on-again-off-again talk did culminate in one decision: to bring in a trustee as chief executive officer and to place the responsibility for the professional operation of the company in his hands, together with an administrative committee that would approve or disapprove anything he might wish to do. The board would now take command; the operation was too big for an impresario and could be run only by the trustees themselves. This decision resulted in the sudden appointment of Anthony Bliss as executive director, a move that was announced to me the same afternoon that it was being presented for approval to a board meeting. A few days before Rockefeller had come to tell me for "humanitarian reasons" that such a move was about to happen, again with no explanation or reasons.

The afternoon of Bliss's appointment both Rockefeller and the then chairman of the executive committee, Francis Goelet, came to see me to break the news and give me the draft of a press release that was to be distributed at a special press conference later that afternoon. I told both gentlemen that it was obvious they were dissatisfied with what I'd done and that I intended to resign right there and then. Goelet looked at me very carefully and acting as spokesman said that he very much hoped that I would not do that. He emphasized that the day-to-day operations of the theater would continue to be my responsibility but that I would now report to Bliss and that this should make it easier to cope with the numerous problems that modern life and finance had brought to the traditional desk of the general manager. I told them I would think about it. They needed to know my decision in thirty minutes and I told them I would let them know.

When they left my office I sat staring straight ahead. All the fascinations and vexations came pouring into my mind, how much had indeed happened since my first day as assistant manager-elect in January, 1972, how the heartache and "thousand natural shocks" had been more than offset by the glories of the company and our work together. I was hurt, bewildered, puzzled, angry. There was a knock on my door and Bliss walked in, looking pale, bedraggled, and nervous. He took a chair opposite me. I didn't say anything for a moment and then rose and asked him if he would like my chair and my job. He protested mightily that this was not the case, that he had been asked to take on his new assignment only days before, that he did not know whether or not it was "five minutes of midnight or five minutes past," and it was obvious that he was in no state to take on the full responsibility. It had been rumored for many years that Bliss harbored ambitions to succeed Bing as general manager but he had left his board presidency under a cloud and until this moment had been relegated to the sidelines. Now he was back, bewilderingly, perhaps, but back nonetheless, and I sensed he needed time to get his feet under him before assuming authority.

But it was not because of this that I stayed. It was because there were still major projects to be completed: the new *Boris Godunov*, the revamped *La Forza del Destino*, Beverly Sills's debut, and the three-week trip to Japan. These were all plans that I had started or was carrying out based on previous work with Gentele and Kubelik. There were the 1975-76 and 1976-77 seasons to finish up. There were the negotiations with Levine to complete his arrangements to become music director. There was the money that needed to be found for all the new production plans. There were so many things under way and so much needing to be done that I could not, in all conscience or desire, simply walk away from them because my wings had been shortened. I was, despite all shortcomings, involved in a job I loved, a job that I was doing better and better and that was the culmination of a life-long dream. Not many people are as lucky. I saw no reason to throw it all away without at least giving the new arrangement a chance to work. I suppose in my heart I knew that it wouldn't and that as soon as it could be done legally I would be out of the picture. I am definitely not the Bliss-Rockefeller-Fisher-Smith type and they were now asserting themselves even though they were doing so without any clear-cut idea of what they wanted to do. I told Bliss I'd give it a try. He seemed relieved.

Later that day Rockefeller, Bliss, and I went to the press conference where Rockefeller, not a terribly articulate man at best, was soon flashing anger at some of the questions and leading himself into some pretty treacherous territory. The press had turned out in droves and were squeezed into the lower press office of the house. Rockefeller, Bliss, and I were lined up against a wall, somewhat like a police lineup, and the questions were coming thick and fast. Rockefeller left after a few minutes, to attend a Guild reception ironically going on just over our heads, leaving Bliss and me to carry on as best we could. Bliss, too, was tongue-tied and matters were getting out of hand. Finally Bill Bender of *Time* asked who was going to be artistically responsible for the company and who was going to have the final say about casting, which, he observed, was in his opinion not consistently good. I picked him up on this and reminded him that casting and artistic matters were always going to be subjected to Monday morning quarterbacking. I reminded him that his magazine had dismissed *Death in Venice* with a short paragraph while *Newsweek* had devoted several pages and photographs to what its critic felt to be a work of monumental importance to the opera stage. I said that this was a perfect example of the differences so valuable in art and that Bliss and I were going to work out a division of duties that would create a partnership between us and that I welcomed his help. The question was asked about a music director and I stated that this was a high-priority item to us both and that I hoped we would have an announcement about this before the season was over. Bliss seemed to welcome my intervention and we closed the meeting as reluctant but acceptable shotgun colleagues.

There is no doubt that Bliss was a bitter pill to swallow. He was a retread and his appointment had been handed to me in a graceless manner, except for Goelet's quiet explanation, and above all it was done without any real plan of where the organization was heading. It was change for change's sake and seemed to be leading nowhere.

The next day the media was filled with stories and Bliss and I were asked to pose for a whole new set of photographs for the national news magazines. The New York *Times* speculated that with his appointment tensions would grow at the opera house, but on the whole he was received as a good partner who might be an effective teammate in coping with the myriad problems faced by the company. It was as good a public launching as could be expected and it now remained for us to get on with the work.

An office was set up for Bliss within a few days of his appointment but in the beginning he occupied it very little. First he became ill with a recurrence of a heart condition that had been bothering him for over a year and when he was around he pretty much went his own way. We met from time to time but he was on a campaign of his own to explore the house and its future. He rarely attended performances but when he did it was not with too great a degree of comfort. We exchanged a series of memos on various administrative matters but it was through one major New York critic I learned that he was pursuing another conductor to become music director of the company. I talked to him about this and suggested that what he had in mind was not a good idea and that it was my understanding that I was to remain responsible for artistic matters and that if he had ideas in this direction he would be better off discussing them with me first. We were always polite to each other but never in any sense intimate. I felt his appointment should be properly explained to the radio public and the week after it was announced I went on the air with a careful and cordial welcome to him. This, too, he viewed with suspicion, although he did thank me for covering this important area of our audience.

Then came the shenanigans that went on with Levine's appointment. In this instance Bliss was negotiating behind my back with Levine's agent, who was delighted to do so, and neatly sabotaging an agreement that Levine and I had worked on for over a year.

I felt it was wrong—and still do—that the ultimate responsibility for

artistic affairs should be in the hands of a music director. I planned to
have an artistic team of Levine, John Dexter as director of productions, and myself making the basic decisions, but Bliss was willing to
turn over all artistic decisions to Levine as a musician, on the premise
that the opera house was basically musical. This idea delighted Levine's agent, who had fought for the same thing unsuccessfully for
Kubelik, whom he also represented, and it went on without my knowledge.

Levine and I would talk one line; Bliss and the agent another. I discovered all this when Levine began to get evasive and the Metropolitan's attorney, to whom I'd turned over my version of Levine's contract, told me that he was not authorized to discuss the matter any
longer with me. Here's your coat, here's your hat. What's your hurry?

Bliss's appointment was announced on November 21. A few days
before, during the thoroughly disagreeable preambles to his coming,
Betty and I had been invited to the White House for a state dinner in
honor of Bruno Kreisky, Chancellor of Austria. We were there at the
suggestion of former United States Ambassador to Austria John
Humes, whom I'd gotten to know during my two winters in Vienna
with Bernstein. Kreisky is an old friend of Bernstein and we met just
before the first general election that brought him to power. I was fascinated by his clear mind and plans for turning Austria into what he described as the Switzerland of the east.

The White House bid was a "must" and we flew down in the afternoon and put up at the Mayflower Hotel. At the appointed time we
went through the elaborate, old-fashioned, but strangely moving and
impressive ritual of the reception and dinner.

Right after the meal and toasts we all rose to move to the East Room
for the entertainment. The tables in the dining room were very close
together and all during dinner I felt the back of my chair touching the
one behind. When I got up I turned too quickly and collided with
Henry Kissinger. I apologized for the bumping and he smiled. I put out
my hand and introduced myself. "Oh, yes," he replied. "You're the
one who runs the opera." Now it was my turn to smile. "Well," he
went on, "your job is a lot more permanent than mine!" And he turned
to walk out of the room. If you only knew, Mr. Secretary, I thought to
myself. If you only knew. The irony was almost too much.

I did not have too much time to brood over Bliss. *Boris Godunov*
was in rehearsals and these were tense days, mostly because of sparse
communication between August Everding, the director, and Thomas
Schippers, the maestro. Everding and I had worked hard with Ming

Cho Lee, the designer, to evolve a *Boris* that kept the dramatic tension throughout the evening.

Everding felt that most *Boris* productions lost their impact by the constant wait between scenes and we agreed that we should use the Met stage's mechanical facilities to their utmost to avoid pauses and let the action flow its natural course. We were committed to using the second Lamm edition of the score, which was really the 1872 version of the opera as revised by the composer himself. This decision had been made by Kubelik in our early pre-planning and I saw no reason to change it. The Rimsky-Korsakov and Shostakovich versions seemed to assume that the composer did not know what he wanted from an orchestral standpoint. Lamm, the musicologist, and other experts felt that Moussorgsky knew very well what he wanted and was, to a large extent, ahead of his time. The only problems presented by this version had to do with the actual sound as it would reflect in a theater as large as the Metropolitan. Too sparse and skimpy an orchestration would sound just that way and Schippers felt that we had to modify the score or beef it up in a way that would give the composer's sound to the audience sitting anywhere in the vast auditorium. The trouble was that he kept changing his mind on details and at every rehearsal he would make new changes and every night the librarians would be piling up overtime with modifications that had to be in all the orchestral parts by the next morning. This meant that every orchestra-stage rehearsal was a stop-and-start affair and progress was very slow.

We had assembled a splendid cast. Martti Talvela, the Finnish basso, was the Boris; Paul Plishka, Pimen; Harry Theyard, the False Dimitri; Donald Gramm, Varlaam; Andrea Velis, the Simpleton; and as the Polish princess, Marina, Mignon Dunn.

The Polish Act, Act II, presented some special problems for which we found a wonderful solution. Early in the summer Lincoln Kirstein asked me who was doing the choreography and I told him that we had not decided on anyone. "Why don't you ask Balanchine?" he suggested. "Balanchine!" I replied. "But you know there really is very little to do and I'm sure Balanchine wouldn't be interested." "Why don't you ask him!" came the reply. "I think he might be." I wasted no time and went to see Balanchine that same afternoon. When we were together I told him that it was time he returned to the Metropolitan, where he had not worked for some years. "Metropolitan," he said, "Metropolitan. I love Metropolitan!" "Good," I rejoined, "because next year we are doing the first new production of *Boris Godunov* since 1913." "Oh, *Boris*," he said. "I love *Boris*!" And he began to sing the opera from the beginning. As he sang he acted out all the parts. I was fascinated until he suddenly stopped. "*Boris!*" he said. "*Boris!* Very boring, *Boris!*" "Boring?" I replied. "How can you say boring? It is one of the most colorful, most moving and glorious operas in the whole repertoire!" And I went on extolling the virtues of the piece. When I had about completed my colorful phrasing I paused for a second and ended by saying, "Besides which, we are doing it in Russian!" "Ah, Russian!" he replied, raising his eyebrows. "Russian you say!" And he paused. "Especially boring!" I must have looked nonplussed because a moment later we were talking about the Polish scenes and I asked him if he would consider staging the polonaise. "But you don't need me for that," he said. "A polonaise is just a polonaise. I'll help your ballet mistress with it but there is no ballet. It's just a polonaise!" And he gestured with his hands and arms to show me what he meant. "But I do need you," I said. "I would like the polonaise to be the best." "I'll think about it," he said. "I'll call you tomorrow," I replied.

The next day I called and he agreed to come. Everding and Schippers were delighted and so was the corps de ballet and all was well until the first rehearsal. At that momentous occasion Balanchine did exactly what he said he would. He staged the polonaise the way a polonaise was supposed to look, only in the setting and lighting it looked strangely like two lines of people walking up and down two flights of stairs. Everding asked me to come into the auditorium, which I did, and I saw for myself what he had done. "Do you like it?" I asked him. "No no, not at all!" came the reply. "I think it's much too static. I'm very unhappy." "Well, why don't you speak to him about it! I agree with you and I know George will be interested in your comments." "Me talk to Balanchine!" he said. "Me talk to the great master? Oh, no. No. I couldn't do that." We were then joined by Schippers, who had his eyes glued to the stage. "Do you like what Balanchine has done?" I asked. "Not at all," he replied. "It will look too flat." "Have you said anything to him?" I asked. "Oh, no, of course not," came the reply. I looked at both of them. "Obviously this is a job for the general manager," I said, "but before I talk to him, do you have some specific suggestions you wish to make?" "Of course I do," said Everding. "I think he can do something beautiful and I'd like to tell him what I think." "Stay right there or go to my office after the rehearsal. I'll see him as quickly as I can." And I made my way backstage.

By the time I reached the area his part of the rehearsal was over and he'd left the theater. I crossed the plaza to the state theater and went straight to his office. He was standing in front of his desk looking down at a sheaf of papers. He looked up when he saw me in the doorway. "George," I began, "I was at your rehearsal." "I told you it was just a polonaise," he began. "Simply a polonaise." And he began the gestures again with his hands and arms. "But George," I said, "I know it's a simple polonaise and I'm not asking for a ballet but I am suggesting that when the curtain goes up on a dance that has been prepared by Balanchine the audience must see something that has your trademark. But don't listen to me. Will you see Everding? He would like to talk to you but he's too scared to do so." "Scared?" Balanchine's eyebrows went right up into his forehead. "Scared? Of me?" "Right," I replied. "Scared of you." "But that is ridiculous," he went on. "I know," I said, "but that's the way he feels. Now, he would like to talk to you. He has some ideas that he wants to discuss but will not do so unless you would be willing to receive him." "Of course I will!" came the reply. "Good," I said. "How about twenty minutes from now?" "Okay," he said. "I'll wait here."

I dashed out of his office and over to mine, where I found Everding waiting. "Come on, Gus," I said, "he's waiting for you and anxious to talk." I took him by the arm and led him across the plaza, put him in the backstage elevator of the New York State Theater, and pushed the button for Balanchine's office.

The next day Balanchine was back and in less than thirty minutes had completely restaged the scene. Now it looked elegant and rich and was still a polonaise although with a little sprucing up and dance gestures that made you think you were seeing more than you really were.

On the opening night Balanchine's secretary delivered a letter to me. In it was a wonderful note wishing us all well and two checks: his fee, which he returned, and a check for $2,500 as a gift to the Metropolitan Opera's fund drive. Such is the measure and generosity of the man who, more than any other, has created this country's passion for ballet.

The opening of *Boris* was, indeed, a glorious event. The production worked in every detail and at the end of the opera the audience leapt to its feet and cheered and bravoed for some little time. I finally had to close it off by ordering the iron curtain lowered to prevent our going into overtime. There was a party after the performance in the Grand Tier, sponored by the Guild, and the atmosphere was golden with success and pleasure. I sat back watching the proceedings until I was asked to speak and when I rose was treated to a long and loud ovation. I felt very good about this.

The next day the critics were unanimous in their praise, one even going so far as to say that if Schuyler Chapin ever needed a memorial to himself he had it in this version of *Boris Godunov*. While basking in this heady wine, however, I kept realizing that such days were numbered and that I better not begin to take them too seriously.

Just a month before *Boris*, Vladimir Horowitz had given his benefit recital for us, the first one ever held in the opera house, and Herbert von Karajan had been one of our guests. It happened that shortly thereafter *Boris* had its dress rehearsal and Karajan asked to come. We went into the auditorium together and he greeted various members of the technical staff with whom he had worked on his *Das Rheingold* and *Die Walküre*.

I was extremely anxious about the rehearsal: it was only the day before that the entire opera had been run without stopping and there were complex moves of the chorus and the stage wagons that needed split-second timing. I needn't have worried: the Metropolitan stage crew and staff are the best in the world and the show unfolded as if it had been running for months. Karajan rarely took his eyes from the stage and at the end of the first act seemed pleased by what he saw. We returned to my office, where I had a sandwich waiting. He had a doctor's appointment and was not planning to stay for the rest of the performance. "Too bad you didn't take my Salzburg production," he commented. "We might have," I replied, "only you burnt up all the scenery." "Ah well," he said, "but this version will not work. The public will not like the starkness and the Lamm orchestration." And he smiled as we shook hands.

I thought of the hours we had spent in cockpits, particularly in the cockpit of that Piper Apache while he was learning to fly. I remembered standing in front of a record shop window in Washington and looking at a display of his recordings, when he pointed to one of them, a symphony with the Berlin Philharmonic, and said quietly but oh so passionately how the Berlin post was the only one he'd ever really wanted and he had it, now, for life, forever. All these thoughts rushed through my mind as we shook hands. "I hope you're wrong," I said. I walked him to the side exit from my office and into the lobby. "Goodbye," I called after him. He turned and waved. He was wrong. Very wrong. I was delighted.

XXII

Sills, Tucker, Nilsson

Von Karajan's reminder of the Salzburg *Boris* scenery turned my attention, later that afternoon, toward another big project that was nearing completion in the scenery shops: the sets and costumes for Rossini's *L'Assedio di Corinto*. As almost everyone in the opera and music world, and many others outside of these two spheres, knew by this time *L'Assedio di Corinto (Siege of Corinth)* was to be the opera that brought Beverly Sills to the Metropolitan.

Three years before, when Gentele and I had picked this opera for Sills's debut, my first order of business had been to contact La Scala and see if its production was still intact. It wasn't. The costumes were mostly available, having been used in another production, but the scenery had been destroyed. Nicola Benois's drawings were there and I asked that they be held for me to see. I had a spring meeting in Milan and thought to combine the meeting and negotiations for *Siege*. I did. The costumes were, for the most part, salvageable and the drawings for the sets were beautiful but not a single piece remained. I contacted Nicola Benois and invited him to New York to see the Metropolitan Opera House and confer about the sets. He came in the fall of 1972 and I explained carefully to him that we wanted a painted set that could be handled both in the house and on tour. I warned him that most designers had a tendency to look at the Metropolitan's facilities and get carried away with all the machinery and gadgets, coming up with drawings that incorporated some or all of the mechanical marvels at the expense of simplicity and without thinking that each production had to play in a repertory situation.

Benois seemed to understand and after some weeks I got a call one morning from David Reppa, in charge of our design shops, asking me to come upstairs at my convenience and look at Benois's models that had just arrived. I did so and was presented with more scenery than Switzerland. There were towers and ramps, fortresses, boats, and ships enough to serve a medium-sized navy. In no way was this what had been asked for and I wrote Benois that same day. He replied that this was what he felt to be right for the Met and I wrote back saying that what he sent was directly opposite from what we discussed. Our letters went back and forth for almost eight weeks and finally I wrote that if he could not give us what we wanted I would have to seek out other designers. This ended the matter. Within a few days I had a note saying that he had rethought the problems and would probably be able to give us what we wanted.

Before *L'Assedio di Corinto* actually got on the stage, however, we had the little matter of a *Ring* cycle, the first one in twelve years, and a revamped *La Forza del Destino* with Levine in the pit and Dexter as director. It was supposed to have been a new production but I canceled that idea as a money saver and because the new designs and production ideas were not acceptable to any of us. The project had been put in the hands of Nat Merrill and Bobby O'Hearn and somehow these good people could not agree about how the opera should be done. I had the feeling they both took the assignment because Gentele had asked them to and were not happy about it. I think I was right because when I withdrew the whole thing there was very little wailing and gnashing of teeth.

I thought we should follow the same route as the last season's *Don Giovanni* and refurbish the old Eugene Berman production. Unlike *Don Giovanni*, though, Berman's *Forza* had never been really successful. For some reason the Inn scene had been completely cut and the Met version played all kinds of tricks with the original. Levine had already decided to restore musical validity to the work and when Merrill and O'Hearn stepped down I asked Dexter to take it on. He turned to David Reppa to help reconstruct what might have been the Inn scene if Berman had finished his sketches and in addition decided to completely relight the whole opera. The costumes all had to be new because of our costume warehouse fire of the spring of 1974. This gave Peter J. Hall, whose stunning work on *Boris* had been greatly acclaimed, a chance to exercise further his imagination and talents. We treated the production as if it were a new one, allowing maximum rehearsal time, and this was imperative for lots of reasons, not the least of which was that Jon Vickers was cast as Don Alvaro, only his third Verdi part at the Met and his first performance anywhere of this particular role. He was surrounded with strength: Martina Arroyo as Leonora, Cornell MacNeill as Don Carlo di Vargas, Bonaldo Giaiotti as Padre Guardiano, Nedda Casei as Preziosilla, and Gabriel Bacquier as Fra Melitone, a part he, too, was doing for the first time. Vickers was nervous and tense and we had to send a coach to his home in Bermuda to help him master the role.

While *Forza* was in rehearsal onstage two dramatic deaths in the Metropolitan family occurred within a week of each other. Milton Cross, for over forty years the voice of the Metropolitan on the Saturday afternoon broadcasts, died after a short illness. Cross had come to represent "opera" to millions of people in the United States and Canada and his passing brought forth a flood of messages from all over the world. His funeral was held on January 6, with the church packed with celebrities, members of the company, friends, and plain music lovers. Two days afterwards I received a phone call in the late afternoon announcing that Richard Tucker had died of a heart attack in Indiana. Like everyone in the music world I was stunned by this news.

Not two months before, as part of an experimental program to establish solid television techniques for transmitting programs of live performance on the stage, we had taped *Cavalleria Rusticana* and *Pagliacci*. Tucker sang Canio in the latter, a role that he loved, and it was an especially brilliant performance. I remember thinking at the time that it was almost like a lightbulb about to burn out. At the end he was totally exhausted and stood backstage before bowing, bent over, trying to catch his breath. Tucker was not the kind of man given to backstage temperament and I thought he looked as exhausted as he obviously was.

Now he was dead, one of the great tenors of his time and a mainstay at the Metropolitan for twenty-nine years. He and I had known each other for over twenty years: at one time I helped take care of his concert bookings and later, at Columbia Records, I supervised his recordings. We got along well, although we often disagreed, and when I came to the Met he was very welcoming, even though constantly referring to me as the "Kid."

Of all his disappointments, and there weren't too many, his greatest was that he never got to sing *La Juive* at the Metropolitan. A strong and religious Jew, Tucker wanted New York to see his interpretation of Eleazar, the rabbi, in this curious but strangely moving and uneven opera by Jacques Halévy. He would go anywhere to perform the work and one such engagement caused us to have a real falling out.

Barcelona had offered him a production in 1974 that meant he had to step out of his Metropolitan contract two weeks before he was properly finished. It happened that the particular two weeks were extremely complicated, both with the repertory onstage and the final and intense rehearsals of *I Vespri Siciliani.* Tucker was singing in *Simon Boccanegra* and asked to be released from his last two scheduled performances. I had to refuse as I had no replacement for him except his cover, William Lewis, who was also covering Nicola Gedda as Arrigo in *Vespri.* Tucker himself was due to sing Arrigo at a later point in the season. I explained how I couldn't release him from the *Boccanegras* but he ignored my comments. He sent his agent to talk, and his press agent, and I told both the same thing.

The matter seemed settled until the afternoon of the *Boccanegra* broadcast when quite by accident I learned that he was leaving that night for Barcelona regardless of what we had discussed. I went to his dressing room to find out if this was true and he admitted it. I told him that he couldn't do that to the house and he told me not to worry, that Lewis was all prepared and would sing splendidly. I told him that I was sure he would be fine but that was not the point, the public had been told Tucker, had bought tickets for Tucker, and were entitled to hear Tucker, and that Tucker had a very firm contract. "Don't worry, kid," came the reply. "Everything will be fine." "Richard," I said, measuring my words carefully, "if you leave here now you leave here for good. This is a flagrant violation of your agreement and if I were doing the same to you you'd have me in court in the morning. I know how you feel about *La Juive* and we have been talking about doing it for you here, but whether we do or not is beside the point. If a contract is to be worth anything it must be honored by both sides." He stared at me. "You'll be okay, kid," he said again. "You'll see. Everything will be fine." I told him I meant what I said. And I did. He left for Spain the next day and I fired him within the hour.

All hell broke loose. Mrs. August Belmont telephoned and later wrote me that I was "impetuous." Members of the board with whom I'd had almost no personal contact began calling and asking what I'd done. Subscribers, finding out somehow through the operatic underground, began assailing me for assassination of character, imperialistic tendencies, and even lack of sympathy to singers. At home the phone began ringing at 3:00 and 4:00 AM with threatening voices saying: "Chapin, get out. You've ruined the Met." This went on for enough nights that we finally called the phone company and had cutoff switches put on our instruments. We were reluctant to do this, having a family living in different places, but it was either that or not sleeping.

Despite everything, I felt my position was correct. A contract is a contract and to me that means both the letter and the spirit. If there are problems, of course one wants to try solving them in an understanding manner. I did many times with many different artists. I was even accused of being "too nice," although I never understood what that really meant. But in the case of Richard Tucker he had done something unprofessional after all avenues to granting his wishes had been explored and found wanting. I saw no reason that the Metropolitan Opera should be made to suffer. We made plans to get along without him in 1975.

During the summer of 1974, well after the 1973-74 season and before the beginning of the 1974-75, the barrage of pressure died down. At the same time we realized that we had hoisted ourselves on our own petards. Whatever Tucker's unprofessional behavior, there were simply not enough world-class tenors around to fill our needs and quite apart from what I believe was our correct position we needed him badly. I began to hear that he was truly sorry for his actions particularly since, I think, he found that the "kid" was not going to be budged.

His agent, Michael Reis, asked to see me and when he came into my office I held up my hand in a stop-gesture. "Michael," I said, "no pressure. I've been through a lot about this and I won't submit to threats of any kind. Your client was in the wrong and hurt this house." "I know," replied Reis, "and so does he. I've come around to talk about the problems. You've no idea what's happened. Tucker loves the Met, adores it; it has been his life. He knows he was wrong and wants to apologize. He'll never do such a thing again." "But I think he will," I replied. "He did the same thing to Bing once. I know all about it. If he's now done it twice who's to say that he won't do it a third or fourth time when he wants to do something else? I'll tell you what we'll do. I want a letter from Tucker, acknowledging what he did and stating in no uncertain terms that he will never repeat such an unprofessional act. I want the letter written in a way that if he ever should try something like that again I will simply turn it over to the press as is." "Agreed," said Reis. "I'll talk to him and get back to you." Which he did in short order and this was followed by a visit from Tucker and the incident was shelved. We proceeded with the 1974-75 season plans that included Canios in the first part of the seasons and Arrigos in the spring, the spring that he was never to live to see.

His funeral was held on the main stage of the opera house and the auditorium was packed with loving and devoted fans. The family asked me to speak for the Metropolitan, and in a sense for his professional life. Two cantors from two synagogues that had been a part of his life were also included in the ceremonies, as was his Great Neck, Long Island, rabbi and Cardinal Cooke of the Catholic Archdiocese of New York, a long-time friend. It was a very moving occasion and when the great gold curtain descended slowly at the end of the services it was a perfect symbol of the closing out of an extraordinary life of a poor boy from the Lower East side who had risen to great artistic and personal fame. We miss him now; we always will.

The revamped *Forza* had its first performance on January 17 and was a marked improvement over the old one. It was a success with both audiences and critics and was proof to me once again, as if I needed proof, that we had the right man in John Dexter to supervise the stage side of the Metropolitan's artistic affairs.

With *Forza* the stage was now clear for the preparations for the *Ring* cycle, the first at the Metropolitan in twelve years. We planned it carefully, trying to keep the casts as consistent as possible. Paul Jaretzski of the artistic administration was back at his Wagnerian post juggling Rheinmaidens, Walküres, and the other assorted dwarfs and demons. He prepared a schedule that showed every part, both large and small, cast with, in most cases, two cover artists.

We were taking as few chances as possible, particularly since we seemed to be in a period of widespread illness and cancellations. But the best-laid operatic plans have an uncanny knack of going awry; a few weeks before rehearsals got going I received a cable from Leonie Rysanek announcing that she had to enter a hospital for an operation and regretfully could not be with us for the season.

This left us a prime hole; Rysanek was to sing Sieglindes to Nilsson Brünnhildes in *Die Walküre* among other things, and her absence was a big problem. While pondering the situation Jaretizki reminded me that Nilsson had once expressed interest in singing Sieglinde in New York and why didn't I ask if she was still interested. We looked at the schedule and realized that we could do this with some performances if we could find an acceptable substitute Brünnhilde. We thought of Janis Martin, who earlier in the season, while singing Marie in *Wozzeck* had told us that she was relatively free around our *Ring* period and if anything went wrong to let her know.

I immediately called Nilsson, who was delighted to sing some Sieglindes, and we contacted Janis Martin, who was indeed free to come from Germany and we were quickly able to recast in an exciting manner. That meant the public would hear Nilsson and Vickers in *Die Walküre*, as Sigmund and Sieglinde, about as powerful a bit of international opera casting as one could want. It was strong enough to make up for the disappointment over Rysanek.

At the first *Walküre* performance Nilsson and Vickers were both in top form and Jon became so excited and involved that when he pulled the sword from the tree he did so with such gusto and strength that the blade snapped off and cartwheeled over and over, landing, thank God, at the edge of the stage before tumbling into the orchestra pit. Such was the force of their performances, however, that no sound broke the tension. At the curtain calls Nilsson was a bit shaken. It seemed that the blade had whipped past only millimeters away from her nose and would have hit her if she had not happened to step back at that particular moment. Considering her accident the previous season with the stairs in *Götterdämmerung* her nervousness was understandable!

There were some memorable performances during the cycle, not the least of which was the final Nilsson *Götterdämmerung* on the Saturday broadcast of March 29. I had a feeling that this might be a very special performance because it might just mark her last one in the United States for some time to come.

Over many years Nilsson and the Internal Revenue Service had been having at each other on the matter of taxes and by 1975 quite a large sum was in contention. The matter was in the tax court, where it had been for some time and all of us thought that her lawyer was going to continue the fight. Quite suddenly, however, he pleaded "nolo contendere" and I had a hunch that Nilsson's American performance days were numbered. We had discussed the 1975-76 season and agreed on *Elektra* but she would not talk about plans beyond that and indicated that she was not even certain whether or not she would be coming back in 1976. With the "nolo contendere" now in the courts I was certain these were to be her farewell performances, if not forever, then for quite some time, and I think she felt the same way. Those who heard the broadcast that afternoon will never forget the vigor and strength of her performance and with the Immolation scene she surpassed even her own previous excellence. The ovation that greeted her at the end is given to few and she was touched and moved by it. Someone took a photograph of the two of us together during the curtain calls and I cherish this picture as a special souvenir of one of the greatest dramatic sopranos of our age.

She left the theater that afternoon and flew out of the country. Shortly thereafter word came that she was unavailable for the 1975-76 season in America and as far as I know there are no new plans for her return.

It seems to me that the whole problem of foreign artists' taxes should be re-examined realistically. I've never known one of them who is not willing to pay taxes but the 30 percent now extracted from their paychecks, regardless of problems, is too much. It's true, of course, that when the artist leaves the country he or she can file for a rebate but the process takes forever, at least a year, and in the meantime the person does without.

In Europe it is understood that a percentage is taken and that's that, but here the government reserves the right to re-examine returns and extract extra penalties and generally makes it both unpleasant and unprofitable for the foreign singer to come. In the days when the U.S. dollar was the stable currency everyone wanted to sing here regardless of taxes but now we are in competition, and sharp competition at that, with an economically viable Europe and in many cases it no longer pays artists to come here. Of course some, the wiser ones, always will, because there are side benefits that are of enormous importance. Each trip helps plug the artists' recordings and keeps their names in front of the music public. But it is becoming more and more difficult to get the good ones to come and to come for any length of time. And what they lose in taxes they want to make up by increased fees.

The whole subject of opera stars' fees is one of constant gossip and speculation. I was severely criticized for giving in to pressures and to a certain extent the criticism is not without merit. But there are extenuating circumstances that I'm sure my successors are presently finding difficult.

The international opera market was jolted mightly in the early 1970s when Rolf Liebermann of the Hamburg Opera moved to Paris to take over the opera there under a mandate from then French President Pompidou to create a world-recognized company, second to none. For decades the Paris Opera was a joke; the question was only how bad each night was in relation to all the other bad nights and Liebermann had his job cut out for him. He had offered me a position in Paris before Gentele spoke to me about the Met, but for many reasons, including my wretched schoolboy French, I thought it wise to decline. Liebermann knew that he would have to spend a lot of money to get what Pompidou wanted and he set to his task with vigor. Fees shot up all over the world as Paris outbid everyone and in doing so drove the basic rates up faster than twice the percentage of worldwide inflation.

At the Met the top fee was $4,000 a performance but this was soon not enough and every major star wanted to reopen the fee question. The problem was simple: pay me what I want or get somebody else. Since the international star market of opera singers is relatively small, perhaps some thirty or forty people, the bargaining power is in their hands and they take full advantage of their new clout. It was a question of pay or no play. If you run a major opera house you pay if you want to give your audiences what they expect. The trustees can wring their collective hands all they like but they had better deal with realities.

I understand that this point was one of the major indications that I was supposed to be a bad administrator. Perhaps so, but in my three years, nearly every major singer of consequence appeared on that stage, as they had done in the past, and they didn't do it for love of the art alone. I don't blame singers. They have a relatively short time span in which to catch their golden ring and they are entitled to everything they can get. Opera managers must bargain like hell, and I did, sometimes even won, but in the last analysis you needed them more than they needed you and some compromise had to be found. It usually was.

Among the roles that Nilsson had to give up in order to take on Sieglinde was Tosca, no easy part, and I wanted to bring someone who would stir up a lot of interest. At lunch one day with Marilyn Horne, in a preliminary discussion for *Le Prophète* for the 1976-77 season, she asked me what I was going to do about the newly vacated Toscas. Before I could answer she told me that only two weeks before she had heard Magda Olivero sing the role in Texas and that the performance was breathtaking. "But Olivero must be in her sixties," I said. "How could she possibly both sing and act Tosca?" With that Horne took off on such a complete critical analysis on the lady's style and technique that I was drawn to listen to every word. After lunch I mulled over what had been said and made a few calls to check Horne's story. Everything seemed to jibe and I was astounded to find out that Olivero had never sung at the Metropolitan.

Hers is a fascinating career, one that has gone on for a long time with great stretches of interruption, and her only appearances in the New York area in recent seasons had been in Newark, New Jersey, with the New Jersey Opera. I cabled her in Spain and asked whether or not she was free in early April and interested in singing Tosca at the Met. I had been told that she was a very great lady and expected to be treated as such. Her reply was gracious: yes, she was free and she was interested, and could I tell her with whom she would be singing and how much rehearsal time was possible. I cabled her that James King was her Cavaradossi and Ingvar Wixell her Scarpia, and that she would have as much room rehearsal as she required but that there would not be time for anything with orchestra or on the stage. There was a pause in our cabling but after a few days she wired again that she understood the situation and would be delighted to come.

Her first day in the theater was unforgettable. Bodo Igesz, who was responsible for the *Tosca* staging, came to me almost with tears in his eyes about what a sensational actress she was and how she was deeply moving in the role. Shortly thereafter Jan Behr, who was doing the musical preparation, came to my office to say the same thing. They were both stunned by Olivero's artistry and this quickly got all over the house. By the first night there was not a ticket to be had for any of the Olivero performances and when, on April 3, she actually made her debut the curtain calls went on for half an hour. *Tosca* being a relatively short work, there was plenty of time and no one worried about overtime. Olivero had, at long last, made her debut at the Metropolitan.

The big end-of-season excitement, though, was reserved for the long-awaited debut of Beverly Sills. As much has been written about this event in the world press as any in recent Metropolitan history, with the possible exception of Maria Callas's first night, and the marvelous part about it was that it measured up to every inch of the expectant publicity. We had many problems to overcome, none of them with the star, but when April 7, 1975, arrived history was made and it will always stand in the record books.

L'Assedio di Corinto is a very tricky work, the first that Rossini wrote to the specifications of the Paris Opera. At its premiere on October 9, 1826, the Corinthians were battling the Turks on the stage but in real life a similar and even more serious affair was taking place in the Peloponnese. Greeks were fighting to liberate their land from the Turks. As J. F. Mastroianni wrote in *Opera News:*

> It was not by coincidence that the libretto by Alexandre Soumet and Luigi Balocchi reflected this contemporary political strife. Public sentiment in Paris during the 1820s supported the Greek struggle for independence. *The Siege of Corinth* came to the stage not only for the pleasure of the operagoing public but as a reminder of the grave political situation in Greece.

The Siege of Corinth was an adaptation of an earlier work of the composer entitled *Maometto II*, written in Naples in 1820. A study of some thirty-five librettos published between 1826 and 1855 show that following the custom of the day each *Siege* production was tailored to a particular cast. Beginning with an 1830 performance in Rome the opera was subjected to endless changes, and for the next twenty-five years no two performances were identical. Even at the Paris Opera in 1836, only ten years after its premiere, it was performed with substantial changes. Rossini's operas were often modified, sometimes under his supervision and sometimes not. The operas were treated with great flexibility which today no longer seems to be tolerable.

For the Metropolitan Schippers used the 1969 La Scala version, which was, in turn, based on Rossini's Paris revision. He planned further revisions and expansions for New York and this is where the trouble began for it was very difficult for him to settle on a final set of orchestra parts and once again, as with *Boris Godunov*, the candles burned late in the music librarian's office. New parts were distributed to the orchestra almost every day of the rehearsal period. This caused confusion and unhappiness until I finally put my foot down and froze any further changes. While we were fighting these battles we were also coming to a head in our negotiations with CBS Television on the matter of a televised *Look-In* with Danny Kaye. While these highly successful children's programs were done just in the theater the atmosphere was relaxed and easy, but the minute television reared its head everyone became tense, and an expert on what sections of the *Look-In* should be taped. We had a number of long production meetings trying to pick the right opera to excerpt, the right singers to demonstrate vocal ranges, and the right star with whom Danny could do a sketch. The only one who fitted that situation perfectly was Sills, but I did not feel I could ask her to do the program while heavily involved in her own debut.

Our CBS-Danny Kaye talks led down to an impasse. Either we had Sills with Kaye or we could forget the whole idea. I did not want to do this. It had been some little time since the Metropolitan had been seen on any television, let alone on commercial time, and I was determined that we were going to get there. While commercial television is not the answer to the Metropolitan's video needs—it never will be as long as commercial television is aimed primarily at the mass market—it is important to have occasional exposure and we needed it particularly at this time when we were going to be reaching out as far as possible to get our financial message across. We also needed to correct a bad balance of payments in the commercial world. When the Bing Gala ran on CBS-TV it cost almost the highest amount of money per viewer reached in the history of prime-time television and this had left a residue of skepticism about the worth of opera in the mass market. While we were not planning to televise an opera, we were planning to televise a program about opera, and to get our message across we needed as much star power as possible. Sills and Kaye together could supply that but the only problem was that the program was scheduled to be taped the morning after Sills's debut and we all thought that she would be in no mood to come into the house at 11:00 AM following her night before.

As the discussions reached the crisis stage I decided to put the problem to Beverly and see what her reaction might be. Among many other things Sills is passionately interested in the problems of America's artistic institutions and I knew she would realize what a special opportunity this program was for us. We discussed the matter at some length and she listened to what I had to say. After thinking for a few minutes she agreed.

"You know what this means," I said. "It means that you will be onstage for most of the morning and afternoon with almost no time to rest." "Don't say anything more," she replied. "If you do I might change my mind." I didn't open my mouth again, just embraced and thanked her.

The premiere night of *L'Assedio di Corinto* finally arrived. The dressing room area looked like the branch of every florist in New York. Beverly's fellow cast members—Shirley Verrett as Neocle, Justino Diaz as Maometto, and Harry Theyard as Cleomene, in principal parts, and Betsy Norden, Richard T. Gill, Arthur Thompson, and Richard Best, in supporting roles—were as eager as she was but the usual tension found backstage before a debut was missing. In its place was a relaxed atmosphere of good cheer and the general feeling that all was going to go well. If any of the individuals felt otherwise they kept their feelings to themselves. Benois's sets and costumes were magnificent, a tribute to a clever designer who painted beautifully and gave the illusion of masses of impressive scenery when there were, in truth, only about four solid pieces. The house was packed to the walls, every standing-room place having been sold weeks before. Cameramen were all over the place, recording reactions of people in the audience to this special night. When Schippers made his entrance into the pit he was greeted with a warm ovation and when Beverly made her entrance the greeting was stupendous. As the evening wore on the audience began to discover that the opera was not just a display piece for a prima donna but a highly dramatic and musical experience where each of the principals had his or her moment in the sun. Shirley Verrett, in her blue uniform and silver helmet as the young officer Neocle in love with Pamira, was in brilliant form and her solos, duets, and ensembles were greeted with great approval. No one liked that more than Sills: at the end of the evening she shared the triumph equally with her and it was obvious by looking at the two of them that their respect and affection were mutual.

When the final curtain fell, pandemonium broke loose backstage.

The crew was moving to strike the set and the television news cameras and well-wishers were making this difficult. Finally the head of the night crew called out, "Mrs. Chapin! Will you please help me clear the stage!" Betty looked a little startled but did as he asked and we moved the hordes back to the dressing room area.

In her dressing room the strains of the evening finally began to catch up with Beverly and after as brief but affectionate a time as possible we took her to the Guild party briefly and then to her car. As we waved good night I was absolutely certain that she would not show up the following morning.

But I was wrong. The next day, exactly on time, she was on the stage with Danny Kaye cavorting through their routines. I went onstage to greet her and she looked up at me with mock hate. We exchanged some one-liners and then I noticed a ring on her right index finger, a beautiful solitaire diamond. "You like that?" she said, looking at me and the ring. "It was Peter's present last night [Peter Greenough, her husband]. It's my debut-at-the-Met present." The stone picked up and reflected the stage lights, casting slivers of color on my sleeve. "Very much," I said, "and I also like your present to us being here this morning." And then before anything more could be spoken I turned tail and ran for the exit.

XXIII

End at the Met: Coda

As things on the stage were getting more and more exciting, developments in the board room and with the officers of the association were getting murkier and murkier. Rockefeller sent for me in mid-April and I went to see him in his office at Shearman & Sterling. Without comment he handed me a draft of a press release announcing the formation of the Metropolitan Opera Foundation, to raise money in support of the Metropolitan Opera Association, with myself named as president. It also stated that I was becoming a member of the board of the Metropolitan Opera Association and would advise, from time to time, on artistic matters. "Who's going to run the company?" I asked. "Bliss and the administrative committee," came the answer. "Why?" I asked. "Do you want chapter and verse?" came the reply. "I certainly do. I've been trying to find out ever since my appointment." He looked at me but made no further comment.

I stared at the paper. He handed me another, this one a memorandum concerning salary. I noticed it was less than the one I was currently earning. "Of course we can discuss this area," he went on, in an attempt at friendly discourse. It came out creaky, stiff, embarrassed, and awkward. "I'll have to think this over," I replied. I rose. So did he. "No, stay put," I said. "I prefer to find my own way out."

As I walked out of the Shearman & Sterling building a total stranger came up to me and asked whether or not I was Schuyler Chapin. I said I was. "I just want to shake your hand," he said graciously. "You've given us some wonderful nights at the opera." I thanked him and went into the subway.

That night I met Betty and Miles for dinner. I handed them the draft of the Rockefeller press release without comment. They were appalled. "What's this all about?" Betty asked. "It seems that the affairs of the company will now be in the hands of the trustees directly. I think they feel I haven't given them a plan to get us out of the financial mess and they'll be more comfortable controlling the place themselves." "You're not going to stay?" Miles asked. "I don't think so, but I don't know yet. It will depend on what develops in the next few days. Now that this is out in the open it gives me a chance to see what they're really seeking."

And I started on this task the very next day. In the morning I asked Rockefeller for a special meeting of the executive committee. I addressed the group but didn't get very far. They all wanted to say things to me urging acceptance of their proposal. Each one spoke in turn, telling me what a great job I had done in raising money and helping to make the Metropolitan a part of the New York community. They went on and on, until they came to the faceless Mr. Smith. "I don't want to be critical," he said, tapping his long fingers together, "but administration is not, shall we say, your forte. You are . . ." and he paused to find the right phrase, "you are . . . a people person." He made it sound like a disease.

I listened to all they had to say and finally asked what they thought I was going to be able to do to raise money with the general manager position no longer mine. "But there will not be a general manager at all," came Rockefeller's reply. "We are doing away with the job. The Metropolitan is too complicated to be run by one man any longer. Bliss will be executive director, as he is now, and chairman of the administrative committee. Levine and Dexter will report to him but he will have no say over artistic plans other than financial." "Do you seriously expect me to be able to raise the money without the position to go with it?" I asked. "In one sweep you are eliminating a ninety-one-year-old title that has always symbolized the Met."

"In the three years you've been here you've become a public personality," Rockefeller replied, as if I'd committed an original sin. "Of course I have, to a limited extent," I replied, "and so would anyone. It's the nature of the job and the nature of the profession." "That's what we must never have again," he answered. "We must never have an impresario again. We've outgrown the need." And as he said this his face took on some passion, even turning a little red in the process. I began to realize that there was more to these changes than met the eye but I did not have much chance to think further about it at that moment. "We all hope you'll stay," came a voice from down the table. It was Laurence Lovett, a member of the executive committee and president of the Metropolitan Opera Guild, a sensitive and hard-working man who was devoted to the Met and to music in general. I looked down at him. "We'll see, Larry," I replied.

And I did think everything over for a few days and called a family meeting of the New York branch over a dinner. Miles and Ted were both there, as was Betty, and when I asked them what they thought they were eloquent in their comments. "You mustn't take this job," said Ted. "You'll be miserable coming into that theater every morning and knowing that you were forbidden to have any authority over it. You'll get ulcers again and you will be frustrated more than you ever have been before." The others spoke their agreements to this thought in their own ways. I was deeply moved, both by their obvious concern and by the practical and worldly good sense that the boys seemed to have acquired over the growing-up period. They were not cynical or wise-ass: they were concerned, thoughtful, and practical. I loved them all for it.

I called Rockefeller the next morning and he came to the opera house to see me. "I'm sorry, Bill," I said, "but I cannot take your offer. I don't believe in it. I don't think you've got any well-thought-out plan and it would be impossible to come into this theater every day with absolutely no authority. And while we're at it, I think you'd be better off sending Bliss to Japan; I think the Japanese would be embarrassed to find they were dealing with a general manager about to lose his job. This trip is of great importance to the Met and must not go wrong."

Rockefeller pulled himself up straight. "If I may use an old navy phrase, the captain of a ship who knows he's going to be retired brings his ship safely into port." I acknowledged that was undoubtedly true but that somehow there was a difference between the navy and the lyric theater. I finally withdrew the suggestion because I realized it was no use talking to someone about sensitivity and feelings who obviously didn't understand them. He is a righteous man, William Rockefeller. He wants to do good because it's his civic responsibility, his duty, something he was brought up to do. His antipathy to the post of general manager almost certainly has deeper roots than just the Met problems by themselves. When his mother and father were divorced his mother remarried George Sloan, a Southern gentleman who was for many years president of the Met board. Mr. Sloan was charming but, I gather, slightly to the right of Prince Metternich and often tangled with Bing on casting. Rockefeller was evidently very fond of his stepfather and resented Bing's remarks about him in his autobiography. Perhaps this is all conjecture; I have no proof, but the vehemence with which he stated that there would never again be an impresario or public personality probably had root cause in the George Sloan affair.

Two or three days went by after our last talk. Several individual executive committee members asked me to lunch to talk things over. They were kind and thoughtful and really seemed desirous of changing my mind. And one of them almost did.

Irving Mitchell Felt, the chairman of Madison Square Garden and an old personal friend, took me to lunch, and then started in as only an old friend could, by telling me that I was a damn fool, that I needed the Met as much as the Met needed me, that we were made for each other and that this business might not work and if I took the new position I would be around in case of problems. "If you leave now they'll never ask you back," he said carefully. "I know what I'm talking about. I have watched similar situations." He made a lot of sense: I loved the Metropolitan with a deep and abiding affection and wanted to remain in a position of helping solve the problems, but not at a price that would destroy my own self-respect. Felt continued to talk along the same lines throughout the meal and I told him that I would think over what he said. He suggested a salary package and new contract with very tempting terms that he said were his own ideas, not those of the executive committee and he'd have to talk with Rockefeller and the rest if I gave him the green light to do so.

Later that afternoon, my head running with his comments and the specific proposals he'd put in front of me, I called his office and told him to go ahead and speak to Rockefeller provided not one single sentence of his ideas was changed and that I was not required at this moment to make a definite change of mind. He called Rockefeller, who, in turn, called me and we arranged to meet the next morning at an extremely early hour in my office.

I spent a sleepless night. I'd explained Felt's proposals to Betty and to Miles and Ted but as I spoke them out loud I realized they still were not right. Certainly the money was attractive and the idea of a firm contract for two years with only myself able to cancel was enormously appealing. Still and all, I felt uncomfortable. There was something wrong and something missing.

The next morning I told Rockefeller I would consider the Felt offer if not one iota was altered and he seemed pleased. Later, in a special executive committee meeting just prior to a special meeting of the board to ratify the new reorganization plan and my dismissal, he must have asked for time because the matter was laid over to the annual meeting of the association due to take place in late June, just after the company's return from the Orient. We were now at a standstill; Rockefeller felt reasonably secure that I would stay but I felt queasy and uneasy, that to stay would be a fatal mistake no matter what the pricetag.

These matters perforce had to be put aside as our spring tour neared completion and we prepared for Japan. Bliss did not want to go and, despite Rockefeller's naval reasoning, I wanted to see the trip through because it had been my baby from the first day and I felt it a very important project for the Metropolitan, artistically and institutionally, and good for the United States cultural position.

The Rockefellers were coming along; some time back they'd asked if I objected to their coming and I said that far from objecting I thought it wonderful and· I still thought so, despite our private wars. Molly Rockefeller is a joyous person; she lights up any room or situation, and the company would have fun getting to know her better. From time to time they'd caught a glimpse of Bill but there was not much general communication. It was also courteous to our Japaense hosts, who were not only presenting us in Tokyo, Nagoya, and Osaka under optimum circumstances but paying us enough money to make the trip and, with careful management, the possibility of ending up better than break-even. The worst that could happen would be a balanced wash; the best, a net figure showing more income than expense. It was also to be the third foreign trip ever made by the Metropolitan. I was determined that Japan was going to be a triumph.

We left for Japan on May 25, 1975, on a sunny, cool morning from Minneapolis, where, the night before, we had finished our 1975 spring tour. We traveled in one 747 for the company and one cargo plane. Our repertoire was *La Traviata, La Bohème,* and *Carmen.* The sets for *Traviata* and *Bohème* were constructed in Japan from our original designs. *Carmen* was shipped by sea since the work was not in the house repertoire for that season and there was plenty of time for it to get there.

The entire Japanese project was a huge undertaking. We were scheduled for the better part of three weeks, two of them in Tokyo, split between two theaters, one performance in our hosts' home city, Nagoya, and the balance of the third week in Osaka. In preparing for the trip we wanted to leave nothing to chance and organized three separate task forces whose jobs were to coordinate and organize the entire effort. The Japanese were extremely helpful but knowing their use of the word "yes" when they really meant "no," and not wanting to put anyone in an embarrassing position, I felt we should double-check everything. The company was, for the most part, eager to make the trip but toward the last minute certain members of the orchestra decided they did not want to go. I said that this was all right with me; we would find quality substitute players and be on our way.

One of the biggest problems was the productions themselves. David Reppa and Rudy Kuntner made several advance trips to Japan and discovered the particular qualities of each of the theaters that might give us trouble. The decision was made to duplicate the scenery of the Cecil Beaton *Traviata* and the Rolf Gérard *Bohème*. The latter was a very old production. *La Traviata*, new in 1966, was one of Cecil Beaton's more lavish creations and had, over the years since its premiere, fallen into shabbiness, largely because of its constant use. Reppa brought in some young designers and they set about painstakingly making new models of both operas from the original Gérard and Beaton sketches. These, in turn, were flown to Tokyo and priced out by our hosts and then turned over to Japanese scenery shops, where they were constructed from thin woods and what looked like rice paper. They were beautifully painted, down to the smallest detail, and when lit looked as good as the original sets must have on the day they were first revealed to the public. *Carmen* arrived safely and initially puzzled the Japanese stagehands, but they soon mastered all the problems.

In Tokyo we were scheduled to divide our time between the NHK Theater and the Bunka Kaikan which meant shifting the scenery from one building to another, an expensive proposition. We tried to minimize our hosts' expenses as much as possible but this trucking must have cost them a fortune.

In my professional life I have never seen a road trip as beautifully managed as this one. Between the incomparable Met group and our hosts absolutely nothing went wrong with the mechanical and technical part of the trip. The entire company, from prima donnas to apprentice makeup men, were all housed in super-first-class hotels, the Imperial in Tokyo, the Kanko in Nagoya, and the Royal York in Osaka. Everything possible was considered to please the company and give them a chance between performances and rehearsals to sightsee and explore the cities. They, in turn, responded to the courtesies and each night was like an opening, with everyone giving their all.

We brought an roster of international singers, including Joan Suther-

land, Marilyn Horne, Robert Merrill, John Alexander, Luciano Pavarotti, Franco Corelli, Adriana Maliponte, and James McCracken, and
gradually throughout Tokyo, and the other cities as well, they became
recognized in stores and restaurants. We were all treated wonderfully
well; we were known as the "Meto."

The only problems we had were really not of our own doing. At our
first press conference, where I spoke a greeting to our hosts in Japanese that I learned under pressure while on the plane, an old friend
from my 1970 trip took me aside and told me that we were going to
have some trouble. There was, at least in Tokyo, a simmering anti-
American feeling and an attitude of country-cousins about our hosts,
the Chibbu-Nippon Company. "They're rather like rich Texans who
might come here, see the Kabuki, like it, decide to take it to America,
bring it to New York, dump it in a theater and say: 'There you are.
There's ma present for ya!' And walk away from the whole thing.
Their hearts are in the right place but they don't really know how to
promote in Tokyo." These comments were later borne out by another
Japanese friend, one of the most successful men in the country, who
suggested that we try to arrange for a television program of one of the
operas. He said that if we did this we would accomplish two things:
show an example of American culture to an enormous audience and fill
every seat at every performance. This was no small undertaking; we
discovered that tickets cost upwards of $50 each for good ones, consid-
erably more than in New York.

I began to think over his suggestions and decided to do nothing about
it until after our opening. This was Sutherland in *Traviata* on May 28
and I noticed that the theater was more than comfortably full but not
sold out. The previous day I had been on a television interview program with Horne, Lewis, and Pavarotti and when we were discussing
the program before going on the air I sensed by the way I was questioned that we were to be in for some shadowy comments about the validity and place of the Metropolitan Opera in the scheme of Western
musical institutions. I warned Pavarotti that the questions were going
to be loaded and he told me not to worry. When it came time for him to
speak he became the most eloquent spokesman the Met could ask for.
By the time he was finished there was not a dry eye in the studio and I
fervently hoped that it was the same way across the country. But opening night, despite all blandishments to the contrary, was not a sellout
and this worried me greatly.

The star of the evening was a surprise. In addition to Joan Sutherland as Violetta, the cast included John Alexander as Alfredo and Rob-

ert Merrill as the elder Germont, a role he has sung hundreds of times at the Metropolitan, on recordings, and all over the country. When the curtain rose Sutherland was given a warm welcome but a subdued one. The same applied to Alexander, but when Merrill made his entrance through the garden gate in Act II the house went wild with cheers and bravos and clapping. Merrill did not know what hit him and kept on singing and acting but glancing furtively into the auditorium to see what was going on. When he took his curtain call the explosion was repeated and he was stunned but pleased. His wife and children had come along on the trip and they, too, were delighted. It seemed that the Japanese knew him well and had known him for many years through records and broadcasts and he was something of a musical folk hero. I was afraid that Joan, who is, after all, a prima donna assoluta, might be put out by all the attention given to her baritone colleague but I need not have worried. She was gracious and delighted to bring him out for solo bows. Not that she was ignored; she certainly was not, and, like Merrill and most of the others except Pavarotti and Corelli, she was making her Japanese debut and loving it.

The matter of appearing on television became more important as the first few days passed. The American Ambassador and his wife had given a delightful reception at the embassy for the company. I rather dreaded the event: most times these affairs can be crashing bores and exhausting but this one was not. Ambassador James D. Hodgson had gone all-out and obviously enjoyed the party himself. I did have a moment to talk with the U.S. Information Agency officers while we were there and they urged me to do everything possible to do a television program. Betty gathered up similar strands of information. She was the one who walked all over Tokyo on her own and with many members of the company and sensed the unique opportunity we had to reach millions of Japanese. I thought all of this made good sense, both from the box office standpoint and from the point of view of our country, and I called a company meeting during the intermission after the first act of *La Bohème* one night and explained the whole situation. I said that there was no money to pay anyone and that there was no obligation on anyone's part to agree but I thought they should know what I'd been told and how important such a program could be for the tour and for our artistic image. I pointed out that no extra work would be involved, only that cameras already built into the NHK Theater would be activated and a performance taped. I asked them to consider that matter carefully among themselves and that I would seek answers the next night. The questions that were asked were all intelligent and detailed and from the general attitude I felt that the proposal was going to be given very careful thought.

It was. By the following evening everyone had agreed and I was able to inform our hosts. Within two days a performance of *La Traviata* had been taped, I had made a brief introduction, and the program was scheduled for the following Sunday night at 10:00 PM on the full NHK Network.

The Monday following the telecast you couldn't beat your way to the box office. Everything that I'd been told turned out to be true and we finished up the tour turning people away.

That was the good side. The bad was that I was coming to the realization that I had lost my battle. On our first Sunday in Tokyo, Rockefeller and I had spent almost two hours together walking in the park of the Imperial Gardens while I went over again the reasons why I thought the committee system for running the Met would not work. He had been with us for a week and had seen for himself the necessity for leadership. I told him that I thought he was doing something as a trustee that he would never tolerate in his professional life, making an amateur decision on a highly professional matter. I said that I wouldn't presume to come to his law office and tell him how to practice his profession and that I was surprised that he thought he had the right to do the same thing with mine. I pointed out that he was perfectly free to get rid of me if he thought I was a failure but not free to destroy a leadership principle on the theory that what is good for a conglomerate is necessarily good for a theater. We talked frankly and freely and I thought that perhaps I was making headway.

I reported our conversation to Betty, who urged me to sit down and write him a letter reviewing everything we'd said so that there could not be any confusion in either of our minds. Initially I balked at this, believing that we had understood one another quite well and could continue the dialogue after returning to New York. She suggested that this was probably not the case and that I better be absolutely clear what I said and how I said it and that the best way to do this was to put it down on paper. The Rockefellers were leaving Tokyo for Hong Kong the next morning. I decided that Betty was right and that I would send the letter to New York, where he would receive it before the company returned home. I sat down that night and wrote the following.

DEAR BILL:

It was good to have you with us during our first Tokyo days and wonderful for the company to have the chance to meet both you and Molly.

It is hard to get the feel of this group from a distance—a board room is one thing, human contact quite another, and the contact is what really counts, particularly in an arts organization that is people rather than things. Molly's bag incident at the airport was terrific and the company's reaction just right. The relationship between you and them got off to a great start.

I also appreciated our walk in the Imperial Gardens and the chance to review the proposed reorganization. I think it might be helpful if I put the gist of my comments to you on paper so that we both understand what my position is regarding the future.

First of all, the idea of running the Metropolitan by a committee or consortium will not work. A theater, unlike other businesses, must be run by one man. The processes by which it is run will vary according to the individual. Bing did it his way; I have done it mine. Mine includes the participation of a variety of talents before final decisions are reached. These include people like Levine, Dexter, Riecker, Bronson and Rodzinski as the first-line administrative team with additional input from Hubay, Robinson, Stayer, Veitch and others.

From the beginning I realized that the role of the general manager would have to change to cope with present problems. He would have to continue to take the leadership artistically but add to that a major responsibility for fund raising. It became obvious that a solid artistic position had to be evolved first, using the best possible people in order to free the general manager for the necessary liaison with the public, the box office public as well as those in a position to give major support. To do this a team was needed, hence the bringing along of Levine, the engagement of Dexter, the appointment of a new chorus master, new rehearsal department personnel, and additional strength in the artistic administration. In addition, it was obviously necessary to create greater integration between the financial department and the other company departments. This has been done and has resulted not only in considerable dollar savings in the operation of the theater but the development of close working relationships between all sections of the company.

The team that exists now is one that I created. More, obviously, needs to be done. The whole area of press and promotion must be overhauled. The Studio and its future must be re-examined, future seasons and possible major readjustments of our present schedules must be thought out. These and many more problems must be examined while still keeping faith with the company and the public.

Japan has shown the profound strength of this organization. If we can capitalize on this trip, perhaps equally important foreign expeditions lie ahead.

Now, however, the decision has been made to restructure the management just at a point when we are moving ahead on all fronts. I realize that this restructuring is in large measure an Executive Committee reaction to our current financial situation as well as feelings of a lack of confidence in my administrative abilities. In addition, you are planning to abandon the title that in itself has high visibility and symbolizes the entire Metropolitan family.

It seems to me that what you are doing is taking my basic team and replacing me with a trustee. In the process, you have turned over the artistic life of the theater to a very talented young conductor and given him carte blanche. . . .

The running of an opera house is a unique combination of many things: an ability to balance conflicting forces, a sense of responsiveness to individuals and their real or imagined personal and professional problems—in short, how to get the best out of other people's talents. Without leadership a group such as the Metropolitan will become factionalized, uncoordinated, and disordered. Despite grave difficulties, great progress has been made in the past three years. To me it seems wasteful and foolish to tear the place apart at a time when we need all our strength and talents to cope with present and future problems.

Therefore, I must tell you that if the Executive Committee's decision is to remain unchanged, I will not be able to remain with the organization, in spite of the tentative understandings we may have regarding a new position for me. Simply stated, I cannot in all good conscience remain a part of a plan that I deeply believe is wrong for the Metropolitan at this time.

Believe me, I have the utmost respect for you and the challenging job you have as president of the Association, but in the last analysis I am a professional in my career area, just as you are in yours, and I see decisions being made that simply do not make sense for the opera house.

If the Executive Committee should reconsider their decision, I would be happy to continue as general manager with the same responsibilities as I presently have and, in addition, would be willing to take on additional fund-raising responsibilities as head of the house, in keeping with the philosophy expressed earlier in this letter and already known to you from many talks.

I look forward to seeing you later this month.

I mailed it off the next afternoon, which happened to coincide with the performance attended by the son of the Crown Prince. This event was carefully arranged, with great detail paid to protocol. During the first intermission, the members of the cast appeared for presentation to His Highness. Unlike royalty in England, the Japanese royal family never goes backstage. The artists go to them, and in our case the artists included Horne, McCracken, Maliponte, Sarabia, and Henry Lewis, who all came after the first act of *Carmen*. It was quite a distance from the backstage to the royal receiving room and they all had to climb a number of stairs. They arrived sweating and still panting from both the performance and the climb and looked on the young prince with politness but obvious desires to get to their dressing rooms.

While they were all on their way it fell to me to keep His Highness in conversation. We were ushered into a rectangular room with two sofas near either wall, a long, low series of tables separating them, and four chintze-covered armchairs at one end of the rectangle. As we entered the room, Betty and Mrs. Hodgson were seated on the far side, the men, both Japanese and American, on the other. The Japanese included a chamberlain, a tutor, and someone who seemed to be an observer. His Highness was seated on one of the chintze-covered chairs, flanked by a translator and secretary, and the seat next to him was vacant. I was beckoned into it and it was obviously my responsibility to keep up the conversation. His Highness was about fourteen, I would guess, with a remarkable resemblance to his grandfather Hirohito except for one adolescent pimple directly under his left nostril. We talked of America, of art and music, of the Metropolitan and anything I could think of to keep him busy. When I began to run out of steam and was convinced that the artists would never show up Betty, from her banishment on the other side of the room, suggested that I ask His Highness about his studies. This was a brilliant idea and soon brought out the fact that he was studying American geography and had just reached the Great Lakes. At this moment the doors swung open, the artists entered, and I made the introductions.

After a few more minutes the intermission bell sounded and His Highness rose, bowed to everyone, put out his hand in an unusual gesture for a Japanese and we shook hands. He walked out of the room, his shoulders squared back, looking every inch a Royal. He also seemed to be having a good time at the opera.

The three weeks in Japan were enjoyed by almost everyone. There are always people who are going to complain for the sake of complaining. Years ago a friend who heads a large business with factories spread all over the country was advising me on some general principles of labor negotiation. He said that usually a group is divided pretty much into thirds—one-third who will go along with whatever management has to suggest, one-third neutral, and one-third against anything and everything. He told me that one must try to move that uncommitted third and realize that the dissidents are going to remain dissidents no matter what you do. We had a few of the dissidents on the trip, including one who sprang to attention, even glee, when he discovered

that we were asking everyone to travel by bus from Nagoya to Osaka.
According to the exact terms of his union's contract, bus riding was
forbidden because it was not first-class transportation. He confronted
me with this violation, together with the somewhat reluctant fellow
members of his particular committee, and demanded to know what I
was going to do about it. I said that I wasn't going to do anything about
it, that we had planned the bus ride deliberately in order to give everyone a chance to see something of the Japanese countryside instead of
only cities, and that we had enough vehicles rented to give everyone
two seats. He smiled in his pleasure at knowing that I was breaking the
agreement and said that he was taking the train and that the Met was
going to pay for it. "Go right ahead," I said, "and enjoy the train.
You'll find that the railroad station is about thirty minutes away from
the hotel and it will be a long ride. But the Met is not going to pay."
"I'll take this up with the union in New York," he said, looking
pleased. "Do as you like," I answered. He did. Evidently his wife
heard of his plans for the train and vetoed. The next morning he was
scheduled on a bus and Betty and I decided to take the same one and sit
behind him. He hardly said a word but his wife seemed to be enjoying
the scenery. When we reached Osaka he bowed his head in our direction and had the touch of a smile at the corners of his mouth. As far as I
know he never complained to the union, although he might have done
so after my departure. I suspect his wife would have been hard on him
if he tried any nonsense.

By the time our three weeks drew to a close we had made some fast
friends, especially Kinzo Sato, the officer of Chibbu-Nippon who
watched over all our proceedings. Sato-san added to our pleasure not
only with his courtesies and attention but with a new phrase for our domestic vocabulary. On our last night in Osaka he came to the performance accompanied by a young man and a beautiful young girl. With
great formality he introduced us to the young man, his son, and we
bowed at each other. Then he paused, looked carefully at the girl, and
said, "And now you meet son's ah, eh, most personal friend . . ."

Our long flight back was broken by Betty's fiftieth birthday party
spread over a two-day period because of crossing the international date
line. By the time we reached New York there, among the several hundred friends and relatives that had come to greet the returning company, were Ted, Hank, and Miles, holding a big "Happy Birthday, Ma"
sign in Japanese. With lots of hugs and embraces we climbed into our
own Fiat stationwagon and headed for the city and another birthday

dinner at Gino's with another cake. By the time we went to bed on that memorable June 15 we had good reason to fall asleep immediately.

Back in New York, back, in fact, to reality, I called Rockefeller, asking if he had received my letter. "Oh yes," he mumbled, "I have it." There was silence. "Well, what about it?" I asked. "What about what?" came the reply. "What about my situation?" "Oh," he said, "well, nothing has changed. My colleagues wouldn't agree at this point to what you suggest." "Is that final?" I asked. "Oh, yes, certainly," he replied. There was a pause. A long one. "Then I guess this is it," I said slowly, "because I meant what I said to you in Tokyo and wrote in that letter. I'm sorry." "So am I," came a laconic reply and he hung up.

And that was that. Three seasons as the boss and half a season as assistant manager-elect had come to a halt. Why?

I think probably there were many reasons, some of them a legitimate attempt at reorganizing a situation that certainly had its problems, and others the making of changes for the sake of making changes without clear definition of either goals or procedures in mind. In many ways the Metropolitan Opera reflects the problems of contemporary American society with the arts. Yes, the arts are fine and important and uplifting and since World War II we've made tremendous strides in making them more accessible to people and in broadening the financial base. But we've never had as compelling a reason to examine our position in this area as we have had in, for example, education.

In 1957, when the Russians launched Sputnik, we suddenly found ourselves outdistanced in science for the first time in our modern history and we were put into a state of national shock. The villian was found to be our educational system that had been developing hardening of the arteries for some years. Congress sprang into action, the several states and cities did the same, and presently we had a whole series of programs devoted to the enlargement and improvement of our educational processes. New campuses sprang up; old ones were lining the Washington corridors for handouts that were generous in coming. Education had become a national focus and it still is, although there are voices now being raised that question some of the action taken during the Sputnik fever. Nonetheless, education was made into a major political and power force by that small, beeping satellite, and nothing comparable has happened in the arts. The arts have been maturing slowly into the national consciousness but too slowly. There is the need to value

what we have, to rethink our major purposes, and to work upon a formula to pay for the arts that takes into account some combination of
public and private monies.

We must face certain facts: the age of unlimited private philanthropy
is drawing to a close. This private sector will never be completely cut
off but over the years it is bound to be curtailed as the tax base changes
and it becomes increasingly difficult for individuals to build substantial
personal fortunes. The role of the foundations is already reflecting this
fact and they grow into the major force in what is referred to as the
"private sector." Partnered with this is the "public sector," a fancy
way of saying government support, and this area is in the process of
growing with each passing year.

Somehow, in the immediate future, we Americans must devise an
arts financial plan unique for us. The common idea is to emulate Europe; if the Europeans support their opera houses and symphonies and
museums why, then, we must do the same. Of course that idea, to me,
is out of the question. We would never accept such a plan because,
among other things, we are too polyglot a people to accept what are
essentially monolithic plans for single nationalities. What's good for
the Germans is done in Germany, for the Italians in Italy, for the
French in France. What's good for the Americans has to be drawn
from all the cultures that make up the country, and our economic system still militates against government handouts as an automatic way of
life. Significantly, too, the arts, until very recently, were always
thought to be the responsibility of the affluent and never were woven
into the legislative tapestry.

As our mechanized age and plastic society begin to bring their own
problems, as the standards of living across every segment of society
are being raised at a rate unvisualized by even the strongest dreamer
thirty years ago, we are introducing many new concerns into our lives
and one of these is leisure time. What are we going to do with ourselves? The work week is already being reduced and sociologists tell us
that within the next five to ten years we may be down to the three-day
week. Leisure time may turn out to be the most destructive force of all,
for boredom and restlessness can be the seeds of adventures begun
merely to create something to do.

Here is where the arts are going to have the biggest chance to grow.
If we are able to stimulate people's interests, even more than is being
done now, and if we have the talents, the theaters, the museums, and
the opportunities for participation either as members of the audience
or as developers of our own talents, we can play a major role in bright-

ening the lives and filling the hours of an ever-wider-spreading leisure class.

The Metropolitan Opera is squarely in the center of this problem. For an institution that came into being in 1883 for essentially insignificant social purposes it has grown over the years to become an institution of important artistic purposes, reaching out to literally millions of people each week of its season. The "millions of people" is true. For over forty uninterrupted years the Metropolitan has broadcast its Saturday afternoon performances live from the stage of the opera house across the entire country. At least two million people listen regularly each Saturday and according to the surveys somewhere between five million and fifteen million hear at least one or part of one opera broadcast each year. Coupled with the figures of attendance in New York and the audiences that attend performances on the annual spring tour, the Metropolitan Opera has a significant constituency. It has helped to develop the taste for opera that is now exploding all over the country with regional opera organizations that are flourishing artistically, and in many cases, are financially healthy.

There are two other major companies in the United States that operate on an economic par with the Metropolitan, the Lyric Opera of Chicago and the San Francisco Opera. The San Francisco Opera is over fifty years old, the Chicago Lyric Opera over twenty-five and the successor to several previous attempts to establish a permanent opera company in that extraordinary city. The "Big Three" cost about the same to run. The catch is that San Francisco and Chicago mount their international season only three months of the year and gear their fund-raising efforts for that limited time period. The Metropolitan Opera guarantees fifty-two weeks of employment to its chorus, ballet company, principal contract artists, and stagehands. The phrase "principal contract artists" means those under contract to the company for secondary or comprimario roles, essential to the building of an operatic ensemble. Dividing gross expenses by three months, even if the expenses are essentially the same as the Metropolitan, brings an operation into viable financial dimensions. The Metropolitan as the oldest and most recognized operatic institution in the country has a significant leadership role to play in the international cultural life of the country and stands unique.

But the Metropolitan is saddled with one expense that is a constant drain and a perfect example of the "edifice complex" at its most careless. The Metropolitan Opera House itself costs $3 million a year at the present time for upkeep—heat, light, electricity, maintenance, and security—and because of the individual situations in Chicago and San Francisco these costs are not a major factor. The opera house should become, for its basic housekeeping, the ward of New York City, but in the light of New York's acute fiscal problems this is highly unlikely. Perhaps it should become part of the national parks system under either the Smithsonian Institution or the Department of the Interior. Three million dollars a year is a significant amount on the Met's budget; it could be of overwhelming importance in saving the company.

When the news of my departure reached the press there was quite a lot of attention given to it and I began to get a stream of mail that went on for over a year. It was extremely gratifying to Betty and me and made us both feel that we were going to be missed. We spent the summer of 1975 at Long Pond in the house that we built in 1972. I was more tired than I thought and the summer winds and the water did great restorative work to body and soul. The awkwardness of my departure was exacerbated by the clumsiness of the officers of the board, particularly the president, and I found myself out of my post without one penny of turn-around pay, a situation hardly believable of an organization of such stature. I wasn't there long enough for any significant settlement but even the usual two weeks' pay in lieu of notice might have been helpful. Their lack of graciousness continued right to the end.

And what about the future? I had hoped to be with the organization for at least ten years after which I had thought of retiring into a consultant position and devoting the rest of my working years to the overriding problem of financing the arts. My timetable was disrupted! When all was said and done, however, the board problems I faced were of great unimportance compared to the pleasures and joys I was granted by the actual job. Not many people in this world are given the chance, however briefly, of living out their childhood fantasies and being paid for them. I was and I am grateful for the chance.

Now I've started on a new phase. As Dean of Columbia University's School of the Arts it is my job to build up this small but potentially important school to take its place on an equal footing with other academic disciplines. The challenge is enormous; the problems curiously similar to many other adventures in the arts. It is a new world for me, never having been to college and in fact not even having graduated properly from high school, and I doubt that I would have accepted the assignment except for the fact that the school is located in New York City, which still is, despite potholes, swollen crime rates, and other major urban ills, the arts capital of the Western world. Here is where the action is and if a great university such as Columbia really wants to play a significant role in the arts, it can be done best here.

I was thinking about this at the beginning of my first term in September, 1976, when I had been asked to address the incoming freshmen of Columbia College and Barnard College on the arts in New York. Some two hundred students jammed a small lecture hall and seemed to listen carefully to what I had to say, even if my remarks were slightly disjointed and not too well organized. At the end of the talk several lingered behind to ask questions the thrust of which were to the point and caring. Later there was a reception where more came up and I found myself in the middle of an eager pro-arts group who fired off intelligent and piercing questions.

One of them, an attractive redhead who looked familiar, asked me a question and then said, "Don't you remember me? I'm Annie Gormley!" I certainly did: Annie Gormley is the youngest of the several daughters of our friend Jim Gormley, pediatrician extraordinaire of Plymouth, Massachusetts. "I liked what you said," she went on, "and I love being here in New York." We agreed to see each other from time to time and shortly thereafter a very earnest girl, who also looked vaguely familiar, came up with some questions and comments and finally said, "You don't know me but I'm Joseph Papp's daughter!" I said I certainly knew her father, whom, as I told her, I respect, admire, and like. "Most people only say the first two words," she rejoined, with a broad smile. Later on a third girl approached and said that I did not know her but I knew her grandfather. I asked who that was and she replied, "Giovanni Pramagiorre." I did a double-take. Indeed I know Giovanni Pramagiorre, who runs one of the best restaurants in New York and it was to his establishment I went as a scared and shy fourteen-year-old on my first solo date. Giovanni had been a father-protector for many New Yorkers over the years and to think that the pretty girl standing in front of me was his granddaughter.

The thought suddenly struck me: what a unique place New York City is and what a unique world the arts. Here, in the course of less than half an hour at a great university I had seen three people representing three different ways of life all converging on the city and all deeply involved with the arts. I had talked with many more; I had sensed the excitement and vitality that ran through them. I had sensed passion tempered with realism; I had, in the words of a famous writer, "seen the future."

As the early autumn sunlight bounced off the branches of trees up and down the campus I suddenly had a sense of joy. Never mind the disappointments; they'd always be there. Take heart from the better things, those values that keep us moving excitably and eagerly exploring our fascinating world.

I thought of Sister Mary Madeleva of St. Mary's College, South Bend, Indiana, her habit flapping behind her in the cold, damp winter slush as she rushed from room to room and hall to hall in her not-yet-finished Fine Arts Center in 1955. Sister Madeleva had determined that the girls under her care were going to be exposed to the finest in all the arts, and she went about creating her center with determination, humor, and stubbornness. I loved her dearly. In my earliest days as an artists' representative I called on her to book her concert series and we had become friends. I knew what the building meant to her and somehow it came to mean almost the same to me. She had battled through the Church, through the college trustees, through the alumni; she had carried her message and the building was a tangible sign of her victory. As we whirled through the place my eye fell on the cornerstone. Carved into the rock was the legend "Art is the Signature of Man."

I asked her who wrote that meaningful phrase. She was always vague about this, never answering the question. Slowly I came to understand that she, a splendid poet in her own right, had written the words herself.

After that there is little to say. I get up every day and somewhere along the line a part of the arts touches my life. I am an incurable optimist. I think it's the way to go. As has been said, the future comes one day at a time.

Index

437